ONLY GOD KNOWS

A Journey of Love, Faith and Joy

EDD L. BROWN

Only God Knows: A Journey of Love, Faith and Joy

ISBN: 978-1-940645-22-3

Courier Publishing
100 Manly Street
Greenville, S.C. 29601

PRINTED IN THE UNITED STATES

To Flo, Steve, Peggy, Wayne, Helen, Bruce, Lynn,
Marcia, Charlie and our grandchildren:
Thanks for your love, your life and your support.
You, with God, have made my life.

This book is primarily the history of my life with my wife, Flo, and our family. However, our story would be incomplete without introducing you to another family, one that had a great impact on our lives and our ministry in California and around the world.

One of the first people I met when we moved to California was Dorothy Warren, the mother of Rick Warren, who is well known today as the author of *The Purpose Driven Life* and the pastor of Saddleback Church. Dot and I helped lead state Vacation Bible School conferences. Over the next thirty years, Jim and Dot Warren became more than friends.

When Flo and I moved to Kenwood, south of Santa Rosa, to work with thirty-eight Baptist churches in four counties, another Jim Warren — Jim Warren Jones — moved his cult, the Peoples Temple, from Indiana to Redwood Valley, close to Ukiah (about 17 miles north), and erected a ten-foot-high chain-link fence around his compound. Jones was bitterly anti-government and anti-Christian. He had made himself the ruler (God) of all his people. Families had to sell homes and cars and give their assets to him for complete control. County officials enforced the law, and Jones' cult sent their youth to public schools. Dot became the librarian for the local high school and began to work with the students from the Jones compound.

Jim Warren and I were given the responsibility of rebuilding Camp Cazadero northwest of Santa Rosa so that youth and adults could be part of a camping and spiritual development program for Christians. The Warrens' children and ours were involved in the reconstruction of the camp as well as leading training conferences.

Jim Jones became frustrated and worried that he was losing control of his people. In two years, he closed his compound. After other moves to southern California, he took more than six hundred of his people to Guyana, South America. Because of complaints from cult members' families, Congressman Leo Ryan, along with others, traveled to South America to investigate Jones and the way his cult operated. The result of that visit was that Ryan was killed, and Jim Jones convinced more than 900 followers to murder their children and babies and then commit suicide.

I only met Jones twice, but, as Dot said, there was something about him that scared me. Flo and I had listened to the reports of the events in Guyana on our car radio while we were returning from a mission conference I was leading for churches in northern California. We stopped at the Warrens and spent several hours with them, watching the news and trying to understand how a self-centered, demented man who claimed to be educated could murder the very people who were convinced he had all the answers to life — for himself and for them.

I continue to wonder how two charismatic Jims who lived within a mile of one another could be so committed — one to the death of his own people; and our Jim, who carried the message of life and love. Jim Jones killed and threatened for obedience, but God loves us and just takes us as we are.

Jim and Dot Warren, because of our parallel work, joined with Flo and me — along with over four hundred volunteers from churches in California and Nevada — to begin to take God's message and help to more than a thousand churches in California, across our nation and to another two-hundred-plus churches in twenty-eight foreign countries.

To know the Warrens and work with them was a major influence on us and our children. If you think your influence does not affect others who need to hear your message, you might be interested to know that Rick Warren and his sister Chaundel's great aunt was Annie Armstrong. Our Southern Baptist annual campaign to support North American missions and meet people's needs was named for her work in reaching out to others.

One Jim for death, and one Jim for life — it is still a great paradox to me.

Hopefully *Only God Knows* can be a help and a challenge to you in your life's journey.

God love and keep you,
Edd and Flo Brown

Table of Contents

One

1926-1932

Who Are You?

If I could have had a say about my birth, I would not have chosen to be born anytime in the 1920s. Why? Because during the first ten years of my life, two international and two national devastating events began, and each one had a direct impact on me and what I eventually became:

Adolph Hitler was building a German base for a world controlled by a pure Aryan race.

Japan was planning to retake Korea and then invade China to dominate the Pacific nations.

The undisciplined spending of the Roaring Twenties in America was coming to an end; the Great Depression would cause havoc and replace the nation's wild good times.

The rains in the Midwest began to cease, replaced by dry, hot winds; the Dust Bowl would ruin the lives of thousands in north Texas, eastern New Mexico and western Oklahoma.

In my most formative years, my family lived in twelve different houses. With that and the above, my life and my future began. I did not give much thought to my past until years later when a friend asked me to dinner.

Charlie, the Syrian pastor of one of our Middle Eastern Baptist churches in California, invited me to lunch at a Syrian restaurant in Orange County. He had moved with his family to California to work with Muslims and other Middle Eastern people and help them know the truth about Christianity, without having to live in fear for his and his family's lives. As we talked and shared our histories and family backgrounds, he looked up at me and point-blank asked, "Who are you anyway, and how can you live with yourself?"

This was not an accusation — just an honest dialogue between two friends about family history. I answered him as best I could, but he could not understand my varied family background and how the racial integration of my family was an accepted fact. There have been moments before and since that I have wondered the same thing: "Who am I, and why am I here?"

One of those moments happened while I was in Rostov on Don, in Southern Russia. I was teaching sixteen young Baptist church pastors and six older church leaders the basics of church leadership and Bible interpretation. It was winter — cold, with heavy snow and ice. I had spent hours in unheated airports and was over ten hours late getting from St. Petersburg in the cold north to the "warm south," which was five degrees below freezing.

The guesthouse I stayed in was not heated at night. My bed had a metal frame with a mesh of coiled springs that sagged almost to the floor. I had two sheets, a pillow, two blankets and a mattress not much thicker than a blanket. Three students of my sixteen-member class were in other bedrooms and no better off than I was, so I just made do. One of those students was from Chechnya, a province just southeast of Rostov. Radical Muslim groups were randomly kidnapping and killing people not of their extreme beliefs. One of our students had been unable to make contact with any of his family for two days. The five of us had spent time in prayer for his family and him before we went to bed.

I was beyond exhausted. I put on as many nightclothes as I could and, surprisingly, dropped into a deep sleep. Six hours later, I was suddenly awakened by loud explosions. At first, I thought it was the rapid fire of rifles. I grabbed my blankets, rolled off the bed and waited. After one or two more shots, I began to seriously ask myself, "Who are you anyway? Why are you here? You are not getting paid to do this."

I was overly tired and now scared. I was ready to get back home. Home then was in Schweinfurt, Germany. Flo, my wife, and I were living there. I was the pastor of a small Baptist church. Our real home was in California, but Schweinfurt was safer and warmer; compared to this, it was home sweet home.

The noise stopped. I got up and carefully searched the dark room to find the kitchen knife on the end table where I had left it. I moved to a window and scraped off enough ice on the inside of the window to see out.

All I saw was a stalled cable car, ten feet outside the window in front of my room. My mind went crazy; my imagination ran wild: "Is the main power out? Is the trouble local? Have the police taken over? Are the railroads and air traffic closed? Will I be able to leave if a civil war breaks out? Why are the others not up?"

While I tried to make sense of what I was seeing and feeling, the conductor and the driver, in no hurry, walked to the back of the cable car. One of the men took hold of two ropes and jerked down the electric contact poles attached to the roof of the cable car as hard as he could. He then released the ropes, and the springs that held the electric connectors to the power lines overhead pushed the connectors up against the lines with a bang. That banging sound, to me was like big guns going off. Big chunks of ice broke off the power lines and hit the top of the cable car, the pavement, and the outside wall of my room. That noise sounded like gunshots. After a few minutes of banging, most of the ice fell, and the electric connections were remade. The driver and conductor returned to their positions, and the cable car made its way up the hill.

As I was beginning to feel foolish and trying to calm myself, there was a soft knock on my bedroom door. "Dr. Brown, hope you slept well; we will have breakfast in twenty minutes."

Relieved but still shaking, I seriously began to ponder, "Who am I? Why am I here? What is driving me?" These questions were the beginning of my search of myself, and now I could find some answers.

My family, like most in America, is a hodgepodge of different nationalities and cultures. To be politically correct, I am a German, Irish, British and American Indian. This was what my Syrian friend could not understand. I later learned that he was worried about his beautiful daughter leaving home for college; she might fall in love with a non-Syrian, and that scared him.

My father, Madison Euel Brown, was the youngest son in a family of eight children. His father was either Swiss or Bavarian, and his mother came from a small Indian village in Arkansas. My grandfather died before I knew him, but Grandmother Brown lived into her late eighties. She was small and quiet and had an inner strength and sense of calmness that fascinated me. She never seemed to be upset about anything that happened to or around her.

My mother, Amy B. Ribble, was the oldest daughter and second child of Tom Ribble and Ida Chandler. Mom's parents lived into their late eighties and were major contributors

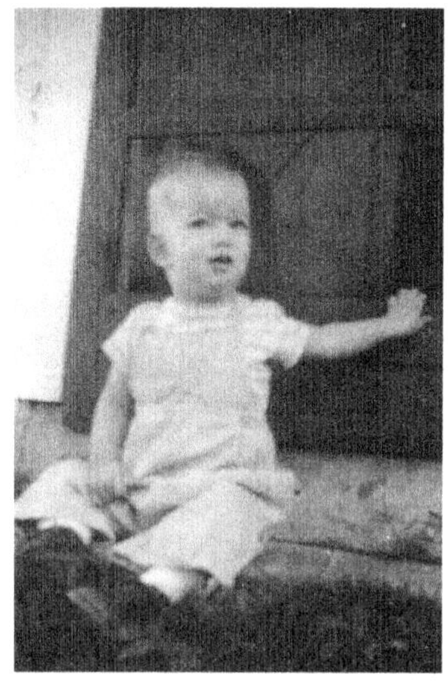

Edd at age two.

to what I am. (Their influence will be shared about later in this narrative.) My grandmother was the steadying influence on my grandfather. Granddad was Irish, Scots and English, with a temper and stubbornness that only she, Ida Chandler, could mediate and control.

My dad was born in 1904 in Buda, Texas, halfway between Austin and San Antonio. His father was a strong abolitionist, and his mother, from Arkansas, was one-fourth American Indian. He was not a popular person in the county. Although it is probable that two of his brothers died at the Alamo, the history of that county only included a simple statement: "The Browns have left and moved north."

My mother's family history goes back to a ten-year-old boy who came from somewhere around London, England. He was on either the second or third ship that landed in the Jamestown area. We do not know if his name was Chandler or if that was his job on the ship. As a cabin boy, he would have been responsible for the candles and lights of the ship. The town of Chandler, Texas, was named after one of his descendants, who sold the land where the community developed to a railroad company for a right-of-way.

My great-grandfather, "Poo" Ribble, became the man of the house when he was fourteen years old. His father had died that year. One of Poo's first responsibilities was to track three horse thieves to Ft. Worth, Texas — over 100 miles from home. He located the three horses and then helped the sheriff retrieve them and return them to the family home on the Brazos River. Poo also helped his mother hide the family in small caves along the Brazos River to protect them from raiders who kidnapped white children to sell into slavery in Mexico.

My grandfather, Tom Ribble, married and had two sons, Carnice and Carson. He moved his family from Graham, Texas, to Hagerman, New Mexico, to homestead on new land. Tom Ribble opened a livery stable and hired himself out as a digger of water tanks (ponds) for farm stock and cisterns for families. In 1905, my mother was born.

Everything went well for them for several years; then an anthrax epidemic killed most of the horses and cattle in New Mexico. Defeated, with almost no money left, my grandfather and the two boys loaded three wagons with what they could salvage and moved the family back to Brazos River country. My mother told of days of walking to keep warm and how, in extreme weather, the family would take turns riding in the cook wagon. To keep from freezing, they kept a fire going with "cow chips" and dry wood they could find.

On their six-week journey, for safety reasons, the family joined with other travelers and cattle herds being moved to better grazing areas. On that trip in 1924, my mother and dad first met. He was returning from Tatum, New Mexico, where he had been working on his sister's ranch, to his family home just out of Olney, Texas. Mom's family was on their way to the Brazos. Because of that chance contact, closer family ties began. Mom and Dad began to see one another. Their courtship was slow because of distance and limited travel options, but in time they became engaged.

The year 1926 was another "boom" year in the United States; the wild free thinking and good times kept the Roaring Twenties alive and exciting. The stock market continued to climb, and jobs were plentiful. Ford Motors made new models, and Henry Ford said, "You can have an auto in any color you want as long as it is black."

Ford, not the government, introduced the eight-hour workday, the forty-hour week, and a five-dollar daily minimum wage. Walt Disney opened his new studio. Georgia banned the teaching of evolution in its schools. SAT tests were approved for college entrance. Gene Turnery defeated Jack Dempsey for the heavyweight boxing title, and Babe Ruth hit three home runs in one game. U.S. Highway 66, which spanned the nation from Chicago to Los Angeles, was opened. Hitler's

"Mein Kampf" was published in Germany.

When my father returned to Texas, he went to work in the oil fields in "Boomtown" Burkburnett. Later he worked on a derrick in the Chalk Hills, drilling for oil just out of Archer City, Texas. It was a great year to get married.

He and Amy B. Ribble started a new life together. They set up their home in a three-room house, four blocks from the courthouse in Archer City, Texas. Eleven months after their wedding, on a cold windy night in December, Mom asked Dad to take her to see a movie at the theater three blocks away. They paid ten cents each for entrance and five cents for a bag of popcorn. After the movie, on their way home, Mom began having birth pains. Dad helped her to bed and rushed two blocks at two o'clock in the morning to wake up the doctor.

He and the doctor hurried back to Mom. At seven o'clock on a cold December morning, I entered this crazy world. I was the first son, the first grandson in my mother's family, and the son of the youngest son in my father's family. My birth was to have been a big event that morning of December 19, 1926; however, because of my small size, I had to be closely watched. In addition to regular nursing, I had to be fed special fortified milk for my first six months of life. Some of the family jokingly began to refer to me as "The Runt" and wondered if I would ever be worth anything. That is who I am and how I began my life.

The doctor or a nurse came for a month to check on me and Mom. In a year, I began to gain some weight and could take baby food. Mom then felt free to invite women from the Baptist church to meet in our home. At a meeting six months later, most of the ladies left early because of a strong thunderstorm. I was watching them leave through our screen door when a lightning bolt struck a utility pole thirty feet in front of me. The pole was split, and the electric wires were broken and scattered. The force of the lighting strike knocked me down and threw me against a wall twelve feet away. One of the ladies had stayed and saw what happened. She rushed to get the doctor. Mom was terrified and tried to control her reaction to care for me. The lady located our doctor, and both rushed back to our home. I was examined from my feet to my head for half an hour. There was no visible damage, although the doctor was concerned about my eyes and my hearing. Mom asked the doctor if there could be any permanent damage.

The doctor, as nicely as he could, said, "Mrs. Brown, Edd has already had two rough beginnings in his short life. I have done all I can and will continue to watch Him. While I feel confident that Edd will recover, I have to admit that ONLY GOD KNOWS what effect this lightning strike and his lack of size will have on him."

That is how I began my life. For six years, animals were my only friends. What other experiences, family traditions and world events contributed to my life and molded me into what I have become?

In 1927, the Chicago White Sox baseball team was charged with 'throwing' a World Series game. The "Ziegfeld Follies" opened on Broadway. Golfers were arrested in South Carolina for playing golf on the Sabbath. Chiang Kai-shek began his revolution in China, and an earthquake in China killed over 200,000 people. Charles Lindberg made the first solo airplane flight across the Atlantic. Ford Motor Company introduced the Model A, and the Berlin Stock Exchange collapsed.

Dad found a new job in the small town of Megargel, Texas, eighteen miles west. He worked at a service station owned by his older brother Ernest. We moved into a large rooming house close to Dad's mom. My mother was gone to Graford, Texas, for three weeks to care for her sister, who was having her first child. My aunts and grandmother took care of me.

Two months after Mom returned home, we moved into a small house with a fenced yard across the street from my grandmother. At the doctor's suggestion, I got a bulldog that became my only friend.

I was two years old and Rex, my eighty-pound bulldog, owned me. I could not go anywhere that he did not go. He was a digger, and Dad did everything he could to keep Rex penned up. Rex would dig under the fence, Dad would refill the holes with boards and rocks, and Rex would dig them out. It was fun for me. I could crawl through a hole, hold Rex by the collar, and take him for a walk, wherever he wanted to go. Mom or Dad would get a phone call from someone saying that Rex and I were two or three blocks from home.

One day, I wanted to go see Dad at work. Rex and I crawled under the fence and walked away with me holding onto his collar. The two of us walked up the road to the highway, which was the main street of our town. We got on the white line in the middle of the highway and started toward the other side of town where Dad worked. Mom at home and Dad at work began to get telephone calls from people.

Dad advised, "Do not try to do anything. If you even approach them, Rex will attack." The result was that the local police came and, with red lights flashing, followed us down the street to where Dad worked. After a spanking and firm warning, I never did that again. Rex was put on a long leash, and the fence was reinforced a lot more than I thought was necessary.

The first big loss in my young life came two weeks later. While the repairs and upgrading of the fence was being done, Dad took Rex to work with him. Two guys who lived out of town were "dog baiters." They raised dogs to fight and bragged that their dogs could whip any dog in Archer County. Dad began to leave Rex at home, but when Mom and I were gone one day, Dad took Rex to work with him.

The two dog baiters came to get gasoline to go to a dogfight. While

Dad was inside, they took their two dogs out of their truck and set them loose on Rex. Even though Rex was tied to a post, he killed one of their dogs and chewed up the other so bad that he and Rex both had to be put to sleep. The two punks were mad and made threats of getting even. Dad called the sheriff, and the two were arrested. My loss of Rex was the greatest disappointment of my young life. It was offset some when my younger brother Charles, who was larger than me, was born.

In 1928, everything was still great in the U.S. Air conditioning was installed in an office building in San Antonio. Alto's on Fisherman's Wharf in San Francisco was opened. Penicillin was discovered. The Graf Zeppelin landed in New Jersey. Hirohito became the emperor of Japan, and Japan began its invasion of China. Very few in the U.S. were even aware of these world-changing events and couldn't have cared less. Radio was becoming the latest "thing" that people had to have. "Old Man River" was the nation's top song. The influenza epidemic that took over 200,000 lives dominated the news.

Oil prices began to drop. The Dow Jones Average hit an all-time high of 381, but the U.S. stock market dropped over forty percent four weeks later. Panic replaced the "spend and enjoy; the world is ours" mentality. In a week, the price of oil dropped to eight dollars a barrel. Dad's job was in jeopardy. Dad called his oldest brother, Eck, a banker in Dalhart, and asked if any jobs might be open in the north Texas Panhandle. Eck was not sure, but with the market still dropping and the price of oil still going down, Dad decided we had better move.

We loaded all we had in our Model T Ford and headed north. Because we had little money, we bought food in markets and ate beside the road. At night, we camped in open fields until we passed Amarillo. Sometimes we stayed in abandoned houses that people had left. We found a place on a small farm east of town to live in, and Dad was hired as a shoe salesman at J.C. Penney in downtown Dalhart.

The land was flat, and the wind blew most of the time. Rain was infrequent, and no more than a drizzle when it did come. Mom had another baby, this time a girl. Vera Nell was a delight; Charles and I enjoyed playing with and teasing her when we were not running through the cornfields or when I was not riding my Shetland pony that a family had left behind when they just gave up and moved away.

Charles and I liked to throw rocks. We would throw them at birds, chickens, fence posts, or anything we could find. One boring day, we were playing around a steel culvert, looking for snakes to kill. A car went by on the road. After it passed, we both threw a rock in that direction.

"I can come closer to a car than you can," Charles challenged.

Since I was the oldest (but not any larger), I replied, "No you can't."

We threw rocks that missed the cars but came close. As we began to get closer, one of us hit the windshield of an oncoming car. Scared, we took off to the cornfield to hide. Fifteen minutes later, Dad and the owner of the car walked into the cornfield. "We know where you are. You better come out, or the trouble you are in will be a lot worse," Dad said.

We knew running was no option. With our heads hanging down, we walked out. We had to apologize to the owner of the car and promise to never throw rocks at any moving thing. Dad agreed to pay for a new windshield. The man left with his own warning. We headed for the house, knowing we were in big trouble. We both got the spanking of our lives and were sent to bed without dinner. We were confined to our house for a week and given the worst jobs Mom and Dad could think up. After that, neither of us ever threw rocks at anything other than a tree stump.

The wind continued. The rain came less frequently. Some people lost jobs, and Dad was one. Many could not buy food; they stopped buying shoes or anything else. We could not pay rent, and our food was scarce.

Dad's brother came to tell Dad that the bank had to repossess a ranch south of Clayton, New Mexico, which was west of Texline, Texas. They needed someone to care for the few cattle and horses still on the ranch. Dad borrowed a pickup, and we moved to the ranch. Like most others, we had very little to move and only a few clothes to worry about. While my folks worried and worked hard to make ends meet, the next year and a half was one of the high points of my early life.

The ranch was located on a stretch of small rolling hills that was bisected by a small river. Our adobe brick house had eighteen-inch thick walls and was a hundred feet up a slope from the river. There were large oak and cottonwood trees surrounding the house. The corrals for the horses, milk cows and calves were close by. I was in heaven with all the open country where I could ride my horse.

Our house had one large room that served as both kitchen and den and two bedrooms, each with a closet. We had a wood-burning stove that was used for cooking and heating, as well as an inside water pump with a sink. The only door was the front entrance to the house. We had a screen door we could use on warm days. The other rooms had non-opening windows. The trees and the thick walls helped with the summer heat and cold winters.

The area around the house was sandy. Quail, ducks, crows, robins and other birds were abundant. Coyotes, snakes, lizards, skunks and other animals were not far away. We had an outhouse (privy) at the back, downhill from the house and away from the river.

Dad had brought wooden boxes and made shelves for Mom in

the kitchen and for our things in the bedrooms. Charles and I had one bedroom. Mom, Dad and Nell had the other one. We were settled in within a week, and I began to roam the country. Dad had a friend of his remake a horse saddle to fit me. At five years of age, I had my own Shetland pony with saddle and bridle. I would ride to the mailbox a mile and a half away. I would ride the fence line with Dad or one of my uncles. I would go after the milk cows, I could and would have lived on my horse, but I had to eat and sleep, so most of the time I stayed close to home.

One day, Dad told Mom that he and I needed to go to our neighbor's place to pick up hay for the horses and cattle. Winter was coming, and we had to refill the barn. It was a five-mile round trip, and we went everywhere either on horseback or by wagon. I thought, "All I am going to do is ride five miles in an old wagon."

As we went to the corral to get the horses, Dad asked, "Think you are big enough to learn how to hook a team to the wagon and drive a ways? Let's just see."

He gave me a rope, but I was not able to catch either of the two horses we used to pull the wagon. He sat on the fence and watched as I missed and missed, catching neither of the two big animals. The rope I used had to be light and short so I could throw it. That was part of the problem; for years after I was born, the doctors were still concerned about my size. I was small and was still referred to as "The Runt."

After five minutes, Dad got off the fence to help. Together, we roped the horses and led them to the barn. We put the harness on them and hitched the horses to the wagon. Dad drove the team out of the barnyard and onto the road (which had no gavel or pavement). He stopped and got off the wagon to check and make sure everything was connected right. He walked around the wagon, climbed up the wagon wheel on my side and handed me the long leather reins. He began to explain how I could learn to drive a team of horses.

"You do not jerk the reins; you pull firmly and slowly and give the horses time to respond. You let them know what you want, vocally and manually."

I sat there, hoping he would change his mind. He waited. I shook the reins and hollered, "Giddy-up!" To my amazement, the horses began to move.

I learned that all I had to do was occasionally slap the reins gently on the horse's rump, and the horses would follow the trail. I began to relax as Dad would point out the trees that were a few miles away. A mother skunk and her two little ones walked close to us in the soft rain that began to fall. A coyote ran across the trail ahead. It was a great way to spend a day.

As we approached our neighbor's house, Dad took the reins. We entered the yard and drove to the barn. The neighbor opened the huge double doors, and Dad backed the wagon just inside. That way, we could load the hay out of the rain. I was tired; it was work for me to drive the team evenly with no problems. Dad found a place at the opposite end of the barn, put a blanket down and suggested I might want to rest while he and the neighbor loaded the hay. I thought that if I was big enough to drive a team, I was big enough to help load hay.

Dad told me to just lie down while they got everything ready. I did and was only going to rest until they began to load the wagon. Two hours later, Dad picked me up, carried me into the house and woke me by washing my face and hands. I was then ready to eat lunch with our neighbor's family. The wife and two girls, one older and one about my age, had prepared a big meal for us. The older girl and their big boy who had helped load the wagon helped me feel at home and kept encouraging me to eat. With cornbread, fried chicken, mashed potatoes and gravy, apple cobbler and fresh milk in front of me, their encouragement was not necessary. We thanked them and left. Dad drove all the way back to our home. The next morning, the neighbor and his son came to help unload the wagon and put the hay in our barn.

The next week, Dad went to a horse auction in Clayton, fifteen miles north. Late the next day, he came home leading an Appaloosa horse that was extremely unhappy. The big horse had on a halter with a heavy rope attached. The end of rope was tied around the horn of Dad's saddle. "Big App" (my name for him) balked, bucked, and tried everything he could to break away; he even tried to bite Dad's horse.

"Open the gate!" Dad called.

I opened the gate to the corral and backed away. Dad pulled, jerked, and fought to get App into the corral. After three attempts, Dad managed to get both horses through the gate. As fast as I could, I closed and locked the gate. Dad dropped the rope from his saddle horn and rode his horse into the horse shed that was attached to the corral. He removed the bridle and saddle from his horse. He slammed the door, took off his hat and muttered words I had never heard. He walked to the horse-watering trough and dipped his hat into the water. He then poured water over his head and stood there shaking. I walked over and looked up at him.

"You okay?" I asked.

He replied, "I have been better, but that damn horse will either kill me or I will kill him. You do not have to tell your mother what I have said, and you are not to repeat those words, okay?

I asked, "What about the rope on the horse? He could get tangled up and even break a leg."

App was rearing, fighting the rope, charging the fence, and scraping his head against the posts attempting to rid himself of the halter on his head.

Shaking his head, Dad answered, "He will quit once he exhausts himself. It may take a few hours, but he cannot keep this up. Let's go see what your mom has to eat."

Mom had been watching. She was more than upset by what she had seen, but she was smart enough to say nothing until Dad had regained his composure and we had finished eating our supper.

I was tired, so Mom let me sleep late the next morning. What woke me was the noise coming from the horse corral. In the middle of the corral was a huge upright pole. Dad had secured the rope, still attached to the halter on App, to the pole. He used a short rope to make App circle the pole until he had tightened himself to the pole. App was then unable to move more than a foot or so. Dad and the horse just stopped and looked at one another.

Dad backed off and waited until the horse had settled down; then he went into the shed and picked up a saddle blanket. He approached App with the blanket and held it in front of the horse for three to four minutes. Dad carefully walked to the side of the horse and laid the blanket on App. App attempted three times to shake it off and then tried to reach the blanket with his teeth, but the rope and halter held his head too tight for him to reach the blanket. Dad walked to the fence and climbed to the top railing. I joined him, and we sat for half an hour. App was watching us all this time, but he had stopped trying to remove the blanket.

"Okay, you get that bucket by the gate, fill it about half full of water, and see if App will drink," Dad said.

I looked at that huge animal and stayed sitting.

Dad laughed, "That horse can't hurt you while he's tied like that if you stay in front of him."

I got the bucket, dipped it in the water tank and, with it half full, started for the front end of the horse. App did not try to move but followed me with his eyes as much as the rope allowed him to move his head.

Very quietly, Dad said, "Just hold the bucket in front of him and let him smell the water."

Shaking enough that the water was splashing, I eased the bucket less than a foot away from App's nose and mouth. App settled down, but I didn't. "Now," Dad said, "Slowly move the bucket up to where he can get his mouth in the water."

I did that and tried not to drop the bucket and run. I watched as the horse began to drink. There was so little water; it was gone almost before the bucket was in position for App to drink.

Dad said, "Okay, go get some more water and let him have it."

I filled the bucket with as much as I could carry and came back. With no hesitation this time, I let App drink.

"Time for a break," Dad said. "Let's see what your mom has for breakfast."

Mom had been watching and replied, "I have been too frightened to cook, so it will be a few minutes. Edd, go to the hen house and get me six eggs."

Charles, my younger brother, grabbed the egg basket, and we headed for the hen house.

"Scared, weren't you?" he snickered.

"Not me," I lied.

"Were too," he said.

Before we could say more and get into one of our daily fights, Mom called, "Boys, if you are going to get anything to eat, I need those eggs now."

We looked at one another and went to gather three eggs each. Charles, grinning from ear to ear, led the way back into the house.

After breakfast, Dad said, "Edd, I want you to give that horse a half bucket of water and, half an hour later, a half bucket of grain. I want him left tied to that post with the blanket on him until noon, and no one, including you, is to go back into that corral until I say so."

With that, Dad left. He hitched up the team of draft horses to a plow and headed to the five-acre high meadow a mile down river from our house. I went to the horse shed, got the water bucket, filled it half full and went into the corral. With no problem, I gave App some water and, later, a half bucket of grain. Too much water with grain, and the swelling could cause the horse some real problems. Even though the horse had almost whipped Dad the day before, Dad wanted nothing to harm that animal.

Charles and I went to the pasture on the other side of the river (which was almost dry) where the milk cows were grazing. We drove them to the barn and put them in the cow pen. My job was to watch over my six-month-old sister Nell, who was learning to crawl and climb. Charles helped Mom. She milked the two cows, and she and Charles cleaned and washed the stalls and turned the cows back out to pasture.

At noon, Dad returned from where he was plowing. He watered App, who was snubbed to the post, and began curing him. The horse was still resisting but not so wildly. Dad released the rope from the halter. He backed away, making sure he stayed in front of the horse. App shook his head and backed up. He looked surprised that he was able to walk away from the post. He nickered, jumped around and began to run around the corral. Dad got a bucket of water and carefully approached App. App backed away but made no threatening moves. Dad just stayed still and held up the bucket. They stood and stared at each other for five minutes. App moved forward, put his head in the bucket, got a mouthful of water and jumped back. Little by little, he repeated those moves. All this time, Mom, who had picked up Nell, was watching in dead silence with Charles and me. In almost a whisper, Dad said, "Edd, get the other bucket, fill it half full of grain and bring it here. Try not to make any unnecessary moves or noise."

I got the bucket, filled it half full of grain and entered the corral. Slowly, I approached App. App stood and watched but made no move. I walked to the horse, held up the bucket and waited. Cautiously, the horse approached. The whole time, App never took his eyes off me, but he ate. He then turned, walked to the other side of the corral, turned back to me and just stared.

"Okay, that is enough for today," Dad said.

Dad asked me to get the two draft horses in the small corral and bring them with their harness out of the shed so we could hook them to the wagon. Those horses were tame enough. All I had to do was open the gate, put out some hay and start them that way. The horses, though they were not huge like App, were still big to me. I got a collar off the hook and dragged it to an overturned steel watering tub. I put a rope on the smallest horse, led him to the tub and then got on the tub.

Dad was harnessing the other horse and watching me. The horse I was working on stood still. I lifted the collar off the tub and tried to get it around his neck. After three tries, I got it on him, but I could not get it buckled. The horse shook his head, and the collar fell to the ground. I got off the tub, picked up the collar, put it on the tub, crawled back on the tub and, with the help of a patient horse, got the collar on again. I was out of breath.

"Dad, I need some help." Grinning, he came over. "Just wondering how long it would take you to ask," he said as he buckled the collar and then helped me put the rest of the harness on the two horses.

We led the horses out to a small wagon that had been loaded with a row cutter sled. With Dad doing most of the work, we hitched the team to the wagon. Dad gave me the reins and told me where we were going to work. I was to drive the wagon with the sled to the field and wait for him there.

I slapped the horses with the reins, drove along the banks of the river for a mile and then turned uphill for another half mile. The field had been planted with "Highgear," a hybrid seed that was developed for greater endurance in drought conditions. The grain was primarily for animal food, but it was sometimes milled and used in baking for human consumption. The weather had brought less rain than normal. The crop was doing fine, but so were the weeds. The weeds were taking up more moisture than were the crops. Dad arrived carrying a water jug and a bucket with my noon meal and hung them on a tree close by.

"You will be here most of the day. Mom sent lunch for you. I will show you how to do want I want done, and then you will be on your own."

I was to ride the sled and drive the horses down the furrows. The blades would cut the weeds and grass under the topsoil. Dad did a couple of rows while I rode on the back of the sled. We then reversed, and I drove. I did all right on the rows, but turning around was a real problem. Turn too quick, and the sled would tip and possibly turn over. Turn too late, and I would cut ten to fifteen feet of grain before I was able to get the team and sled back in position to cut out the weeds and not the crop.

We did two more rows, and Dad left with a simple statement: "Just do the best you can, and try to leave some grain."

After my first couple of trips down the rows, about half the weeds remained and half the crop was destroyed; but then my horses and I developed a rhythm and more of the crop survived. I stopped for lunch and watered and fed the horses. As I was getting back on the sled, I saw a black car approaching our house. The road was a mile from where I was working. We had not had anyone come to our house in a car since we moved there four months ago. I just stood there and stared and wondered what was going on.

Before we moved there, a car usually meant we were going to move again. I hurried as much as I could and finished my job. When I arrived at the corral, no one was around; the car was there, but no one was outside. I heard laughing and joking coming from inside the house. I hurried to get the team inside the corral and hoped I could get the harness off them by myself. I could then turn the horses out to pasture and find out who was in the car.

One horse was tame enough to let me lead him to the up-turned tank. I wrestled most of the harness off, but my arms were so tired I almost fell off the tank.

"Looks like you could use a hand," a familiar voice said.

I looked up and could not believe who I saw. Tom, Mom's youngest brother and my favorite uncle, was leaning on the fence and watching. I dropped whatever I was holding, ran to the fence, climbed to the top and jumped into his outstretched arms.

The questions just flew. How long would he be there? Why had he come? What was going on? Tom backed off, saying, "Just hold on; we will get to all that. First, we need to unharness those horses."

We unharnessed the horses, rubbed them down, and opened the gate so they could run. Tom was the youngest of my four uncles. He was ten years older than me and had been away working on Dad's older sister's ranch, south of Tatum, New Mexico. He was going to stay with us for three weeks and then go back to Dalhart in time to get back in school. I forgot how tired I was, and we went into the house where my grandfather and grandmother were waiting.

When they asked about my day, I told them about riding the cutting sled, and my grandmother just had a fit.

"You put my six-year-old grandson on that thing with those awful horses?" she blurted out at Dad.

"Grandma," I said, "the horses know me. I can jump and the horses will stop, but I didn't have to."

She smiled at me and said, "Okay, but I still don't like it."

The talk around the dinner table for an hour after the meal was about the lack of rain and the question of whether there would be enough moisture to have any crops that year. I listened but had no idea what they were concerned about. I had a horse, miles of open country to ride, enough to eat, two good pairs of boots, enough clothes and a good bed to sleep in. I had loving parents and my favorite uncle. My younger brother was a pain, but we got along together most of the time. Old folks worry because they have to take care of the younger ones, but it was no big deal to me.

My grandparents left in the car early enough to get home before dark, just in case the wind got up again and blew the sand. The next day, Tom and I rode the fence line to look for breaks and downed posts. We looked for any place where cattle rustlers might have come through. Other days, we just looked at the country and found a few new calves. Tom would pick the calf up and put it crossways on the saddle in front of him. With the bawling mother following us, we would take both back to the corral across what had been the river.

In three months, the river had become a creek and was now almost dry. We had to use a team of horses and a Fresno Scraper (a digging tool) to dig out the sand. When we first started digging, we only had to remove a foot of sand to find water; but in just a few weeks, we had to dig four or five feet, and even then only half of the hole would fill with water.

Uncle Eck, who worked for the bank in Dalhart that owned the ranch, came to look things over. He and Dad decided that some of the cattle must be sold. There would not be enough grain and hay to feed them because of so little rain. I remember their concern, but I thought this was just part of ranch life.

We had two good saddle horses. With Tom there, we had to have another saddle horse so he could help round up the cattle and new calves. We either had to break App to ride or find another horse. Dad tried to work with App. The horse would let the saddle blanket be put on, but it took two days to get him to accept a saddle. Even then, he would not let it be cinched. As Tom and I watched, Dad shook his head walked off.

Tom got a bucket of oats and "soft-talked" the horse, patting him on the nose. After three or four tries he got the saddle on App and was able to get one cinch halfway tight. We left App that way and ate lunch. Tom and I went back, and he was able to get both cinches of the saddle on and tight. App would not take a bridle, so Tom decided to ride him with a halter. He put the halter on App, and I held the one rein.

Tom began to pet App, talking to him while he slowly mounted the saddle. App just stood. I handed the rein to Tom and backed away. No one moved. Tom kneed the horse, but nothing happened. He kneed him again, and App began snort and shake his head, slowly moving to the rails of the corral. App began to rub against the post to get Tom and the saddle off. That did not work, so App began to buck, but not hard; he just wanted that thing on his back off. After a few minutes, App stopped.

Tom looked at Dad and asked, "What do you think?"

"It is up to you," Dad replied.

No one moved, and the horse looked frozen. "Okay," Tom said. "Edd, open the gate."

I was too scared to move, so Dad gave a gentle push. "Go, do it and get back out of the way."

I ran to the gate on the outside of the corral and swung it open. App was almost there before it was open enough for him to get through. That horse ran as if he was on fire — up the road, across the meadow, down the hill, across the river, and up another hill — and disappeared.

"What we going do Dad?" I asked.

"Nothing — we just wait. Tom will come back on the horse or he will limp back. If the horse comes back by himself, we will go find Tom. So we wait," Dad answered.

We waited. In twenty minutes, Tom and App came over the hill. Tom was still in the saddle. App was sweating and had foam in his nostrils and mouth. Tom rode him across the river and into the corral; he then removed the saddle and blanket and began to rub the horse down.

"Edd, bring me a little water, will you?" Tom asked.

I looked at Dad. He nodded. I was scared but went for water and took it into the corral.

"Let him drink slowly," Tom said. Between App's huffing and puffing, I let App drink about a half of bucket of water.

"Later, when he cools down, we will give him more and then feed him," Dad said.

That evening, Dad told us he had known the horse would be rough and hard to break, but he had never dealt with a horse this stubborn. He did not know if our time spent would be worth our trouble.

"I don't know either, but he is one good piece of horse flesh," Tom replied.

"I think he likes me," I said.

"Sure he does," Tom said. "You aren't big enough for him to be afraid of."

That statement was disturbing. I did not want people or anything to be afraid of me, but being referred to as little began to rankle me.

The next day, Dad went to plow a small area for a fall garden while Tom and I rode the fence line. Tom was on App with a halter that worked fine. The horse did not like anything on his back and balked a little, but he did not buck. Tom and I raced the horses some just to keep them loose and tired enough that we could enjoy our ride. The ranch was just over two hundred acres. The fall rains had not come, so the cattle had to be sold; otherwise, they would be so weak that they could not survive the winter.

We had been gone three hours and were starting to head back to the house when we saw dust in the air a mile away. We talked about what it could be, and Tom decided we ought to check it out. We put the horses into an easy lope and, in a few minutes, came to a spot where two thirty-foot lengths of fence had been cut out. We saw a small truck rushing down a trail that led to the road a mile away. We found the remains of two cows that had been skinned and butchered. We repaired the fence and were careful to not step in any tracks or mess up anything around the area where the cows had been butchered.

Tom asked if I would mind staying there by myself for a while. He would ride to the house to let Dad know what had happened and get word to the sheriff. I did not mind. I just needed to move the cattle away from the fence so no tracks would mess up the area. Tom gave me his water and what was left of our lunch and took off. I rode my horse to where twenty head of cattle and a few calves were standing and herded them half a mile down a small hill. I rode back to a huge rock beside the fence line, got off my horse and climbed to the top of the rock. I could now see the area where the fence had been cut and see the livestock for a mile. I ate the two lunches, drank some water and laid back. Without planning to, I went to sleep.

I have no idea how long I slept, but I was awakened by a dog barking. I sat up and saw Butch, our big collie, come lumbering up the hill. Behind Butch were four horses. For a minute I was concerned, but then I knew that Butch would not be so friendly if there was any danger. As the horsemen got closer, I recognized App (gosh, he was big!) and saw Tom was on him. Dad on his horse and two others I did not know were also coming in my direction.

They stopped and made sure I was all right, and we all went to the area where the fence had been cut. The two other men were sheriff's deputies. They got off their horses and began to look around. They found tracks of boots and tires and made plaster casts. They took pictures out of their saddlebags, laid them out beside the casts and began to compare the likeness.

"Same bunch," they said. "Did you see the truck? What color was it? How old do you think it was? What did you do?"

We answered as best we could and all rode back to the house just before sunset. Later, we learned that the two men were raiding local ranches, butchering two or three cattle at a time, and taking only the best meat. They were cutting up that meat and selling it to cafés and restaurants in other communities. Tom and I were the only ones who had seen the truck. With the plaster casts of tire treads and boot prints, prints from the other sites and our description of the truck, the sheriff was able to track down and arrest the two guys.

Two days later, Dad decided that he would ride App. He went to the corral and was able to get a halter and blanket on the horse. App would still not take the saddle from Dad. App bucked, kicked and almost got Dad before Dad got over the fence.

Tom was plowing a new patch of field for planting next to the area where I had run the cutting sled. We heard a noise and ran outside. The draft horses were running at breakneck speed down the hill toward the barn. Tom was on the plow, trying to stop them and hanging on. The horses flew by the corral and through the yard and finally stopped, exhausted, at a water hole in the riverbed. Tom got off, unhitched the two-wheel plow, took up the reins, and made the horses run up and down the dry riverbed until they almost fell. He drove them back to the plow, re-hitched them and went through the gate of the corral. He unhitched the plow, unharnessed the horses, put them in the other corral and came into the house.

"Dumb, stupid animals, anyway," he said.

"What happened?" Mom asked as she put a plate for his dinner on the table.

"That black mare began to smart around again. She got one of the reins around her neck and swung her head to get it off. The other horse began to push back, one thing led to another, and they ran. Once they ran out, I unhitched the plow and worked them up and down in the sand until they nearly dropped. I doubt it will change her; she did that once before. She is one spooky horse," Tom explained.

Things became routine for a few days. We cut and gathered wood, fed the cattle, gathered eggs, slopped the hogs, milked cows, rode the fence and enjoyed the country even though there had been no rain.

Dad had almost given up on App. Tom could ride him with a halter, but that horse got his haunches up every time Dad went into the corral. A few times, App even tried to bite and kick him. Dad left App alone. Our routine was fine, and we were enjoying having Tom with us.

No one knew how it happened or who left the screen door unlocked, but it happened. Mom's screams scared everyone. Dad and Tom were out working cattle. Charles and I were playing some game. He and I jumped up and ran to the front door to find Mom in hysterics.

"What's wrong?" I asked.

Mom could not answer; she just pointed. Nell had made her way out the front door, crawled over fifty feet and gone under the low railing into the horse corral. She had stopped and was just looking around, and App was moving in her direction.

"He could kill her," Mom moaned.

Without thinking, I rushed out the door, ran, and dived through the fence rails. I grabbed Nell and threw her out of the corral fence. Exhausted, I fell down. I was as scared as Mom was. Mom picked up Nell and took her to the house to make sure she was all right.

After she examined Nell, Mom looked back at the corral and saw me still sitting where I had sat after getting Nell out. With Nell in her arms, she came back to the corral and calmly (almost in a forced whisper) said, "Edd, get out of there before that crazy horse gets to you."

I was still stunned by all that had happened and even more so by what had not happened. I just sat. Mom had calmed down and was holding Nell. She began to convince me that I needed to get out of that corral and away from that horse.

I was almost in shock; nothing seemed real. I felt something wet on my neck and tried to brush away whatever it was, but it kept coming back. I turned and looked, and App was standing there nuzzling me. I was totally unnerved, and Mom more so.

Not knowing what else to do, I carefully turned and rubbed App's forehead. He backed up a few steps but kept his head down close to me. I slowly stood up and turned to rub his forehead again. He did not move, nor did I for a few minutes. I began to breathe normally and backed a few steps away from App. He followed me, but not threateningly. I stopped, and he stopped; I began to jog, and he stayed with me. I went fast, and he ran with me; I slowed to a crawl, and that big animal slowed, too.

I picked up a short rope, and App let me put it around his neck. I led him to the fence. I climbed the fence and eased on to him. He just stood, turned his head and looked at me. He turned his head back and began to walk around the inside of the corral.

All this time, Mom was watching. She was holding onto Nell so tightly that it was only when Nell whimpered that Mom realized how hard she was holding her. Mom walked to the fence of the corral, smiling and greatly relieved.

"You okay?" she asked. I nodded. "Well, I think you may have a new friend," she said.

Later in the house, Mom warned that I must continue to be careful of the horse until I could trust him and that I was not to embarrass Dad when he came for supper that night.

After lunch, I went back to the corral with a carrot. I sat on the fence and held it out to App. He came over to get it and let me put the rope back around his neck. I gently pulled him along the side of the fence and climbed on his back. With no bridle and no halter, I rode him around the corral for next twenty minutes.

I got off App to do my daily chores. I fed the chickens, slopped the hogs and cleaned the hen house. Later, Tom came in from digging deeper waterholes in the creek bed. After he had his lunch, I asked him to help me put a bridle on App.

"Are you crazy? That horse will not let either of us get within a mile of him with a bridle," Tom said.

"Maybe, maybe not, but will you help if I can get him to the fence?" I asked.

"Okay, if you can get him that close, I will help," he replied.

We headed for the corral. I climbed to the top rail and whistled, and App came running. I gave him a half apple, put the rope on his neck and crawled on the horse's back.

"I'll be damned!" Tom muttered as he came through the gate and approached App and me. I patted App on the neck and began to talk to him. He stood still while Tom caressed his forehead, slipped the bridle into his mouth and put the harness part over his head behind his ears. Tom then quickly backed away, waiting for the horse to erupt and throw me off.

App shook his head, brushed it against the fence once and settled down. "Tom, get on your horse and open the gate; maybe App will follow you," I said.

"Okay," Tom said, "but you stay close. You want a saddle? And when did that horse get 'App' for a name?"

"I don't want a saddle, and App just comes when I call him," I replied.

Tom got on his horse and reached over to open the gate. I gently kicked App and leaned the reins toward the gate. I followed Tom out of the corral, across the river and up the hill. We went slowly for a mile and then turned back to the house. Mom was outside watching. I could tell Mom was holding her breath and was scared that App would break into a run or start bucking. Nothing happened, though; we rode to the river bottom, I let App drink from a shallow pond, and we returned to the corral. I edged App to the fence and crawled off him. I took the bridle off him and then went into the shed and brought out some grain to feed him.

Tom closed the gate and went back to work, muttering, "Craziest, thing I ever saw."

That evening, Tom told Dad what had happened and how surprised he was. Mom shared how scared she was, and of course Charles chimed in, "I wasn't, but Edd sure was."

Dad looked at me and asked, "Were you scared?"

"I was worried more than scared, but App seemed to accept me. With Tom leading and us staying mostly on sand, I wanted to try," I said.

"Okay," Dad replied. "I was ready to get rid of him. He will never accept me, but if you will promise to always let me know before you go anywhere with him and if you will feed, water, and curry him on a regular basis, he can be yours."

I gasped. I knew I had heard wrong. I had no saddle and no real knowledge of the responsibility I was asked to agree to, but I was so overwhelmed and overjoyed to have my own horse that I would have agreed to anything. The next morning, when I went to bring in firewood and gather the eggs, Dad was in the barn and had my saddle on a workbench.

I walked over and looked at him with all kinds of questions in my eyes. He looked at me and smiled, saying, "Can't have a cowpuncher riding bareback when we move cattle, can we? I can make the cinches long enough and can adapt your saddle to fit that horse."

"Dad, he is App, not 'that horse,' " I said.

"Okay, App it is," he laughed.

Over the next few days, App and I — along with Dad, Tom, and three of our neighbors — rounded up over two hundred cattle and calves. We herded them into a ravine and began to separate out the unbranded cows and all the calves. You could hear the bawling from the cattle for a hundred miles.

A big fire was built and branding irons were heated. The cows and older calves were roped first; they were pulled close to the fire and forced to the ground with all four legs tied. With the red hot branding irons, they were branded. The small male calves were castrated and would become just dry cows.

My job was to ride in a circle and keep the herd from scattering.

At first, I had a lot of trouble with the cows and calves that would not stay in the herd. If I waited too long to head them off, I would have three or four to chase instead of one. I had not yet learned how to use App as a cowpony, so some of the older hands began to help and make suggestions: "You use too much bridle; use your knees," and "Let the horse lead," and "Trust him to learn."

After a couple of days, App and I began to merge. He was a born cowpony and had an uncanny sense of how to respond to my kneeing. My problem changed from guiding him to simply staying in the saddle as he began to take over the job of overtaking and turning back the cows and calves.

Four days later, we had driven the herd to a railroad holding pen. We returned home after five days and four nights of eating camp food and sleeping on the ground with only our boots and hats off. I was ready to go home. I was so tired I could not eat; sleeping was all I wanted to do.

At home, I noticed that Mom and Dad began to have more and more private conversations. I knew from the way they looked at each other that some major decisions had to be made and we were going to move again. I could tell Mom was not herself and Dad was working longer.

One day, I was at the outdoor pump getting water for the chickens. One of our dogs ran by and knocked the bucket over, and I blurted out, "You S.O.B.!" (I did not use the initials). Mom heard. She came outside, grabbed me by my shirt collar and dragged me into the house. She snatched up a washrag and soap and started scrubbing my mouth out. It burned and hurt. I cried and washed out my mouth two or three times, and it still burned.

Mom said, "I don't want to ever hear you say any words like that, you hear me?"

I nodded my head. I could not talk; I still hurt and could not stop crying, but I did go back to water the chickens. All the cowboys I had been with on the cattle drive used words like that (and some others I had never heard before), and it was all right.

Later, Mom came out to where I was. She was crying and saying she was sorry, not for cleaning out my mouth but for picking up the lye laundry soap instead of hand soap. Then she said, "Those cowboys can talk how they want, but no son of mine will never talk like that." To this day, many of my friends, Navy buddies, and classmates often remark about my very limited use of profanity of any kind.

The rest of the year was mostly routine. We gathered wood and took care of the remaining livestock. Still, there were always unexpected events to break any boredom that might be created with no radio, no telephone, no automobile and almost no friends other than the animals.

I was feeding the chickens and gathering eggs early one morning when I saw that the corral gate was open. I knew I had closed it the night before. Dad was still eating breakfast. I took the eggs in and asked Dad if he knew why the corral gate was open. He wanted to know if I had checked everything. I told him I had and that all I could find wrong was that the four horses were gone. The pen for the cows was okay. We went out and looked around, but the horses were nowhere to be seen. Dad looked at the gate and then at the post where the gate was supposed to be tied.

"Looks like you have a problem," he said. "Come take a look."

I walked over and saw what he had found. We used a rawhide (heavy leather) tie to secure the gate, and it had been chewed in two. "Guess who did that," Dad said.

I knew who. For over four months, the horses had never bothered the rawhide; only App would do such a stunt. "Guess I better get my boots on and get a rope," I said.

"You better get a jug of water and something to eat. I bet you have at least three to four miles to walk before you find those horses. Take a halter; App may let you catch him," Dad said.

"How can I get on him out there? He is twice as tall as I am," I shrugged.

"Don't really know; he is your horse, remember?" Dad replied.

"Yeah, I know," I grumbled as I went into the house.

Mom already had a lunch and a water can ready. I got the rope and halter and headed across the river and up the hill. It seemed like a week to me, but in two hours I had located the horses. Sure enough, those stupid (the worst word I could safely use) horses had gone to the far corner of the fenced area, close to where the two cattle rustlers had been.

I whistled, and App came trotting over. Using the apple I had brought, I was able to get my rope around his neck and lead him to the large rock I had slept on a few weeks earlier. I pulled App up close to the rock and climbed on. Just like my American Indian ancestors, I rode bareback and drove the other horses to the corral. I had been gone six hours and surprised everyone by getting back so early. Dad and I changed the rawhide to a double barbed wire latch held together around the post with a bolt and double nut closer. This meant that it took more time to open the corral gate, but neither of us wanted to spend another day walking to catch our horses.

Fall came. The weather cooled, but the rains did not come and crops began to die in the field. For two months, Mom seemed to be having difficulty getting around and rested a lot more, but she was in good spirits. She seemed to be doing better now and was not as sick as she had been. With the dry weather and the continuous wind, we were all tired and sluggish.

Uncle Eck came to the ranch. Sam Ed and Billy Neal, my two cousins, came with him. I had not seen either of them since we moved to the ranch. While the adults talked, Charles, our two cousins and I walked down the river for a mile. We walked across the dry riverbed up a large sand hill on the opposite side. The sand hill was over a hundred feet above the river and sloped at a twenty-five degree angle to the bottom. We had a few old fenders from wrecked cars and a few boards we used for sleds to slide into the river. Since there was now no water, we just sledded or rolled down the hill. We used long ropes to pull what we were using back up the hill to ride or tumble down again.

When we had sat down to rest at the top of the hill, Charles spoke up: "I hear something, sounds funny."

We laughed and told him it was sand in his ears and made jokes about his imaginary sounds. Then Sam Ed, the oldest, stood up. He walked around a bit and then spoke up. "Listen," he said.

We stopped talking and could all hear a low roar that began to grow louder. The noise sounded something like calves or cows bawling, pigs squealing, rocks falling and other weird sounds.

Sam Ed said, "I don't like what I hear. We better get to the other side of the river as fast as we can."

We picked up our stuff, left the sleds and boards and started down the hill. About halfway down, Sam Ed grabbed Charles, put him on his back and hollered, "Run now and don't stop!"

I looked up; coming down the riverbed toward us, less than a mile away, was a mass of logs, cattle, and other stuff in a wall of rolling water at least ten feet high. We ran, we fell, we got up, and we ran some more. We pulled and pushed one another until we were on the other side of the then dry riverbed. We stopped at the edge of the river, so traumatized by what we were seeing that we did not notice the water rising around us. Then, above the roar of the river, we heard Dad screaming at us as he ran in our direction, "GET BACK, GET BACK NOW! "

Sam picked up Charles, and we climbed up two more banks; we turned around and saw that where we had just been standing was now covered in swirling water over six feet deep. We climbed up another ten feet to meet Dad, who was so out of breath that he could hardly stand or talk. We were safe; we stood in awe as we saw trees, sheep, snakes, cows, pigs and debris we could not identify sweep by.

Slowly, the river began to return to its normal banks, and some of the animals that were fortunate enough to survive walked out of the mud and past upturned tree branches to clear ground. Snakes didn't even notice us; stunned, they just headed for any place to hide. Dad regained his breath and strength. He looked us over to make sure we were okay and then said, "Let's go home so your Mom and the others will know you are all right."

Halfway back, we met Uncle Eck and Mom. Mom was crying. She handed Nell to Dad. She then grabbed us and began to settle down. All the way to the house, she kept crying on and off. Over and over, we kept telling Mom we were all right.

"I know, I know, but I had to see for myself," she replied.

We boys were filthy and, when we got to the house, could not go inside to eat or get our clothes until we cleaned up. Mom brought out clean clothes and towels. We took them and went to the large windmill a hundred feet from the house. A hundred-gallon wood water tank was mounted on a platform fifteen feet off the ground. This was our secondary water supply for the garden and animals. We hung our clean clothes and towels on the frame of the platform, climbed the ladder to the top of the tank and jumped in. We splashed around for awhile and then scrubbed the dirt, sand and filth off us.

As the dirt and sand fell off, so did the horrors of the day. We even began to made jokes about the experience. We looked over the edge of the water tank to make sure no one was there; then we climbed down and dried off with the clean rags and towels that Mom had brought. We turned around to dress and saw that all our clean clothes were gone. We looked all around the platform frame and in all the trees, but all we had were our socks --not even our dirty clothes were left. We found some bailing wire and broke it into pieces just long enough to go around our bodies; we then took the rags, towels and socks and looped them over the wire, covering ourselves as much as we could while we continued to look for our clothes. Dad, Uncle Eck and Mom walked up and began laughing.

We were humiliated.

"WHO STOLE OUR CLOTHES?" we shouted.

"Don't know, but we found them and will return them to you for a price," replied Uncle Eck.

We knew then we in trouble. We had no clothes, and there was nothing we could do to retrieve them. Catching on Billie Neal asked, "Okay, what do we have to do?"

"All of you gather together at the base of the windmill, and we will take your picture. Then we will give you the clothes we found," Uncle Eck laughingly said.

We looked at one another. Charles started laughing, and soon everyone began to laugh. We lined up at the base of the windmill, and the pictures were taken. Those photos were later enlarged and hung in the front window of the Dalhart Bank for a month.

An amazing day, fraught with danger we had never dreamed of, ended in a hilarious good time. It was a day that not one of us would ever forget.

A few days later, the river was almost dry, and the mud between the house and the corral had dried. Dad came running in, grabbed his .22 rifle and started shooting just as he cleared the door.

Dad shouted, "Got one, wounded another. Edd, come on!"

I had no idea what was happening but grabbed my hat and went. Two coyotes had raided the chicken house. They had killed one hen and broke a leg on another. A dead coyote was across the riverbed. A wounded one, a young pup, was lying on the ground and trying to get up.

We killed the chicken with the broken leg and took it to Mom. She would dress and clean it. We would have fried chicken for supper.

Dad tied a rope around the neck of the dead coyote and asked me to go and saddle App. We had built steps inside the barn to enable me to saddle him. I put a rope around App's neck and led him inside; with more problems than usual, I was able to get the bridle on him. I had real problems getting the blanket and saddle on. I could not figure what was wrong.

"Dad, is something is wrong with App?" I asked.

"He smells the coyotes. Give him a little time. You be calm and he will be, too," Dad replied.

I readjusted the bridle and rubbed App on his forehead. I got the currying brush and rubbed his back and flanks. He then accepted the blanket and saddle with no problems. However, when we got outside of the corral and App saw the dead coyote, it took all I had to calm him. Dad handed me the end of a twenty-foot rope and told me to drag the dead animal a mile away, downwind from the house. We had neighbors three miles downriver. I needed to find a ravine or some kind of terrain where I could dispose of the dead animal. App was skittish all the way, and I had to be careful of the way I went to keep from hanging the dead animal on rocks or in brush. Finally, I found a place. I slid down off App, untied the rope and pushed the coyote with my foot into a gully fifteen feet deep.

Once that was done, I began to relax. I turned to remount and saw that my stirrup was head-high. There was no way I could get back on that horse. I rolled up the rope I had pulled the dead animal with, picked up the reins and started leading App back to our house. I was soon on a trail just above the riverbed and saw a place where the trail went between two small cliffs. I stopped and tied the rope to the reins. I led App twenty feet down the trail to where I could climb up a short incline and dropped the reins (trained horses stand when their reins are on the ground). I climbed up the slope with the end of the rope in hand and walked back to a spot directly above App. I stepped out over the saddle, dropped six inches and was on board. I coiled the rope, pulled the reins up, untied the rope, separated the reins and put them on the right side of App's head. We made it home with no problem.

The coyote pup that Dad had injured was tied between two trees, its two front legs bandaged. A pan of water was beside him. Dad had roped and tied him so that the cub had very limited movement. I had no idea how Dad had been able to get a muzzle on that wild pup. Even though the animal was secured and had two injured legs, he was still wild and dangerous. A few weeks later, the young coyote was bought by a neighbor.

It was just one more normal day on a ranch in northeast New Mexico. The day ended with fried chicken, mashed potatoes with gravy, fresh veggies out of Mom's small garden and hot apple pie.

Winter was close; the tree leaves changed color and dropped. The wind began to blow more often and harder, but there was still no rain. One day, Charles and I got on App and rode to the mailbox two miles up the road. While App would let the two of us ride, he would not permit us to ride double with a saddle. This was the first time Charles and I had gone bareback to the mailbox together on my horse. The mailbox was set high enough that I could reach it and retrieve the mail. If I was in a saddle, I could keep one foot in the stirrup and not fall. That day, with no saddle, I leaned over to open the mailbox, got off balance and fell off the horse. I had no way of getting back on. Charles laughed at me for my fall but then realized he was on the horse by himself and the reins were on the ground.

He began to cry, "I can't ride this horse by myself. You don't care if I get hurt."

He carried on. I had to do something.

"Okay, Charles, just move forward to where you can get hold of App's mane," I suggested.

"I can't! He will buck me off!" he cried.

"No, he won't, but you will fall off if you stay where you are," I tried to reason.

Slowly, Charles inched forward toward App's mane and held on. I put the letters in the front pocket of my overalls and picked up the reins to lead App. Charles was complaining the whole two miles back to our house.

One of the letters was from Grandma Ribble in Texline. Granddad was coming to the ranch in few days. He would stay long enough to help Dad get everything taken care of so we could come to Texline and spend Thanksgiving with them. We were excited and began to make plans to go. Extra water was put in the tanks and ponds, and more food was laid out for the chickens, cattle and horses. The neighbor three miles downriver agreed to come by every other day, checking on things and caring for the livestock if necessary.

When Granddad arrived, we were ready. On the way to Texline, the conversation was dominated by the weather: the continuous wind, the lack of rain, and the crop failures. I was aware of what was being said but was more interested in enjoying the ride in the new car. I watched Rabbit Ear's Mountain come into view and then slowly disappear as we left New Mexico and entered Texas. We turned right off the highway when we entered Texline. Granddad drove across the railroad tracks and went a hundred yards. He then turned left and entered a large yard with huge trees in front of the house. In the backyard, between the house and barn, there was a tall windmill that was pumping a lot of water into a large open storage tank.

"So far, we have been fortunate," Granddad said. "We have plenty of water. The wind has been continuous but not excessive, and it looks like our crops will be okay. The Harvey House by the railroad buys our milk, cream and butter. We sell our eggs and some vegetables at the farmer's market on Fridays. We are so much better off now than a lot of our friends and neighbors."

Grandma added, "Don't understand why, but God has blessed us. While we are grateful, we hurt for others who are hurting so much."

One event of that day has plagued me much of my life. The wind had stopped, and the windmill was quiet. While dinner ("supper" to country folks) was being prepared, Charles and I were looking for something to do. We fooled around the water tank, got our feet wet and climbed a fence. We threw corncobs at the horses but were still bored and looking for something else to do.

"Bet you can't climb up the windmill," Charles said.

"I can, but you can't; you aren't big enough," I replied.

"I am as big as you. I can do anything you can and more," Charles snapped back.

"Okay — prove it," I replied, and we headed for the twenty-five-foot-high windmill. I climbed the thirty steps to the top, sat on the edge of the platform and hung my feet over the side. In a few minutes, Charles made it. He sat down beside me and said, "Kind of high, ain't it?"

"Yep," I said.

"Scared?" he asked.

"Some," I replied. I began to point out landmarks and to wonder how big Grandpa's farm was.

We began to hear voices below: "They were here just awhile ago; they can't be far."

Charles and I looked at each other, covered our mouths, smiled and kept quiet.

"They know that dinner is ready; they will not want to miss that," we heard.

We looked at one another, grinned and shook our heads. Charles began to giggle. Mom looked up and saw our legs hanging over the platform, some twenty-five feet above the ground.

"Oh no!" she cried.

Granddad quietly said to her, "Sis, don't say anything; we cannot scare them."

He walked out far enough to where he could see us and we could see him. "Boys, your grandmother is ready to put dinner on the table, and you need to come down," Granddad quietly said.

"But I am scared," Charles said.

Grandpa took over. "Okay, here is how we will do it. Edd, I want you to crawl — not walk — over to the ladder, come down two steps and wait until I tell you to move. Okay now, crawl … Do not walk … Now, you wait until I tell you to move." I nodded my head and did what he said.

"Now, Charles, you do the same thing."

"But I am scared," Charles said.

"I know, but you will be all right if you do what I say. Now crawl to where Edd is," Grandpa directed.

Charles carefully lifted his legs, rolled over on his hands and knees, and moved toward me. As he got to me, Granddad said, "Now, Edd, move down two steps and help Charles get his feet on the ladder."

Under Granddad's direction, we safely climbed down off the windmill. While Mom was trying to compose herself, a brisk wind blew. The windmill turned into the wind, and the blades began to whirl. If Charles and I had still been up on the top deck, we could have been hit by the whirling blades and been badly injured or even killed.

After a big dinner and a lot of good joking and playing, Mom and Granddad walked outside. Mom just stood and looked at the windmill. I was close by, but neither noticed me.

"I just don't understand," Mom said.

Grandfather responded, "I hate to say this, Sis, but I have had this fear since Edd's birth: *that he will never be worth a damn.*" With that, Granddad walked off. Mom began to cry, and I walked away, stunned.

On our way home, everyone was tired and subdued. All I could remember of that day was what my Granddad had said: I was not worth a damn. I faked sleep so I would not have to say anything.

The next day, clouds rolled in from the west. The wind picked up, and we had a few flurries of snow. We harvested what little grain we had, stored it in the barn, gathered as much hay as we could and tried to winter in. More wood was cut and stored; a pig was killed, butchered, salted down and hung in the smokehouse. We had to have a fire going continuously for three to four weeks so the meat would be thoroughly smoked. Slabs of bacon, links of sausage and ribs were placed in a large box filled with sugar and salt. The hams were wrapped in heavy cloths that had been boiled in the big black pot Mom used to wash our clothes outside.

A new addition to our regular chores was a fun one. Dad and I built a drop trap to catch quail. The contraption was a box eighteen inches long, a foot wide, and eight inches deep. There was no bottom board. The top had an eight-by-four-inch opening running lengthwise. That opening was covered by another board that was suspended off-center like a seesaw. This seesaw rested against a stop board to keep it from opening. When an object was placed on the shorter part of the seesaw, the weight would cause the trapdoor to open, and the object would drop into the bottom of the box. A short stick with an arm extended out over the opening was nailed to the head end of the box. We placed the box ten feet outside the big window of our main room. We had scattered grain around the trap and hung a head of grain on the arm over the opening of the box.

We went inside and watched to see what might happen. Two sparrows came, ate some grain and flew away. Some other birds came and did the same. Charles and I were watching and it was getting boring.

"Look," Charles said. "I turned to the window and saw a large bobwhite (a type of quail) eating the scattered grain. It pranced around, swinging its white topknot, and jumped up on the box. It then reached for the suspended grain, moved to get a bite and disappeared into the trap.

"We got one!" we shouted.

"That is all you will get if you keep hollering like that," Mom said from the cook stove.

We quieted down and began to count. When we had counted five quail, Mom asked us to go and remove the head of grain but not to disturb the box. We wanted to see inside, but every time we acted like we were going to check in the box, Mom would tap the window and shake her head. Dad came in an hour later, and we boys, of course, tried to be first to tell him we had caught five quail.

"Well, let's go see," he said.

We followed him out to the trap. Dad tilted the trap up just enough to slide his hand under and pulled out one bird. He broke the bird's head off and continued until all five were removed. Mom brought boiling water out to us, and we scalded and de-feathered the birds. Dad gutted the birds with his knife and washed them in the hot water. We rinsed out the pan and took the quail inside. Mom floured the birds, cooked them with gravy and served them with hot biscuits and fresh vegetables. We enjoyed our dinner. Charles and I talked about how we could eat like this all winter. Mom and Dad just smiled.

Winter set in. Snow began to fall. The Depression became worse. We had food, water, a warm home and enough clothes to keep us warm; many did not even have that.

One icy morning, Mom was up early to get eggs. Before she made it to the hen house, she slipped on some ice. She caught a rail on the corral fence to keep from falling, but she broke the heel off one of her only shoes. Dad tried to repair the shoe, but nothing worked. He decided we would have to get it fixed or replaced. The nearest cobbler was twenty miles away in Texline. The next morning, the snow had stopped, the sun was out and the wind had quit blowing.

"You up to making a trip with me today?" Dad asked as we ate breakfast.

I wanted to know where and why we were going. After Dad told me "Texline," my answer was, "Sure, if we get to eat lunch at Grandma's house."

We finished breakfast, saddled the horses, filled some water cans, packed some food and extra coats in the saddle bags, and headed off across country. Dad was on his horse, and I was on App. We followed the river for three miles, turned west and started across the plains in a slow lope. The cool temperature and clear sky made it a great day for riding, and the horses wanted to move. We gave them their heads (loosed our hold on the reins) and let them run. They had run enough to satisfy themselves in thirty minutes and settled into an easy walk. Birds were out; dove, quail, and even an odd roadrunner would appear by the trail. We saw coyotes running and a mother skunk with two or three babies out walking. A small herd of antelope went across our track as if we were not there.

"I never want to live anywhere else," I said.

Dad's reply shook me. "I like it out here, too, but you will be six in two months and have to start to school next fall. There are no schools within fifteen miles and no bus to pick you up."

"But Dad, I can read and I know my numbers. Isn't that enough?" I asked.

"We will just have to think about that," he said as we put the horses into an easy lope.

We arrived at Texline and found the cobbler in his shop. Dad gave him the shoe and explained that we lived a three-to four-hour horse ride away, that Mom and two young kids were alone, and that she had no shoes to wear. "If possible," he asked, "could you fix the shoe today so we can get back home?"

The cobbler looked around a minute and said, "Okay, I will do it; but it will cost you three dollars and may be a little late by the time the glue sets so I can shape and attach the heel."

"We really need to get back tonight, and I appreciate you doing the best you can," Dad said.

The man suggested we come back around four o'clock, and Dad gave him three dollars. We left and went to Grandma's house. Dad and Grandpa worked outside, and I helped Grandma fix us lunch. I even helped do some of the cooking.

After the meal, I helped clear the table and dried the dishes. I was tired; I lay down on a rug in the living room and fell asleep. Two hours later, I woke up and wandered outside. A breeze was blowing, and the windmill was pumping water. The blades were humming. As I looked up, I vowed never to ever climb one of those things again. I wandered into the fields and saw new sprouts of grain and corn. They looked real puny to me, like they were sick. I went back to the house because it was almost time to get Mom's shoe.

"Grandpa," I asked, "what is the matter with the new sprouts of the crop you planted?"

"Son," he said, "we have had no rain since the seeds germinated. If it does not rain in a few days, they will die, and we will have no crops to harvest."

"Wow," I thought, "that would be tough."

Dad and I left and went to the cobbler shop. "Be just a few minutes more, young man; if you won't touch anything, you can look around and watch as I trim and finish your mom's new heel," the cobbler offered as he turned on one of his electric brushes.

I walked through a small half gate into the back of his shop. I saw the forms he used in his work and the knives he used to trim leather on the half-finished boots and shoes. The few minutes it took for him to shape and attach the heel to Mom's shoe was not long enough for me. He handed the shoe to Dad, who thanked the cobbler, shook his hand and left.

Dad put Mom's shoe in one of the saddlebags on my horse; the saddlebags on his horse were full of the meat, flour and canned fruit Grandma had insisted we take home with us. The sun was already low in the western sky as we walked the horses out of town.

"It is going to be long while before we get home. You up to doing some real riding?" Dad asked.

Man, what fun! "Let's do it," I replied. I let App have his head and kicked him in the ribs. Across the prairie we flew until the horses decided to slow to a fast walk.

"Dad, these horses seem to know where we are going even though we have never been this way before today."

Dad grinned and replied, "If you ever get lost and can't find your way, just give them their head and they will get you home."

"Wow, they must be smart," was all I could think. About halfway home, we stopped at a windmill and let the horses drink. We loosened the cinches and let the horses rest. We rested on a log and ate the meal Grandma had prepared for us.

It was too dark to go fast, so it would take over two hours to get home. When I had climbed back on App, Dad came and tied my boots to the saddle stirrups; he then put a rope around my waist and loosely tied that to my saddle horn. He took my reins from me and tied them to the lanyards attached to the back of his saddle. That way, he said, I could sleep.

Sleep? Not me. No way was I going to sleep, and for about fifteen minutes I didn't. The next thing I knew, Mom was putting my pajamas on me and putting me in my bed. I had slept for two hours, lulled by the rhythm of my slowly walking horse.

The snow was not heavy, but the wind became a problem. It blew hard and seemed to never quit. Dust turned the snow dark brown. When the snow melted, the ground looked dead. A week before Christmas, Dad asked Charles and me if we would like to get a Christmas tree. We had been housebound for a week. Just getting outside was enough for us.

Dad had removed the blades from the sled that I had ridden to cut the weeds out of our crop. He had replaced the blades with wood outriders. We harnessed two horses and hooked up the sled. We rode the sled two miles upriver on a snow-covered trail to a forest of cedar trees. Mom had packed hot chocolate and cookies for us. It took longer than necessary for us to agree on a tree. Charles and I had to cut and trim the tree we picked; that agreement was made before we left home. Our tree was six feet tall. We removed some lower branches with a small hatchet and attempted to cut the tree down with an axe we could hardly handle. With our flailing the axe, Dad knew we would be there all day. He took over cutting the tree and loaded it on the sled. It was beginning to snow. I took the reins to start the horses, and we walked back to the house with our Christmas tree.

Mom and Nell had popped popcorn and colored it with the juice of wild berries that grew along the banks of the river. Charles and I drew a large star on a cardboard box lid and colored it with crayons. Dad held Charles up; after two or three trials (while Nell and I laughed and kept telling him he was doing it wrong), Charles finally attached our star to the top of the tree.

We had lunch ("dinner," we called it) and then spent the rest of the day threading the various colors of popcorn on three-to four-foot lengths of colored thread. Dad went outside to take care of the live-stock and to bring in more quail from our box trap. Mom found three candles, and each of us kids helped to light one. We placed the candles on the adobe brick windowsill. We all, including Nell, bundled up in our coats, went out into the snow and looked through the window to see the candles burning and our Christmas tree. The snow only added to one of our most beautiful and meaningful Christmases. Every night until the tree was removed, we went outside. Most of the time, we did not talk or make jokes; we just looked and then went inside to bed.

A day later, Dad and I rode our horses to the mailbox. As we approached the road, we could see a large box sitting on the ditch bank. It was from Sears Roebuck, and it was addressed to us. Dad tied it on the back of my saddle. I could not wait to get home. Charles and I ripped the wrapping off; on the side of the box, we saw in big letters: "DO NOT OPEN UNTIL CHRISTMAS DAY."

"Mom, that is three days away," Charles whimpered.

"Too bad. You will have to wait," Mom replied.

Dad pushed the box under the window next to the Christmas tree. For three days and two nights, we enjoyed imagining what that box might contain. We kids had no idea who might have sent the box. We were afraid that Santa would never find us because only a few members of our family knew where we were. On Christmas morning, Charles and I got up at five o'clock and were made to go back to bed. Finally, an hour later, we were allowed to stay up and open our presents.

Nell was first. She crawled to the tree and began to pull the popcorn off, totally ignoring her presents. Even after Mom got Nell's doll for her, Nell went after the popcorn and tried to feed it to her doll. The more we laughed, the harder she tried to feed the poor doll.

Charles grabbed his gift and threw paper and ribbons everywhere; he found his new jeans and shirt inside. I was next. I grabbed the long box and opened it to find a Red Ryder BB gun. I did not care if I got anything else. Mom had helped us kids get Dad a heavy jacket and new leather gloves. Dad helped us get Mom a new winter robe. We kids all had new clothes, and Charles got a wooden train set with a circular track. Dad cooked flapjacks (pancakes), ham and eggs for breakfast, and we all laughed, joked and had wonderful time.

After breakfast, Dad and I bundled up. It was snowing again, but we did our outside chores. When we were sure all the animals were fine, we fed and watered them. We went back into the house and played Chinese checkers. All day, we had cocoa and cookies. Charles and I put on our new clothes with warm jackets and went outside. Later, we were joined by everyone in a friendly family snowball fight.

The next morning, Dad and I went to feed the animals. I took my new BB gun and was ready for anything.

"Now hold on," Dad said. "If you are going to keep that gun, here are the rules. You do not point that gun at anything you do not intend to shoot. You do not shoot at anything unless you need to kill it or drive it away. You do not point the gun at any human or animal, unless they are a danger to you. You keep it clean and unloaded, put up on top of your clothes box where no one else can get to it."

Dad found an old tin cup and placed it on a stump behind our outhouse. He handed me a small box of BBs and showed me how to load the gun. He told me to practice until I could hit the can three times in a row. It was lunchtime before I could quit.

The snow was light and dry. The wind continued to blow. All we could do outside was take care of the animals and bring up more wood. We had to keep the stove going day and night. The wood burned fast.

A week later, the sun came out and the snow disappeared, but the warm weather was not welcomed. We needed any moisture we could get, and warm weather would not help.

Mom decided that, while it was warm, she would visit our neighbors who lived four miles to the north. Dad put the canvas top on the wagon and hooked up the team. Mom and I carried out blankets and our lunches and stored them in the wagon. Dad handed Nell, who was secure and asleep in her cradle, to Mom. I was given the reins, and we headed out. Charles roamed around in the wagon and played with Nell when she woke up.

It was a clear, cool day. We enjoyed watching rabbits, skunks, coyotes, quail, hawks, and other animals out enjoying the spring-like weather. The horses were in good shape and wanted to move. I did very little other than keeping them on the right road. We had snacks and fresh water, and in two hours we pulled into our neighbor's yard. The father and son came and helped Mom out of the wagon. Mom took Nell and went inside the house. The father and son then drove the horses and the wagon inside their barn. They removed the harness from the horses and turned them loose into a small pasture. I had my Red Ryder BB rifle with me, and I stayed in the barn to kill rats.

When Mom had finished her visit, our friends fixed us a lunch and gave us food to take home. Our horses were harnessed and hitched to the wagon. With Mom driving, we headed home. I should have noticed but I did not: our two horses were reversed. The feisty brown mare would not work on the right side of the team. Before we were outside the yard, the other horse pushed her, and that spooky mare acted up. Before Mom could react, the team became unmanageable. We had a runaway on our hands. Mom turned the team into a plowed field. The loose soil made it difficult for the horses, and the weight of the wagon made it sink into the plowed earth, but the horses kept trying to run.

"Drop Nell and Charles out the back of the wagon now!" Mom hollered at me.

I grabbed Nell's cradle, leaned out the back of the wagon and carefully dropped the cradle into one of the furrows. I then grabbed Charles, who was not going to jump, and pushed him out.

"Now you jump, and then I will!" Mom shouted.

I jumped. Just after I hit the ground, the horses, out of breath, stopped. I ran to Nell, expecting her to be screaming. I was shocked. She lay there, still in her cradle, kicking her feet and laughing. She acted like this was the funniest thing that had ever happened to her. I picked up the cradle with Nell still laughing and took her to Mom, who was in shock. Mom was unable to move from her seat on the wagon. Charles looked at Nell and started laughing, and Mom began to unwind. She climbed down off the wagon, hugged me and cried until she actually believed we were all okay.

Our friend and his son arrived to make sure we were all right. They unhitched our team from the wagon and drove them into the barn; then they brought their own horses, hitched them to our wagon and moved it into their yard. We all went into the house and had coffee, hot chocolate and cookies. They discussed why the attempted runaway had happened. After a bit, I mentioned that the mare was placed on the wrong side of the team and always acted up when that was done. After an hour, the team was realigned and hitched to the wagon. Mom wanted me to drive this time. We made it home just before dark.

Dad and Mom began to have more and more private talks. Mom urged me to learn my numbers and helped me read books that came in the mail. Dad and I shelled corn, fed the animals, carried "cake" (a compressed mix of feed and minerals) to the cattle and broke ice so the cattle could get to water. We cleaned the barns and chicken coops, repaired and oiled the harnesses, and watched the weather.

Neighbors began to move away. More houses were vacant. The snow came in short flurries with little moisture. The river had gone underground. We had to dig over six feet to find any water, and it lasted only a day or two. Things were not getting any better, and Mom was having more sick spells. In December, I had my sixth birthday. I knew that most of their talk was about my going to school. I did not need school. I could read some, and I knew how to count money. I could ride and care for horses, and I could herd cattle. What else should I need to know?

A month later, Uncle Eck and Granddad Ribble came to see us. Charles and I were sent to clean the stalls and the chicken house. After an hour, we were called inside. Mom said that Uncle Eck had something to tell us.

"The ranch here is going to be shut down for awhile, and you won't be able to live here any longer. We will have to move you to Dalhart," he explained.

I was shocked and scared. "What am I going to do? Where will we be? What about App?" I cried.

"That is what we want to tell you," Uncle Eck continued. "We have a house east of Dalhart that we need someone to live in. It has a barn and enough open land for you to keep App with you. There is a school bus that comes by your house and will take you to school and bring you home. Your mom has been having some sick spells; this way, we will have her close to a doctor to take care of her. Your family will have a car. Your dad can go to work and take you to movies and other places in town."

Mom had been sick, and I wanted her well. If App was with me, I would be happy. A week later, Dad and I rode in the two trucks with milk cows, workhorses, App and Dad's horse. Uncle Eck would bring Mom, Charles and Nell the next day.

Two

1931-1932

School and the Dust Bowl

In his book "The Worst Hard Time," Timothy Eagan does a superb job of giving a verbal picture of the background that led to the Dust Bowl tragedy. He tells of the many lives and families that were affected and the devastation that occurred in that section of United States. While I cannot add anything to his excellent book, I will try to let you see part of those days through the eyes of a young boy who lived through "The Worst Hard Time."

When we moved to Dalhart, we had a large rambling house with a bedroom for each of us. There was a living room with no furniture, a dining room with a small table and four chairs, and a kitchen. Some cooking utensils had been left by the previous owner, along with two bed frames with springs. The barn also had a few tools. Outside, the fences and buildings were covered with hundreds of tumbleweeds. We had a deep well that pumped enough water to care for our few horses and milk cows. We would have enough water to take care of our mandatory weekly bath in a number three washtub. All water would be emptied around trees and plants. No water was ever just thrown out. It was the most important resource on the place, and none could ever be wasted.

Dad went to work for the local bank, delivering bank notices of delinquent payments and repossessions. He was also the unofficial custodian of repossessed and abandoned property. He made regular trips to farms and houses in an impossible attempt to prevent people from breaking in and taking what few things might be left. Most people who were passing through used the houses and barns for a place to spend the night before moving on. Some were destructive, but there was little to steal that was worth anything.

We planted a small vegetable garden on the leeward side of the house to protect the plants from the wind and hot sun. We watered the plants at night to conserve water. Some clean unused water was used to wet sheets that we hung over windows and doors at night in an attempt to keep the sand out. We had few possessions, but no one else had much more. We were grateful to have food to eat and have a house to live in.

That summer, only the calendar changed. The wind and lack of rain remained the same. The XIT (named after the ten original counties of the Panhandle in North Texas) held its annual rodeo and reunion at the Dallam County Fairgrounds at the edge of Dalhart. I would go to town with Dad and walk to the fairgrounds.

Tribes from New Mexico, Oklahoma and North Texas would come each year, set up tepees and wigwams and dance. They brought exhibits of jewelry, beadwork and special foods.

I did not have any money, but I walked and watched. As I have mentioned, I was not just a small kid; I was a scrawny runt. Security people stopped me everywhere I went. While that was a minor nuisance, it turned out to be a blessing for me. Dark-eyed mothers watched as I was stopped by security and questioned. After I had been given permission to go and continue looking at the displays, the mothers would ask why the security people had stopped me.

I would tell them, "They think I might be abandoned, a runaway or lost."

The mothers would hug me or pat me on the head and say, "You too little be by self." Then they would give me a drink or a bite of whatever they were selling and tell me to have a good time but be careful. On other days when I would pass by, they would call me to come over because they had something for me.

The Indian kids and I played games together. Their favorite game was their own variation of kickball or soccer. They were good, but I was clumsy. I enjoyed my days and became a part of their group; I was even invited to eat lunch with them.

After two weeks, when the rodeo began, most of the Indians who were not entered in some part of the rodeo loaded their teepees on small wagons and went home. At the rodeo, I liked the calf roping, bronco busting and bull riding, but what I really went to see were the clowns.

When the rodeo was closing, another sandstorm came. There had been airplane cloud seeding, cannons shooting blanks into the air, special prayers, rain dances, sermons calling for repentance, and everything else people could think to do to bring rain. Instead, all we got was wind, sand, tumbleweeds and, of course, more sermons.

One afternoon of a following week, Charles and I were home alone. We were out working and had finished cleaning the henhouse. As we started to our house, a wicked wind began to blow. This was normal, so I did not pay it much attention. Charles stopped, turned, looked up and said, "We better go get on our horses and get the cows and other horses into the barn."

"Why? It won't get dark for six or seven hours," I said, and I kept walking.

"Look!" he insisted.

I turned. On the western horizon, I saw a rolling, mile-high sheet of red sand and trash.

"Ain't no cloud," Charles said.

We turned and rushed to the barn. I grabbed a halter; there was no time for a bridle or saddle. I climbed the fence and got on App. Charles crawled on his Shetland, and we took off as fast we could to the backside of the twenty-five acre pasture. We rounded up the two work horses, the two milk cows and the three calves and ran them back to the corral. We put the cows and calves in their barn and the four horses inside theirs. We checked the water and filled the tank. We closed the barn doors and the corral gates and ran to get inside our house.

Around two o'clock that afternoon, the sand descended. We made it onto the porch, which was enclosed with clear plastic, and the sun disappeared. I reached for the pull chain for the light, but everything went black. We had no electricity, and it was totally dark.

"What did you do?" Charles hollered.

I had only touched the light chain. It was like I had suddenly gone blind. Years later, our family went to Carlsbad Caverns. When we were several hundred feet underground, all the lights were turned off; we were in complete darkness. That was what we were experiencing around two o'clock in the afternoon four miles east of Dalhart, Texas. We searched and found a small candle and lit it. Our snack in the kitchen was already too gritty to eat, and our water had a thick film of dirt on top.

"Wish I had a gizzard," Charles laughed. "I am hungry."

For those who may not know, chickens, turkeys and other foul have gizzards that filter out sand, dirt, and other crud from the food they eat off the ground and elsewhere. This keeps the filtered material out of their stomachs.

The wind howled. The house shook. We could hardly breathe, and we were scared out of our minds. We had been in bad storms before, but nothing like this.

I thought of Mom and Dad. They were somewhere between

Clayton, New Mexico, and Dalhart in an old Model A car with a ragtop. Mom was getting more tired all the time. I did not know much about praying, but I tried; I asked God to take care of them and, if he could, to take care of Charles and me, too. I had no idea of what else I could do. Right then, our small candle went out.

The wind continued to blow. The darkness was complete. Charles remembered that Dad had a modified railroad conductor's lantern somewhere in a cabinet on the closed-in porch. Dad used it to check on the horses and cows at night. We searched in total darkness and had to holler to each other to be heard. Charles began to feel along the wall, going to the right. We had to be careful at the porch door; we did not want it to come unlatched and blow open. The wind would tear it off its hinges. I went the other way, keeping one hand on the wall. Charles let out a yell. He had bumped into a cabinet in one of the corners. He opened the cabinet door. Stuff fell out and sounded like a window had been shattered. Charles was almost crying.

Then a light came on. Charles had found Dad's lantern and turned it on. What had broken was an old dish we used to feed milk to a couple of cats that had a full-time job of keeping down the rat population. Using the lantern, we returned to the kitchen. I found a kerosene lamp and matches, and we had light enough to get by. We opened the icebox. There was leftover meat and potatoes, fresh milk and cornbread. Our problem was eating fast enough to keep the sand out of our food.

We had no idea what time it was. We knew the clock was wrong. It showed three o'clock in the afternoon. It seemed to us that we had been without light for hours. We knew there was another clock in Mom and Dad's bedroom; however, we were not going in there in the dark, and we knew we were not to move the kerosene lamp while it was burning. We turned off the lantern and waited.

After three hours, which seemed like days to us, the sandstorm moved on east, the sun began to shine, and we were able to turn off the lamp. The wind died down enough that we could check on the horses, cows and chickens. They seemed more scared than we were. We opened the gates, but neither the horses nor the cows would leave. The chickens stayed on their roosts in the henhouse.

Just before the real dark came with the setting of a blistering hot sun, Dad and Mom drove up. We ran to the door to let them in. They were as worried about us as we were about them. There had been no way for us to communicate with one another. Mom checked the house and Dad, the outbuildings. Everything looked good to them.

In answer to our questions, they explained that around one o'clock that afternoon, they had started home from the ranch. The ranch still had to be looked after. They were in Texline when the sandstorm hit. They drove to our grandparents' house, and as they pulled into the driveway, everything went black. Dad had eased the car to where he thought the back door of the house should be. Granddad had seen a flash from the car lights. He called for Grandmother to get the lantern and come to the back door. He ran, opened the back door and began to holler as loud as he could so Mom and Dad could follow his voice.

Mom and Dad were less than twenty feet away and could hear a noise but could not understand. Once or twice they saw a small flash of light. They eased themselves in that direction. Halfway there, they could hear Granddad, and they followed his voice and the flickering light into the house. It was two hours before they could safely leave.

They drove home over sand-covered roads as fast as they could to check on us. Mom gathered all the sheets off the beds and soaked them in water. She tried to get some of the sand out while Dad hung the sheets that were still wet over the windows of our bedrooms. We all were tired and relieved. Mom put clean, dry sheets on our beds, and we went to sleep. When Charles and I got up in the morning, we looked at our beds, pointed at the once-clean sheets and laughed. There were outlines of the occupants in sand. Even with wet sheets, the only thing in the bedroom not covered with sand was a sculptured relief of us where we had slept.

The wind dropped to a steady breeze, and we were able to clean the sheds and chicken house. We removed some of the hundreds of tumbleweeds on the fences and let the animals out.

Later that week, Dad had to go to town, and I went with him. While he was taking care of business, I walked around. Very few people and fewer cars were out. Only a few businesses were open.

I saw a wagon turn a corner a few blocks away. I wandered in that direction. A man stopped his team in front of a horse-watering trough. The trough had been placed there for the XIT Reunion and had not been removed. Someone had been keeping it filled with water.

While the horses were drinking, the driver went into the small grocery store. The haggard mother and wife just sat in the wagon. Two kids, four or five years old, looked out from under the canvas cover. The man came out of the store with a twenty-five pound sack of flour. He took out his knife and cut the string that closed the sack. His wife handed down a shallow tin pan, and the man filled the pan with water from the horse trough and began to make a paste with the flour. "What is he going to do?" I wondered.

He handed the pan to his wife. She took a spoonful of that paste — with no salt, with nothing but flour and water from a horse tank — and began to feed the two children. The owner of the store ran out, shouting at the man that he had called the sheriff and that the man was not to leave until the sheriff got there. The sheriff arrived and talked to the grocery man. He reached in his pocket and gave the store owner some money. He then walked over to the man at the wagon and told him where he could go that people would give him some food.

While this was an extreme case, there was a constant moving of people in wagons, in old cars, or on horseback. Many rode the rails on trains (under the boxcars) trying to find some way to feed themselves and their families.

I went back to the bank where Dad was. We got in the car and headed home, and I told him what I had seen. His reply was that I had better get used to it, because it was going to get worse. He explained that even if the sand quit blowing and the rains did come, it would be two or three years before there would be any crops or real recovery.

A week later, we went to Texline to be with my grandparents. I was given a small horse to ride and instructed by Granddad to herd cows away from a break in the fence line along the railroad track. I sat on my horse, watching the cattle trying to feed on grass that was dry and mostly gone. Along the railroad tracks, the grass was green and five or six inches high. I decided to let the cows graze along the tracks. When I heard the rumble or whistle of a train, I drove the cows back into the pasture.

Grandpa came out when I had let the cows graze the second time and roared at me about letting them though the broken fence. I could not understand; the cows were safe and had good grazing, but he was mad. All I heard as he walked away was, "I hope that someday you will learn how to do things right."

Most everyone trying to live in that area at that time lived close to a breaking point. They lived with constant fear and uncertainty, day in and day out. The situation had taken a toll on the people's ability to cope mentally, emotionally, spiritually and physically. The least little thing would cause them to snap, and Granddad was not the most docile person anyway.

I drove the cows to the barn and gave them some of the small amount of hay. I helped with the milking of twenty-five cows by keeping the hay in the toughs and carrying the milk into the milk room. We had dinner with my grandparents and went home. Mom asked me if Granddad and I were having problems. After I explained what had happened, she reminded me that he was under a lot of pressure. I needed to remember that he loved me but was having a difficult time telling me.

It turned cooler, and the hopes of rain increased, but rain did not come. Even as bad as things were (and they would not improve soon), we were not without better events and some entertainment. We had picture shows at the theater, with gifts of Depression glass and dishes as prizes. The rodeo and fair were still annual events. Individuals, families and civic groups continued to find ways to entertain and give hope.

The Ladies' Sewing Society in Dalhart planned an event called a "Tom Thumb Wedding." It was to be a mock full wedding. They made dresses, tuxes and everything that a regular large wedding should have. There were to be bridesmaids, a best man, a ceremony, a reception and even a ball with music. I was not aware of any of this; I was preoccupied with beginning my first year of school in a few months.

I helped Mom find a box of her clothes among the boxes we had not opened. I thought nothing of it and went out to play. A few days later, she called me inside and began to hold up different colors of cloth against me. After trying some of her dresses and colored flower sacks, she hummed to herself and sent me on my way.

Mom's youngest sister, Elsie, who was in college in south central Texas, came to visit. The two of them worked together for three days and then called me inside. They made me take a bath and put on clean underwear, and they dressed me up to look like some child movie star

I never heard of — Little Lord Something or Other. I had a ruffled white shirt, a funny coat, and black pants that had white stripes down the sides of the legs. They put a goofy-looking tie on me and had me stand in front of the mirror. I did not recognize myself. It looked horrible to me, but Mom and my aunt smiled.

Then my aunt said, "When we get him some new shoes, it will be perfect."

"Perfect for what?" I wondered as they carefully undressed me. "Who needs shoes?" I had two good pairs of boots — old, yes, but still good. Plus, I did not like shoes anyway.

A few days later, when I learned what was going on, I wanted to get on App and ride as far away as I could; but Dad kept telling me that I better not do anything to upset Mom or I would be in big trouble. I knew she was getting fat, but we all were eating much better than we had on the ranch.

The next week, Mom took me to a beauty parlor with a room full of women. I was to have my hair not cut but done. The lady doing my hair kept telling me to sit up so she could do my hair right.

She should know that I did not want to be seen. I wanted to crawl under the big wrap around me. Besides, all I could hear was, "He is so cute! We made the right choice."

"Cute" is not what a six-year-old cowboy who has his own horse wants to be called. I thought I might just run away. Let them try to find me. What would I do if my friends saw me in a beauty shop? I would never live this down. When I got out of the chair, I wanted to get out of that place as fast as I could, but all those grinning ladies gathered around. Some patted me on my head, and others even hugged me. I hated every minute of it.

"Tell them thank you," Mom said as she stood between me and the door. I did say the words, but they should know I did not mean them. Dad's warning was still there, so I smiled and waved to them as we left. Mom seemed happier than I could remember. It was worth it, I guessed. As far as I knew, none of my friends had seen me.

A week later, Mom and Elsie dressed me again in their (not my) new outfit, and we went to the theater. I had no idea about what was going on.

"Where are we going?" I asked.

"A rehearsal," they answered.

"Rehearsal for what?" I wanted to know.

"The Tom Thumb Wedding," Aunt Elsie replied.

"Who is Tom Thumb, and whose wedding is it?" I asked.

"You will see," they laughed.

We went inside the theater, and a large woman came over. She called me by name and asked me to come with her so she could show me what to do. She said I would not have to talk at all but just follow directions. I thought maybe this would not be so bad. I would just follow instructions and get out of here. Other ladies and dressed up kids began to arrive. We were all lined up and waiting.

Once everyone was present, I was called and placed in front of the line. I was with a girl who was dressed up like she was going to be buried or something.

"Now, everyone, listen up," the big lady said. "Edd, you and Patty will lead. You will walk down the center aisle together. When you get to the front, you will separate. Edd, you will go to your left; Patty, go to your right. Young men, you will follow Edd, and young ladies, you will follow Patty. When you get on stage, Edd, you and Patty will go and stand in the two circles on the stage floor. The rest of you will go and stand on marks on your side of the stage. Okay, music! Now walk slowly and stay together."

For the first time in my life, I was involved with other children that were not my relatives. I slouched and stayed as far away from Patty as I could. "Edd, hold your head up and walk; don't drag your feet, or we will have to do this all over," the big lady said loud enough for Mom to hear.

I knew I had better do it right. Dad was going to ask Mom how she was feeling and how I did. Both answers had to be good, or I would be in big trouble.

How we all made it to the stage without someone stumbling or falling was a mystery to me, but the real shocker came when we stopped at our assigned places. The big woman told Patty and me to step forward two steps and hold hands. I did not know any of the kids, much less Patty. At the thought of holding Patty's hand in public, I nearly wet my pants.

Slowly, I reached out without looking. Some way we got our hands loosely together. From there on, I hardly remember anything. I became a robot and began to breathe only when we finally marched off the stage, with me still holding Patty's hand. I hoped she was just as glad as I was that we were done.

"The costumes are great; you can put them away until the actual wedding. Now, everyone, give the kids a big round of applause and hugs," our leader said.

I had lipstick all over on my cheeks. On our way home, I had questions, but Aunt Elsie put her finger to her lips. She and Mom talked all the way home while I just sat. We had one more rehearsal that was not too bad. We were not dressed in those icky clothes, and I did not have to hold Patty's hand.

The night of the big show it dawned on me. The "Tom Thumb Wedding" was open to everyone in the community, and people were encouraged to come and stay for a reception that followed. I also learned it was the one of the biggest social events of the year.

Since Patty and I were the star attractions, we would have to stand in a reception line, and everyone in town would expect us to act like a husband and wife. There was no way that I was going to let a girl kiss me. I would only hold her hand as we marched on and off the stage. These icky clothes would later be burned if I could find a way to do it.

The big night came. Aunt Elsie, Mom and I went early. I would be dressed at the theater. They went into a public restroom to change their clothes. I was told to wait on the steps outside. I would later be dressed in the ladies restroom.

A lady came up to me and asked, "Young man, can you read?"

"Yes, ma'am, I can," I answered.

"Then why are you sitting on the steps to the women's restroom?" she asked.

"My Mom told me to," I answered.

"Where is your mom?" she snarled.

"Inside there," I said and pointed at the restroom door.

The red-faced lady walked off. For some reason, I began to feel a lot better. Mom came out. She and Aunt Elsie took me inside the restroom and dressed me in my suit, and we left for my "execution."

"Now, boys and girls," the big lady said, "we are all here and ready to go, but there is one change in the way we rehearsed. Edd, you and Patty will not go in first but last. I will be with you and let you know when to walk in. Okay, let's give the people a big show." With that, away she went.

The lights were low. The music started, and I was ready to run, not in but out. Our twenty escorts made their way in; then the lights were dimmed and everything got quiet. My hopes went up.

"Good," I thought, "something is wrong and I won't have to do this stupid thing." Then all the lights came up, the organ began to roar, and Patty and I were pushed into the aisle toward the stage. Everyone stood and began to clap. To this day, I do not know how I made it to the front with Patty hanging onto my arm.

All I remember about the rest was that there was singing by some kids and individuals, that others did some kind of dancing, and that Patty and I had to answer some dumb questions. The rest just happened. After what seemed like an entire day to me, it was over. Patty and I, holding hands, were led offstage and out of the theater through the standing and clapping crowd into the building next door. We stood in line for what seemed like hours so that people could come and hug and kiss two embarrassed, tired kids.

Patty and I had to feed a piece of cake to each other and were first in line to eat. There was music and some dancing, mostly by Patty without me. There were even more hugs and kisses as people came by our table. After a final "thank you" and more applause, we could finally go home.

I do not remember ever seeing Patty or the big lady who gave us directions again. I won't go into the jokes and jabs I had to put up with for the few weeks at home before school started.

The weather changed, the wind blew less, and the sand seemed to settle. The tumbleweeds (Russian Tea Vines) did not cover as many fences. Some of the farmers who were left began to prepare their land for new crops. Scattered clouds appeared and moved on with lighting and thunder but no rain.

My first day of school came. I was dressed, but I was not ready. Mom walked me to the school bus stop and waited until she could push me on board. The bus door closed, and Mom went back to the house. I was scared more than I had been at that so-called wedding. The school was new to me. I had not even seen the buildings, and I had no idea where to go. A young lady stood in the bus parking area with some kind of board in her hand and was calling out names.

When mine was called, I stepped up. She asked me to wait. Three others were also asked to wait. The bus was unloaded and driven off. The lady told us she was to be our teacher and asked us to follow her to our room. Twelve other kids were already there. Tables with puzzles, books, crayons and paper and one with a big globe of the whole world were in the room.

Our teacher, Miss Ann, asked us to take our seats. She asked each of us to stand and tell her where we lived when she called our names. Some lived close to the school, while others lived farther away than I did. Miss Ann told us where she lived and what she liked to do and what she wanted to help us learn in our first year of school. We were given a few rules and guidelines about where the restrooms were, where we were to hang our coats and where to put our lunch pails.

"Now, go look at the tables and pick the one you would like to work at this morning. After lunch, you can move to another table if you want." She smiled, stood and waved us away.

I began to relax and went to a huge puzzle table. The puzzles were about outdoor work and numbers. I began to feel good about more learning.

After lunch, Miss Ann asked us to share why we chosen our tables and then let us go to other ones. I went to the big globe, mostly because no one else was there. Miss Ann came and showed me the U.S. and Texas and pointed out the area where we now lived.

"This is fun," I thought. "I am going to like school." When I got home, I jumped off the bus and ran to the house to tell Mom what I had done and that I was happy to be in school.

The weather began to cool, with very little rain. The air was more breathable and smiles more noticeable. People were nicer. The world was beginning to look good again.

Mom tended her garden. She looked funny to me, but she was

happy. Charles had stopped bugging me as much. Nell was walking and getting into everything. Dad was busy with housing problems for the bank, and I was having a ball at school.

At Thanksgiving, we went to Texline for the family get-together. Mom's brother Carson and his wife, Jo, from New Mexico were there. Elsie had come from Central Texas, Tom was home, and we had a great time. The crops were coming up, and the little rain kept the sand and dust down.

The water tank out back at the base of the windmill had a lever with a float attached. When the tank was full of water, the float would rise and the lever would close the valve, shutting off the water to the tank. Sometimes the valve would stick, so a large board was laid over the water from one side of the tank to the other to enable someone to reach the valve and clean it. The valve was now stuck, and water was running over the side of the tank into the yard. I walked the board and was cleaning out the valve.

I heard something and looked around, and there was Nell. She had crawled up onto the board. Before I could say or do anything, she hollered, "I come," jumped into the water and went under. I dropped everything, jumped off the board onto the ground and rushed to where she had gone underwater. Her dress was all I could see. I leaned over and grabbed the hem of her dress, hoping it would not rip loose. I pulled her to me and lifted her out of the water. I sat down on a stump holding her. She was cold, but she was breathing. In a minute, she opened her eyes and began to shake. "Edd, I cold," she murmured.

Now I had a big problem. Dad's words echoed in my mind: "Don't you do anything to upset your Mom." Fine, but Nell was freezing and I had to get her inside. Covering up the truth a little, I went into the screened porch of the house.

"Grandma," I said, "Nell got wet playing in the water, and she is cold. Can you hand me a towel?"

"What happened?" Mom asked.

"She is okay, Mom. She was too close to the tank while I was cleaning the valve and got water all over her. She is wet and cold but no problem," I said.

Grandmother handed me a towel and Aunt Elsie, grinning, got out of her chair. She took Nell to her room, dried her off and put her in dry clothes. It wasn't until a month later that Mom learned what really happened.

Most of the relatives went home after Thanksgiving, but our family stayed over Sunday. We went to a church that met in a dugout. The worship center was in an eight-foot-deep basement with four-inch-thick concrete walls. Windows were in the walls two feet above ground. The room had a concrete floor and roof. The walls and ceiling were painted off-white and the floor a kind of dirty brown. They had an upright piano and homemade wood pews to seat thirty-five people. The church had a preacher every fourth Sunday of the month. On other Sundays, one of the four deacons was responsible for the service.

A young man by the name of Wallace Amos Criswell from a Baptist college south of Amarillo was the preacher who came once each month. Years later, he became the pastor of the First Baptist Church in Dallas, Texas. I enjoyed church with Brother Wally. He was friendly and was often the guest for lunch with my grandparents and me.

On Monday around noon, the sky began to darken like it had before. This time, there was no wind, and the clouds were coming from the east. No one could understand or explain what was going on. In a few minutes, we heard a strange sound like bees buzzing that gradually got as loud as an airplane.

We went outside and watched the darkening sky. A huge grass-hopper landed on my sleeve. Before I could brush it off, two more hit me. Suddenly dozens more were in my hair and eyes; they were every-where. Everyone began to slap at them, and we rushed into the house. We picked the pests off each other and watched the destruction going on outside. Everything green — weeds, plants, leaves on trees — just disappeared. Then, almost like magic, the hoard moved on.

We walked outside. We could not take a step without crushing grasshoppers. They were in the hay racks, in the feeding pens, floating on the water, and matted on the mouths of horses and cows. The chickens and turkeys were happy; they were gobbling up grasshop-pers as fast as they could. All the hope of yesterday's day of family rejoicing was wiped out in less than an hour.

We hated to leave, but Dad had to be back at work and Mom was going to see her doctor. The grasshoppers had hit Dalhart and most of the Panhandle of Texas. They had covered western Oklahoma and southeastern New Mexico. Nothing was left to hold the soil. Sandstorms only needed a breeze to begin.

In the first week of December, Aunt Elsie came to live with us. Mom had trouble moving around and was tired all the time. Later, Grandma came. I was having a ball. There was no work to do outside besides just watering and feeding the animals. There was no fruit on the trees; the garden did not exist. School was fun, and Aunt Elise was helping me read and answering nearly all my questions.

I was out riding App when a car drove up. Mom was rushed into the car, and it drove off. I did not know where she was going or why, so I chased the car. I was afraid I would never see Mom again. I ran to the house and asked Grandma where Mom had gone. I did not even get to say goodbye to her.

Grandma took me into front room, sat in her chair, picked me up and held me. She said that Mom would be back in a few days and that I would have a new person to play with. Charles and Nell were with relatives. I felt like I had been abandoned. I could not ride App; he had too little food and water. Grandma was nice and a good cook, but I had no one to play with.

When I went back to school, my teacher came to the table where I was and sat down beside me. With patience and understanding, she listened to my story of feeling that I was alone and not knowing what I could do. I could not ride my horse and I was scared of being alone. Grandma continually hugged me and told me that things would be all right.

Five days later, in a sandstorm that was lighter than normal, Dad drove to our house. Grandma went to the car. She took some kind of bundle from Mom, cooed over it and came into the house. Dad helped Mom get out of the car, and they came inside. They went straight to the bedroom with just a quick smile at me. I wondered why I was left out. Mom usually hugged and held me, even when she had only been gone for the day. I went outside, but Dad came and asked me to come back inside. "Your mother wants to see you," he said. "Now, don't run in and don't jump on the bed."

I slowly walked into the room and stopped, not knowing what to do. Mom looked up and whispered, "Come here." I walked over, and she laid the sheet back. With a big grin on her face, she said, "I want you to meet your new brother."

Dumbfounded, I looked as she removed the blanket and saw a small, red, wrinkled face and hands that looked like chicken feet.

"That is my brother?" I exclaimed. "Where did he come from? What is his name?"

"His name is Donald," she replied. "He is why I have been gone. Now I am home, and we will all help him grow up to be as big as you."

I do not remember Christmas of 1933 or much else of the following few months. The weather remained cold, windy and dry. My grandparents never recovered from the loss of their crops. They gave up the farm in Texline and moved five miles east of Dalhart, where they had two deep-water wells.

Dad was able to purchase a small house for us just east of Dalhart. The house was small and needed work to become livable. It was close enough to town that Dad could walk to work and I could walk to school. We could even come home for lunch if we wanted.

The most difficult part for me was having to let App be moved to Granddad's new farm. There was no place for a horse at our new home. We were not renters; it was ours. We had our own home. It was not the best nor in the best location, but we would hopefully not have to move again. We continued to have sandstorms and grasshoppers, but they were less destructive.

My second grade at school was fun. I made new friends. I began to read out loud and learned how to divide and multiply numbers. I could walk to town and visit the "roundhouse" a mile down the road. The roundhouse was where the big locomotives were cared for. The engine would be driven onto a big round table with train tracks on it. The huge table would then be turned, and the engine would be driven onto the pad where it was to be repaired.

I made friends with some of the workers. Because there were no insurance warnings posted in those days, I was allowed inside to watch the big cranes move parts and tools to the men rebuilding loco-motives. The only rule was that I could not move without permission from the foreman. When a locomotive was ready to be put back into service on the rail lines, the turntable would rotate the repaired loco-motive, which would then be backed out into the waiting area. It was then ready to move freight or people across the country when needed.

For a seven-year-old boy, this was big stuff. One of my favorite memories is of the time I was asked by the foreman to come and help him. Sometimes the mechanical gears that worked the turntable platform would get the tracks an inch or two off-center. The men had an eight-foot long, four-by-four-inch post they would use to move the roundtable a few inches to line up the tracks.

"Edd, get over here! I need some help!" the foreman shouted.

I looked at him like he was crazy, but he kept motioning for me to come on. I rushed over. He handed me a huge pair of gloves and told me to plant my feet and lean into the big post like he did. I put my gloved hands on the post; when he and I pushed, that huge locomotive moved three inches and was lined up with rails. I was given the gloves as my pay for helping. I never used those gloves but lost them in one of the family moves later on.

Dalhart was the main switching line for two major railroads that went north and west from North Texas. Produce, manufacturing supplies, household goods and other cargo was stored in sealed boxcars on short rail lines. Switch engines would move the freight cars from one rail line to another and hook the railcars to trains going in different directions.

At home, Mom made curtains. Dad bought paint. We scrubbed and painted. We cleaned windows. It was our first home, and we wanted it to be nice. Even with rain uncertain, we planted flowers and cleaned up the yard. We did not live in the nicest part of town, but we couldn't have cared less. It was the nicest place that we had ever had, because it was ours.

On a cool Sunday morning, I asked Mom if I could walk downtown. The stores would be closed, but she said it would be okay if I promised to be careful and back in time for lunch.

I walked the rails of the railroad track as far as I could. I crossed the highway and walked down Main Street. There was no wind, and the sun was out. It was a nice December day. I walked to where there were no stores. I wanted to see the front of the big building I was standing behind. On a corner, I could see a sign that said it was a church building. I knew that my Uncle Eck, Aunt Maude and cousins went to some church; maybe it was this one. I crossed the street so I could see the front of the building. I was staring at the huge entrance when a nice lady stopped and asked if I was looking at the church.

"That is a church building?" I asked.

"Yes, it is. Would like to see inside?" she answered.

"I don't know. I have only seen a dugout for a church," I answered.

"We have children your age who come every Sunday. You could come," she said.

"But I don't know anyone," I replied.

The nice lady held out her hand, and I took it. While we shook hands, she grinned and told me her name. "Now you know someone, so let's walk inside."

Holding hands, we crossed the street and walked into the biggest building I had ever seen. "My, you could get a hundred people in here," I stammered.

"Well, a few more than that. How old are you?" she asked.

"I am seven today. It is my birthday, and Mom is baking me a big cake. Granddad and Grandma are coming this afternoon for my party," I told her.

"My, you are a big boy," she said. (I would love her forever because she did not call me little.) "I have a room downstairs for boys and girls the same age as you. Would you like to come with me and meet them?"

I would have followed her anywhere.

We entered the First Baptist Church building and went to a room that was like a schoolroom. There were a dozen boys and girls my age who were busy at tables that had picture books. I learned that the books were Bible stories. My new friend introduced me to two boys, and then she went to the front the room.

"All right, young people; let's find our seats, and we will sing some songs," the teacher said.

They sang the same songs I had learned in Texline.

"We have someone special here today that I want you to meet," my new friend said. "Today is his birthday. We want to welcome him and sing 'Happy Birthday' for him." She walked to me, put out her hand and asked, "Edd, will you come up front with me?"

Since that dumb Tom Thumb wedding, her invitation did not bother me. I went with her. On a small platform was a red chair that I was to sit in. Everyone sang "Happy Birthday to You" and then added a line: "God loves you, and we do, too!" I began to think that maybe Granddad was mistaken; I just might be worth something to someone someday.

After a Bible story, almost everyone but me went to the big church. I walked home because I did not want Mom to worry. Mom asked all kinds of questions and was really pleased with my report.

"Mom, can we go there next Sunday? The people are real nice and my teacher is great," I said.

"I think we might just do that," she answered.

I have had more than seventy birthdays since Dec. 19, 1932, but none have been more impressive than that one. The First Baptist Church of Dalhart became a major source of learning and love in my life, and it helped make me what I am.

The year of 1933 began in the same manner as the previous year had ended: cold with a lot of wind and no rain. More hoboes rode the rails and more houses were left vacant. There was less money for food and clothes. Cardboard or newspaper filled the bottom of shoes because there was no money for resoles. Clothes were washed one day and worn the next.

The Empire State Building had been completed. "The Star Spangled Banner" became our national anthem, and the sand continued to blow. That year, someone tried to kill the president of our country. I did not know who Mr. Roosevelt was, but I thought no one should try to kill him. Dad liked him, so I did, too. Some little guy named Adolph something was now head of some country I never heard of across the big sea. A few of our people were concerned, but he could not bother me, so what did I care?

In February, our family attended a service at First Baptist Church. After church, we went to Granddad's new farm. Grandmother had cooked a huge meal. Just before we sat down to eat, she looked out the window. She went to the cabinet, took out two extra plates and asked me to hold them for her. We went to the stove, and she filled them with huge amounts of food. She led me to the kitchen door, which faced the railroad three hundred feet away. She opened the screen door and pushed me outside.

"Edd, take this food to the table where those men are sitting. Come back and get two of the metal cups at the well, fill them with water and take that to them as well."

"Grandma, those guys are bums; can't you see?" I protested.

She nodded to me and said, "Yes, they are; but can't you see they are hungry human beings? No man or woman will ever come by my house and leave hungry. Now go."

Granddad had built a large table around a tall cottonwood; at Grandmother's insistence, it became a regular stopping place for hungry men and women who had nowhere else to go. That day after church, we had a great meal and time together. For some reason, that dinner tasted better to me than any I had eaten in a long time.

After we finished eating, Charles and I took off to the barn. I whistled, and App came running. We gave him extra greens left over from lunch. Charles and I sat on the fence and patted his head. We then got on the ground and began to chase the calves. We heard a car come to a quick stop on the gravel area in front of the house. We looked and saw the sheriff get out of his car and rush inside; then he and Dad ran out. Dad got in our car and followed the sheriff, with his red lights flashing, into town. Charles and I started for the house. Granddad came out and stopped us before we could get there.

"What's wrong? Where is Dad going?" we asked.

Granddad took us over to the hobo table and told us, "We don't know for sure what is going on. The sheriff received a call that a house was burning close to your home. We have no telephone, so he came here to let your Dad know."

Charles and I went back to the fence, climbed back up and waited. Dad came back three hours later. He looked beaten and had terrible news. Our new home, along with everything in it, was now ashes. The fire department could do nothing; they arrived too late.

Stunned, Charles and I went back outside; we kicked clods of clay, threw rocks at anything we could find and waited. We did not know what to think or do. Dad and Mom came out. Nell and Donnie were with Grandma. We all sat down at the hobo table and talked about what happened. We had lost everything — all our clothes, our toys, everything we owned. We had no place to live. We had no beds and no money. We had to stay the rest of that week with our grandparents. Charles and I slept on the floor on pallets in front of the fireplace. Mom, Dad, Nell and Donnie were in the guest bedroom.

On Monday morning, Dad rode to work with a neighbor, and Mom and I went in the car to see the remains of our house. We walked around the ashes, looking for anything that was salvageable. Mom found some of her limited amount of jewelry; I found a few forks and knives, a number three wash tub and some other small items. While we were sorting through the ashes, a large car pulled up in front of what used to be our home. A man Mom knew from church came over. He looked around, and then he and Mom talked for about ten minutes. Mom called me over. She introduced me to "Mr. Jones" (sadly, I cannot remember his real name). Mr. Jones put his hand on my shoulder as we looked at the black debris.

"Kind of a mess, isn't it?" he commented.

"Yes, sir, it is. I don't know what is going to happen to us," I replied.

"I don't know either, but you and I can start right now. Let's see if your mother will let you go with me, and I will buy you a big hamburger."

I looked at Mom; she, knowing what was going on, nodded her head. As the man and I left, Dad drove up. He waved at us and went to stand with Mom.

I began to feel some better. I was sitting in the front seat of a big, beautiful car with no brother to hassle me. We drove downtown and went into a restaurant. We sat at a table with a white tablecloth and bright water glasses. A pretty lady came and asked what we wanted.

"How about two big hamburgers with a coffee for me and a chocolate milkshake for my young friend here?" Mr. Jones said.

When she brought my milkshake, it was so big that I had to take it off the table to drink out of the straw. She came back with the biggest hamburger I had ever seen. Grandma and Mom were both great cooks, but this meal became special to me. We were there an hour, and my host never hurried me. He talked to me as if I were big enough to understand what had happened and the problems we would have to overcome. He looked directly at me and said, "Always remember this! Neither God nor God's people will ever let you down. This is hard for you to understand now with all that has happened; but one day, even this will make some sense to you. Come, I have a friend I want you to meet."

As we were leaving, the waitress came over and hugged me. She kissed me on the cheek, and I did not mind at all. Afterward, Mr. Jones and I walked down Main Street and went into J.C. Penney, the store where Dad had worked before we moved to the ranch in New Mexico. A salesman came and greeted us and asked if he could help. Mr. Jones asked to see the manager. The manager came over; he and Mr. Jones exchanged greetings and talked for a few minutes.

Mr. Jones then turned to me and nodded toward the manager. "Sir," he said, "I want you to meet this friend of mine. This is Mr. Brown (I was quite excited to be called 'mister'). He has had a run of bad things happening these past few days, and I was wondering if we could help him in some way."

Smiling, the manager replied, "I think we may be able to do something."

The manager took my hand, and we three walked into the center of the store. An hour later, I had a new pair of boots, three pairs of socks, two pairs of pants, three shirts, a hat and two new sets of underwear. They took my old clothes off me and put them in a bag; then they dressed me in my new ones. I cried, laughed and hugged everyone who would let me. We left with Mr. Jones carrying the two bags. We got in his car and drove to my grandparents' home.

I thanked Mr. Jones a dozen times if not more, and he just smiled. He patted me on my head and shoulder, and I was glad. He then shook my hand and said again, "Don't you ever forget what I told you — that God and God's people will never forsake you!"

I do not recall ever seeing that man of God again, but I have remembered his words to this day.

We were still with Granddad and Grandmother when Uncle Tom came home from CCC camp. Charles and I moved into the attic with him; Nell was in the living room; and Mom, Dad and Donnie were in the guest bedroom. It was still cold and windy. The sand moved one way one day; then the wind would change direction, and the sand would move back. A standing joke was, "I lost two acres of land last week, but three acres came back yesterday."

Two weeks later, Dad found a vacant house east of town and close enough that I could still walk to school. We had a barn and a corral for the horses and milk cows, and App could come home. The days got warmer, and the winds and sand increased. There were still no jobs.

Dad became the auctioneer for the bank. We kids ended up with more toys, peddle cars, scooters and dolls than we could use or give away. As people moved, they took only the things they absolutely had to have to survive. They left furniture, appliances, bedding and toys. No one wasted what little money they had on any unnecessary items. When an auction was over, whatever was left was donated to help charity agencies; what the agencies could not use was given to anyone who wanted it.

Another "norther" blew in. It moved sand by the tons and tumbleweeds by the thousands. The weeds blocked roads, hung on posts and covered barbwire fences for miles. The gate to our cow shed was blown off, and our three milk cows were gone. Dad asked me to find them and bring them home that day. I saddled App and was ready to go east. Livestock usually group together and head downwind.

I was ready to ride but realized there was no way I could open the barbwire gates that would enable me to go through the fields where the cows might be. The wind had blown tumbleweeds hard enough against the fence that they matted against the three strings of the four-foot-high barbwire fence. The winds packed dirt and sand into the matted tumbleweeds. The sandy weeds were three or four feet high along the barbwire fences. I rode App over five miles and found our milk cows. I drove them back home over the fences of eight different properties. There was no need for the gates. Some of our neighbors never found their cattle or horses.

I did not have to change schools; I just approached my school from the opposite direction. My size set me up to be the punching bag for the school bullies, and in some instances, even the girls got on the bandwagon. Two things other than my size made me the target for some in the class. First, I was excused from taking exams; thanks to Mom and Aunt Elsie, I could read and do numbers better than anyone else in the class. Second, some of the girls who had been part of that Tom Thumb Wedding the year before began to hound me about that.

Two factors kept me from striking back. One was that I was never to hit a girl. If I did and Mom found out, I would suffer something a lot worse than girls hitting me. The other reason was simply survival. I knew that if I fought back, I would really get beat up; so I just whimpered, cried and put up with my tormenters.

One morning, just before lunch, our teacher left the classroom for a short conference. No adults were around, and three of the girls began to torment me, saying things like, "He ain't purty at all, is he? I had rather kiss a cow than someone like him."

I got up from my desk and started for the door. One of the girls suggested they get me; another girl said something as they ran up behind me I did not turn around but tried to ignore them. One of them pushed me, and I fell forward. I grabbed for the desk and missed. My head hit the corner of the heavy oak desk, and I fell to the floor.

All I heard was, "Oh, God! What are we going to do? We may

have killed him!"

I was knocked out for two or three minutes and did not know where I was or why I was lying on the schoolroom floor. My head hurt. I rolled over and began to rub my head. I had a two-inch cut right where I parted my hair. If you know anything about scalp cuts, you know that the blood comes fast. Even with a small cut, you bleed as if your head had been cut off.

The girls started screaming. The boys backed away. I sat up, continuing to rub my face and head. I was dizzy and could not stand. I rolled over and remained on the floor with my back against the bloody corner of the desk. Our teacher and the principal rushed into our room, and the first thing they saw was a bloody kid they could not recognize sitting on the floor by the desk. My teacher let out a word I did not know. She sent the class to their chairs and tried to get some order.

The principal called another teacher into the room; the other teacher knelt beside me, washing my hands and face and trying to carefully clean my head. I still had no feeling. I was glassy-eyed but felt no pain other than a headache. After I was cleaned up as much as I could be, they sat me in a chair.

"What are we going to do? He has blood all over him!" my teacher said.

Some way, I was able to mutter, "I want to go home."

"You will go soon," the principal said.

I was later told that some of my records were misplaced, but I was too woozy to help. Someone (it could have been one of the kids) told them my full name and address.

My teacher said, "We cannot take him home like this (I was bleeding through the bandages again). We must call Mrs. Brown and tell her what happened and let her know that Edd is not injured as badly as he appears to be."

The other teacher said, "I think a friend of mine lives next door to the Browns. She is a nurse and has a telephone."

The principal, with that information, went to his office. He returned a few minutes later and reported that the neighbor was home and would help.

They cleaned me up as best they could and helped me into a car, and the principal drove me home. The wind was blowing as always, and sand was thick. Blood dripped from the wound onto my face and clothes, and the sand stuck everywhere. I rubbed my face and cried. I was not hurting that much, but I was humiliated. I did not want Mom or anyone else to see what those catty girls had done.

When we arrived at our house, our neighbor, the nurse, stood on the front step. She had convinced Mom to wait inside, but the front door was open. The principal asked me to wait in the car. He wanted to tell Mom what had happened and reassure her that I was fine. The blood had stopped, but with the sand and blood, I was one scary-looking kid. The neighbor had agreed to stay as long as needed. If I had to go to a doctor, the principal would take me.

The nurse came to the car and helped me get out. I walked to the house on my own. I had quit hurting and tried to make a brave entrance. Mom looked terrified, so I laughed and asked if she thought I would make a good clown for Halloween. She did not know if she ought to cry, laugh or get the paddle and use it on me. The nurse and Mom took me into the kitchen, sat me in a chair and began to take off my bloody bandages and clothes. They washed my head with a special soap and cleaned my face again. I was fearful that they would undress me and make me completely naked in front of everyone, but I did keep my undershorts on. The nurse cleaned the cut and pulled the skin together with gauze and tape. She said that I would live but that I should not sleep for six hours.

When everyone left, Mom fed me some soup and asked me what happened. At first, she was angered; but she later told me that what happened was an accident. The girls did not intend to hurt me. If they came later to say they were sorry, I was to thank them. I was to get on at school as if it never happened. The rest of the year was uneventful. The story of my fall was known all over the school, and I was not harassed any more that year.

Three

1934

A Move South

The wind and sand did not quit. There were more cars, wagons and whatever transportation families could find leaving to take them anywhere or nowhere. There were fewer people showing up at bank auctions and more houses abandoned, so Dad's job was coming to an end. For the first time in our nomadic family life, I was not unhappy about our move.

We loaded everything we owned into a small trailer, pulled behind a Model A touring car. Electra, our new home, was 140 miles south in Wichita County, Texas. Dad had located a job as a night manager at an oil pumping lease in Megargel, thirty miles west of Electra. We stayed in Electra only three months. During those months, Charles and I were introduced to chiggers. We had no grass in our yards in the Dust Bowl; but in Electra, we had a green lawn around our house and water to care for grass and flowers. A warm gentle rain came, the first real rain we had seen in months, maybe years. Charles and I frolicked all day in the cool, clear water.

That night, we began to break out in what Mom thought was a rash; however, it was no rash. It was chiggers, little red bugs that are almost invisible to the naked eye. They got in the pores of our skin and festered there. Overnight, we developed sores all over our bodies, especially around our private parts. Later, they became small abscesses that itched horribly. If scratched, they became worse. Mom tried different salves, the bluing she used to bleach clothes, Epsom salt baths and anything else people recommended, but nothing worked. We could not wear clothes, and bed sheets were agony. For three days, we could not sleep or eat. We just knew we were going to die. We didn't die, but we did become very aware of a new pest we would have to live with in north central Texas.

Before school began, Dad found us a house close to the ranch where Grandma Brown then lived. It was closer to Dad's work and was on a small creek. There was also a school bus stop nearby. We liked the open country, and I could now have App with me. Our neighbor had a cotton field. Two weeks before school began, I asked him if I could pick cotton. He agreed and let me have an old cotton picking sack that Mom cut down for me. I picked cotton for the two weeks and made three dollars. For the first time, I had worked for my own money. I hung on to it for weeks.

The fall rain came early. One night, the entire family awoke scratching and trying to find some relief. Thousands of fleas had been dormant under the house, but the rain and cool weather had awakened them. They invaded our house. We used oil, gasoline and whatever we could to kill the fleas and survive their invasion. A week later, Dad found a house in Megargel, and we moved. If I have the count right, this was now the tenth house we had lived in during my seven years.

App was kept on the ranch where Grandma Brown, a widow, lived with two of my aunts. I was able to ride App at least once a week. Our small house in Megargel was three blocks from the center of town, a half-mile from my school, and four blocks from the Baptist church and across the street from the Methodist Church. Best of all, there were no chiggers and no fleas.

I began my third grade in school, and bullies came out of the woodwork. I became the punching bag for them. One day, on my way home, two of my tormenters were waiting for me. It had not been a good day, and I was already mad. I looked at the two and said to myself, "I will not run. They can beat on me, but I will not run. They are not going to beat on me anymore."

I dropped my books and bowed my head, but not to pray. I was close to the bigger boy. I jumped at him, rammed my head into his stomach and sent him flying five feet. I then turned to the other one, and he ran. I watched both of them run and screamed, "You (deleted word) better learn now to leave me alone!" I looked around to see who might report my language to Mom. I was feeling like Superman as I walked home.

While the life change was welcomed by Dad, Mom was not as happy. While she was glad that the bullying might stop, she was rightfully concerned that I would move too far in the opposite direction. Unfortunately, I did. The principal and I became well acquainted that year.

The news of the world began to catch up with me. I was selling newspapers on the streets of Megargel on Saturdays. This time, my size helped. People asked questions like how old I was and if my parents knew I was there; their concern helped me to sell all my papers within an hour. I made enough money to go to the ten-cent picture show on Saturday and buy a double-dipped ice cream cone for a nickel. I saved enough money to buy a bicycle for five dollars. I began to read the papers that I sold and learned that a woman named Amelia Earhart had flown an airplane across the Atlantic Ocean and that Lindbergh's baby had been kidnapped. That weird guy named Hitler, who wore a funny mustache, was still some kind of ruler in Germany and was building camps to hold people he did not like.

I made friends with the people in our small town and most at least acted as if they liked me. During recess and lunch breaks at school, we would have ball games, and someone would be appointed to choose sides. You don't have to guess who the last one chosen was.

Our family began going to the small Baptist church. I met some nice people my age and made some friends. I began to learn about God and Jesus and how I ought to live to become a better person. The church began a program called "Royal Ambassadors." It was like Boy Scouts but was church-based and focused on Bible principles in daily life. We went on camping and fishing trips and to R.A. meetings with boys from other churches.

That fall, eleven boys went with our counselor and pastor on an overnight fishing trip. We were only ten miles from home, but we were camping. We fished, cleaned what we caught and cooked them over wood fires. When the sun disappeared in the west, we sat around the campfire and told stories.

Our pastor talked to us about our lives and how God loved us even if no else one did. While I was closely listening to what he said, the log that three of us boys were sitting on moved. I lost my balance and fell backwards off the log. I tried to break my fall with my right hand. I fell on a mesquite limb, and a thorn pierced the palm of my right hand. Our counselor and the pastor immediately came to see if anyone was hurt. I did not even feel the thorn in my hand.

I stood there looking at the thorn in my palm and the crazy branch attached to the back of my hand. The pastor, with the help of the counselor, carefully pulled the thorn out. I was still in more wonderment than pain. Because it was a puncture wound, they began to press and massage both sides of my hand to make it bleed. They then soaked my hand in warm salt water.

"I think we had better take you home," the pastor said, "and get you to a doctor tomorrow."

I replied, "I don't want to go home. They will take me to a doctor who will want to give me shots."

Regardless of my objection, that is what happened. Two days later, the pastor came to our house. I was outside playing and thought he had come to talk to Mom. She was a teacher of a children's Bible class on Sunday mornings. Instead of talking to her, he came outside to see me. We sat on benches and talked about the campout, the fishing and the good time we all had.

"It was fun, but I ruined it for everyone," I said.

Quickly, the pastor replied, "Oh, no, you did not ruin it. When I drove back to camp, everyone — and I mean everyone — wanted to know how you were. Then one boy asked if we could we pray for you. We did, and we sang songs before we went to bed. This morning before breakfast, they wanted to pray for you again."

The pastor prayed with me and left. I sat for a long time and could not believe that I was that important to him or those boys. Maybe, someday, I might be worth something.

I began to enjoy school but was unsure of myself and hesitant to participate in class. In Dalhart, I fit in. I was a cowboy in a cowboy town and could ride a horse with the best of them. Even my granddad agreed that, for a kid, I really knew how to "set a horse" (how to ride right). Very few had horses in Megargel, and the Dust Bowl had not ruined all their crops or forced people out of their homes. Here, fewer people rode the rails in search of food or jobs, but the Depression was as real in Megargel as anywhere else.

Even with the same economic problems, I was out of my element. Questions were about cities, governments, social problems and sports with rules, like football and baseball. I froze up after trying to answer a few questions with the limited knowledge I had. I dropped from the head of my class in Dalhart to close to the bottom of my class in Megargel. My teacher, who was a friend of one of my aunts, came to see Mom. She brought me "readable books" that Mom could help me read.

They enrolled me in a private home school that taught elocution for an hour on Saturdays for six weeks. Dad would take me with him at work. Out in the open country, he would let me drive the pickup across the fields where there were no fences. We checked all the oil pumps that lifted the oil from deep in the earth to storage tanks. We checked the rod lines that operated the pumps. We would then return to the pump house, and he would help me read the books and explain them to me. I began to learn geography and history, and Dad used the newspaper that I was no longer selling to help me understand more about our world.

I did not move to the head of the class, but I did move up a long way up from the bottom. In December, the weather was cold but we all went to church on Sunday mornings. Because the kids I knew went to a fun special learning time before the evening service, I went Sunday nights as well. Mom wanted to me to go because I enjoyed going, but she was worried one night because it was below freezing. She and Dad suggested that, instead of me walking to church, we all go that Sunday night. There was a place for everyone in our family. Dad and Mom sat with the adults; Charles and I, with the youth; and Nell and Donnie, with the children. As we left for church, I began to feel uncomfortable. I had been listening to the pastor's sermons, and he had privately talked to me and Mom. He wanted me to understand what it would mean to me to become a Christian. Dad had listened, and his only comment was, "Don't do it if you don't really mean it."

That evening, the service began with some of my favorite hymns. I loved to sing. I was not very good, but I enjoyed music. I do not remember much of what the preacher said, but there was that uneasiness, an eerie feeling in me. I knew I was not ill, nor was I scared, but there was a kind of wonderment that would not go away. The pastor finished his message and said a prayer. He then asked everyone to bow their heads and to ask God what He wanted us to do with our lives. Something clicked inside me.

My pastor had rushed to me when I fell off the log. He came to see me, not my parents, the day after he came back from camping. The pastor continued, "If you feel God wants you to be his servant and you are willing to give your life to Him and to trust Jesus to save you, come and let me know."

Nothing could have held me back. I knew that was what I wanted and what I had to do. I went forward and told him how I felt. He asked me several questions, and I must have answered right. He asked the people to sit and had me stand with him. He asked me more questions in front of the church. He then asked the church to express their desire. I was accepted for baptism and, after baptism, as a member of the First Baptist Church of Megargel, Texas.

Normally that ends the service, but instead of dismissing the people, the pastor asked everyone to sit for a few minutes. He went to Mom and Dad and explained that there was to have been a baptism that night, but the person who was to be baptized was ill and unable to be there. The baptistery was full of warm water. He would have one of the deacons go and start his car and have it warm. He would baptize me in the clothes I had on. His wife would wrap me in my wet clothes with a blanket, and he would put me in his car and drive me home. Dad said it was fine, and Mom asked how I felt. I had no problem at all. I was baptized that night and started a lifelong up-and-down journey with God. Not really understanding what was involved or where it would take me, in December of 1936, I made the first public commitment of my life.

The next year, Texas was one hundred years old, and celebrations took place all over the state. Mom, Charles and I, along with our friend Mrs. Bacon and her two daughters, Theresa and Barbara, went to Fort Worth and Dallas for the Centennial Fair. We kids rode the Ferris wheel, the electric bumper cars and the roller coaster. We ate popcorn, ice cream and other stuff until we were almost sick. We spent the whole day at the celebration and that night with family in Fort Worth.

The next day, we went to Dallas to see the giant fireworks display in the Cotton Bowl. On a super large movie screen, we watched a film about the hundred-year history of Texas. That night was the first time I spent a night in a motel. We had a great time, and I did not mind spending my money for rides and food.

The last morning, we went to the carnival and walked through the midway. Hawkers were selling everything imaginable. They promised fantastic cures for everything. The sideshows had unusual animals and some acts that we kids were not old enough to understand. One such show was "Sally Rand and her Fans," direct from Chicago. We kids laughed.

"Must be hotter in Chicago than here if she needs that many fans," Charles said.

One fellow standing in line heard and remarked, "Yeah, could be, but she could have left some of her fans there." He laughed and walked off. We looked at one another and wondered what in the world was he talking about. After more sideshows, we had lunch, and Mom drove us back to Megargel. Grandmother Brown had kept Nell while we were gone.

My first day back in school, I was asked to share with my classmates. I told of the rides and the history show. I tried to explain the fireworks and then mentioned the Sally Rand show. For some reason, my teacher interrupted and said we needed to get back to our lessons.

Dad had been meeting with the owners of a different oil lease. They had asked him to go look at a new oil field fifty miles north. Dad asked us if we would like to go. We kids wanted to go, and Mom agreed. We spent the day driving around the area of K.M.A. The town (if you could call it one) was named after three men who had leased the property to form an oil company: Mr. Kemp, Mr. Munger and Mr. Allen. The town had two cross streets, six oil well service businesses, a liquor store, a telephone office, two small eating places, an ice cream parlor and two churches. Kadane Corner, closer to where we would live, was even smaller. Dad's new job, if he wanted it, was to be the field supervisor of the lease for Consolidated Oil. The company offered to build us a new house and pay Dad a good salary and give him two weeks paid vacation a year.

Our friends the Bacons had moved to K.M.A. We visited them, and we liked the area. The people we met were nice and friendly. Dad took the job, and we moved to K.M.A as soon the new house was built.

School in Megargel was becoming more interesting, and I was gradually becoming accepted by the boys my age and older. At recess one day, we were playing workup softball. When a batter made an out, every position would move up one place. You could get to bat two ways. You could either work your way up by the outs made by the batters, or you could change positions with the batter by catching a fair fly ball.

As usual, I was the last one to get to play and was in the outfield. The batter hit a long fly ball, and we all thought he had a home run. Everyone was sure I could not get to the ball in time to catch it. I surprised not only them but myself. I turned and ran to where I thought the ball would land. I got there in time to catch the ball in the air one-handed. No one was more surprised than I was.

I went to home plate and took my turn at bat. Everyone moved up close to make sure that I did not hit a ground ball through the infield and get on base. The pitcher knew he had an easy out and lobbed a ball over my head. The second ball was right down the middle over the plate. I swung the bat and hit the ball perfectly, and it sailed over every player on the field. I had two more at-bats before I made an out.

I was on my way back to my position in the outfield when the next batter hit a ball and someone hollered, "Edd, look out!" I turned, and the ball was almost in my face. I threw my right hand up to protect my face and caught the ball. I calmly walked back, pitched the ball to the catcher, took up the bat and batted until recess was over.

After that, I was not the first one chosen for games, but I was no longer the last. I tried to learn to play the French horn in the school band, but I could not distinguish the difference in the tones. My teacher tried and wanted to help, but the lightning bolt that knocked me down had left me with hearing problems.

In the fall of 1937, our house in K.M.A. was finished. After Christmas, we moved into our new home. App had a barn and corral. We had chickens, a milk cow and acres to roam. The house was new and small. There was one room for cooking and eating, a small living room, two bedrooms and a screened-in porch. Mom, Dad and Nell had one bedroom. We three boys shared (and fought in) the other. When the weather was nice, we boys slept on the screened-in porch. We had a well with a pump and water inside the house. The water was hard and tasted bad. We bought drinking water by the barrel; it was delivered to us every week.

I had a few friends from Megargel who now went to Valley View School. I had met others at church in K.M.A. My school bus stopped a mile from our house and took thirty minutes to get to Valley View School. I was the new kid; with help, I found my classroom and was looking around. A black-haired girl my age walked up and asked, "Are you new here?"

"Yes," I answered.

"Good; you need to meet some people. I am Rita Glenn Storie. Who are you?"

"I am Edd Brown," I replied.

Rita introduced me to three or four others. Jack, I had met at church; but most of the others I did not know. After I met several people, Rita turned and told me she wanted me to meet her best friend. She went and took hold of the arm of a cautious, reserved brown-haired girl about my height.

Rita said, "This is Florene Nelson, my best friend. You can be her friend, too, and I won't be jealous."

Florene became "Flo" to me (and no, she never sold insurance). I had seen Flo at church but had not met her. Flo and I just stood and looked at one another for a minute or two. We were two slightly embarrassed ten-year-old kids who could not think or dream then that a shared life lay ahead for the two of us.

I finished my fourth grade at Valley View. One Sunday, Dad had to work, and I rode App to K.M.A Baptist Church. Our friends the Bacons from Megargel lived close to the church building. They let me tie App to a post behind their house. I now knew several of the kids in church from school.

After Bible study, I stayed for church. When the service, which I

Flo at age ten.

enjoyed, was over, the pastor gave an invitation for any who wanted to join the church to come forward. I lived here and liked the people and did not want to be a stranger. I went forward and tried to explain to the pastor that I wanted to be a member of the church and move my church letter from Megargel. The pastor was confused. He knew that I had already come forward to make a public decision to become a Christian. Mr. Bacon sensed the confusion and came and told the pastor of my baptism and confession at Megargel, which Mr. Bacon had personally seen. The pastor then explained my decision to the church. After a few more questions, I became a member of First Baptist Church of K.M.A., Texas.

The church had varnished pine tongue-and-grove flooring. The wood flooring had been installed over the clay floor that had been used for several years. They had put down untreated four-by-six timbers for floor joists and nailed the pine tongue-and-groove flooring to them. No vents were put in the floor or the edge of the stucco building. The pine timbers began to expand and buckle, creating ridges in most of the flooring up to one inch high.

Mr. Bacon was a carpenter and builder. He was asked to take charge. Several strips of flooring were removed in six or eight locations. The door and windows were left open, and electric fans were brought by members to dry out the old clay floor. Men cut openings in the walls of the building beneath where the new flooring would be installed. When I could, I helped install the new church floor.

School was great. I made some good friends and liked my teachers. The school superintendent, Mr. Brazill, was the music director at our church. That summer, the church attendance had grown. We needed more space for children and young people. The church had been given a wooden warehouse. Men from the church, along with men from the company that donated the warehouse, salvaged as much of the lumber as they could. They moved and stacked the lumber at the back of the church property.

School was out, and I did not have a lot to do at home. I asked Mom if I could ride App to church and help to remove nails and sort the lumber.

"You think you can do that?" she asked.

"No, but I can learn," I answered.

"Okay," Mom said, "but be careful and be back in time for supper."

I had no tools but knew Mr. Bacon would have plenty. I saddled App from the platform that Dad and I had built and headed for the church three miles away. I went the back way, following the river as much as I could. When I arrived at the church, Mr. Bacon asked if I wanted to help.

"Yes sir," I answered.

I put on leather gloves, and he handed me a claw hammer and took me to a huge pile of assorted lumber filled with rusted, bent nails. He showed me how to place the boards on sawhorses to keep them from bouncing when I hammered the nails. He helped me learn how to use the claw end of the hammer to pull nails out of the boards. He watched as I tried to take the nails out of the lumber. He picked up a hammer out of his work chest and led me over to a stack of boards ten to twelve feet long. He placed one of the boards on his sawhorses and began to remove the nails. He picked up another and told me to watch closely as he did two more boards. He then asked me to do the same and watched as I began to pound at the nails.

"Slow down and hit easy," he said. "Use your arm, not your wrist." He coached me for ten minutes. He then took me back to my pile of lumber and went to help someone else. I worked every day for two weeks, driving out old nails and sorting and stacking lumber.

When there was nothing else I could do at church, I told Dad I wanted a job. Dad had met Mr. Burns, who had a cotton crop along the Wichita River two miles away. He was looking for someone to clean the weeds and space the cotton plants to get the best possible cotton from his crop. I went and talked to him. I admitted that I had no experience but said I was willing to learn.

"Come back at seven in the morning, and we will see what we can do," he said.

Early the next morning, I took my new hoe and file and was there early. Mr. Burns was pleased that I was there early and ready to work. He asked me to chop some weeds along an irrigation bank. He watched and then came over to show me how to swing the hoe and not use it as an axe. He took his hoe and asked me to follow. He started down a row, swinging his hoe with a rhythm and moving his body in the same motion. He did two rows, and then it was my turn. He walked with me, giving me instructions. He was not critical, but helpful. I thought I was killing more cotton than weeds, but he never said a word. We stopped at the end of a row and sat under a tree. He took out his file and demonstrated how to sharpen my hoe.

"When you chop cotton, don't rush. Develop your own rhythm. Work only one row at a time for a couple of days; once you learn that, we will go to two rows at a time. If you learn how to do that, I will pay you a dollar a day and feed you lunch." He handed my hoe to me and left.

It took me over three hours to feel like I was walking and swinging the hoe in rhythm. A dollar a day for an eleven-year-old boy was big money. I worked for Mr. Burns for four weeks. When he paid me my wages, he put in an extra five dollars because he could depend on me to be there early every day.

Because larger oil deposits had been found deeper in the earth, larger and taller drilling rigs were moved in. With the drilling rigs came more people. Valley View School ran out of room and had no place for the additional students.

Archer County School District decided to reopen Eagle Bend School, which was three miles from our home. It was a three-room school. First and second grades were in one room; third and fourth in grades were in another. The fifth, sixth and seventh grades were in the largest room, which also doubled as the school auditorium. I began my fifth grade at Eagle Bend. Flo's father had helped start the school and had taught many of his own family there during the school's early years. We had sixty students and surprisingly few discipline problems. Many of my classmates from Valley View and friends from church were in my classes.

We had good teachers; we also had good softball and basketball teams and some good tennis players. We competed with other small schools in Archer County in the three sports and in choir and speech recitals. I participated in all of the activities. Our small school led the district in most events and finished second in all others during the three years I was there.

When I was in the sixth grade, Mom was elected the president of the Parent-Teacher Association. They sponsored three or four major events each school year and awarded scholarships to deserving students. The school held its annual drama and music program, and I had a major part. I was a young black plantation girl (yes, a girl!). The auditorium was packed. Our presentation was about the problems of a then-typical southern plantation home and was enjoyed by parents and guests. The parents were more than pleased, and it helped them accept the moving of students from Valley View to Eagle Bend.

After the program, a meal was served. Many of the mothers and students stayed to help the officers clean up when the meal was finished. Two things happened that provided the ones who stayed a lot of fun. One was that some of the parents were guessing who had played the part of the young black girl. I had cleaned my face and changed clothes, and I had a ball listening to them trying to figure it out. One of the students in the play told them who it was. I was congratulated and good-naturedly booed and joked about. The entire evening was open bonding and fellowship.

The second thing that happened was that one lady who had recently moved from a larger community with a much larger school approached my mother. The lady had helped some that evening, but mostly she had stood around and watched. In time, she came over to Mom, who, as president, was the hostess that night.

The lady asked, "Mrs. Brown, how long have you been president of the PTA?"

Mom answered, "This is my second and last year."

"What would I need to do if I wanted to become eligible to be president?" the lady asked.

Mom, without answering, took her hands out of the hot soapy dishwater, dried them off on a towel, turned, took off her apron and then tied it around the lady's waist.

Mom backed off and replied, "That."

Embarrassed, the lady looked around; then she began to laugh. "Boy did I ever ask for that," she said. She kept the apron on, turned to the sink, rolled up her sleeves and began to wash the dishes. She and Mom became the best of friends, and the entire group went home that night feeling good.

I graduated from the seventh grade at Eagle Bend. WPA workers had finished the high school building at Valley View, and I began high school there. That same year, Dad leased three acres across the irrigation ditch from our house. Charles and I planted, watered, hoed and picked our cotton, and we made close to a hundred dollars each that summer. Because of the war in Europe, cotton prices were high, and there was a big demand for our crop.

Workers for the oil fields were becoming scarce. Many young men in our community, and even some women, had been drafted or had enlisted into the armed forces. Hitler had invaded Austria and was moving into Poland. Concentration camps were being built in Germany. England and France were fighting to survive. Japan had invaded China and was moving south toward Singapore.

K.M.A. petitioned the Postal Service for a Post Office. It was approved, but the community had to have a name and it could not be initials. So "Kamay" was born and our own post office was opened.

I had very little contact with Negroes and had no feelings about them one way or the other. Mr. Burns had recommended me to Mr. Wells, a friend of his in our church. Mr. Wells asked me one Sunday after services if I would be interested in working for him a few weeks that summer. He would pay me a $1.50 a day. His wife would feed me three meals a day if I would come and move in with them for three weeks. I was free at that time, so I took the job. His plot was not overly large, but it would take me a month or more to work his fields. When I asked him about the time, he told me that four other workers would be coming and that he wanted me to be the foreman of the group. He had other crops he had to care for, and Mr. Burns had told him that I could be trusted to take over. I was pleasantly surprised.

On my first day, he sent his son, who was a year younger than me, to the field to work. We took an hour lunch break and worked four more hours. At supper, Mr. Wells asked his son how our day went.

"Dad," he said, "I have hoed cotton for three years and know how to do it well, but I cannot keep up with Edd."

"What Mr. Burns told me must be true. We will know more in a couple of days," Mr. Wells said as he went to milk the cows.

I had my own small room. I cleaned up at the outside shower and went to bed. The son and I worked the next day, and I slowed down enough so he could keep up.

At noon, an old Ford Model A loaded with tents and bedding pulled into a flat area under some large shade trees. A middle-aged black man got out and went to the house. Mr. Wells came out, and they talked for a few minutes before coming to where I was sitting on a log. Mr. Wells introduced me to Mr. Henry. I put out my hand to Mr. Henry to shake. He looked at me and smiled and took my hand. I told him I was glad to meet him. Mr. Wells excused himself and left. I did not know what to do. Mr. Henry noticed my embarrassment and broke the silence.

"Since we are going to be working with you, let me get my family settled, and we will meet you in the field in thirty minutes."

I could think of nothing to say, so I just nodded and went to the house to get my hat and water bottle. I went to the field and sat under a shade tree, sharpening my hoe. In twenty minutes, Mr. Henry, his wife, his son (who was about my age) and an older daughter came with their hats and hoes.

I knew I had to say something. "Sir, I am only sixteen years old. I don't live on this farm, and I am not old enough to be a foreman for a man old enough to be my father."

He looked at me, smiled, put a hand on my shoulder and said, "Son, you were hired to do a job. Me and my family were hired to do a job. Why don't we forget about what we can't change and go to work?"

"Yes, sir," I said, and we went to work. Mr. Henry and I each took two rows, the others took one, and we began to chop cotton. I started out slow, because I needed to know their pace. At the turnaround a quarter of a mile away, I began to pick up the pace, and they stayed with me. We stopped, drank some water and caught our breath.

Afterwards, I headed out at full speed. Mr. Henry stayed with me, and the others were not far behind. I asked if everyone was okay and if we needed to stop to sharpen our hoes. Mr. Henry suggested we wait until we had finished the round. That was fine with me, so we headed out. We worked until lunch time. I went to the house. Mrs. Henry had stayed at their campsite the last round to fix their lunch. We took an hour break and worked until sundown. Two days later, we moved to another field a mile away.

Mr. Henry and his wife came to me and said, "Son, we have two questions. One, we want to know how and where you learned to chop cotton. Two, would you eat lunch with us, instead of going all the way to the house?"

I was overwhelmed. I told them that Mr. Burns had not told me how but showed me how, and that he had worked with me until I learned.

"He must have been an experienced teacher. I have never worked with anyone close to your age who can chop cotton like you," Mr. Henry said.

With a compliment like that, I could not turn down the invitation to have lunch with them. In ten days, we finished our jobs early but were paid for the full time for which we were hired. The Henrys moved on, and I had an amazing new understanding of some of God's good people whose skin just happened to be darker than mine.

A company named Buffalo Oil bought the oilfield where we lived and wanted Dad to stay and manage it for them. They were going to begin drilling deeper to increase production. They would also increase Dad's salary and build us a new larger home. Mr. J. B. Tobman, one of the principal owners of the company, was a Russian Jew who had to flee the country when Stalin ousted the very people who had supported him during the Russian revolution.

When Trotsky fled to Mexico, Tobman escaped through Southern Europe and came to the United States. He found a job in Pittsburgh at a junkyard. He cut up the body of two old cars, welded them together and made living quarters for himself. He cooked his own meals and did any kind of work he could find; in five years, he had saved enough money to buy a half-interest in the junkyard. Two years later, he bought the other half. He and a close friend enlisted several other immigrants to join them, and in five years, they created a corporation that would later become Bethlehem Steel International.

Because of the Lend-Lease Act, a program in which the United States provided resources to Great Britain and other Allies, the demand for oil was increasing. Mr. Tobman and the others who had joined him bought our oil field. He personally visited the lease and took time to visit with Mom and Dad. He would often take extra time on his visits to sit down and share about his life with Charles and me.

For the largest cash payment in Texas oilfield history up to that time, Buffalo Oil Company bought the lease where Dad worked and where we lived. In four months, our new home was built. We had a large living room, a dining room, a large kitchen with a gas stove and a refrigerator. We had running water with a hot water tank. We had three bedrooms and two indoor bathrooms with toilets, tubs and showers. A large screened-in back porch was also included.

Our former house was completely remodeled, upgraded and enlarged. The Coats family, our neighbors who had lived a mile away, moved in. Mr. Coats was hired as Dad's assistant. There was a one-hundred-square-foot garden area between the two houses. We had a huge storage tank for water and a corral with a barn for our two cows and horses.

It was like a palace to us. We could now have church and school parties in our home for the first time. We also had a concrete-lined storm cellar (a "fraidy" hole, some wise guy called it). When we were afraid of storms, we would run to cellar. In Tornado Alley, no one minded being known as being afraid of high winds and tornadoes. The cellar was also used to store canned food and cured hams and bacon for both families.

I worked in the oil field for twenty cents an hour, two afternoons a week. I helped clean tools and carried water for the three crews laying pipelines, which would transfer oil from the wells to the six-thousand-barrel storage tanks located in the center of the lease. I also painted "Christmas trees" (called that because of the different colors of the valves and pressure gauges) on top of the wells. The gauges controlled the amount of oil that flowed from the deep wells into the storage tanks.

One afternoon, I was painting a Christmas tree when I heard and felt a roaring explosion a mile away. It almost knocked me down. One of the roustabouts (oilfield general workers) was welding a discharge pipe to empty the sludge and grime from a storage tank. Someone had left one of the lids of that tank open. When a small breeze blew, the suction of air pulled a spark from the welding torch twenty feet away up through the drainage pipe into the empty oil tank. The spark ignited the gas, which exploded. The tank was knocked off its platform and became almost as round as a ball.

Dad was at another well. He shut down the valve that let the oil go from that well to the tanks and rushed by me on his way to another well. As he went by, he signaled by rotating his hand in the air for me to shut off any open valves near where I was working and to make sure that another well close by was shut down.

Local oilfield fire units arrived in about twenty minutes and began to spray water on the other tanks to cool them down. The other tanks were full of oil and some covers were open. They would not explode like the empty one that had been filled with gas; however, if they became hot enough, they would expand and allow the oil to escape through open covers or weld leaks and burn.

After thirty minutes, Dad climbed the ladder steps to the walkway and, with the fire control team covering him with three streams of water, closed the openings to the other five tanks. The fire team then began to spray foam on the burning tank to cut off the oxygen. Having lost its source of oxygen and been cooled by the water, the fire was put out. For two hours, the fire team pumped water and foam onto the tanks so the gas would not reignite.

That spring, our church addition was completed, and the congregation continued to grow. The pastor asked me to help advertise our vacation Bible school. I had no idea how I could help. He wanted me to ride App at the head of a church parade. I would carry the American flag for a mile through town. There would be eight cars of young people, children and parents following me. The cars would have banners on the sides with the times and dates of the VBS. Some of the older youth would walk along with us and pass out pamphlets with full information, including invitations to the adults for an adult Bible study.

I agreed to help. The day before the parade, I curried App more than he needed. I oiled and polished my saddle until it glowed. The next morning, I arrived at the church early and was ready to go. I was on App and was handed the American flag with no problem. I unfurled the flag, and App went crazy. I pitched the flag to someone and rode App for a few minutes before he calmed down; then I dismounted.

I took the flag and went to the front of App. I held up the flag, still rolled on the staff, and began to slowly unroll it. I shook it and moved it across App's forehead. With the help of one of the men who had horses, I held the staff of the fully furled flag and mounted App. Everyone held their breath; I was ready to throw the flag and hang on, but App just stood. I sat for three minutes and then gently nudged App with my knees; with my left hand, I shook the reins, and he began to move. I asked the pastor to ask the first two cars behind me not to blow their horns; otherwise, App might run.

We went to the road and made our way the mile through town. I have no idea how many were in the parade or how many watched. I was concerned about App behaving in a new situation and about finding a place to rid myself of the flag and not be taken to task for dishonoring our national symbol. After the parade, I had to move away from the crowd that gathered because I had no idea how App would react.

On the morning of Sunday, Dec.7, 1944, my friend Fred Minix and I were sitting in his dad's new car. We should have been in church, but we were not. Fred was showing me all the new gadgets on the car. He turned on the radio and began to change stations, but the same message was being broadcast on all stations. We then began to listen to something about bombs at a place called Pearl Harbor. An on-site reporter came on, and we heard of the destruction and how the U.S. was now at war. We had no idea how much our lives had changed in that hour, and there was nothing we could do to change it back. Six of us young people — Jack and Wanda, Mack and Betty, and Flo and me — had begun to run around together. Flo was the girl that Rita had introduced me to. None of us were dating; we were just six high school and church friends doing things together.

High school was different because we were in classes instead of grades. The mix of grades there was much like I had encountered at Eagle Bend, with three classes in one room. We had good teachers, but the war effort and the allure of higher-paying factory jobs made for a high rate of turnover, which did not help my education. I had six different English teachers in three years, and four for math. Even though John Nelson, Flo's older half-brother and the pastor of a small Baptist church, was one of my teachers, it is a wonder I learned as much as I did.

One of our new history teachers was a German American. She was not a Nazi, but she had respect for what Hitler had done for Germany and dismissed the reports coming out of Europe as propaganda to inflame the West to support the war.

Our high school had some good athletes who had grown up on farms and in the oilfields. Hard work was nothing to us. We stayed in shape the year round, and no team could out hustle us. We won two district championships in six-man football. Our senior year, we moved up to eleven-man teams and won all but one game: Crowell, Texas, beat us and went on to win the state championship in our division. We won most of our baseball games, even though there was no league play for baseball.

Flo was elected school queen for our homecoming, and she chose me to be her escort. We had begun to move toward a casual dating relationship while we were juniors in high school.

Mr. Tobman's company sold the lease where Dad worked to Gulf Oil, which wanted to bring in its own crews. Dad began to work on a wildcat drilling rig. These rigs were owned by companies looking for new oilfields. Many of the wells they dug were dry holes. They would move on to other areas that had been "doodle-bugged," a process of checking for oil by sending loud sounds deep into the earth. To put it simply, instruments on trucks parked over the tested areas would measure the sound waves that returned to the surface. The process would give back evidence of a particular type of rock deep underground. That dome of rock could be over a pool of oil.

In the beginning, the odds of finding oil that way were less than fifty percent. As better equipment was developed, the finding of oil greatly improved.

Our family had to give up our house on the lease and moved to a rental just off the campus of Valley View High School. I was less than five minutes away from classes. Most of the school graduates were already in service or were waiting for their orders to report.

We had eighteen in our graduating class. Flo was valedictorian; I graduated. Since we had become something of an item, she asked me to walk with her in our graduation ceremony. To keep her from being taller than me, she wore flats and I wore my new cowboy boots.

After the ceremony, Jack, Wanda, Mack, Betty, Flo and I left for Wichita Falls in my family's car. Dad had to have the car early the next morning to take the drilling crew to work. We went to some movie and sat on the back row. We necked, had popcorn and watched some of the movie. We then went to our favorite late-night restaurant and stayed until it closed. We got in the car and started back to Kamay. The car was hard to drive and made a funny noise. I stopped, and we all got out.

One of the guys from Valley View was angry because Wanda was with Jack and not him. He had knifed one of the tires. At one o'clock in the morning, we lifted out the spare tire, located the jack, removed the flat tire with the lug wrench and put on the spare. We had to find a place to get the tire repaired. Dad was using our car to go to a new drilling rig site that had only a bulldozer track for a road. There was no way he could go to work without a good spare tire.

At two in the morning, we found an all-night service station. The owner agreed to fix the tire between taking care of customers. Fortunately for us, there were few. By three o'clock, we were on our way home. Wanda's home was the first stop. Her mother met us at the door, and I don't think she believed our story. Betty was next, and we had no problem with Mr. Bacon. It was almost four o'clock when we took Flo home. Mrs. Nelson was waiting. She accepted our explanation, and I went home with the notice from her that I was to be in church Sunday morning.

We all had work to do on Saturday, so there was no time for rest or sleep. We made it to church Sunday morning and spent most of our time keeping one another awake. We went home as soon as we could and took afternoon naps.

The week before my high school graduation, Dad had accepted a new job in New Mexico with the Maljamar Oil and Gas Company. He would be leaving the next week. Mr. Tobman had bought an oilfield, a refinery and truck transports. Dad was to be the resident field manager.

Flo and I had what we thought may be our last date the night before Dad and the family left for New Mexico. Maljamar is located between Lovington and Artesia on the southwestern side of the state, over three hundred miles away from where we were living. I had no car and was waiting for my orders from the Navy. All high school seniors were expected to register for the draft for military service. Rather than just registering, five of us volunteered for different services. I had volunteered for the Navy. Flo and I had agreed to write and to try to stay in touch, but neither believed we would see one another again.

Edd as a young seaman.

All the family except me went

with Dad. I stayed at the house to load the truck. With the help of two high school classmates, I loaded our furniture, clothes and everything else, and we left early that morning. We drove all day, stopping only for fuel and meals. We arrived at Maljamar late that evening. Workers on the lease came and unloaded the truck, and then my high school friends turned the truck east and headed home.

Maljamar had four houses and a small church. Most of the workers had homes close to the refinery, three miles south. The Maljamar community had a convenience store, a barbershop that was open only one day a week and a service station; all other services, businesses and public schools were in Lovington, thirty miles east. Maljamar had just over 150 people, most of whom worked for the oil company. Others owned or worked on cattle ranches. There was an abundance of wildlife in the area, including quail, doves, hawks, owls, crows, rabbits, squirrels, foxes, prairie dogs, antelope and a few deer. Of course, there were also horses, mules and cattle on the ranches.

On top of the cap rock, half a mile east and two hundred feet high, hundreds of miles of flat prairie land filled with cattle, sheep and goat ranches began.

Mr. Ellis, Dad's former boss and close friend, lived in Artesia, which was forty-five miles west of Maljamar. He was the Texas-New Mexico supervisor for Buffalo Oil Company, which had bought out Maljamar Oil and Gas.

Mr. Ellis hired me to work on the lease until I went into the Navy. I would be paid the same as the other general workers. I received a dollar an hour, with double pay for any hours over forty in a week. I would have time off as necessary to take care of my Navy enlistment. Dad would be my boss and supervisor. (What else was new?) I drove trucks, unloaded hundred-pound sacks of special drilling cement from boxcars and moved rock from one job to another. I helped build roads to new drilling sites and "tailed" (guided) a forty-foot-long drilling pipe onto pipe racks adjacent to the drilling rig. The drilling pipe was made of thick steel, strong enough to carry a hundred-pound drilling bit and hundreds of lengths of drilling pipe thousands of feet deep into the earth.

The pipe also served as the delivery system for drilling "mud," a lubricant for the bit as it drilled through rock and shale. My job was to make sure the pipe was stacked in an orderly and safe way. I used a thick rope to guide the drill pipe and protect the threads from damage so the "sticks" of drilling pipe would be ready to be set upright on the drilling deck.

Once all the sticks were on the drilling deck, a new drill bit was screwed to the first section of the drill pipe to go into the well. Other drill pipes were attached to the line of pipe that carried the bit. When all the drilling pipes were connected, then drilling could be continued thousands of feet into the earth. Safety and efficiency of a bit exchange depended on how the sticks were stacked and handled.

One week when we were bringing in a well (drilling through cement and the rock cover over the oil pool), I worked seventy-two hours; I had sixty dollars of regular pay and eighty-four dollars overtime. For a seventeen-year-old in 1944, 140 dollars for a week's work was huge money. The month before I left for the Navy, with my overtime, my check was ten dollars more that my dad's.

I came home from work one day, and Mom handed me a letter from the Navy. I had volunteered rather than waiting to be drafted. It included vouchers for round-trip train tickets from Hobbs, New Mexico, to Dallas, Texas. I would be in Dallas four days. My supervisor (Dad) did not want to argue with the military, so I went to Dallas.

I was given a full physical and passed. I was one inch above the height requirements and five pounds over the minimum weight. I was given a Morse code exam and did fine until halfway through. As the speed of the transmission picked up, the dots and dashes began to merge and I had to think to write out the words. The examiner allowed me three different attempts, but nothing improved.

The testing officer asked, "Have you ever had any ear damage?" I told him of my experience with the lightning when I was a child.

"It seems to me that you have lost some of the elasticity of your ear drums, and it has slowed your hearing. We cannot use you for the job we had in mind. We will forward all this and other materials to the Santa Fe, New Mexico, recruiting office. You will be hearing from them in two to three weeks."

I was disappointed; however, I now had two extra days before returning home. I had written Flo and asked if I could come by if I had time. She did not turn down the idea. I used the extra days to go to Kamay. I stayed three nights and two days. I spent as much time with Mr. Nelson as I did with Flo. I enjoyed hearing about the history of their family, their migration from Denmark and his life. He shared about how he had ended up in Texas and endured the Depression.

Almost as an afterthought, he said, "I know the world is in a mess, and you will be in the Navy soon. Neither of us have any idea what will happen in the next few days or years, but I want you to know that if, in the future, you and Florene get serious and maybe even marry, I would be a happy man."

I was honored and replied, "I don't have any idea what will happen to me or to us, but I do thank you."

In my own heart, I was sure that Flo liked me; but once I was gone, there would be other guys who were more intelligent and more available than me. She would know and maybe even begin to love one. Granddad's comment about me not being worth a damn came back, and I wondered if I even deserved someone like Flo.

I made my train connection and returned to Maljamar to work. Two weeks later, a letter with an invitation for me to come to Santa Fe arrived, with bus tickets enclosed. I went and passed all exams. I was sworn into the Navy, making the second public commitment of my life.

I returned to Maljamar to get everything done for me to leave. My orders would arrive in two weeks. When I arrived home, Dad and Mom were packing to go to Dallas. Dad had a meeting with some oilfield executives. He and Mom were going to stop in Megargel and see Grandmother Brown. They would then visit Mom's sister in Graford, continue on to Dallas and return home in a week.

"Come with us, Charles. Nell and Donnie will be with family in Tatum, and you can help Dad drive," Mom said. I had nothing else to do, so I went.

We had a great time visiting family. Two of Dad's younger sisters kept embarrassing me with jokes and demonstrations of how I ought to treat Flo and where my hands should and should not go. They over-emphasized the reasons I needed to watch out for girls around Navy bases.

I had sent a letter to Flo, saying that I might come to see her again and explaining why I was now going back to Dallas. Dad finished his meetings in Dallas, and we headed home. They let me out of the car at a major highway intersection eighty-five miles south of Kamay. I hitched a ride and arrived at the Nelson house three hours later. Even though I had mailed Flo the letter, she and her family were surprised that I was there. I stayed visiting with her two more days, and then went back to Maljamar.

My orders were there. I was to be in Santa Fe in two days. I arrived at the induction center and was assigned a bunk. I was given instructions for meals and told to be ready to move out the next morning.

There were twelve of us new recruits. We walked the streets around New Mexico's old capitol square and talked to the American Indians who had displays of their jewelry laid out on blankets under the museum porch.

At eight o'clock the next morning, a bus pulled up. We loaded our stuff and were driven five miles to the train station. I had never been further west than Santa Fe. I found a window seat and watched the hills, valleys, rivers and landscape features pass by as we crossed western New Mexico and Arizona. We had bunks assigned, but I stayed glued to the window until it became too dark for me to see.

The farther we went, the more barren the land was. I marveled at the table-like mountains and spires of colored rock that appeared. Not one of the twelve of us had ever been to California. We expected the scenery to change when we crossed the Colorado River. It did change, but not in the way we thought it would. It was dryer; the sand blew, and even the cacti looked worse. Was San Diego going to be like this?

As we crossed the desert, I saw the largest fields of oranges, corn, tomatoes and other crops that I had ever seen. We crossed irrigation canals that ran for miles. Only after we passed through El Centro and made our way through the mountains in the west did the fruit trees and vegetable fields disappear. Hundreds of trucks, carrying all kinds of produce, traveled west on highways that ran alongside the railroad. We ate our last meal in the dining car, stuffed our clothes into our suitcases and were ready to depart the train when it pulled into San Diego.

After getting off the train, we twelve from New Mexico, along with others from all over the United States, lined up until our names were called. We were directed to different Navy buses; we climbed aboard and were taken to the San Diego Naval Training Center.

If you have read this personal history, you know that I was taught from birth to think for myself — not just to recognize problems, but to figure out solutions. In the Navy, we had to think and act as a unit; it was an entirely different world.

FOUR

1944

Welcome to the Navy

The bus I was on stopped at the entrance of the training center. Shore patrol officers came on board and rode with us to a large open area. We were ordered off the bus and into some kind of loose formation. We were marched (they marched; we stumbled) to barracks, where we were assigned bunks.

A chief petty officer came and welcomed us. He would be our training officer for the next two months. He introduced two other petty officers and told us which one we would be assigned to. He instructed us to take off all our clothes, including our underpants. We were then ordered to place everything we had brought with us in our suitcases and put them on our bunks. A mattress was rolled up on one end of each bunk. Pillows and blankets and sheets were folded and laid out on the other end. Our suitcases were to be placed in the middles of our bunks. I was glad to have a lower bunk.

We were marched into an adjacent building, physically examined again and given inoculations against more diseases than I thought existed. We moved to a huge room and walked through a line where uniforms, underwear, shoes, hats, stencil equipment to mark our clothes and toilet supplies were handed out according to their (not our own) estimation of our size.

We returned to our barracks and were told to dress in our work uniforms and put anything the Navy had not issued us into our suitcases. I filled out the forms on my bunk and attached the mailing form to the suitcase. My suitcase would be picked up while I was at the chow hall and would be sent back to my home. I began to dress in my new work uniform as best I could.

A new sailor thought he would get a head start on the night and began to make his bed. One of the petty officers walked over to him and, in a voice loud enough to be heard for a mile, demanded, "What is your name, sailor, and where are you from?"

Everyone stopped and listened. The young man muttered something.

"Are you deaf? I asked you a question, and I want an answer. Speak up!" the petty officer shouted.

The new recruit shouted out his name and where he was from.

"Good; now I want to know who told you to mess up that bed," the petty office demanded.

"No one, sir, I just thought …"

That was as far as he got.

"You do not call me 'sir.' I am not an officer. You learn my name, and you will not do anything in this Navy until you are told, understand?" the petty officer said loud enough for us all to hear.

"I understand!" the new sailor shouted.

"Wow," I thought, "I better be careful or I will be in big trouble." While I was mulling this over, we were ordered to fall out in ten minutes. I scrambled to grab my cover (hat) and went outside. Our names were called, and I was assigned to a position in our formation.

Lesson number two from our leaders began: "Now, we are going to march to the mess hall, and I mean march — not run, not walk. MARCH. If any of you cannot count to four, you can learn now."

At the mess hall, I was given no choice of what kind or amount of food to eat. We had beans, bread, some meat, some cooked and fresh vegetables, and coffee. When we finished eating, we were told where and how to take our metal trays and utensils. We were watched as we scraped our leftover food scraps into the garbage cans. If there was more food on my tray than the officer watching thought necessary, I would be pulled aside and made to explain why I had not eaten the good food Uncle Sam was providing for me, free of charge.

Outside, we were lined up and marched back to the barracks. We were sent to our bunks for inspection and given a detailed demonstration of how to make our beds, including how to put our pillowcase on our pillow. We were instructed how to pack our sea bags and wrap them in our hammocks.

We stayed in that barracks for three days. For ten hours each day, we were in sessions to learn what was expected of us. We were told what we would be learning in the next two months. We were informed that there would be no liberty for four weeks, and if we messed up, we could even lose that privilege.

We were ordered, "Store your goods in your sea bag, make your bed and be ready for an inspection in thirty minutes."

I wrestled my clothes and my two pair of shoes into my sea bag. I wrapped and tied my sea bag into my hammock. I stood at attention at the head of my bunk and was closely inspected by our petty officer. It had been one long, tiring day. When that inspection was over, the petty officer announced that lights out would be out in forty-five minutes. I wanted to cheer, but then I realized I had to go to the "head" (bathroom) to brush my teeth and then lay out my clothes for the next day. Eighty of us had four double heads set up for ten sailors each to use. I had to get busy.

Three of us from Valley View High School ended up in the same unit even though we had been inducted in two different states. We were placed in separate platoons and did not get the opportunity to do more than acknowledge one another.

I had been separated from family and friends before, but never like this. I began to wish I had never joined this Navy and could go home. Even if I could not go home, anywhere would be better than this. Tiredness took over, and I wasn't aware of anything until the petty officer walked in and shouted at the top of his voice, "Hit the deck formation in thirty minutes!"

We scrambled and made it to the head. I shaved, dressed, made up my bunk and assembled with the others outside on a dark, foggy morning. It was wet and cold. None of us had expected this. Our names were called, and then issued orders: "Right face (some turned right), forward march, count off!" We started shouting, "Left, right, one, two, three, four," over and over again. Some actually marched part of the way to the mess hall for a breakfast of beans, eggs, potatoes, two slices of bread with butter and jelly, and all the coffee we could drink.

The rest of the day had us marching to different buildings for orientation. We learned ship names and their purposes. There were lectures on Navy language, regulations and safety. We had one thirty-minute break in the morning and one in the afternoon. The next two days were a repeat of the first. On the fourth day, when we returned from breakfast, we were called to formation again. We were instructed to pack everything in our sea bags and prepare to move. We loaded our sea bags on a truck and formed up outside the barracks.

Our chief petty officer, whom we had not seen since we were first introduced, was there. He and the two platoon leaders took position. Roll was taken, and all were present and accounted for. The chief called our platoon leaders to take charge. We were formed into ranks and marched a mile to barracks where the truck with our sea bags was waiting.

The platoon leaders called out names. We unloaded the truck and moved into our new housing. The next morning, we were called out at five o'clock and ordered to dress in running shorts, shoes, an undershirt, a sweater and a knitted wool watch cap. It sounded to me like we were in the north, not San Diego. When we had assembled outside in the fog, I thought maybe our pea coats should have been included.

After we were formed up, instead of marching, we were led by our chief in a slow trot. We ran for fifteen minutes, and then the chief picked up the pace. We made two trips around a half-mile track. Our physical training had begun. We jogged back to the barracks and had thirty minutes to clean up and re-dress.

We were called to formation and jogged in cadence to the mess hall for breakfast. The next two weeks were repeats of the same, with daily additions of training. We practiced firefighting, anti-aircraft gunning, hand-to-hand combat and crawling under barbed wire with live fire overhead and smoke bombs exploding around us.

We climbed up and down rope ladders and rope nets from small boats and ships. The obstacle course was a bear. I was in good physical shape from my work in the oilfields and was normally in the lead in most training, especially on the rifle range, but the obstacle course nearly whipped me. I was not tall enough to reach the ropes and ledges and had to jump two or three times to get a hold and pull myself up. The chief assigned me a buddy to push me up, and I then made it.

There were more lectures and more practices for everything, as well as a twenty-mile hike with full packs. We were trained over and over again in first aid and rescue. We spent two days learning the process of using gas masks in a tear-gas-filled hut, and we fired pistols and rifles.

At the end of four weeks, we were given a weekend pass. While many of my shipmates went to bars and took in the town, I visited my family and Flo's family in San Diego. I had great meals and personal travel guides to the parks, beaches and zoo.

The next four weeks of training were more intense than the first. We practiced swimming and rescue tactics. I learned how to abandon ship and spent a great deal of time in the ocean and surf for strength training. I was given more time on the rifle range and was the backup rifleman for our unit's shooting team. If one of the four members had to drop out, I would be on the team.

We had more free time for recreation. There was an intramural football contest among the companies. My friends from Kamay, Carl Kent and Darrell Craft, and I decided we wanted to be involved. We three had played high school football together for three years and had become the core of our team. I became the quarterback, my first leadership responsibility in the Navy. With the chief's guidance, we selected three other players. We beat every team we played, some by huge scores. All the players on our team were given two extra days of liberty.

I graduated from boot camp and received my ten-day leave. I bought my tickets and mailed my trip information to Mom and Dad. I had written Flo about getting leave, but I could see no way of getting to Kamay. My train was two days to El Paso, Texas. From there, I took the bus north to Artesia, New Mexico.

My parents were there to meet me. When I got off the bus, my parents just stood back. Others were running to greet their family or friends, but my parents, instead of coming to meet me, just watched as I gathered my sea bag. They were both grinning and almost laughing. I could not figure out what was going on. I started toward them. When I was close, they stepped back and aside; behind them stood Flo. I dropped everything. We hugged and kissed, and my family and several spectators joined us.

Mom had written Flo and invited her to come and stay with us while I was home. We drove to Maljamar. Charles, Nell and Donnie were there and were as excited about Flo coming as they were about me being home. I spent the rest of the day answering questions about everything they could think of. In the end, even Flo and I were tired enough to call it a day.

Flo and I spent most of our time with Mom. Dad had to work, and my brothers and sister were in school. Flo and I walked the trails in the area, watching the antelope and deer walk among dwarf oak trees no more than five feet tall. We talked about everything but our relationship and the future. We just liked being together. We played board games with the family. Dad drove us over the lease, and I showed Flo the wells I had worked on. When he could, Dad let me have the car. Flo and I would drive to Hobbs, Lovington, or Tatum to visit Dad's family.

The day before I was to return to San Diego, Dad made arrangements for me to have the car. Flo and I spent the day walking the streets in Hobbs, window shopping, and occasionally stopping for ice cream or coffee. We went to the theater in the afternoon, had dinner and started back to Maljamar.

We turned off the highway onto a trail that followed the high ridge of the cap rock overlooking the valley and Maljamar. I parked on an overhanging ledge. The day was cool, the skies were clear, and we could see for miles. The sun was setting; the multiple colors of the sky were reflected off the floor of the valley. We got out of the car and leaned against the hood. In silence, we watched the sun set. The flickering lights of the faraway houses, derricks and refinery glistened and made a picture no one could ever paint.

Flo put her arm around me and whispered, "It is beautiful."

"Yes," I replied.

I put my arm around her and pulled her close. As we stood there watching, I began to shiver. In a minute, it got worse. I began to shake and sweat and felt dizzy.

"Let's get you home now," Flo said as she pushed me to the driver's seat of the car.

It was only a two miles trip, but I was sick by the time we got to my house. Mom got the thermometer, and I had a fever of 103 degrees. Dad got on the phone and called three or four numbers. He was given the number of Hobbs Air Force Base Hospital. A doctor answered, and Dad told him my name and my problem. A military ambulance was dispatched. I was taken to the hospital at the Hobbs Air Force Base. In the next hour, I was prodded, stuck with needles and x-rayed. I had double pneumonia. I was moved to a private room and given medication and sleeping pills.

The next morning, the chief doctor, a lieutenant colonel, came and talked with me. Since I was Navy, and they did not want to cause any friction between services, I was to remain in a private room in the officers' ward. I was the lowest ranking sailor in the Navy, but here I was to be treated the same as captains and majors.

Many of the officers had been in combat in Europe and the Pacific. They were bombers and fighter pilots, navigators and engineers. I was surprised and overwhelmed by the acceptance I received from those older and experienced men and women. The few non-officers who were responsible for my care seemed not to resent the fact that I was not in the general ward for enlisted personnel. After three days, I was mobile. I was escorted by my officer friends to their chow hall and asked to participate in their table games. I enjoyed the recreation options as my health improved. I loved listening to their stories about their battle experiences and their jokes about having to put up with a common Navy swabbie. This was a big time for a seventeen-year-old just out of boot camp. I would be eighteen in two weeks. Mom and Flo came every day to visit. Flo had called home, and the manager of the post office where Flo worked had given her an extra week to stay while I was in the hospital.

I was slowly recovering. The day Flo was to return to Kamay, Mom brought her to the hospital and left her there. Flo and I went to the eating area. With officer privileges, I had twenty-four-hour access. We then walked the grounds and went back inside. I was tired and lay down on my bed. Flo sat at the foot of the bed while we talked. The head nurse, who was not happy that a sailor kid was being treated like an officer, walked in. She did not look at me but turned on Flo.

"Young lady," she barked, "you get your rear end off that bed now! This is a hospital, in case you didn't know." She then turned on her heel and stomped out.

Mom returned and visited with me for a few minutes. Flo kissed me goodbye, and they left. I was in the hospital another week before I was ready to be discharged.

Dad had a ten-day vacation and wanted to leave Friday evening for Albuquerque to take advantage of the weekend to stretch out the time he could be gone. My discharge from the hospital was set for the following Monday. I went to my friend the major and told him my situation. "That will be no problem," he said. "Come back in a couple of hours."

I went to the mess hall, visited with my friends and then went back to the major's office. He handed me some papers to read and sign. One was a forty-eight-hour pass, beginning on Friday. My discharge from the hospital was listed for Monday. Enclosed were my traveling orders and vouchers. I was to report for duty at San Diego Naval Base in two weeks.

He explained that I was not yet ready for duty. He would sign in for me and file my release form for the hospital an hour before my forty-eight-hour pass expired on Monday. There would be no reason for me to return to the hospital. He stood, shook my hand, wished me luck and dismissed me.

I called Mom. She had the car and would be there in an hour. I packed my bags and said goodbye to all the doctors, nurses, orderlies and my other officer friends. I was waiting outside when Mom drove up.

We drove to Hobbs to do some shopping. We parked and went into a small restaurant. I ordered a hamburger and chocolate milkshake, and Mom had a hamburger and Coke. I needed some socks and underwear, and we had to cross a street to get to the store. The cars and trucks moving by with their horns and engine noises hit me like someone had rammed me in my back. I froze. I could hardly see or breathe. Mom looked at me, smiled, took my arm and led me across the street to the store. I was embarrassed and worried.

We waited outside the store until I got control of myself. We finished my shopping and drove home. It took me another day to adjust from near-isolation to dealing with the outside world. Finally, everything was ready for our trip. Dad came and cleaned up, and we headed north to Albuquerque. Over the next five days, I lived through the Ribble family reunion, my eighteenth birthday and Christmas with the most loving family a person could have.

All that was missing for me was Flo.

Five generations of the Ribble family.

I returned to San Diego and

had to explain to the shore patrol and three officers that I had not gone AWOL but had my papers. They finally looked at my Air Force doctor's orders, and I was permitted to retrieve my belongings that were already in the brig. I then went to my temporary quarters.

I had been approved for radar school. Because I was late returning from leave, I had missed my class and had to wait two weeks for the new class to begin. I was assigned to KP duty. I went to firefighting school for my third time. I polished brass at the commander's home. I picked up trash. I was ready for radar school to begin. I did have liberty every weekend and became involved with the young people at the First Baptist Church (the "White Temple") in downtown San Diego.

Radar school was located at Point Loma. One of my classmates and my best friend from Valley View High School, Jack Keel, was also in radar school. He was part of our group of three couples who dated and ran around together in high school. In addition to our class training, we were required to stand watch at the radar station on Point Loma. One night, I had the four-hour watch, and Jack had liberty. The next morning at breakfast, he said, "Bet you can't guess who I saw on my way to town yesterday."

I had no idea but played along. After a dozen guesses, I gave up. Jack smiled and said, "I was getting off my bus and bumped into an older man waiting for a different bus."

I shook my head and waited, "Okay, who was it?"

"It was Mr. Nelson," he said.

Jack Keel and Edd.

"What? I can't believe that!" I replied. "I was with Flo and her family a month ago and not one word was said about their moving."

"He has a job at the aircraft factory as a night watchman. He, Mrs. Nelson and Norma are here, staying with their daughter Ora," Jack said. Nothing was said about Flo.

I was not sure he was telling me the truth, but I let it go. On my next liberty, I went to Ora's apartment. I walked up the stairs and knocked on the door. It was opened, and there stood Flo. Before I could catch my breath, she smiled and said, "Well, hello, sailor. Would you like to come in?"

Seldom am I caught without something to say, but this was one of those moments. I just nodded my head and accepted her invitation. Ora, Flo's sister, worked night shifts and did not want to leave her son, John, and daughter, Jackie, alone at night. Ora had found a job opening for Mr. Nelson at the plant where she worked. He sent in his work history, and the company hired him. They moved to San Diego within two weeks. Flo was planning to contact me after they had moved. She had a job as a family advocate with the American Red Cross in downtown San Diego. She and I picked up dating with Jackie and her boyfriend, Bud. We went to the church where I had been going. Flo had already made friends with many of the young people. My aunt and cousin lived in Loma Linda. We spent as much time as we could with them and my eight-year-old second cousin.

I finished radar school and moved to Camp Elliott, eight miles northeast of San Diego. This was the main processing center for sailors assigned to ships and bases in the Pacific. After I had been there two weeks, I was called into headquarters. I identified myself and was led into a separate office.

An officer spoke up, "Radarman Brown, your group will be moving to Treasure Island in twenty-four hours. You will come here in the morning before that departure. You will pick up all relevant information and take it to the processing personnel upon your arrival. You are dismissed."

I left hoping I had heard right. All identification cards for my group were collected and held by the shore patrol. We could not leave the base without our identification, but we could have guests. I called Flo, and she came over after work. We had dinner together at one of the restaurants on base, and we walked and talked with other couples.

When it came time for Flo to leave, Jack, who was not in my group, came to say goodbye to Flo. He then took me aside and said, "Edd, Flo cannot go this late on that bus by herself, and there's no way she should walk several blocks to Ora's house this late at night."

I did not have identification and could not go. Jack was not leaving for two days. He handed me his ID and insisted I take it and go. He suggested that Flo and I stay with a large group of people when we left. I could get with some drunks when I returned; the guards would not look that closely at that kind of group coming in.

I took his ID, and Flo and I fell in with three couples who were crying and carrying on. I flashed Jack's ID and Flo's pass, and we were waved onto the bus. In town, we took an intercity bus to Ora's. It was one o'clock in the morning when we got there. We sat on the stairs until three-thirty and talked about how our paths seemed to cross with no effort on our part. It was what we had hoped for but had not believed possible. We did not become engaged but came close.

I left for Camp Elliot, arrived back at the base with a busload of drunken sailors and had no problem checking in. I showered and met Jack at breakfast to return his ID. Neither of us had any idea where we were headed or when we might see each other. We shook hands, and I left with, "See you in Tokyo."

I went to the office, picked up the records of forty-eight sailors and stored them in my traveling bag. I joined my group at the base bus terminal. I called roll to make sure I had the right forty-eight sailors, and we boarded the train for San Francisco.

Eight hours later, we arrived at Oakland train station and were put on buses. I again counted forty-eight sailors and hoped they were the right ones. We were bused to Yoruba Buena Island and assigned bunks in a large room. After we had checked in, some smart guy read our orders; we were at the wrong place. We were told to stop unpacking, to replace what we had laid out on our bunks and to wait. I was called into the processing office and informed a mistake had been made. We were to go to Treasure Island. I did not tell them what I thought but thanked them for the information, returned to our group and explained why we would be moving again. We sat on the bunks; some read, and others tried to sleep. At ten o'clock in the evening, we were called to board the bus at the front of the building. Again, I counted forty-eight. We rode the short distance and arrived at Treasure Island in front of one of the largest barnlike structures I had ever seen.

A chief petty officer came on board and said, "Radarman Brown, make yourself known." I raised my hand. He beckoned me forward, and I handed him the package for forty-eight tired and unhappy sailors. For the first time all day, I began to relax. We were called by name and led to a section in the center of the cavernous building. There were over a thousand sailors bunked there.

The buildings had been built for the World's Fair years before. Offices, processing centers, small stores and food dispensers were all throughout the building. There was limited personal space. The mess hall was impossible to describe. Around the clock, hundreds of sailors and other personnel lined up to eat.

There were no drills and no watches to stand; we just had to wait, sleep, read, walk and wait. Sailors actually tried to get on KP duty just to have something to do. Liberty was easy to get but became boring.

Four of us started going downtown to the Seamen's Center at the First Baptist Church. They had excellent programs, meals at cost, some cots for overnighters and entertainment by various individuals and Christian groups; but even that was limited and became routine. Like everyone else, I was bored and tired of going to town, eating, coming back, reading, and arguing with others as bored as I was. It began to rain; it was cold and damp even inside, and I was miserable. I went to the processing office and asked a clerk if he had any information on when I might be shipped out. I was fortunate to find a clerk who took time to see what information they had. He found a typed note that read, "Delayed until further notice."

I asked for leave papers. He gave them to me, and I went to my bunk to fill them out. Several members of my group found out what I was doing and began to joke about how stupid and naive I was. No one could get leave just before he was going overseas. I put up with their remarks and turned in my request. Two days later, I was told that a notice for me to report to the processing office was on the board.

I went, having no idea of what I would learn. I knew the guys had been right. I was not going to get leave just before being shipped overseas. To my astonishment, I was handed an approved order for a fourteen-day leave. I would get my leave papers once I produced a valid ticket from either the bus or railroad company and a baggage check stub.

I went to my bunk, grabbed my raincoat and headed for the door. Two or three asked where I was going. "Just out," I answered. I caught the bus to the train station and then took the tram to town. I walked a block to the bus station, bought a round-trip ticket and was left with four dollars. I returned to the barracks and packed my sea bag. I stored what I could not pack and returned to the bus station. I checked my bag to Tatum, New Mexico. I then returned to the processing office with my ticket and the baggage check stub and picked up my fourteen-day pass. I ate an early lunch with the guys and showed them what I had. I told them I would see them in two weeks, picked up my carry-on and left. I returned to the bus station and cashed in my ticket. The agent was glad; all the busses were full, and my seat was needed. I went to retrieve my sea bag, but it had been sent to New Mexico on an earlier bus.

I took the red line trolley to the end of the line, south of Oakland. I started hitchhiking the fifteen hundred miles to Tatum, New Mexico, where my parents now lived. While hitchhiking was discouraged, there was no regulation against traveling that way. I knew that when I was twenty miles away from the base, people would go out of their way to help me get to where I was going. The war in Europe was being won, we were on the offensive in the Pacific, and most people wanted to do something to encourage and help service people. I caught two rides to Bakersfield and one ride up the mountain into the snow at Tehachapi.

I took another chance and went into a hotel lobby on Main Street. I explained my situation to the desk clerk. He permitted me to spend the rest of the night on a couch with a blanket in the lobby of the hotel. He woke me early and gave me coffee and a donut before I had to leave.

I had been on the highway less than ten minutes when an oil delivery truck stopped. The driver opened the door and asked where I was going; I told him I was headed to New Mexico. He replied that he was not going that far but could get me a long way down the road. I crawled in and had the roller coaster ride of my life.

The present freeway down the mountains to Mojave did not

exist. My driver was headed for some small town on the Colorado River and needed to make up for lost time. There was then a safe and sane speed limit in California. He violated both criteria all the way to Indio. I thanked him for the ride and got out of the truck. The heat there was like a blast from a furnace. The temperature when I caught the ride in the truck was freezing; it was now 105 degrees. I had on my raincoat and was in my winter wool uniform. I found a service station and went to the restroom. I washed up and stored my raincoat in my travel bag. I bought a cold drink and went back to the highway.

A nice, large air-conditioned car pulled up, and three businessmen who were on their way to El Centro stopped and offered me a ride. They had snacks and some cold drinks, including beer. I turned down the beer but enjoyed the cold drinks and snacks during the cool ride. The men were land developers looking at prospects in Southern California. They insisted on buying me dinner, and I accepted.

Later that evening, I was tired. I spent five dollars for a room, took a shower and slept for nine hours. The next morning, I went to the bus station and, for twenty dollars, bought a ticket to Roswell, New Mexico. I had three dollars left. I boarded the bus, found a seat by a window halfway back and settled in for the long trip. The people were exceptionally nice. They wanted to know where I was from and where I was stationed; they asked other questions, but I had been instructed not to talk about certain things.

When we approached the Arizona border, the driver announced that anyone who had fresh fruit needed to eat it; otherwise, it would be confiscated at the entry station. I had oranges, apples, bananas and more fruit than I could eat given to me. I slept halfway to Phoenix. In Phoenix, we had an hour break, and a young couple on the bus insisted on taking me to a restaurant for lunch. The bus continued east as it got dark.

One of the passengers had given me a book; I tried to read but slept most of the time. We made our one rest stop and continued on. Twenty minutes later, a car with flashing lights pulled around the bus, slowed down in front and waved it to a stop. A woman got out of the passenger side of the car, and you could tell she was unhappy. The driver opened the door, and the woman stepped up and blistered him with some "Navy" words. The bus had left while she was in the restroom, and everything she had was in the bus luggage compartment.

The driver apologized, and we continued on our way to El Paso. When we arrived at El Paso, the place was overcrowded. You could hardly move. My bus to Roswell, New Mexico, would leave in twenty minutes. Even though I was in uniform and had priority, I did not want to get out of line.

A young lady came and asked where I was going. I told her, and she said she needed to get to Artesia, New Mexico, halfway to where I was going, for a job interview. The bus was oversold. There was no way a single woman out of uniform was going to get on that bus. With a big smile she asked, "Would you marry me for a couple of hours?"

Embarrassed, I looked around, but no one seemed interested in us. "They will let me on if I were your wife. All you have to do is help me get on the bus and sit beside me," she said.

Since so many people had helped me, I agreed. The bus driver opened the door and called all military couples to board first. I took the young lady's package in one hand and her arm with the other. We were third couple to board the bus and sat close to the front. I began to feel guilty as people smiled at us when they boarded. An hour later, as we approached New Mexico, my traveling partner took a piece of paper out of her purse, wrote something with a pen and handed the paper to me.

"This is your divorce paper. It has been a great short marriage." She gave me a quick buss on the check as she left the bus in Artesia.

On our next break, the bus driver was finishing his run and asked if he could buy my lunch. He had a son somewhere in the Pacific and wanted to do something. I made it to Roswell and caught a bus headed east to Tatum, seventy miles away. My family's new home was two blocks from the bus stop. Mom knew I was coming, but I was home a day ahead of the bus schedule. My brothers and sister did not know I was coming; my arrival was to be a surprise.

I changed into some old "civvies" and walked three blocks to where Dad was working at the service station and auto repair shop he now owned. While we waited for night worker and visited with each other, I pumped gas for a couple of cars. Finally, the night worker came, and Dad and I walked home.

After our meal, my siblings and I walked the sidewalk of the town's main street and just talked. We made stupid jokes and had a good time. It felt good to be home, even in a new location. It felt great to be in my own bed, even in a new house, and I slept good and hard.

The next morning, after the kids went to school, I went to the sweet shop that doubled as the local bus station and picked up my sea bag. My bag's arrival had caused quite a stir in the Tatum community. Two hours after I had retrieved my bag, everyone in town knew that Mr. and Mrs. Brown's son, who was in the Navy, was home on leave. Dad's relatives and friends came by with food and visited. I had only been in San Diego for training and San Francisco for assignment, but that made no difference to them. I was their sailor, and that was enough.

Three days later, Tom, my favorite uncle, came by to visit. He had been at White Sands proving grounds outside of Alamogordo, New Mexico. He and one of my other uncles, Willard Rodgers, Mom's brother-in-law, had been the concrete contractors for a government project. It was so hushed up that Tom could relate very little about what he did. He had been in the observation shelter, which he had helped build, when a bomb on a hundred-foot-tall steel tower was exploded. The blast obliterated the tower, crystallized the area and left a hole in the ground thirty feet deep and half a mile in circumference.

"Don't ask me any questions; I cannot say any more. Just know that you may be home sooner than you think."

After seven days of visiting my family and having a blast with my brothers and sister, I headed for San Diego. Mom and Dad insisted on paying for my bus ticket.

For three days, I was with Flo and her family. She took time off work, and we visited Balboa Park, Old Town, Coronado and the local beaches. We reached an understanding about our love for one another and vowed to do all we could to make our relationship something more than a few hurried visits. She insisted on paying my bus fare to San Francisco.

On base, I reported to processing and was given a copy of my orders. All leaves and passes were cancelled, and we were to be packed and ready to leave out at ten hundred hours in two days. Although my buddies were envious of my fourteen-day leave, they hoped that I'd had a good time. Later on the troop ship, I was asked for more details.

Early the next morning I was first when the postal exchange was opened. I had been there several times before and had looked at almost everything they sold. Once or twice, I had looked at rings but not paid that much attention. This time, I was serious. I had asked Dad for a check from my account, and I asked the clerk for information about engagement rings.

She showed me several and then picked up one. "This is not one of our more expensive rings, but it is my favorite. I hope a certain young man will soon buy me one just like it."

She handed me the ring and I too was impressed. I bought it. The young lady offered to wrap it and send it to Flo for me. I paid her and asked her to put my note to Flo in the ring box. I wrote, "I love you, and I hope you will accept this ring for our engagement."

Then that old horror of my grandfather's words broke through: "You are not worth a damn." Why should Flo want me? I then added to the note, "If this is too much or too soon, I will pick the ring up when I return from overseas." Flo claims she never saw that note.

The next morning, a bus pulled up to the outside door of our building. My name was called, and I picked up my sea bags and boarded the bus. We were taken to a huge dock just to the left of the Oakland Bay Bridge on the San Francisco side. We left the bus as our names were called. I walked up the gangplank and saluted the flag atop the mast of the troop ship. It was four decks down to my quarters. I placed my gear on my assigned bunk. Forty of us were instructed to unpack, make our bunks and store all else in our assigned lockers. We were restricted to our quarters until the ship was underway.

When we were away from the dock, the all-clear was sounded; we could then come to the top deck. We made our way topside and watched as we left the docks in San Francisco. We went under the Oakland Bay Bridge, and I had a hollow feeling as the ship passed by Alcatraz Island.

I had crossed the Golden Gate Bridge several times, but it looked much larger on our way out to sea. The others and I began moving to the stern of the ship as it sailed under the bridge. With very little talking, we watched the bridge and the coast of California disappear in the fog. I really do not know how to explain how I felt. There was a satisfaction in doing what I knew I should. I was also fearful that I might not be good enough to do the job I had been trained to do.

Even with dozens of others around me, I felt lonely and scared. I prayed that God would let me see that rusty old bridge again.

The rolling waves and cross tides lasted for ten miles out into the Pacific. The continuous rise and fall of our ship caused a lot of good food to be fed to the fishes. I went below, but the rocking seemed worse, so I went back topside and began to explore the ship. What I saw at first bothered me. We had no escorts. There were only antiaircraft guns and three or four small cannons on our ship to protect us. I was relieved when I remembered that we were only going to be on this ship to Hawaii. Our second day away from San Francisco, a small plane flew out from the coast. It was pulling a target on a long cable for the antiaircraft guns to target practice. The gunners on one side were able to shoot at the target for twenty minutes, and then the other side had their chance as the plane circled around and pulled the target down their side of the ship. We could not tell if the gun crews hit the target. There were tracer shells and sudden motions of the target that could have been the result of bullets. A shout went up when one target folded and fell into the water. The plane headed back to shore.

The water became smooth and the breeze, cool. It was chow time. I went below to our assigned mess hall. There were beans, bread, Spam (which I like) with mashed potatoes, Jell-O, pie and, of course, coffee.

Two days later, I was on the deck when Hawaii came into view. Everyone crowded the rails, and some of the old hands pointed out various landmarks for us, including Diamond Head and Waikiki Beach. We entered Pearl Harbor, and I could not believe what I saw. I had seen pictures and short films, but this was the real thing. Battle-damaged destroyers and cruisers and aircraft carriers with wrecked planes on deck were everywhere. The area was like a giant beehive; barges ferried food, supplies, equipment and personnel back and forth. Most of the ships were being repaired to return to the battlefront where I was headed. Other ships had been shot up too bad to be rebuilt. The Arizona, with its hull decked in flowers and leis, reminded us again of the cost and the necessity of our mission.

The current news was about a world that seemed to have become even crazier. Hitler was killing thousands of Jews, Christians, gypsies and any other supposed enemies to achieve his goal of a pureblood Aryan race and a "Thousand Year Reich." The Japanese were still convinced they could and would win the war, even though General Doolittle had led a group of U.S. pilots to bomb Tokyo. The emperor and the country's military leaders knew that, because we were a "mongrel race" of mixed descent, we could never be equal to the pureblood Japanese warriors.

In some ways, the U.S. had not done much better. Thousands of Japanese-Americans were rounded up and sent to internment camps in the deserts of California and other places to keep them from spying on or abetting the enemy of their adopted country. No, we did not kill them; but businesses and farms were lost, families were separated, and mixed marriages were looked down upon.

On the positive side, General Eisenhower and his staff had finished plans for D-Day and were waiting on the weather. Our Pacific air forces needed a place for bombers and escorts to land after attacking Japan. The small island of Iwo Jima was chosen, and plans were made to occupy the island for refueling and emergency landings for our planes.

Germany suffered a major defeat in Russia. It began to look like the tide of the long and costly war was turning in favor of the Allies; however, our stubborn enemies were positive that there was some way they could win. Their leaders tried to convince their people and the world that their losses were just part of a long campaign and that they would eventually win.

The boson's pipe sounded, and it was announced that our unit was to be ready to come on deck and disembark. I went below, picked up my sea bag and climbed back to the top deck. I was directed down the gangway and herded into a large Navy bus. The bus went to downtown Honolulu, and we were ordered to disembark at a large hotel on Waikiki Beach. Four of us were assigned to a room. We each had a bed, and the room had a bath with a freshwater shower (There were saltwater showers on the troop ship.). We showered, dressed in our white summer uniforms and explored the beach and surrounding area until dinner. After enjoying a superb meal served by waitresses, we were confined to the hotel. The next morning, twenty other sailors and I were taken to the USS North Carolina. This battleship was my taxi to Ulithi, a remote island in the South Pacific, where my ship was waiting. On our second day out of Pearl Harbor, loud explosions rocked the ship. Again, the older sailors told us greenhorns to relax; what we heard was the ship's sixteen-inch guns having target practice. If I remember right, the ship had four batteries of three sixteen-inch-bore cannons, with two batteries forward and two aft. These, along with antiaircraft and smaller guns, were fired at least twice a week to keep the guns and the crew in shape.

My unit was billeted close to the galley and had flexible eating hours. For five days, we sailed south. Occasionally, we had thunderstorms and a few rain squalls; however, my trip was peaceful until I began to have symptoms like I had experienced in Maljamar. I was sent to sick bay. A medical officer gave me an examination and sent me to bed. I was kept there until I was transferred to my ship.

FIVE

1945

USS Escambia (AO-80), A Navy Fleet Oiler

My first week on board the Escambia was spent in sick bay, with a chief pharmacist's mate carrying out the orders from the doctor. In a few days, I was up and ready for light duty.

We were in port at Ulithi Atoll, one of the main supply and support bases in the South Pacific. Because we were in port, I was assigned to limited duty on a supply boat that visited different ships to pick up food for our galley. Our "floating service station" would be at sea with the fleet five to six weeks at a time. We had to have enough food on board for two months. Many thousands of barrels of diesel fuel in lined fuel tanks filled the hull. The ship also carried aviation gas, lubricating oil and, in some cases, replacement personnel for other ships. Possibly the most important role of the Escambia was that of "mail ship." Whatever else happened, the mail had to go through.

After we were fully loaded, we headed for the Philippines and fueled ships of all sizes and descriptions. For identification, in addition to our name and numbers, we had painted in bright colors on our smokestack a large relief of a smiling duck standing on a floating fuel barrel. He was holding a fuel nozzle, waiting for a ship to come alongside to be fueled. One of our shipmates had worked at Disney Studios and received permission from Walt Disney to have the painting done on our ship. The Navy approved the insignia. Our ship with its smiling duck became recognized all over the Pacific.

I had three duties as one of three radar operators. I was on surface radar when we were in a convoy; I had sky or air radar when we sailed by ourselves or with a small group of ships; and I supervised voice communications on the bridge with the ships that we would be fueling.

One of my radar responsibilities was either on the bridge (the command center of the ship) or in an adjacent room. While this arrangement had its advantages, there were always multiple officers in and around the area. My air or sky radar equipment was in a room on the top deck of the ship. The room was heavily armored; the doors were made of half-inch-thick reinforced steel. I would be in isolation and in direct phone contact with the gunnery officer or the captain of the ship. I would identify approaching planes as friendly or unfriendly and relay the distance and elevation of the approaching planes to the officer in charge. The information would be used to set the distance and height for the shells fired from our ship.

Normally, we would leave Ulithi with one or two destroyers as escorts. At special times, there would be two mine sweepers ahead of us and three or four other oilers alongside. Occasionally, an ammunition ship or other specialty ship would be added. This is a convoy's most vulnerable time. The convoy has to cruise at the speed of the slowest ship.

In addition to our regular duty of four hours on radar watch and eight off, we had submarine watch for an hour at sunup and sundown. Since there were only three radar operators, our duty times were not

"Floating Service Station" insignia.

that flexible. In normal situations, we had time to rest, eat and sleep; however, when fueling time came, which lasted from daylight to sundown, we could have duty as much as sixteen hours a day for four continuous days. Fortunately for us, the cooks kept the captain and the bridge officers supplied with sandwiches and coffee. The captain insisted that others on the bridge were to be included. When we had transferred our loads of fuel to other ships underway at sea, we would head back to Ulithi, where we would tie up to merchant ships, fill our tanks and replenish our supplies before heading out to sea again.

My first trip was good training, a personal shakedown cruise. Some have asked why I was assigned to a fleet oiler. I later learned that the Navy, in looking at my short life history, discovered I had lived and worked on oil rigs and had been around gas and oil wells. From those experiences, I knew the dangers of unseen gas and explosions. I had also been to four firefighting schools before being sent to the Escambia.

The trip to the Philippines was no problem. For others, especially those on the islands, it was hell. We had good weather, and I had time to get acquainted with my shipmates.

We received orders to turn away from the islands at battle (maximum) speed. A Japanese fleet was coming around the south islands of the Philippines, planning to catch us between land and our

The USS Escambia at sea.

fleet. They would use us as cover for their ambush attack. We were able to get out of the way and would return to refuel the fleet after our battleships had driven the Japanese fleet back to their home base.

We returned to Ulithi, reloaded and headed out. My second trip was to Okinawa. On our first day anchored in the Okinawa Harbor, a typhoon blasted the island. Even the fighting on the island was curtailed. We had been rushed into the harbor for shelter and safety. I again was assigned to our supply boat. There was fighting in the hills a few miles away. It was good to be off the ship, even if I did not get to go ashore. We received our supplies and returned to the Escambia as fast as we safely could. Machine gun shells ricocheted off rocks in the hills too few miles above us. Mortars and light artillery shells that exploded were constant reminders of the war in which we were involved. The winds became more severe, and the waves in the harbor rose several feet. Even the shelling in the mountains stopped.

At noon, we were still anchored in the middle of the harbor. We received orders to follow a convoy out to sea. We were the farthest into the bay and the last ship slated to leave. The channel leading out to the ocean became so rough that we were ordered to come about (turn around), put out both anchors and keep our boilers hot. We could be ordered to move at any time.

I was on voice radio, receiving messages. I listened as other ships reported having difficulty in maintaining headway. An order from our captain sent all men not on watch to their quarters. There were to be no personnel on deck. All sea hatches and openings were to be secured. That meant that those of us on watch were in for a long night.

It was late and dark; I was on surface radar, with a break from voice radio. On my radar screen, the waves and wind-driven rain gave out ghost signals. It was difficult to distinguish between them and real moving objects. Around eighteen hundred hours, a huge blip (red dot) appeared on my screen. I grabbed my phone and called the officer of the deck, who happened to be the captain. He rushed in.

"What do we have, Brown?" he asked.

"Not sure, sir. It looks big. It has a strong blip and will be on us in five minutes."

"Well, we can't move," he said.

He went to the voice box and ordered all hands to be prepared for a possible ramming and damage control. He had just returned to his place at the forward windows on the bridge when a lumber barge that had broken from its moorings came in sideways and crashed across our bow. Plywood, sheeting, rolls of roofing, flashing, two-by-fours, big timbers, nails, metal connectors and all other kinds of other materials flew over and around us. The captain got back on the horn and let everyone know what had happened. He told everyone that, from what he could see, there was no major damage to the ship. The winds dropped, the rain let up, and all hands could move about the ship.

After ten hours of continuous duty, I was ready to hit my bunk. After breakfast, the entire ship had to be checked for damage. The ship was inspected and found to be in good shape. Our orders came. We were to proceed four hundred yards to meet a harbor tug and fuel it, which was unusual. The tug needed fuel to move ships, and there was no other place they could get it. The storm damage on the island had destroyed the fueling station, and the docks were damaged and unusable.

We fueled the tug, and it became our guide to get out to sea. The tug pushed us around with its mammoth engines and maneuvered us out of the harbor. On both sides of the harbor entrance, there were boats, barges and huge cargo ships stranded on sandbars at least a hundred feet from water. Seabees with bulldozers cut canals under the hull of the ships; the movement of the water would enable the ship to be pulled into the newly made canal and towed to sea.

Our ship and twenty others formed a single line two miles long and were ordered into the China Sea. Three mine sweepers and five destroyers escorted us away from the island. I was excused from watch because of my all-nighter. I went to the outside signal bridge.

All ships including ours were ordered to man guns and break out rifles. The rifles were not for shooting people. Our enemies now were mines. We were to explode the mines that had broken loose from their moorings. If the mines came in contact with any ship, they would explode. They could not be left to drift in and around the harbor entrance or at sea to sink our ships. The irony was that most of the mines were ours. They had been planted by our mine-laying ships outside the harbor to keep the Japanese ships and submarines from entering.

The few of us who had access to the signal deck watched as the mine sweepers and destroyers exploded mines. Some of us even had a chance to shoot the mines with our rifles if the mines came too close to our ship. Even though we were empty of the fuel that we carried for other ships, our containers continued to hold gas fumes, which made us a potential floating bomb. As I knew from my oilfield days, oil burns, but gas fumes explode.

After two days, we joined a small group of five ships — two escorts and three tankers — and headed south to Ulithi. The island of Turk had not been occupied by our forces, although the occasional American plane would slip in, drop a few bombs and fly away. I do not recall any of the planes being shot down or ever hitting anything with their bombs.

Our next assignment was east of the Philippines. We and three other oilers were escorted by a cruiser and three destroyers. We moved into position and waited for the fleet. A day later, we were again ordered to move out of the area at battle speed. A much larger Japanese force was making another run around the southern island. They were still trying to flush out our fleet into an ambush. Any fueling operation would not only put us in an impossible situation but would become a hindrance to our fighting ships. The standard plan for a fighting ship at sea was to top off all fuel tanks every three days. This would enable the fleet to fight without worrying about refueling.

While the Philippines, Iwo Jima and Okinawa were being secured, the armed forces were in the process of developing detailed plans for the ultimate invasion of Japan. Our planes were regularly bombing Tokyo, Yokohama and other strategic military targets. Rather than seeking peace, the Japanese government began a *kamikaze* (holy wind) war.

Young men took an oath to give their lives to the Emperor and to do all they could to keep the American barbarians from destroying their country and gods. Not too far from Tokyo, close to where the kamikaze pilots were trained, there is a giant brass Buddha. The young men would make their vows and rub their hands on the base of the statue, believing they would receive a special blessing for a happy afterlife. The highest honor a warrior could receive came from sacrificing himself for his Emperor, who was the earthly symbol of the gods he served and worshiped.

A Japanese pilot would shout his prayers to the winds and strap himself into a bomber, which had only enough fuel to get him to his target. The pilot was

Third Division, AO-80, "The Bridge Brigade."

to select an American ship and fly his bomb-loaded plane straight into it. The worst disgrace for a pilot and his family was to be captured and returned to his country. His family would have already buried him. He had been sent on a holy mission and had failed. Suicide was the only honorable way out.

We reloaded our hull with fuel and went north to begin supplying other ships. There were times that we were fueling aircraft carriers while airplanes were taking off and landing. Other times, we would be fueling a battleship at the same time that the battleship was fueling a destroyer along its opposite side. We fueled for three days straight. We were southeast of the Aleutians, out of radio contact and hoping we were out of range of any Japanese scout planes.

We received an emergency order to cease all fueling. We were divided into three different convoys that were separated by twenty miles. The weather people were predicting a super-sized typhoon with fierce winds headed in our direction. I had no idea which way we were headed. I was on TBS, our short range radio, and was just relaying information.

What happened was no one's fault. It had never happened before. We were given orders to move away from the typhoon, and our fleet was moving that way as fast as it could. Suddenly, the typhoon reversed direction, and our fleet sailed directly into its eye (center).

There were too many ships and too little time for the convoy to turn away. Everything was lashed down; every opening was closed and locked. All hands were confined to quarters. Those of us on watch were made aware there may be no relief for hours. The winds began to howl, and the rain came in barrels. The only vision the ship had was what I could see on our shadowy radar. As before, the heavy rain and high seas made it extremely difficult to sort out the ghosts from the real blips showing ships or debris on my screen. I kept the captain, who was on the bridge, as current as I could. One of the other radar men came in, and I went to man the TBS. We could look at the radar screen only so long before our eyes would get foggy and all blips and ghosts would run together.

I went into the bridge and picked up the voice radio control. A shout came over the speaker: "Man overboard!" The voice identified the ship as one that was a half-mile ahead of us. All our search lights went on, but we could see nothing. In five minutes, another oiler a half-mile behind us came on and said, "We just picked up one sailor!" Everyone cheered and slapped hands, and our spirits lifted.

After another hour on radio, I had to have a break. An officer was standing close, and I asked if he could relieve me for five minutes. He looked at the captain, the captain nodded, and I went to the head bathroom that was reserved for officers. In this weather, those restrictions were not valid. I returned to the bridge and began to get seasick. I opened the hatch to the signal bridge and went out to the rail. I don't know what I threw up; I had not had anything to eat for hours.

I stood there and watched a ship crest a forty-foot wave a hundred feet from us; the ship was being pushed directly toward us. I again had to hold my head over the rail.

When I looked up again, the wind had pushed the ship a hundred yards away. The bridge deck where I was standing was thirty feet above the main deck. The water from the waves splashed over me. In a few seconds, I was soaking wet. I began feeling well enough to go back inside. I took over the surface radar and tried to give some directions to the helmsman.

The inclinometer that measured the tilt the ship endured in a roll was on the bulkhead to my right. The red line for a roll was forty-eight degrees. Beyond that, the ship would not be able to right itself; it would roll over and sink. I watched the arrow hover around forty-six degrees for three minutes. I started to press the button to call the captain. Before I could lower my finger, the arrow began to move back, first to forty and then to thirty-five. We were then caught by a thirty-foot wave, and the inclinometer moved in seconds to twenty degrees list in the opposite direction. For four more hours, we fought the vicious wind and massive waves. The radar was almost useless because of the huge waves. At times, the "screw" (propeller) would come completely out of the water, and the entire ship would go into a vicious shudder; then the screw would hit the water, the bow would plunge down into another trough and rise up on another wave, and the shaking would start again.

I had to take a break again and asked one of the other officers to take over. I went into the radar room to be alone for a few minutes. A large metal case of spare parts had broken from its ties and was sliding from wall to wall as the ship rolled. I was in no shape to secure it. I sat on the metal case and rode it back and forth as it moved with the ship.

My buddy with whom I had been exchanging duty became seasick; an officer took over for him, and he headed for the radar room for a chance to calm down. He opened the door as I slid by.

He slammed the door and left. Later I learned that when he opened the door, he was feeling sick for the first time in his five-year Navy career. He wanted to get by himself to see if the sickness would go away. When he saw me slide by, I looked up, and all he saw was two red eyes with a green face. He just made it to the edge of the signal bridge before he began to throw up.

At first sight, he thought I was a corpse; when I looked up, I looked like one, and that was all it took to make him start throwing up. He and I were not the only ones. Several career sailors were seasick for the first time after years in the Navy. The heads had to be scrubbed and aired out for days before the smell was gone.

Around daybreak, we came out of the storm. The waves dropped from thirty to fifteen to ten feet. The heavy rainclouds were replaced by sun and cool breeze. The convoy moved back into formation, and the damage was unreal. Aircraft carriers had their flight decks crushed over their bows. Planes on deck and in the lower hangers had broken loose and were extensively damaged. Ship masts were down. Radar antennae were gone. Boats on decks were gone or damaged beyond repair. We lost a boat, two life rafts and some fuel hoses, but we were in better shape than most.

The admiral requested damage reports from all ships and wanted an additional report from fleet oilers on how soon they could begin fueling. The oiler responses varied -a day, two days, maybe ten hours.

"Captain?" I asked.

He signaled for me to wait while he talked to the deck crews in charge of fueling and damage control; he then turned, smiling. "Brown, tell the admiral we will be ready to take our first ship in four hours."

I looked at him; the question must have been on my face, because he responded, "Go ahead and tell him. We can show those others what a real oiler is like."

"Yes, sir!" I keyed the mike. "Control, this is Rebus (our call name). Our captain informed me that we will fuel our first ship in four hours."

I had to repeat the message twice. All hands were turned to, and we were ready and waiting when a cruiser and an aircraft carrier pulled up, one on each side. I looked aft, and two battleships were lining up to be next to come alongside.

Seven hours later, after we had fueled the last battleship, the TBS came on. "Rebus, stand by. The admiral will want to speak with you."

"Rebus waiting," I replied.

A deep voice answered, "This is Admiral Halsey. To whom am I speaking?"

I nearly dropped my mike.

"Radarman Brown, sir," I replied.

"Radarman Brown, how many crew do you have on your ship?"

I guessed and said, "Two hundred."

"How much ice cream can you eat?" the Admiral asked.

I thought I must be hearing things, but again came the same question. I answered, "It has been awhile, sir; maybe a pint or more."

"I think you can do better than that. Anyway, I am sending fifty gallons to your crew. This is my way of saying thanks to your crew for the excellent job you have done." He hung up.

I signaled one of the officers to get the captain, and we explained what was going on. The captain notified the fueling officer that the cable line used to carry the fueling hoses back and forth between ships was to remain connected to the battleship until two cargo nets had transferred fifty gallons of ice cream to the Escambia AO-80. When the transfer was completed, my work was done. I walked out onto the signal deck. A high-ranking officer on the outside signal deck of the battleship across from me stood erect and saluted. I saluted back. He then waved, turned and went inside. I cannot be a hundred percent sure, but I still believe it was the admiral who saluted us.

We had more ice cream than we'd had in weeks. While we appreciated the ice cream itself, the reason we received it and the fact that it came from the admiral himself meant a lot more to us. It made the last few days worth all our time and trouble.

At dusk, we separated from the convoy and were on our way to Ulithi while many other fleet oilers were still in their repair stage. At Ulithi, we immediately reloaded with fuel and supplies and were moved west several hundred miles. We anchored in a deep lagoon with clear blue water. Most of us took advantage of two warm peaceful days and swam. There was very little going on.

One of our spotters reported two high-flying planes. Both looked like bombers. We grabbed our field glasses and watched. There were no fighter escorts, and the two bombers were headed towards Japan. We were anchored in an area close to Iwo Jima. Maybe the new airfield would be used for their return flight. The next morning, our radio operator, who was our news source, published our weekly paper with a huge headline: "ATOM BOMB DROPPED ON HIROSHIMA."

Everything that my Uncle Tom had told me (and not told me) in New Mexico over a year ago immediately came to mind and began to make sense. We had to wait two days to get more of the details, and by then another atom bomb had been dropped on Nagasaki.

Emperor Hirohito and the Diet of Imperial Japan realized that their entire nation could be wiped off the map. Japan agreed to an unconditional surrender. The war in Europe had been over for months, and now it was over in the Pacific. That night, we broke out signal guns and phosphorus shells and fired them into the air and water. We had extra food and drinks and an outdoor movie, and most of us stayed up all night. A day later, the fleet was split up, with a small force going to Tokyo Bay for the official signing of the surrender by the Japanese.

One week after Japan's official surrender, we entered Tokyo Bay and anchored not too far from Yokohama. Mt. Fuji was covered with snow, and the skies were clear. The super battleship and the kamikaze fighter planes that Japan had depended on to keep foreign forces away were now battle-scarred, unmanned, and useless. The ruined battle-ship was anchored just inside the breakwater. After we had anchored the Escambia, those of us who had not had liberty at our previous docking were to have a twelve-hour day pass.

None of the others who had liberty were my close shipmates. I would be by myself. I stayed with the group as we moved from our liberty boat to the loading docks and boarded the train in Yokohama to make our way to Tokyo. There, the rest went their way and I went mine.

General MacArthur and the heads of occupation forces had taken over a major hotel as their command center. It was in the geographic center of Tokyo and well-guarded by military police.

The strategic bombing of Tokyo was unreal. For miles, there was nothing but burned out factories and business. The hospitals, the palace and the surrounding gardens were mostly untouched. Most government buildings had exterior damage but the insides were still usable. A few passenger trains and some of the subways were still running. Buses powered by charcoal burners carried people from place to place. There were Jeeps and other U.S. military vehicles everywhere.

The only guns I saw were pistols worn by our military police and machine guns mounted on Jeeps moving around in the traffic. Even though I was alone, I felt no danger. I saw very few military uniforms and felt no Japanese animosity. The people were kind and friendly. They acted and looked relieved that the war was over. I went to the fish market and was amazed at the amount of fish for sale.

Downtown in a clean, well-stocked market, I bought several yards of pure white silk, some scarves and some knickknacks to take home as souvenirs. I ate at a very clean, cheap restaurant and then waded through hundreds of kids who wanted to sell or trade favors for cigarettes.

I walked for hours through the palace gardens and along the undamaged city streets where stores were open for business. A few blocks away, other businesses were beginning to open in the cleaned-up neighborhoods. In ten hours, I was walked out. I caught the train back to Yokohama and boarded a water taxi back to my ship.

The next morning, I located with binoculars the ship of Jack Keel, my best friend from high school. I talked one of our signalmen into sending a message to Jack's ship to find out if anyone could get a message to Jack. To my surprise, a message came back. Jack could ask a supply boat to come by my ship and drop him off the next morning. The boat would pick him up on its way back to the ship that afternoon. Since I had already used my liberty, I could not leave my ship. The next morning, Jack came. We had two hours together. We laughed about our promise to see one another in Tokyo and agreed that Kamay, Texas, would be better. We shared stories from home until his boat came and we parted.

In three days, we were given the best orders we'd had in eleven months: "Proceed to San Francisco Bay at your best speed."

Everyone was anxious to go. We stood our regular watches and spent a lot of time cleaning and repainting the ship. We were excited and even accepted our duties and orders with a smile. We had loaded a full supply of food and could eat as often and as much as we wanted. The captain knew the ship would be decommissioned and moth-balled, so he asked the engine room officers to spare no fuel and move us home as quickly and safely as they could. I don't think we set any records, but we made it to San Francisco in eight days.

The guys in the ship's maintenance division made our ship's victory banner. The size and length of the banner showed how long our ship and crew had been at sea and in combat. The top of the banner, which began at the front mast, was six feet in height and over a hundred feet long. It continuously tapered down to a four-inch-wide red, white and blue ribbon flapping over the stern of our ship. We were ready to enter San Francisco Bay. Seagoing tugboats met us two miles outside the bay and, with horns blasting, escorted us under the San Francisco Bay Bridge. A cheer began at the bow of our ship and continued to the fantail as we traveled under the now absolutely beautiful Golden Gate Bridge.

Another tug with a huge banner reading "WELCOME HOME! JOB WELL DONE!" had joined us just inside the Farallon Islands. All along the shore and wharfs, there were foghorns blaring, whistles blowing and fireboats spraying their full force of water in the air. Horns and sirens were going full blast to welcome us home. We were escorted to an anchorage in the western part of the bay next to Angel Island.

Liberty was in two sections, beginning the next morning. This time, my section was first. Two officers and four of us "non-coms" (non-commissioned officers) boarded our liberty boat to Fisherman's Wharf landing. We walked, we laughed, we joked. We found a large restaurant that was not crowded and entered. The waitress, the management and even the cooks took time to come to our table to welcome us home and thank us for our service. The menu was so large and varied that it took us several minutes to decide what we wanted.

I had not had fried chicken in almost a year. Others wanted steak, hamburgers, ham and fresh milk. We had different kinds of pie and ice cream. For an hour, we sat and talked to whoever stopped by. We then took the trolley downtown and went to the USO to be brought up to date on what was happening.

Edd (left) and a pal on shore leave.

Two of us had friends who lived close to the First Baptist Church. Without knowing if anyone would be home, we walked to their home and knocked on the door. The father and mother were both home and insisted we come in. We were fed again while we visited and waited for their son and daughter to come home from work. We answered and asked many questions. We all told jokes and shared about our experiences. Their nineteen-year-old daughter came home first. When she saw us, she burst into tears and nearly squeezed the life out of us. Her brother came in a few minutes later; while there were no tears this time, we were hugged again. They insisted that we stay for dinner. I began to feel like I really was back in my own country, that I was experiencing the real thing and not a dream. While my chicken dinner at the restaurant was great, that meal (and I cannot remember what it was) was the best I had eaten in months.

The second day, with no radar to work, I was assigned to the food stores boat. The supply center was a forty-minute ride to an area near where the present San Francisco Giants stadium is located. We had our shopping list from the cook signed by the captain. The chief petty officer at the stores shed took the list, grabbed a large flatbed cart and signaled for us to bring two more carts. We moved into the storage section. Our carts were loaded with sliced bread, canned vegetables and fruit (real, not dried), eggs, fresh milk, whole potatoes, steaks and roasts. All of it was the real stuff, not canned. The chief, on his own, kept adding extras. Finally, our food order was completed.

It took us twice as long to return as it did to get to the warehouse. Our cooks were thrilled, and our on-ship meals greatly improved. Our joke was that the bread had no weevils, so it had no food value.

The second day was the reverse. We unloaded onto barges everything we could except ammunition and explosives. The third day, with all hands on deck, our ship was escorted by two fire tugs to a section of the bay marked off with flashing red buoys. We anchored in the middle of the marked-off area. The fire tugs backed off but kept their water pumps running. A barge was towed alongside. We loaded slings with five-inch and three-inch shells and thirty millimeter anti-aircraft shells. The slings were picked up by the cranes, and everyone held their breath while the slings full of ammo were transferred to the barge. An inspection was made of our ship to make sure all ammo was removed, and then our ship returned to our anchorage. I was now assigned to deck watch and voice communications.

Six

1945-1946

Flo and Home

I anxiously waited for my forty-eight-hour pass. I had decided to take a chance and go to San Diego. My pass was approved. San Diego was a bit further than the four-hundred-mile limit on that short of a pass. I made round-trip reservations on an airline to Los Angeles because there were no seats available to San Diego. I would go to San Diego from Los Angeles and back to Los Angeles by train. Flo did not know for sure that I was coming. I left the ship on the early boat, rode the bus to the airport, ate a sandwich at the air terminal and boarded the plane.

I was going to be gone two days, so I carried a change of underwear, a pair of socks, my razor, a comb and my toothbrush. The plane took off and flew into a heavy rain squall. It bucked and rolled, and I got sick. I called for a barf bag, but no one could move. My shoes were wet from the rain, and I had taken them off. I threw up into my shoes and onto the legs of my uniform.

Once we cleared the weather, one of the stewardesses brought me towels from the galley. She brought me soap, and I went to the restroom to clean out my shoes. I used the dish soap to wash off my uniform pants as best as I could. When I came out of the restroom, the stewardess asked me about the ribbons on my uniform. We had been issued new uniforms and combat ribbons. She helped me clean up a little more and brought me crackers and coffee. I began to feel better.

At Los Angeles, I took a taxi to the train station and was there fifteen minutes before the train left for San Diego. There were no seats, and Navy uniforms were everywhere. A sailor moved out of a seat at a table in the dining car, and I took it. I ordered a Coke and spent my last dollar. I began to talk with the sailor across the table from me. His ship had been hit by a kamikaze and was so damaged that he had been transferred to another ship. Several replacements on our ship had experienced the same. How our conversation got around to friends, I have no idea, but Jack Keel's name came up.

"You mean that Texan from some place called Kamay?" (I almost dropped my Coke.) "He is in the second car in front of this one," he said.

I could not imagine that being possible. When we arrived in San Diego, my new friend led me to the right car, and we got off just behind Jack.

"Sailor, you sure are a long way from Texas," I said just loud enough for Jack to hear.

Flo at age twenty.

He turned; we laughed, shook hands and hugged. The questions flew. He was on his way to Camp Elliot until his next assignment came. I was returning to San Francisco.

I caught a bus to one of the worker housing areas. I knocked on the door and Flo's sister Ora answered. Instead of asking me to come in, she turned and said, "Flo, I think you should come here."

Ora reached out, gave me a

hug and walked back into the kitchen. Flo came, put her hands on her hips, shook her head, grabbed me and pulled me inside. A year earlier, I had mailed her the diamond engagement ring with the note that she said she never saw. I looked, and she saw where I was looking. She held up her hand in front of me so I could see the ring on her finger. We again hugged. I had a blessed time for as long as it lasted. The family had to go to bed to be ready for work, and I had used up sixteen hours of my pass. If it took that long for me to get back to my ship, I had less than twelve hours left.

Flo and I sat on the steps and talked and then went for a walk outside. She had to work the next day and went to bed. I took the couch. The next morning, we ate breakfast. Flo went to work while I visited with the family.

Mr. Nelson's job was coming to an end in a few weeks, and they would move back to Kamay. Norma, the youngest daughter, would go with them. Flo had a good job. Ora wanted her to stay, and Flo planned to do that. I went downtown, and Flo and I had an early lunch. I was out of money, so she "loaned" me ten dollars. The train fare to Los Angeles was seven dollars. I rode the train and then the bus to the airport and tried to check in. Even with my prepaid ticket, there were no seats.

The clerk, a nice-looking young lady, saw the ribbons and battle stars on my uniform and whispered to me, "Sailor, you take the seat at the end of row two and get where you can see me. When I nod in your direction, get up, get in line and get on that plane."

"How much time do I have?" I asked.

"Twenty to thirty minutes," she answered.

Not knowing if I would get on the plane, I went to the telegraph center and sent the following message to the Escambia AO-80 in San Francisco Bay: "I am having some travel difficulties but will report to the ship as soon as possible. Signed, Radarman Edd Brown."

The message would be wired to the San Francisco office and then telephoned by voice radio to my ship. I bought a Coke and sat in my assigned seat, waiting for the young lady to signal me. I had only fifteen cents left from what Flo had given me. The plane was to be loaded in five minutes. I was nervous; I knew I was in trouble if I did not make it back to the ship on time. I had almost given up when the young lady looked my way and nodded. I ran; she handed me my ticket with a big smile and said, "God bless. Have a good flight!" I could have cried.

The flight was smooth and on time. I rushed out of the airport, jumped on the downtown bus and was relaxing when it dawned on me that I had no way to get to the ship. I would have to sleep on the beach or on a bench in the park and wait for my ship's boat to come in. Both choices were more dangerous than walking the streets of Tokyo.

I boarded the trolley and was three cents short of the fare. The conductor said, "Give me what you have and get on board."

When I arrived a half-mile above the boat dock, our ship's boat was there. I ran, hollering, but the boat pulled out. I was out of breath and ready to give up when I looked up and saw that the boat had turned around and come back! I ran to the dock and jumped in the boat.

"Thanks for coming back for me," I said. The helmsman looked at me like I was crazy, "Huh? I did not know you were in the area. Joe left his bag on the dock, and we had to come back to pick it up."

We headed for the AO-80. I boarded the Escambia, changed clothes and walked to the bridge ten minutes before I was to be on duty. The TBS (voice radio) signaled on; I picked up the receiver and copied, "To Escambia AO-80, I am having travel problems. I may be late, but I will get there as soon as I can. Signed, Radarman Edd

Brown." I thanked the caller and almost keeled over in relief.

I had deck watch that evening and had been given a firm warning: if I let any of our crew on board with whiskey, I would end up in the brig. In addition to my sidearm pistol, I had a short wooden oak club. I used the club to pat down the pea coats that we all wore in the cold damp weather. If I noticed an unusually large object under the coat or under the pant legs of the uniform, I would lightly tap the object. If I detected a ring that sounded like glass, I would strike harder. One time, I broke a bottle of whisky, and the offended sailor began to curse me.

I held up my hand and told him, "If the O.D. (officer of the deck) hears you, you will go to the brig now, not me."

He picked up the broken glass and went to change his clothes. I never told anyone about the incident. A few of his buddies began to rile me. That was a minor nuisance, but I stayed out of the brig.

My thirty-day leave came with no travel restrictions, so I headed south to San Diego. I spent two unhurried days with Flo and headed for Tatum. This trip was now routine. I hitchhiked some but rode the train most of the way. I was expected, and my Uncle Bill Duncan had a temporary job waiting for me.

Because of oil deposits being discovered, housing in Tatum was becoming a big problem. Bill had bought three old houses off some ranches in the area. He had moved them into Tatum and planned to remodel them as rentals. He needed laborers, so I worked for him two weeks.

I spent my evenings and weekends with my cousins and other family. They filled my time with picnics and trips to the mountains and farmlands. For a few days, I was able to ride horseback and help round up calves on Bill's ranch. This work outside in the open air was the best thing that could have happened to me. Charles took me to

Hobbs to board a bus to El Paso. From there, I took the train to San Diego.

Flo met me at the train station. For a week, we double-dated with Flo's niece, Jackie, and Jackie's boyfriend, Bud. Flo and I discussed when and where we would be married. We agreed August would be the best time. We both wanted to be married in the Baptist church in Kamay, Texas, where we had met and grown up. Her family was now there, and my family would come to Kamay from Tatum.

I reported back to my ship. It had been moved to Richmond to be decommissioned. Most of the officers and older seaman had already been discharged. There was only a skeleton crew left on board. All electronics had been removed and shipped. The antennae were to be removed, and the masts that carried them, stripped and repainted. The mast became my task. I was mounted into a sling chair and removed most of the rust with scrapers and wire brushes. I red-leaded the bare areas and spray-painted the mast and side arms.

Our decommissioning party was paid for from the earnings of our ship's store. A large restaurant in Berkeley was reserved, and a local women's college brought fifty young ladies to the party.

There were only forty crewmen left on the ship. We had an unlimited amount and choice of food. A small dance band had been hired. I never learned to dance and did not drink alcoholic beverages. Most of the crew drank, but the girls were under the watchful eyes of their chaperones and did not participate. I sat and watched and was joined by three of the girls. We talked, joked and had a good time. I was asked why I was not drinking or trying to get fresh with the girls.

I told them there were two reasons. One was that I was a Christian; the other was that I was to be married in a few weeks. Two of the girls were Christians. One was engaged and did not think it right for her to be involved in the close dancing. Around midnight, the girls were escorted to their bus and returned to their college dorms.

The sailors had no plans. Four of us took a cab back to the ship and went to bed. The next day, we were moved to processing, given our back pay and our new orders, and dismissed. I opened my orders and saw that I had four weeks leave before I was to report to the El Paso Navy recruiting station.

I called Flo and told her that I would be there in two days. She told me that if I was going to be in Texas, she was not going to stay in California. I could not buy tickets to any destination. The trains, busses and airlines were booked solid. I shipped most of my stuff to Tatum. I kept a change of summer uniforms and toiletry articles in a small bag and hitchhiked. I had no difficulty getting rides. I made it to Los Angeles in eleven hours. I spent the night in a motel somewhere on the north side of the city. The next morning was so foggy that I could not see. I was able to get a ride to a place called Downey, which I was told was a few miles east of downtown Los Angeles. From Downey, there is an inland highway that goes east to San Diego.

The driver of the car that picked me up was a salesman not too much older than me. We stopped, and he bought breakfast. As we moved slowly through the fog, he asked me about my plans. When I left Maljamar to go into the Navy, Mr. Tobman had sent Mr. Ellis to see me. I told the driver I had been offered a full scholarship to Tulsa University if I wanted to study petroleum engineering, and we talked about that for a while. I then shared my growing conviction that I was not to go that direction. What I thought at that time was that I wanted and needed to work with people. I would like to become a high school teacher and coach men's sports.

"Okay, why is that?" he asked.

I told him of my grandfather saying that I would never be worth anything. I also told him about the time our house burned and the words of the man I never really knew: "Neither God nor God's people will ever forsake you."

"You really believe that?" my driver asked.

I shared what had happened on my travels — how rides, meals and money were always there and how Flo and I had become convinced that God kept putting us together without any effort on our part for His purpose.

"I just feel like I ought to help others on their way," I said.

"You base a lot on coincidence. While I wish you luck, I really would like to talk to you again in about ten years. By then, I think you will have changed your mind."

He stopped and let me out at the intersection of Imperial Highway and Telegraph Road on the edge of Norwalk, California. There were two service stations there that were surrounded by bean fields. The fog had not lifted. I went into the restroom of one station and then asked the attendant how I could get to San Diego.

A customer looked over at me and grinned, "Sailor, we have all the sailors in San Diego we need. Why in the world are you going there?"

I told him why, and he replied with a laugh, "Great, I am headed there. Come with me."

I finished my coffee, and we left. We drove through Tustin and then Capistrano, where I learned about the annual migration of swallows. Four hours later, my driver let me out two blocks from where Flo lived.

Flo, Jackie, Bud and I did the town and stayed up all hours. Two days later, Flo and I boarded the bus and bid everyone goodbye. We were sure we had left California for a long time. We talked and slept most of the way to Phoenix; there, we had a forty-minute rest stop. Flo and I needed and wanted to walk. We used the restrooms and went outside in the open air and sun. We walked a ways, bought and ate some food, and then started back to the bus station.

One of the men on the bus ran to us. "Come now, hurry! We are holding the bus for you."

We ran with him to get on the bus and learned we were over five minutes late. Another man had stood in the door and would not let the driver close it until we were on board. We thanked the driver and the two men. Red-faced, we turned and thanked the passengers.

One passenger spoke up, "That's okay. After you are married, maybe you will get some sense."

They had been told I was being discharged from the Navy and that Flo and I were headed to Texas to be married (their facts were a little off). The passengers clapped, and our driver even joined in. At all our stops to El Paso, people bought us drinks and snacks and wished us luck. We transferred at El Paso for Roswell and then, with no problems, made it to Tatum.

All my relatives had to meet Flo. Some had met her when I was in the hospital in Hobbs, but most had not. We spent six days in Tatum and went on to Kamay.

A weird but happy event occurred. Mack, who had been in the Army in Europe, came with Jack from San Diego; Betty and Wanda came from the Dallas Medical School; all six of us (including Flo and me) arrived in Kamay within a two-day period. The Valley View High School Six were together again. We

The "Valley View Six." Edd and Flo are at left.

went back to our old special places, but they seemed so different from what we remembered. They were just not important anymore. We attended church as a group and had a great welcome. Wanda and Betty had to go back to school in Dallas, so the rest of us went with them. We drove in the Keels' 1946 Ford sedan. We stopped three times to visit friends and relatives on the way.

Wanda and Betty lived on the ground floor of their dorm. They checked in just before curfew that evening. Fifteen minutes later, they opened the window of their room, and Flo crawled in. We three fellows went to a motel close by and spent the night.

The next day, we drove to Fort Worth and visited my aunt, my cousin and my now eleven-year-old second cousin who had moved there from San Diego. We went to northern Fort Worth, had lunch at a steakhouse, and headed back to Dallas.

At the eastern edge of Fort Worth, the highway went down a steep hill. A traffic light was at the bottom. I was driving slowly and tried to brake when the light turned red, but the brakes would not work. I shifted to a lower gear, but the car only slowed gradually. I tried the brakes again, but still nothing. I began to honk the horn to warn the other cars that I was in trouble. There was an older couple in the car ahead of us. Just as their car began to stop, we rear-ended it. We were traveling at five miles an hour, and there were no cars coming from cross streets, so a major accident was avoided. When we stopped, an angry man came running back. I got out of the car as quickly as I could.

"Mister, my brakes went out. I am sorry," I said.

Jack and Mack had joined me, and the man backed off. He looked us over and asked, "You guys just back from overseas?" We told him we were.

"Okay, let's see if there is any damage," he suggested.

Fortunately for us, the bumpers had met. The man's wife and our three girls were out by then. We were asked the typical questions about our service, and I apologized again.

"No damage, no problem. My wife seems okay. Just get those brakes fixed before you hurt someone," he suggested.

We found a place to eat and settle down. We spent the rest of the day at a lake north of town. We took our two nurses back to their dorm and drove back to Kamay. Jack made arrangements to have the car brakes fixed. With help from our friends, Flo and I set our wedding for August 9, 1946.

The next morning, I picked up my gear and said goodbye to Flo and her family. I caught the mail ride to town, boarded the bus to El Paso and reported at the Navy recruiting station.

"Radarman Brown, we have been expecting you. Here are your orders."

I took the folder, found a chair and sat down. I read, "Report to Camp Elliot in San Diego, California, for further assignment."

I could not believe what I was reading. I looked up at the recruiting officer. He just shook his head and held up his arms as if to say he had nothing to do with it. I thanked him and left. It was eleven o'clock in the morning, and my train did not leave until four that afternoon.

The Catholic churches were celebrating All Saints Day. The streets were so crowded that I could hardly walk. The sidewalks were worse.

After walking an hour, I located an old-fashioned ice cream parlor with large glass windows overlooking a park along the Rio Grande. I set my bag down and, with the owner's permission, stayed until three o'clock. I ate various types and flavors of ice cream, some given to me by the owner. I watched people outside enjoying their day. I was feeling sorry for myself and knew something was wrong. I was to be discharged in two weeks. That could be done in El Paso.

I boarded the full train and found a seat at a window next to where a young woman was sitting. She wanted the inside seat so she could talk to her friend across the aisle. The train pulled out on time. The two ladies were married and were having problems, whether real or imagined, with their husbands. I hoped that was not what Flo and I were headed for. They asked me what I thought, and I told them that, with no experience, I had no thoughts. I tried to sleep and spend time in the dining car to get away from their angry, detailed discussions. Two days later, I reported to Camp Elliot. Everything was on hold. I had nowhere to go and nothing to do.

I learned that President Truman was negotiating with leaders of the Longshoreman's Union to prevent a threatened strike, which would close all commercial harbors along the Pacific Coast. Truman had frozen all discharges. All Navy personnel on the West Coast were ordered to report to their bases for duty.

Stalin was flexing his power in Europe and Korea. Truman was already upset. He challenged the union, saying that if they called a strike at this time, he would break the union. In addition, he would charge the officers of the union with obstruction of justice. He would use Marines to protect non-union workers. He would use Seabees to man the loading docks. The Army would provide laborers, and the Navy would move cargo from port to port. Right or wrong, Truman's policy of "The buck stops here" worked.

Three weeks later, discharge by the number was back in practice. The numbers were reassigned according to time in service and time in combat situations. My old number was to have come up in two weeks. My new number was now several weeks away.

I spent my time at Elliott working KP and going out to dinner with Flo's relatives and her friend who worked for a wholesale jewelry company. Flo's friend helped me design Flo's wedding ring. Ora, Jackie,

Bud and Jackie's brother John kept me from being too lonesome.

After two weeks, a note was on my bunk: "Report to Processing." My orders were not for discharge. I was to report in two days to the captain of a seagoing tug that was tied up at the downtown harbor. I found the location, called a taxi at Navy expense and reported for duty.

I would be the only radarman on a seagoing tugboat. The tug was to move two support and repair barges to the East Coast. I would be in charge of the radar and assist at the helm and voice communications of the tug. We had a crew of eighteen people, who were divided into three watches. As the only radar operator, the assignments for my watch and other duties were flexible. Instead of bunking on the tug, five sailors and I were moved to one of the barges anchored close to Point Loma. Our job was to protect and maintain the barges. One was a machine shop; the other was a carpenter's shop. Both barges were complete with tools and wood and metal dressing machines.

The barges were twenty-five feet wide and seventy feet long. Both had huge working areas. The one we would be on had a full galley with enclosed living quarters. The interior was insulated. As the highest ranking sailor, I was responsible for the care of the floating machine and carpenter shops.

I had two immediate problems: no boat and no communication with those ashore or on our tug. With the reassigning of people to their new responsibilities, we had been forgotten. For two days, we were out of food and fresh water. No one had made contact or brought supplies.

One of the sailors found a Morse code book. I wrote out the dots and dashes and took what I had written to the sailor on the top deck. A signal light was on the bow. We had some idea of how it worked. I had the mate practice using the signal light. A dot was a short flash;

a dash was twice as long as a dot. There was a crew on duty at Point Loma lighthouse. We turned on our light and signaled them until they responded. I read off the dots and dashes instead of the letters: "Radarman Brown to Tug. We have no food or water. We need help now."

We received an answer from the lighthouse, and a boat with food arrived in three hours. A water carrier arrived in two hours. We sat for three more days with no liberty and no mail. Flo only knew that I would not be in Kamay for awhile. We both began to wonder if we would be able to keep our August wedding date.

After five days of waiting, the tug captain received orders. The tug was to tow the two barges through the Panama Canal and on to the naval base in New Port News, Virginia. All personnel eligible for discharge were to be released from duty there.

The tug came. We hooked a twenty-foot cable to a huge triangular steel flange. Both barges were hooked to the flange, one with a thirty-foot cable and the other with a 150-foot cable. We left San Diego and headed south.

We were not a harbor tug. Our ocean fleet tug was built to tow battleships, aircraft carriers and other large ships out of danger or to move them around in ports. Our tug had two super-sized diesel engines with fabulous maneuvering power as well as speed. I was on radar to keep us away from shore and on course.

The radar I had was outdated. When rain squalls came, the ghosts totally overrode the pips. The captain and I decided that in rough weather I would go to the flag bridge, the highest deck, where I could use visual sightings from the lighthouses. On clear nights, we watched for boat lights. When close to shore, we would use radar.

On our third day, a locking pin on the flange broke, and the furthest barge broke loose and began to float north. The boson mate used a windlass to pull the cables and flange onto the deck of the tug. The closest barge was pulled alongside the tug and secured. We had stopped our engines and were drifting. Three sailors in a small boat boarded the barge that had broken loose. They pulled the loose cable high enough to keep it from fouling the screws that pushed and maneuvered the tug.

With one barge secured, our tug went after the one that had broken away. The captain and helmsman moved the tug upwind from the loose barge. The captain used twin screws to maneuver the tug next to the runaway. Four sailors boarded the barge. The flange, now repaired, was reconnected to that cable. Slowly, the tug moved away to pull the cable taut. Everything seemed to work; the barges were reconnected to the flange and maneuvered back into towing position.

We were a day late getting to Panama and waited until the next morning to join the traffic through the canal. We had to secure both barges to opposite sides of our tug. Because of the lessons we had learned from the breakaway barge, that task was finished in a few hours. We were ready to move into the canal.

I had been in the Pacific in the heat and cold, but the hot weather and humidity of the Caribbean were more than my body could handle. I wore a cover (hat) at all times. I did not wear shorts or short-sleeved shirts. In spite of my coverings, the heat got to me. One day, I was on deck helping the deck hands wrap cable with treated cord to keep the cable lubricated. For two hours, I wrapped cords around cable; then, I began to get dizzy and almost fell. A seaman grabbed me, and another caught the paddle I was using.

The chief pharmacist's mate took me inside. He literally hosed me down with fresh cool water and tried to get me to drink. Nothing would stay on my stomach. He undressed me down to my skivvies and put me in a bunk with ice packs on my head and under my neck.

When I began to cool down, he tried to get a syringe in my arm. Every time the needle penetrated my skin, I would pass out. He gave up and began to spoon-feed me salty fruit juice and water every fifteen minutes. After two hours, I began to feel better and was able to sit up to sip from a glass.

My heart rate and blood pressure were soon back to normal. I was kept on the bunk for five hours and then permitted to walk; however, I was to sit down and rest every thirty minutes. I was just an observer as we went through the canal and was only allowed outside if I stayed in the shade. I watched as our ship and others were lifted and lowered through the locks.

After three hours of being towed by "mules" (special electric towing machines), we went through the inland lake and Atlantic locks and were lowered to sea level and tied up at a Navy dock. The two barges remained lashed to the sides of our tug. We placed a gangway from the tug to an open door of one of the barges and from there a gangway to the dock. My section had watch, but I was excused from duty until the next day. After breakfast, I was ready to go ashore.

I had been reading my Bible regularly. I made no show of it, but if someone walked in on me, I did not hide the Bible nor turn away. If they wanted to talk about what 1 believed, we talked. If they asked questions about religion or Christianity, that was fine; however, I drew the line on arguments, and I did not drink alcoholic beverages.

While we were in San Diego, two of my shipmates had given me a lot of trouble about my narrow, dull life. Those same two came to me in Panama and made an outlandish request. Their request was, "When we go ashore, we want you to keep our money and not let us have any of the money you are carrying. If something happens and our money gets stolen, it will be our fault and not yours."

I thought that either they or I must be stupid. Here in Panama, we had been paid in cash for the last three months. Even with half of my pay being automatically sent home, I still had two hundred dollars; and they had three times as much.

I reluctantly agreed, and we left the tug. I had over six hundred dollars inside my uniform. I was the most protected sailor in Panama. The six of us going to town were under strict orders to stay together. I could not even go to a rest room unless two of the crew went with me. Our agreement was that they would not get any of their money until we returned to the tug.

We walked the streets and listened to the hawkers; we passed bars, restaurants, gambling halls, and questionable hotels. A little farther on, in a separate part of town, was the red light district. Shore patrols were at each entrance to keep servicemen out.

We located a restaurant with a covered patio in a nice section of town. The waiters and cooks seemed decent, and the tables were clean and orderly. We decided to take a chance. The food on the tug was fine, but it was just food. We ordered the bacon-wrapped sirloin steaks with French fries. We had bottled Cokes to drink. The plates were large platters. The steaks were cooked on an outside charcoal fire. Handmade tortillas were cooked on polished granite slabs. Our steaks filled the platters and were three-quarters of an inch thick. The meal cost us a dollar and a quarter each. The steaks were medium and medium rare. For two hours, we ate steak and all the French fries we could hold.

We headed to the center of town, where the results of the national election was being announced. We watched as bar owners, pimps and police met and publicly exchanged uniforms and job roles. Business never stopped for a moment.

The inevitable came: "I need a drink — just one, and then we can move on."

I stayed with them for two reasons. First, I had their money, and they were not going to let me out of their sight. Second, I was not going anywhere in Panama by myself. We went into a good-sized bar. Drinks were ordered for everyone, including Cokes for me. We sat, drank, ate peanuts, listened to some tangy music and watched girls dance. I was bored, but my buddies were not yet ready to leave. Thirty minutes later, three of the hostesses moved to our table and began to talk to us. After a few minutes, they realized I was a "dead fish" and ignored me. When one of our guys was nearly drunk, the girl in his lap tried to frisk him to find his money belt. I thumped the table and made hand signs to let him know what was happening.

The girl was so wrapped up in what she was doing that she did not notice my tipoff. The sailor stood up, grabbed her hand and pushed it away; we had to hold him back to keep him from doing more. The former manager, now the cop, was called in from outside. The former cop, now the manager, came to our table and told me I had to leave or be arrested for disturbing a business. I agreed to leave; and with me carrying their money, the others left, too. I may be the only sailor who ever got thrown out of a bar for not drinking.

A USO was three blocks down the street. A large warehouse had been converted into a recreation hall with a large kitchen and multiple restrooms. I herded our guys to the restrooms; then we had coffee and doughnuts. After three or four cups of coffee and several doughnuts, the other guys began to settle down. We were sitting at a table in the back, opposite the entrance, when the front doors opened.

We sat and stared as 240 young and middle-aged women walked in. Some went to the restrooms while others got coffee or tea and began to mingle. We had three extra chairs at our table, and three of the ladies asked if they could join us. The women were on their way from England to Australia. They had been recruited by a matchmaking company and had made commitments to marry men they had only met by mail and wire service. They had sailed from London the week before and were staying overnight on the ship docked in Panama. This was the only time on their trip they could get off ship. At ten o'clock that evening, they would have to board the bus to go back to their ship.

We visited for awhile before the other sailors (who had been drinking more than they should) were ready to go back to our tug. Most of the crew members were already on board when we arrived at the dock. I started across the gangway and bumped into Baskin so forcefully that it nearly knocked us both off into the water.

I recognized my shipmate and apologized, "Baskin, I am sorry. I did not see you."

My black friend laughed, "Dark blue uniform, black guy, no moon … Kinda blends, don't it?"

We danced foolishly around each other and then went to the galley, had coffee and shared about our day. When it became late, I went to my bunk and Baskin went to his watch for the night. The next day, our section had duty. I returned the money to its owners. I split the guard on the barges into two sections; each member of our crew could spend as much time as he wanted on shore inside the base and Post Exchange.

The following morning, we were underway with the barges in tow. We sailed by Cuba and were heading up the Florida coast toward our destination when a radio message came. Our destination had changed; we were to go to Green Cove Springs, southwest of Jacksonville, Florida. Ten hours later, we were escorted up the Greene River for several miles by small harbor craft. We anchored in a large lake a mile offshore. We were issued a motor launch and some food, and the water tanks were filled. The tug was released from the barges and moved out the next morning. Six of us, with me in charge of the two barges, were left in Green Cove. The tug went to Newport News. We had no orders; we knew nothing. We were again in limbo.

The next morning, a chief petty officer came to give us our orders and information. We were again the custodians of the two barges, with me in charge. We were to do daily cleanings, to remove rust and to repaint. We would have eight-hour workdays, and our work would be inspected every other day. Our motor launch was for Navy business only, such as daily trips to the main base for mail. It could also be used to acquire supplies for meals, tools and other materials as needed, once approved by the chief. The chief had no information on how long we would be there.

We were given leave; however, two people had to stay on the barges at all times. We divided the crew into two watches. Two others and I took the first watch so three could go on liberty. I took the ones on liberty to shore. We three who were left tried to make the place livable. We stored our food supplies. We had no cook; everyone could eat what and when they wanted. All cooking utensils, cookware, plates, cups, glasses and other items used in the meal preparation had to be cleaned and stored; otherwise, the sailor who left them out would forfeit one day of liberty. As ranking sailor, I set up a running inventory. Everyone would know when we needed to replace food and what special items and other supplies we could get at the base stores.

During my first liberty, three of us took a bus to St. Augustine to see the early settlements of the Spanish. We went to the city and ate a real meal, walked the streets, explored the beach and then returned to the tug. We developed a time schedule for the boat to take members of our crew to the base and a time for it to be at the wharf to pick up crew members returning to the barge.

Three days later, the chief returned with news. Our tug was at Newport News. All were to be discharged as soon as our records were sent to the local base. The problem was that our records had been left in Panama. They had to be sent to Newport News, approved by commanding officer of the tug and then sent to Navy processing in New Orleans. When approved, they would be forwarded to the base where we were. The Navy expected the paperwork to be done in two weeks; in the meantime, we were to continue our work.

There were restaurants on the base, so we began to take turns going over for meals and movies. The chief did not agree that such activity was "Navy business," so we used the mail run as a time to double up on our time ashore. We would pick up mail and leave a voucher for the food items at the commissary. It took time to put in a request and get it approved, so we would go see a movie and then pick up what we had ordered. It was a different item every day.

For several days, I took the boat with one or two guys to pick up anything we needed; the two others would go on liberty. One day, I was picking up two sailors returning from liberty. I tied the boat to a buoy and caught a ride on a boat going into dock. I went to the post office. I had tried to keep Flo up to date on what was happening. I picked up the mail and went by the processing office. I looked through the names. Four of our six were on the list to report to the processing center at ten hundred hours the next day. My name, even though I had the most points for discharge, was not listed.

I went into the office and asked to see the officer in charge. He came to the desk, and I asked why my name was not on the list. He pulled my records, frowned and said, "You are registered as regular Navy, and that is not handled here."

"What?" I asked. He again gave me the same answer. After ten minutes of searching records, he agreed that I was not regular Navy.

He asked me to come back to see him the next day.

When I arrived at the barge, the chief was there. He either ignored or did not notice that I had been over and back in the boat by myself. After he had looked over everything, I told him that four of our guys were on the discharge list and they were to report to the separation office the next morning. He wanted to know how I knew and why my name was not on the list.

"Why was I not told?" he asked.

"Chief," I said, "I have no idea why you were not told, but those are their orders."

He left with the notice that he would be back in the morning to check their bags. We helped the guys get their stuff together and ate a big breakfast since there would be only two of us left.

The chief came, approved everything and left. I took the guys ashore and asked the dock guard if I could have ten minutes dock time to run to the post office. He told me where to tie up the boat, and I literally ran. I went to the separation office and asked about my discharge. A civilian clerk handed me a packet. I opened it, and all my documents for release and final pay were there. I was to report tomorrow for separation. I almost forgot the mail, but when I picked it up there was a letter from Flo, who wanted to know what was going on.

I went back to the dock. I told the dock guard that I had to get a plane reservation for the next day. He told me that he was not busy and to take my time.

The only seat available was a flight to New Orleans. Since that was halfway to Kamay, I took it. I went back to the dock and told the guard what had happened. He responded, "You sure are a lucky guy" (I have cleaned up his language a little), and he wished me luck.

"Fellow," I replied, "I appreciate what you have done, but there is more than just luck involved."

I jumped into the boat, started the engine and went to the barge. The chief had come back to discuss with me what we should do about the maintenance of the barge. Could two sailors handle the job?

"Chief, there will be only one; I will be leaving at ten hundred hours and have to catch plane in Jacksonville at fourteen hundred hours," I informed him.

"You have orders?" he asked.

"Yes, sir. I picked them up this afternoon," I replied.

He started to ask me how but backed off. He checked my bag and left. The next morning, the last man on the barge took me to the dock. I went through the separation routine, signed my name on four copies of my papers and picked up my back pay and separation bonus. After nineteen months of active duty, I left and headed for Kamay, Texas, and Flo.

I arrived at Jacksonville Airport and had time to walk around, still in uniform but with separation papers in my pocket. I did not even have to acknowledge or salute officers.

My flight to New Orleans was delayed because of weather. I did not get to New Orleans until three o'clock in the morning. I was tired but so wired that I could not sleep. I took a bus to town, went into an all-night café and ordered coffee. This was my first time in Louisiana. The waitress brought me my coffee and a plate of little sugary donuts. I picked up the coffee and, holding it in both hands, took a big swallow. I thought my head would come off. My throat burned, my stomach began to turn, and tears rolled down my face.

The waitress came back and almost cried, "I did not know you wanted coffee plain. Most sailors want it heavy with chicory. Let me get you some water and plain coffee with lots of cream."

She came back and stayed until I began to feel almost human. I was more than awake. I thanked her and insisted on paying for both coffees even though she protested.

I caught a city bus to the northwestern edge of New Orleans and stepped out into the street. I put up my thumb, and a bus stopped. I backed up when the door opened. The driver asked where I was headed. I told him Wichita Falls, Texas. No one here would know about Kamay.

"Hop on; I am going about halfway," he said.

The driver told me to make myself comfortable and sleep a while; we could talk later. I moved back a couple rows, lay down crossways and slept for two hours. I woke up when he pulled into a service station to get gas and something to eat. There, I found out that the driver had been in Europe and was part of D-Day. He and two other ex-G.I.s were starting a new bus line between Dallas and Houston, and he had been in New Orleans to pick up one of their new busses. They were looking for drivers, and he said to let him know if I was interested later on.

He let me off just south of Dallas. I caught a ride with a family headed north. We got to Wichita Falls around four in the afternoon. Flo and I were to be married in four weeks. I had to get clothes, go to Tatum, come back to Kamay for the wedding and try to be accepted into college within six weeks.

I went to a men's store that I had used before and bought a suit, two shirts and a pair of shoes. The suit had to be altered. I went to a hotel and spent the night.

The next morning I slept late. I went to the main post office and asked when the mail for Kamay would be picked up. The carrier had not been in, but they were expecting him around two o'clock. I left a note for the carrier, went to pick up my suit and came back to wait for the carrier. He knew Flo from the time she had worked at the post office. I rode to Kamay with him.

Flo's dad had moved an older wooden freight car to a lot in Kamay. He had removed the undercarriage and converted the rail car into a kitchen and a bedroom. He had added a living room and a bedroom to the side of car. He, Mrs. Nelson, Flo and Norma lived there. They were expecting me. I spent two days with them, sleeping nights on the couch. With help from our friends and family, Flo and I finished our plans for our wedding.

I left my new clothes with the Coats family, who had been our neighbors when Mr. Coats and Dad were working for Buffalo Oil Company. The Coats had sent word that I was to stay with them.

I took a bus to Lubbock. From Lubbock, I hitchhiked to Tatum. Two ladies about my age had stopped and offered me a ride. They had insisted I sit up front with them so we could talk. The car was a nice size, so we were not that crowded. They were going to Tatum for an annual barbecue and dance at one of the ranches a few miles out of town.

I learned down the road that the ladies made this an annual event. They were traveling prostitutes. They offered me cigarettes and whiskey they had in the glove box. One offered to ride in the backseat with me while the other one drove. I thanked them for picking me up and told them, "I am getting married in a few weeks, so I must turn down all your invitations."

"Wow, you sure are not like any of the other sailors we have met, but that's okay. Who do you know in Tatum?" the driver asked.

The one next to me buttoned her blouse and pulled her skirt back down as I told them who my relatives were and what my Dad did.

"I bet we see you at the barbecue. You are related to half of the county," the driver said.

Three hours later, she stopped in front of our house. I knocked on the door. No one came. I heard a sound like a kitten meowing. There was some kind of movement going on, but I did not want to just barge in. I waited, and Mom came out of one of the bedrooms. She was carrying something in her arms.

She looked up and said, "Thought that might be you; come on in."

Concerned about the casualness of my welcome, I walked in. Mom met me just inside and handed me what she was carrying. I took the bundle and was more than astonished at what I saw.

Mom took my arm, pulled me to her and said, "Meet Janie, your new sister."

Janie fit perfectly in my arm; her head rested in the palm of my hand, and her rear end sat in the crook of my elbow. I nearly dropped her. My first reaction was wondering why I had not been told. Mom's answer was practical and comical at the same time.

"We did not know if you would get the information with all your moving around on different ships." Mom added, "We did not know how you would react and if you would want her."

Carnice "Prof" Ribble.

That was funny to me, so I asked, "What could I or you have done if that were the case?" I then assured Mom that, if she wanted my opinion, I thought we ought to keep her.

Two days later, Mom's brother, Carnice "Prof" Ribble, an economics professor at Hardin Simmons University in Abilene, came by on his annual recruitment trip to youth camps in New Mexico. He was headed to a camp in the mountains

south of Albuquerque. He asked me to go with him to visit my grandparents on the Isleta Reservation in Los Lunas. He spent a day visiting
with Dad and Mom; then he and I drove to Los Lunas and spent a day
with my grandparents. We went to Mountainair to the youth camp
and Prof did his thing. We spent the night and stopped the next day at
another youth camp close to Cloudcroft.

In four days, we were back in Tatum. Prof may not have recruited
anyone else, but I was ready to go to Hardin Simmons. He left to go to
another camp and would be back before going on to Abilene.

I found a job driving a dump truck for a road building contractor
for two weeks and made some good money. Prof came back to our
home a week before I was to be in Kamay for my and Flo's wedding.

There was no housing left for married students at the University.
Prof and Ginny Mae had no children. They made up for this by
"adopting" students and helping them get a college education. He had
already registered Flo and me, but I needed to get my G.I. application
and Flo's and my class requests in.

Prof and Genie May closed off a large area in living room with
movable blinds. Flo and I would live with them until further arrangements could be made. I went with Prof to Abilene and, after several
problems with notaries, was able to get Flo's and my marriage license.
I completed our enrollment in Hardin Simmons four days before our
wedding.

I went to Kamay. Flo and I met with our pastor to complete final
arrangements for our ceremony. The day before our wedding, Jack,
Wanda, Mack and Betty took us to Wichita Falls for a reunion.

Mom and Dad had been delayed and did not get to Kamay until
the morning of the wedding. We had our wedding at nine in the
morning. The church had no air conditioning, and it could be hot in
August. We had to catch a bus in Wichita Falls by noon to go to Dallas

for our honeymoon.

Jack and Wanda took me to the Coats' house, where I had spent the night. The next morning, Effie (Mrs. Coats) fixed a big breakfast. We all went to our rooms to dress, and I opened the packages of my new clothes. There were no socks and no tie. I went into the front room and told Effie. She went to her bedroom and came back with a few ties and a pair of socks. Henry, her husband, and I were the same height, but he outweighed me by sixty pounds. The socks were so loose that I had to hold them up with a pair of Effie's garters. The ties, which I had never seen Henry wear, were as old as I was. Effie helped me pick out a neutral one, and it did not look bad. I packed my bag, and we headed for the church. It was already getting hot. Hand fans advertising funeral homes were laid out on the benches.

I was ushered to the Bacons' home to wait until the wedding was to begin. Ten minutes before the wedding, Mom and Dad drove up. Alterations were made to my clothing, and I was escorted into the church through the back door. Jack was my best man. Flo's sister sang, and the pianist began playing one of Flo's favorite music pieces instead of the wedding march.

When Flo walked in with her Dad, I was in a trance. Flo was always beautiful to me; but that day, as she came down the aisle, she was the most beautiful woman I had ever seen or dreamed about. I had to control my emotions to keep from gasping out loud.

Brother Sartian, who had been our pastor for six years, did an

The newlyweds depart.

excellent job. We were pronounced man and wife. We led the procession out the front door, where Flo would let me kiss her. We said our brief goodbyes at the church. We hugged our parents and our friends and thanked everyone. Jack and Wanda took us Wichita Falls to catch the bus to Dallas. Flo and I did take some time to change into traveling clothes. We would wear our wedding clothes as dress clothes for the next several months.

I had now made the third public commitment of my life.

Seven

1946-1950

Hardin Simmons University
Southwestern Baptist Theological Seminary

Flo and I arrived in Dallas, a few blocks from our hotel. We checked in and then walked the streets and had a relaxed evening meal. This was our first free time in weeks; we did not need to rush.

Our hotel was nice, but air conditioning was a dream. At eight that evening, we returned to our large fourth floor room, which had nice décor, comfortable chairs and a large bed. We looked through wedding gifts and read a few cards. At nine o'clock I took a shower and changed into my new pajamas. Flo went for her bath. When she came out, I was again speechless. She had made a gorgeous nightgown from the yards of white silk I had bought for her in Tokyo. I stood and I stared; I could not speak. No pictures, no books, no stories could have prepared me for this. I was more nervous than I had ever been in my life. I was afraid to even touch her, afraid she might break or disappear. After we had hugged and kissed for a short time, one of us suggested we try the bed. The details of what followed are our own private fond memories.

Late that night, the noise of garbage trucks, taxis and sirens was cause enough to shut the window. Our room became so hot that we took turns sleeping on the floor with just sheets under us. It was ten in the morning before either of us could get much sleep. We showered, dressed and went to late breakfast. From the way we acted, no one had to guess that we were newly married.

We spent three days in Dallas visiting family, going to church and exploring the city. We returned to Kamay and packed for our trip to New Mexico. My sister Nell had been at our wedding with Mom and Dad and had stayed in Kamay with friends. Mr. Nelson took us to get Nell and then drove us to Mankins for us to catch the bus. We were going to my parents' home in Tatum. It took us six hours to get to Brownwood, Texas. Charles and Mom were to meet us and take us to Tatum, thirty minutes away. We were tired and hot. After we had waited for half an hour, I asked the ticket agent if there was a hotel close by. There was one two blocks away. We dragged, pushed and carried our luggage two blocks and entered the hotel lobby.

The lobby would have made a perfect old-time western movie set. A stairway with wooden banisters curved around the walls up toward a high ceiling. The furniture was at least a hundred years old. The clerk, an older man, looked up from a book.

"Whatch'all want?" he asked.

"A room with two beds, sir," I answered.

"Got one on second floor. You got eight dollars?"

I handed him a ten-dollar bill. He took the bill, held it up and then asked, "How y'all related?" (Flo and I did not look much older than Nell.)

Pointing to Flo, I said, "This is my wife, and (pointing to Nell) this is my sister."

"Hmm, okay, I guess," he said as he handed me the key and my two dollars.

We made two trips to get our luggage up the stairs. The room had a dim light and looked like it had not been used or cleaned in a week. We decided to sleep on the sheets with just our shoes off. When we had just lain down, there was a knock on the door.

"Who is it, and what do you want?" I asked.

"It's me, Charles. Mom and I are here to take you home."

Tatum is less than hour away from Brownwood, but neither Charles nor Mom had remembered that there is an hour time change at the New Mexico border.

Charles helped us wrestle our bags downstairs and into the car. We arrived at our house in Tatum thirteen hours after we had left Kamay. Mom had a bedroom for me and Flo. Nell had her own room. We went to bed. Janie and Dad never woke up during all the commotion.

The next day, Janie would not leave me or Flo. She would cry until one of us picked her up. We carried her everywhere we went for two days. We enjoyed it as much as Janie did.

Dad and Mom had made plans for us to go to the mountains west of Artesia to get fruit and then to Muleshoe, Texas, for fresh vegetables. They planned to buy and prepare enough canned goods to last us our first year of college.

Prof came a week later from another student recruiting tour. The next day, Flo and I went to Abilene with him. We moved only our clothes and personal items. We would live with him and the other family members. We all would share the costs of food and utilities.

Prof and Ginny Mae, Prof's wife, had a houseful of people in addition to Flo and me. A new professor lived upstairs in a garage apartment. The Christophers — two brothers and a sister-in-law of Ginny Mae's from Easley, South Carolina — lived in two back bedrooms of the house. All eight of us ate breakfast and, when possible, dinner together. Flo and I worked in the school cafeteria at noon and ate our lunch there.

There were three bathrooms for the eight of us. Our work and class schedules were staggered — and with a few adjustments, we did fine. Flo's and my bedroom was behind two moveable screens in a large wing of the guest and living room. For six weeks, we lived that way — then the professor in the garage apartment moved. Tom, the oldest brother, and his wife moved to the garage apartment. That left a bedroom for me and Flo. At midterm, a house trailer in the school trailer park became available. Flo and I moved there. We had one big room with a small kitchen. The bathhouse was thirty feet away, but we did have running hot and cold water in our trailer. There were ten trailers in our park, a block away from the campus.

Four months later, we moved to what became known as "Baby Row Apartments." The university had been given eight barrack buildings when an Army Air Force base closed. The barracks were modernized and converted into eight two-story buildings, each holding six one-bedroom apartments. In our junior and senior years at Hardin Simmons, we lived there with fifty ex-military families. Our oldest sons, Steve and Wayne, were born during those years.

Flo and I enrolled and took two classes together the first semester. She was a straight A student. I made B's and a few C's in most classes. The next semester, I did have two A's. After our son Steve came, Flo decided she needed to stay at home with him.

My history of multiple English teachers in high school caught up with me. I struggled and was getting desperate. Flo and I would be included when professors were invited to dine with Prof and Ginny Mae. One guest was an English professor who lived a block away from Prof. She invited me to come for tutoring once a week. She worked with me on basics for two to three hours for four weeks. While my skills improved, I have continually struggled with English and especially with writing.

The University Baptist Church, just off campus, decided to begin a program for the ex-military and other young adults that were flooding the community. I was asked by the church to be the leader of a committee to develop a weekly program for that age group. I had been involved in such a program at the First Baptist Church in San Francisco and had been ministered to by a similar group in San Diego; however, I had no experience in developing or leading any type of program. The pastor and deacon chairman helped me enlist four individuals to develop a program to reach out to our age group.

On our committee was Jwell Spencer (a male Indian who was a superb piano player), a male student from the town of Buffalo, a new woman professor, two mission students, and two male ministry students. We began with thirty young people at a Sunday night fellowship after worship.

Our committee members were great, and we shared what we hoped to accomplish. We asked all who attended our first meeting to become involved by helping us come up with ideas and plan what they would like to do. After refreshments, a dozen students stayed and offered to help clean up.

We soon had fifty young people, including couples and singles, each Sunday evening. To begin our second year, we planned an outdoor welcome for new and returning students. We had over a hundred reservations, and fifty more joined us. The event was an outstanding success. Our volunteers led skits and music, encouraging audience participation. We closed with an old-fashioned country meal provided by the older couples of our church.

That year, one of the lecture halls at the university burned. The administration rented the church

Edd with first son, Steve.

education building for classroom space. The university agreed to provide custodial care for the building.

I was hired and had my first church-paying job. I was the head custodian for the rooms that the university was renting. Four young men from Hawaii, students at Hardin Simmons on work scholarships, were assigned to help me. For six months, cleaning toilets was my occupation. When the new building on campus was finished, so was my job. Because of time restraints with multiple classes, I also had to give up my leadership of the young adult outreach program.

My G.I. bill paid me ninety dollars a month. Flo and I paid forty dollars a month for rent and utilities, thirty dollars for groceries and ten for tithing. We had no car, so we did not have that expense; however, our firstborn, Stephen, was on the way. I needed to find some part-time work.

In our sophomore year, we visited Flo's parents for Thanksgiving. I paid eight dollars for Flo's round-trip bus ticket. She and Steve, our six-month-old boy, rode the bus. There was no money for me. I hitch-hiked and had to wait thirty minutes for her and Steve at Mankins, where her father picked us up.

I was able to get a job selling suits and other clothing at men's store in downtown Abilene during the Christmas season. I worked six hours a day for six weeks and made four hundred dollars. Dad and Mom came to our barracks home after Christmas and, without our knowing until they were gone, paid the forty dollars we owed at a small

Flo's family at Thanksgiving.

market.

I had four years of college provided with my G.I. bill. I increased my hours of classes from fifteen to eighteen. With two summer schools, I could graduate in three years and have at least one year on my G.I. bill for graduate school.

I changed one of my minors to music education and began to sing in the church choir. My ignorance of music was astonishing. The early ear damage from lightning also put me at a disadvantage. The professors were patient and encouraging, and I worked hard to learn the basics.

A local pastor called and invited me to lead the music for a revival meeting in his church, twenty miles south of town. I was to begin Sunday evening and lead the congregation in singing every night and at both services the following Sunday. I went into the church building twenty minutes early and met with the pastor and the visiting preacher. We went over the program, and the service began. There were five or six in the choir and maybe twenty in the congregation. We stumbled through the first song. The pianist set the tempo and played as if I were not there. As the service progressed, she and I began to work together, but the church people just sang their own way. The invitation was some better, but not much.

The next night, fewer were at church, and the music and singing were dead. On Tuesday night, if any singing was done, it was by myself and maybe five others. I am not a soloist. If people in the choir or congregation did not sing, everyone would have a good reason for staying home.

On Wednesday morning, the pastor called and, as gently as he could, told me he had to cancel my involvement in the revival. I knew it was going to happen, and I understood why, but Granddad's "never worth a damn" came roaring back into my head. My very first time out, and I had blown it. I was simply not good enough. I thought seriously about quitting school. I would never be a teacher or leader. I wondered if Mr. Tobman's offer was still open; I could move to Tulsa University.

Flo had not gone to the meetings. Our son was all she could handle. She would not let me be alone. She kept telling me that it was only my first time and that most people were not successful at anything with just one try.

On Monday morning, the pastor called and asked if he and the visiting preacher could come by our apartment. I really did not want to see them, but I could not think of any reason to prevent them coming. The visiting pastor was to catch a bus for home around one that afternoon. At eleven that morning, they came. The pastor explained that there had been serious difficulties in the church the previous week, which made for a bad beginning to the revival. It had nothing to do with me.

He continued, "After I told the congregation why you were not coming back, some of the people became upset with themselves and their rejection of your leadership. You were a victim of their orneriness, and nothing that happened was your fault. The people insisted that I come and apologize to you for the way they had acted. They then took up a thank-you offering of sixty dollars and sent it by me to give to you."

The two prayed with us and left. Flo smiled, and I cried as another memory came to mind: "Neither God nor God's people will ever forsake you." I looked at the gift (equal to two weeks of normal income for us), and the joy overrode all the negativity I was focusing on. Flo and I held each other, and I began to refocus and forget about quitting. Five weeks later, I began being asked to go with student preaching teams to different churches. I soon had more invitations to lead music than I could handle.

I needed to find work. I would work a week or a month or more — whatever each job required. I took any job available. I painted houses, hung wallpaper, and coached basketball and baseball for the YMCA. I sold home insulation and window coverings. I worked at a nursery making leis, funeral flower blankets for caskets, corsages, and church and home flower arrangements. I was also a part-time salesman and delivery boy for the nursery. I later managed and cooked in a small restaurant just off campus. I had three students from the university as waiters, waitresses and dishwashers. Summer came, business was slow, and the restaurant closed. This variety of jobs gave me the opportunity to learn people and business practices in a way that I could never get in any classroom; plus, they paid our bills.

I found a new job at the Armor Foods Company mill across town. For ten weeks, I worked seven hours five nights a week, powdering eggs for forty cents an hour. My job was packing the powdered eggs. The eggs were candled to make sure they were okay. They were then cracked by a dozen women working around one big metal bin. There were six bins. Each of the six bins held 150 gallons of raw shelled eggs. The eggs were gently whipped until the whites and yokes were thoroughly mixed. The eggs were then pumped under pressure through hose nozzles that fogged the eggs into the top area of a large heat-controlled vault. As the moisture was removed by the heat, the dried eggs floated down to a combination of continuous mechanical sweeps and conveyor belts. The belts with augurs carried the eggs to the packing room. I would move the receiver tube over a barrel or a box and fill the containers with the correct weight of powered eggs. The containers would be sealed and labeled. Another conveyor belt would take the container of eggs to either shipping or storage.

In addition to my salary, I was allowed to take no more than a pound (three dozen) of powdered eggs home each week. If the eggs were prepared right, they were fine; not good, but fine. We had them all the time in the Navy. For cooking, they were excellent.

Wayne, our second son was born. Flo and I learned one more important lesson: Contraceptives only have a chance to work if they are removed from the dresser drawer. I was in my junior year and was leading music on Sundays or at special meetings two or three times a month.

I graduated in three years with a B average. I still was not positive about the direction of my life. I drove to Fort Worth and spent time with the registrar of Southwestern Baptist Theological Seminary. He listened, and we talked. He encouraged me to come and take a semester of beginning courses. Perhaps then I would know if God was leading me into some type of ministry. I asked for an application.

I drove back to Abilene. Flo and I talked, and she made one thing clear: I should do what I felt was right, but she was not cut out to be a pastor's wife. I did not feel that a pastor was what I should be; however, I was being slowly convinced that I was to be in some kind of ministry.

I received a letter from the First Baptist Church in Tucumcari, New Mexico, inviting me to come to their church and talk to their minister search committee. The church was looking for a second staff member and they were interested in talking to me.

I talked to Prof, and he said, "I know the church and the pastor. It would be a good place for you;

Second son, Wayne.

however, I want you to think about something. If they ask you and you decide to go, you could cut off any further education. Now, if you go just a year or even a semester to the seminary, that will go on your resume and will open twice as many doors for you in the future."

With two boys, Flo was not eager to move that far away from parents and friends. I wrote the pastor in Tucumcari, thanked him for the invitation, and told him that God was leading me to get more education and experience before I moved to full-time church ministry.

One of Flo's sisters, Gertrude, lived in Dallas. She had been in touch with us and knew we were planning to move to Fort Worth, where there was no available housing. She wrote that she and Myron (her husband) would be at our home the following Friday. They were going to load our things into their and our cars and move us into their home until we could find a place to live. They did not ask us if we wanted to live with them, and they knew that we had two small boys. They came, and we moved into their house with their two children, Roger and Myra.

I went back to the place-ment office at the seminary and completed my enrollment. The lady at the desk handed me a note that had come from Bowles Memorial Baptist Church in Grand Prairie. The church was looking for a part-time music and education director.

The church was halfway between the seminary and where we were living in Dallas. I drove by the church. The building was small, but the community around it was

Flo's sister, Gertrude, and children.

growing. I stopped at the church building, but no one was there. I walked around the block and knocked on the door of one of the houses. A lady came to the door, and I introduced myself and asked if she knew anything about the church.

She said she was a member and that the pastor was away. He lived just down the street and would be back in two days. I thanked her and went home. Two days later, I went back and talked to the pastor. He asked me to come the following Sunday to meet some people and talk to the search committee. Flo and I went and met with the church people. I met with the committee.

The pastor told me the church would be given the information about us. If the church then wanted to move forward, he would contact me. A week later, we were asked to return. The church voted for me to come on staff the following week. I accepted and began my work.

Vacation Bible school was coming up. The planning and administration of it was handed to me. My only experience with VBS was riding my horse in a parade to promote it, although I had read a book on how to prepare for, staff, and conduct a vacation Bible school. I decided that the best plan for me was to go by the book, and it must have worked. We broke all attendance records for VBS at the church. I was elated. The parents, children and pastor were well pleased.

The woman who had given me the information about the church came to my office. I was planning music for the week. Without any greeting, she stunned me with the angry demand, "Why did you have our pastor here every day in VBS and made him talk to all those kids?"

I was not sure I heard right and asked her to repeat. I lit a firecracker. She told me that if I was going to stay in her church, I had better learn to listen and quit putting my work on the pastor. I just thought she was having a bad day and let it go.

The church grew, and so did I. My music training in college was focused on public school music and only loosely related to what was done in churches. It took me two months to learn that volunteers and early learners were adults who wanted to be treated as adults and coworkers, not as students. Half of my training went out the window. I majored on hymns and meaningful special music programs. We had to enlarge the choir area. We were out of space.

Flo and I moved to an apartment complex in Grand Prairie, on the main highway between Dallas and Fort Worth. I do not remember what the church paid me, but I needed a part-time job, and our car needed work. An automobile and body repair shop was across the highway from our apartment. I met with the owner and asked if I could exchange my work (painting his customer's cars) for his work (overhauling my engine and fixing my brakes). He was way behind in his painting, and we struck a deal. I could work when I was not at the seminary or at church and when no one else was in the shop.

Four weeks later, I was wet-sanding a coupe and heard brakes screeching, tires skidding and car horns blowing. I dropped everything, rushed outside and saw our four-year-old Steve in the middle of the four-lane highway. Flo's mother was there and was so scared that she could not move. Traffic was almost at a standstill. I rushed to Steve, picked him up and ran with him into the house. I left him with Flo and went back to the highway to tell the waiting people that he was scared but fine. I also added that, as soon as possible, we were moving. They were relieved that there had been no accidents and that the child was okay. His parents would recover.

The next day, I went to the Veterans Affairs office in Dallas and applied for a G.I. home building loan. In a week, the loan was approved. I hired a contractor who was a member of our church, and in six weeks, we moved into our new home.

Our church was in the process of putting up an education and office building. I worked with the men and made some good friends. Flo and I were feeling good and enjoying our own home; we felt we were where we should be. Unknown to us and most of the members of the church, my lady "friend" was more than unhappy with me. I was in with the wrong group in her church. I had worked with the county commissioner and had enlisted several men from the wrong group to build a ball field on the edge of our community.

The Trinity River flooded, and I had enlisted several of our people to help those caught in the floods. We mudded out and cleaned the houses as well as we could. In doing this, I had (according to my critic) neglected my church work. I also had a part-time job. That was fine; she understood that, but I was working for a public high school and had been hired by a non-Christian board member to drive the school bus.

The church was still growing, and the open spirit was excellent, but an undercurrent within the church membership was building. Two months later, the pastor came to our house.

"Edd, we have a problem. Mrs. (omitted) has gone through our church records and found an article in the bylaws that requires any new staff member, including the pastor, to serve ninety days and then be voted on by the church to stay or be removed from office."

"I have been here six months," I said.

"I know," he replied. "She has most of her family with her. One man told me she was not going to back off until you leave. He said that he would not vote against you, but that was all that he could do."

"Okay," I said, "You have my resignation. I will not start my ministry and have on my record that I was the cause of a church split."

"What shall I tell the church?" he asked.

"That I quit. They are smart enough to figure it out."

He shook his head and said, "I don't like this and may get fired myself, but you will get a full month's pay. I will then go with you to meet other pastors and let them know that none of this is in any way related to you, your work or your character."

Later, Flo asked me what I was going to do. I answered, "Pack up. We are going to Grandpa and Grandma today."

Steve and Wayne heard and began to shout in excitement; they headed for their bedroom and started throwing clothes on the floor to take with them. While I had heard and understood the pastor, that old feeling of not being worth anything still came back. "Maybe," I thought, "I should just forget about what I thought was my call to ministry."

We stayed with Flo's parents in Kamay for a week. We never went back to the church in Grand Prairie but remained friends with most of the congregation. We later learned the lady's real motive: She had convinced the church that her nephew should be called as music director.

I went to work in a dye factory that dyed Army and Navy uniforms for people who wanted the uniform quality but not military colors. I continued classes at the seminary. To feed my family, I took any job I could find. I delivered new phone books in the suburbs and worked for the post office during holiday seasons. Any kind of job was almost impossible to find, and my G.I. education funds were running out. Our 20-year-old Chevy had seen all the road it could safely see. I could not drive on the ice-covered highway, and I missed too many classes at the seminary. I was failing in one class and borderline in another. Rather than have that bad period on my record, I withdrew from the seminary.

I was a member of the Naval Reserve, but job hunting and family took up all my time. I could not attend the necessary required meetings. I received a letter from the Navy Department with an honorable discharge, along with an official notice stating that I was not recommended for reenlistment. Two weeks after I received that notice, my reserve unit was activated and sent to Korea. We were ever thankful that I had been unable to attend my required training meetings.

While I was still questioning my life, my ministry and what to do, Pastor Taylor of the First Baptist Church in Grand Prairie called. He asked me to come to his office to talk to him. I went, having no idea what he might want. He told me that their church music director was leaving and that the church would like me to serve as interim music director until a replacement could be found. They would pay me a little more than I had been getting at my previous church. I accepted and led the music for four months that included a special Christmas music program.

A concert music director from a major city (I do not recall his name or where he was from) attended our service one Sunday morning. After the service, he came and asked if he could talk to me. He was very kind and asked if I would mind if he gave me a couple of suggestions.

"You have a natural ability, but you are too rigid. Relax! While you relax, control the movement of you wrist."

He then demonstrated and had me practice for ten minutes while he hummed.

"Good. Now do it that way, and you will do all right." He shook my hand and walked away.

Eight weeks later, the new music director was called to the church. I again had no job and no income. I walked the streets looking for work with cardboard in my shoes because I could not pay for resoles. Our refrigerator had only enough food and milk for breakfast for our two boys.

Even though I was no longer the music director at First Baptist, I sang in the choir. There was an unwritten rule that if you missed rehearsal on the Wednesday night before the choir sang the following Sunday, you sat out. I had not made it to the Wednesday night rehearsal — and so, for the first time in several weeks, I sat in the pew with Flo. For some reason, we had not made it to Sunday school where she normally gave our weekly offering. Five dollars was our tithe (about thirty dollars today). It was all the money we had, and I had four mouths to feed.

Since Flo did not give our tithe money in Sunday school, I had the five dollars with me. The offering time came, and the ushers moved down the aisle. The offering plate came by, but I could not let go of that five-dollar bill. There was a new usher on duty, and he made a mistake: Instead of sending the offering plate down the next row, he sent it back down ours.

"Okay, God, that's enough," I whispered, and the five-dollar bill went into the offering plate.

Flo has said many times that she was glad it was me who was holding the money, because all she could think of was our two boys and no food. We walked out of church and started for our car. Mr. Cook, the father of one of our seminary friends, called out, "Edd, wait up!"

He and his wife came and asked if we had plans for lunch. We told them that we had no plans, and they asked us to go to their home and have lunch with them. When we were in our car, Flo and I almost cried with gratitude. We followed them to their home. Flo helped to prepare lunch, and we had a great meal.

Mr. Cook was a commercial delivery driver for Planters merchandise. He not only had peanuts but also cookies, assorted snacks and items from the entire varied line of their merchandise. He insisted that we take four big sacks of food home with us. Mrs. Cook packed all that was left from our lunch and included a quart of milk for the boys. We had never mentioned our situation. It took the drive home and the rest of the afternoon for us to absorb what we knew God had done.

The next morning, when I went to get the mail, there was a letter from Bob and Gene Campbell, our close friends from Hardin Simmons. A year before, they had been on their way from the seminary to a church in south Texas. They had stopped at our home, visited and spent the night with us. Their note said, "Thanks for helping us. For some reason, you are on our minds this morning. We felt like we needed to send you something. Enclosed is a check for seven dollars." (Today it would be close to forty dollars.)

We sat, read the note again, and then cried and thanked God for what had happened.

One of our friends in Bowles Memorial Church was a salesman for Manor Bakery in Dallas. He had a bread route in the community where we lived. He had left loaves of bread and cookies for the boys with a note: "Manor is expanding, and they need drivers. With your school bus experience and sales ability, you should be able to get on."

I dressed and went to apply. I was hired by a good Methodist layman. I went to Sears and talked them into selling me a pair of cushioned black work shoes on thirty-day credit. I went to work on the following Monday.

From that day forward, our family was never without adequate income. We have not had all we wanted, but we have always had more than we actually needed. Some may say it was good fortune or a coincidence — but Flo and I know and unashamedly say that the giving of that five-dollar tithe opened the door for God to honor His promise to care for His own if we would just trust Him. The job and the shoes happened within a week after the five-dollar bill (which was not really ours) went to where it was supposed to go. Within three weeks, we paid off our debts and began to breathe easier, marveling at how God was in control of our lives.

I had worked for Manor Bakery a year when my back began to really bother me. I went to the doctor; after examining me, he had bad news: "You have rheumatoid arthritis in your lower back. You cannot continue your present job. The basket and bread are more weight than you are built to handle."

We had to have another car: Our 1940 Chevy had 120,000 miles on it. Our boys were outgrowing all their clothes. While we owned our home, we probably would have to start over. The possibility of now having to look for new job clouded my thinking. One of the men on my bread route was the supervisor for a large national insurance company. They were looking for an adjuster to work the western part of Texas. With my Navy background and sales abilities, he was convinced that I was the person they were looking for. He told me that, in the past five years, he had not been turned down for any request for new workers he had recommended. He was going to attach a personal letter about my background with my application and send both documents to the company bosses.

"Don't quit your job yet. It may take some time to get everything processed," he said.

I told Flo, and she was relieved. If I were hired, I would have a company car that we could use for personal needs. The salary was beyond belief, and I would get three full weeks of paid vacation.

Three weeks later, I was on my bread route and found a note on the insurance man's door. He wanted to see me when I came by on my next delivery. I returned and was excited; however, when I entered their living room, I could tell from the way he and his wife were acting that there was going to be bad news. Everyone involved in hiring for the company had agreed that I was perfect for the job, but I was nineteen days too young. The age cut-off for new employees was December first; my birthday is December nineteenth.

He had argued with them but was told, "If we give nineteen days now, it will be twenty and then thirty. If we do not stay with what we have, there will be no age requirements at all."

He apologized, and his wife came over to give me a hug. On the way home, I began to think about God being in charge, but my disappointment did not lift. I decided to seriously rethink finishing my education at the seminary and seeing what might happen. I went back to the bakery the next day and gave my two weeks' notice.

My route supervisor said, "If you are going to quit, just do it now!"

The Methodist sales manager called me in and asked what was going on. I explained what my doctor had said and told him that, after praying, I was convinced I needed to get back in school and finish my education. He wanted to know when school would start. I told him I needed to be there in six weeks. He asked if I could work those six weeks as a vacation temporary. I had no other job, and since I would be working multiple routes, he would be my route supervisor. I would have full income for another six weeks. In those six weeks, we were able to replace our thoroughly worn out 1940 Chevy. The fourth week, we put our house on the market. It sold in a week for what we owed on it. I went to the seminary and reenrolled and then went to housing to see if they had anything to offer. There was nothing.

I was walking down the steps to my car when the young lady with whom I had just spoken came running out of her office, waving a sheet of paper.

"Edd, wait! This just came in. This lady called and wants a student with small children. Go!"

I jumped in my car and hurried the fifteen blocks to the address she had given me. I got out of the car, looked over the upscale neighborhood and walked to the front door. I rang the door bell. A nice-looking, well-dressed middle-aged lady came to the door. She wanted to know who I was and what I was doing there. I explained that I was a seminary student and had been given this address to look at a possible place for my family and me to live while I was in school.

"I just called ten minutes ago," she said.

"I know. They gave this information to me ten minutes ago," I replied.

She invited me in. She wanted to know Flo's and my background and all about our two boys, and then it was settled. She took me to a garage apartment at the back of her large brick home. The apartment was on ground level, built beside and onto the back of the garage. It had a large kitchen, a dining area, a living room and two bedrooms with adjoining baths. There was a small deck with steps going down eight feet to a large grassy yard surrounded by a six-foot-high fence and bordered by blooming flowers and shrubs.

The lady told me I could have the apartment for fifty dollars a month, including utilities. If I wanted to mow her yard, she would take fifteen dollars off the rent. I took it. I paid her seventy dollars for two months and agreed to take care of the yard. I could not believe this. It was perfect for us, and I asked when we could move in.

"Anytime," she said, and handed me my key.

As I left, two other cars pulled up to look at the apartment.

The next day, I went back to Fort Worth with Flo and our two boys to look over the place. She and the boys were as impressed as I was. I took Flo and the boys to stay with my aunt, and I went job hunting.

I tried three businesses with no success. I then had two job offers: One was at a bakery, and another was with a utility company. Both would have wreaked havoc with any school schedule, so I put them on hold.

My last stop was the personnel office of the Fort Worth Star Telegram. They did not know of any openings, but if I wanted, I could go upstairs and meet an older gentleman who was the supervisor of the advertising department. I went and introduced myself; I then told him why I needed a job and that my first priority had to be finishing my graduate degree. I had to find a job that I could fit into my education program. He told me that the paper had no jobs like that. We talked a few minutes more, and I asked for an application form.

"Here it is, but it won't do you much good," he said, handing me the form.

"Maybe not now, but something might come up," I said, and I handed him my completed form.

He looked it over, put it in his desk, shook my hand and wished me luck.

The day I rented our apartment, I had also rented a mailbox. I used that address on all my applications for jobs. I left the Star Telegram and went to my aunt's home to visit for awhile. Flo got in the car, the boys crawled into the backseat, and we headed north. We spent the weekend with Flo's parents and went to the church in which we had grown up and were married. We had lunch with friends and drove back to Fort Worth on Monday morning. Flo was tired and wanted to go to Grand Prairie so she could begin packing for our move.

I wanted to go by the new apartment to take a break and let the boys play. I also wanted to go to the post office. She consented, knowing it would be a waste of time. I did not expect any mail, but I had never had any dealings with mailboxes that had to be opened with combination locks, and I wanted to practice. The box was at eye level, and something was inside. I fumbled and eventually opened the box. There was a letter from the Star Telegram asking me to come in the next day because they might have something. Early Tuesday morning, I went to the newspaper office and was again sent upstairs to see the gentleman I had spoken to four days before.

He smiled, asked me sit and said, "I like your attitude. Maybe we can work out something."

He picked up a two-inch stack of cards on his desk and said, "These are unpaid bills for advertising. I will pay for your gas and give you twenty percent of all you collect. You are to tell the people that they cannot advertise in our paper again until these are paid. If they want to send in advertising, take it — but they must pay you for it in advance. You can start tomorrow."

He handed me a city map and a note to the service station where I was to fuel my car. I picked up Flo and the boys and told Flo what I had been offered.

At home, we did not have a lot to move — but even with a borrowed trailer, it took most of two days. I began my job and worked early mornings and afternoons. I collected just over one hundred dollars the first day and seventy-five the next. I sectioned off the map and completed all my work in one area before moving to the next. Before classes started, I worked a minimum of eight hours each day.

When classes started, I cut back to five hours. I would go to work early and then go to class. At noon, I would have lunch with Flo and the boys. Afterward, I would work the accounts close to our home for two hours and then attend a late evening class or go to the library. I had very few late night calls. I had time for family and my classes. I was picking up regular advertising in addition to my collection work. My schoolwork was not exceptional, but I maintained a B average.

Two days before Thanksgiving, I came home to find the kitchen table covered with grocery sacks. Some were filled with bottles of milk and other drinks. I asked Flo where all this food had come from. She told me that her Sunday school class at First Baptist in Grand Prairie had adopted us for Thanksgiving and that three of the ladies had brought the food to us. Our cabinets and refrigerator were overloaded. We called some of our seminary friends and invited them to Thanksgiving dinner. Two couples with small children accepted, and we had one more glorious Thanksgiving Day.

The time arrived for our third son, Bruce, to be born. I took Wayne and Steve to my aunt's home, and she spoiled them for a week. On one of our worst stormy nights, I rushed Flo to the hospital. Within three hours, Bruce was born.

One night before Christmas, Flo and I had been singing carols with a group outside on the Hardin Simmons campus. Flo's hands shrunk from the cold, and her engagement ring fell off her finger and was never found. When I was leaving the hospital the night Bruce was born, I had Flo's wedding ring in my pocket, but I somehow lost it shortly afterward. We now had three boys, and my wife had no rings to show that she was even engaged or married! We later bought some single bands to replace what we had lost.

Four days after his birth, Bruce and his mother came home. We moved to seminary housing just off campus. The wives in the other apartments helped Flo, and Flo's mom came for two weeks.

Six months later, I was called to the newspaper manager's office. I was being promoted and was given a specific section of the city to work. My section included downtown Fort Worth and the area where we lived. The transition would happen in two weeks. All my work at school and on the job was current. I had been able to work out a deal with an auto sales company, and we had bought a new four-door

Dodge large enough for our growing family.

Bill Atchely, a friend and classmate, was the president of the Tennessee Baptist Convention's annual training, to be held in Knoxville. He and another friend, Sam Deboard, approached me about taking my car to go to that meeting. They would take care of gas and food. I took a week of vacation from work and school. We three drove to Sevierville, Tennessee, where Bill's family owned a mortuary. I had driven most of the way and was beat, so I went to bed.

Bill had meetings and Sam had families to take care of the next day. Bill's brother knocked on my door. He came in and asked me if I had any problem with being around dead bodies. I had been around a few while I was in the Navy, so I was okay. He asked me to go with him to a place called Pigeon Forge, in the Smoky Mountains. I agreed to go.

A few miles before Gatlinburg, we turned onto a mountain trail and followed a creek for a mile, finally stopping in front of a shack that looked ready to fall over. I had been raised in the Dust Bowl during the Depression, but I had never seen poverty like this. Vine-covered trees grew so close that the sun barely peeked through. The privy door was halfway open, and the smell almost knocked me down. The inside of the shack was just as bad. One small room served as bedroom, kitchen and living space. Mold and mildew were everywhere. It looked as if no one had cleaned anything, including the sheets and covers on the bed, in weeks.

Third son, Bruce.

I was given rubber gloves. We placed a clean bed sheet we brought from the mortuary next to the body of an older woman. Another clean bed sheet from the mortuary was placed over the woman. We used those two sheets to protect us from any physical contact with the body as we carefully lifted the woman onto the sheet we had laid out beside her. We then folded both sheets into a sort of sling, moved the lady onto the gurney, loaded her into the ambulance and delivered the body to the mortuary.

The remoteness of the area staggered me. On the plains in the west, we knew where everyone lived or could live. Where there were trees or a windmill, there would be a house or a barn. Where this older lady had lived and died, anyone could have lived less than a half mile away and would have had no way of knowing if there was any need for help.

The next day, Bill and I went to Knoxville for the conference. I had never been in the southern part of our country and was overwhelmed by the greenery and the humidity. Smoke and black ash covered the buildings. I knew coal was the fuel for homes and businesses, but I never dreamed of the extent to which smoke and ash could cover homes or even a city.

The day we were to leave, Bill's family gave us eggs, hams, apples and other foods. We drove back to Fort Worth in time for me to rest, wrestle with the boys and get back to work.

My new area of work cut my time on the job by four hours a week, so everything looked better for us. Since I no longer covered the entire city and was given several repeat advertisers, my income increased. Two months later, I was called into our boss' office.

"How many hours a week do you work?" he asked.

"I do not keep a log, but it is close to twenty-five or thirty hours," I answered.

"You keeping up your schoolwork?" he asked.

"I am in the B area and am doing okay," I replied.

"What else are you involved in?" he wanted to know.

Most afternoons, when the weather permitted, I took Flo and our three boys to a park for a picnic. I would make two or three calls while they played. I would come back, and we would go home. I did not tell him any of this; however, I could not make sense of where the conversation was going.

"Okay, here is the problem. There are five of you working in collections and advertising. You are the only part-time temporary employee. You work a third of the hours they do, and yet your paychecks are equal to or up to a third larger than theirs each month." (While this information was supposed to confidential, it had gotten out.)

"Maybe it is because I work when I work and don't drive all over town doing my job," I countered.

"That may be, but in order to keep our regular employees happy and working, we cannot let one part-time worker make more than our four regulars. I don't want to, but I have to cut your commission to fifteen percent," he stated.

"So I make more money for you and get penalized and paid less. That is stupid," I said.

"It may be, but next month's check will have to be figured that way," he replied.

I was angry. I liked my job but evidently was too good at it. What was being done to me now was discrimination against initiative and good honest "horse sense." I was not in any union (I had only been in one during the time I worked at the egg powdering plant) and could do little to change my situation. I thought of quitting.

I had a two-week break from classes and used my extra time to make more calls. Even with my five percent cut in commission, my check was still a third larger than those of the full-timers.

Life has a way of balancing out. The Star Telegram was involved with Billy Graham's Fort Worth Crusade. Amon Carter, the owner of the Star Telegram, wanted the paper to back Billy Graham in every way possible. I was able to personally meet and talk with Billy Graham and his staff. I sang in the choir, worked some as an usher and met with small groups in different churches in town. I was an extra in the filming of Graham's first movie, "Mr. Texas." I made very little money with the Graham Crusade, because large agencies handled most of their advertising; however, to be with the team and participate in their prayer meetings and learn how they operated was worth far more to me than money.

My cousin Eddy Marie, who had lived in San Diego, now lived in Fort Worth. She and her mother had kept Steve and Wayne when Bruce was born. Eddy worked as a hairdresser in a beauty shop three miles away. She called me one day and whispered so softly that I could hardly hear her.

"Edd, listen closely. I have just a little time. There is a young fellow in our shop with a gun. He has made no threats but is angry at his wife. Will you come?"

I thought, "Why me? Why not the police?" All the way to the beauty shop I tried to come up with an approach. I prayed hard for guidance and a sense of calm. I parked a block down the street. I walked to the door and opened it. The beauty shop lights were on, and I commented as I walked in, "You folks open this late? My wife is looking for a hairdresser. I saw your sign and stopped by to see when she might be able to come."

The young man looked at me and tried to hide the pistol he was carrying. I tried to ignore him, but the young man kept following me with his eyes. I asked him if we had met before. He ignored me but made no threatening moves, so I kept talking.

"You are dressed like you may have been in the Army. Were you?" I asked.

"Yeah, four years, and it stunk," he sneered.

"Me, I was Navy, and I learned the hard way that killing never settles anything."

"Guess you might be right," he said.

I looked him. "If you believe that, you want to hand me that gun?" I asked.

He looked at me and handed me the pistol. I made sure the safety was on and put it in my pocket.

"You gonna call the cops?" he asked.

"What for? You did not threaten me. You want to talk?" I asked.

"Guess we can," he said, and he sat down.

The shop lights and sign were turned off. With just the street-lights providing illumination, we talked for twenty minutes. Mostly, I answered his questions about my relationship with God and how it had made Flo's and my marriage one of love and trust. After that, he was ready to talk to his wife.

He moved over and joined his wife, who had remained silent during the conversation, and they quietly talked. They both then promised me that they were going to talk to a friend of theirs who was the pastor of a church close to where they lived. With that, they left.

Eddy hugged me and cried. "I could not call the police. They were just two nice mixed-up kids who needed to talk to someone. I hope you are not mad at me for calling you."

"Mad? No. Scared? Yes, and I will think up some way to get even."

We hugged and I went home. The next morning, I took a good look at the pistol. It was fully loaded, the safety worked, and it had a good balance. It had only one problem — the firing pin had been removed. I had no idea what that kid did in the Army, but he knew nothing about pistols. This gun was useless as a weapon.

Eight

1949-1954

From Woodward, Oklahoma, to Springfield, Missouri

Steve had developed a growth on his neck just below his right ear. The doctors had placed him in the local hospital for tests. He was examined by six different doctors. A biopsy was performed, and they agreed to try a new mycin-based drug to see if it would kill the infection.

The next day, I was contacted about going to a church in Woodward, Oklahoma. The pastor was on campus to talk to me about joining their staff as music and education minister.

I had been recommended to the pastor by Dr. Bill House, my religious education professor. Brother McCracken, the pastor, and I talked three times over two days, and then he left. Four days later, he called and invited me to come to Woodward to lead the music for a church revival. I talked to the Steve's doctor. He saw no problem with Steve's health that would interfere with my being gone a week. Steve still had a sizable swelling on the right side of his neck and face that the doctors were attempting to cure.

I let the pastor know I would come, notified the paper and my clients, and drove to Woodward, Oklahoma. The town of Woodward is in the heart of Tornado Alley. A few years before I was asked to visit, they had a bad twister that had killed over a hundred people. Almost every family in town had lost relatives or had major injuries. Most talk was about the thunderstorms and past deaths and damage.

Because of the threat of a storm one evening, our church service was canceled. I stayed in a home that had a large, well-furnished room upstairs; the room had been rebuilt after being blown off during the last bad storm.

One night after our church service, I went with eight of the members to a small restaurant where we enjoyed coffee, snacks and fellowship. It was late when I got to bed, and I was having trouble going to sleep. I finally dozed off in the midst of heavy rain, thunder and lighting. Two hours later, I was awakened by a loud rumbling sound. Visibility was zero. The weird roaring became louder, like that of an approaching tornado. The roaring suddenly increased so much that I grabbed my pillows and blankets and was ready to roll off the bed to the floor. I was shaking and worrying about Flo and the boys and what would happen to them if I was the victim of a storm. I was at the edge of the bed, ready to drop to the floor, when the rumbling train sounded its warning horns. I did not sleep much that night.

On Tuesday, I tried to call Flo. I could not get her. I called back Wednesday, and she answered.

"I called last night and missed you," I said.

"I know, I was at the hospital," she replied.

"You had to take Steve back?" I asked.

"No, Steve is okay. I was there all night with Wayne."

I was really troubled by what she told me. Wayne had fallen out of the backseat of our neighbor's car and hit his head on the curb. The doctors kept him awake all night and watched him for convulsions. After a thorough exam, they sent Wayne home. I was 150 miles away, and my wife was alone with three small kids, two of whom were hurt or sick. I was going home.

Flo sensed what I was thinking. "There is no need for you to come home. Wayne is fine. Our neighbors have Steve and Bruce. You stay there until you finish what they asked you to do."

"Okay, but I am coming home Sunday afternoon." Disturbed, I hung up.

We finished the revival on Sunday morning. With a nice check for my services, I headed home. On Monday morning, I went to the doctor to get a report on both Steve and Wayne. Both were doing fine, but we needed to closely watch Wayne for two more days.

On Friday, a letter came from Woodward First Baptist Church. The members had voted for me and my family to come and be a part of the church as soon as possible. I answered and agreed to be there in four weeks. I turned in my resignation at the Star Telegram, effective in two weeks — and in three weeks, I finished my coursework at the seminary.

For us, moving was simple. We had very little furniture. I had two suits. Flo had maybe five dresses. I bought Steve and Wayne matching overcoats and caps, and we had plenty of baby clothes for Bruce.

The church in Woodward sent two men with a truck to help us move. We moved into a nice house on the main street going through Woodward. It was the largest home we had ever lived in. My salary was three hundred dollars a month, with house and utilities included. The money was about the same as I had been making at the news-paper; however, we now had a house with utilities provided, and I was doing the work I felt God had been leading me to do.

On our first Sunday, I led the choir and the congregation in music. The pianist, the choir and I had worked together for a week. We were well-acquainted with each other, and the worship service was great. At the close of the service, Flo and I joined the church. Brother McCracken, the pastor, asked the church members to remain seated.

The pastor then dropped a bombshell! He announced that he would be resigning as pastor and would be leaving to go to another church in four weeks. Everyone in the congregation was stunned. I was shocked. I was twenty-four years old and in my first full-time ministry position. In addition to the education and music programs, I would be responsible for our Sunday evening services, which were broadcast on the local radio station. I would also teach a thirty-minute Bible study on the radio each Tuesday morning.

My first few weeks were taken up with adjusting to full-time ministry, making our house livable and learning my additional church responsibilities. We bought some furniture and other items to make the place feel and look like a home. I spent most of my time learning what I would need to do when the pastor left. We would have guest preachers coming to preach most Sunday mornings. Most would not be there for Sunday or Wednesday evenings.

Because of the distance they lived from the church, many farmers and others did not attend Sunday evening services. To increase attendance, we began an after-service fellowship with fifteen of our young people. We played contemporary church music and had a sharing time, some games and light refreshments furnished by the church. Parents and older youth who were waiting on the young people began similar programs of their own.

Our evening service attendance also began to increase. We focused on music and personal testimonies, and included a brief message. In six weeks, our evening service attendance had increased by fifty percent.

Over the course of four months, with the help of the deacons and church members, we grew in membership and attendance. We reorganized the Sunday school and set up a training program for new leaders and teachers. The church rallied around Flo and me. Even with no pastor, our church grew. I began to get invitations from neighboring churches to lead music for special services and revivals.

Our director of missions for the association asked me to help set up a leader training event for twelve of our churches. We did three workshops and trained three leaders from each church, one for children, one for youth and one for adults. These trained leaders would be the teachers for a week in their own churches. More than fifty people responded at our kickoff meeting. At the end of the week when the reports came in, we had sixty newly trained Bible study leaders in our twelve churches. Our church took over the pastor's home next door to care for additional youth and adults.

In five months, the church called a new pastor. The church bought a house five blocks away for the pastor. When H.B. (only initials will be used) came, he and I seemed to get off to a good start. I was able to relax and enjoy my work and focus on personal contact with people in town and in the farming community.

Two car salesmen were in our church. One was sales manager for the General Motors dealership, and the other owned the Chrysler-Plymouth franchise. The sales manager was a deacon, and his wife was a Bible study leader. The owner of the other dealership was not a member, but his wife was very active in the church. I spent most of my time with the owner, because he wanted me to help him clarify some problems he was having with Christianity.

At first, this did not raise any questions, but it later became an issue between H.B. and me. When H.B. was being interviewed by the pastor search committee, I was asked by the committee chairman to sit in on one of the meetings. In response to one of the questions, H.B. answered, "Some members of the church where I am now pastor think I am a dictator, but I am not."

He was not a dictator; he just insisted that everything be done his way. He had been an officer in the Navy during World War II, whereas I had been a lowly seaman. He was also at least fifteen years older than me. For two months, we got along fine. I took care of my responsibilities in the office, led the music on Sundays and taught a young adult Bible class that we had recently started. Our new class began with five couples. After two months, we had twelve couples attending regularly.

I am a people person and spent most of my time out of the office with people. I would finish my office work and then let the church secretary know where I would be and when I would be back. My timing was guesswork at best. Farmers, ranchers and businesspeople could not function effectively on my schedule; I had to work around theirs.

My Bible teaching began to cause trouble between H.B. and me. According to him, the people in my class were not living right. Some played cards; others went to motion picture shows. Some took their families out of church for less spiritual events. Some participated in "mixed bathing" (people of opposite sex swimming together in public), and others drank wine. I was their Bible teacher, but I was apparently not strict or conservative enough in my teaching of the Bible.

One week, I was leading a training event for twenty of our teachers and leaders. Right in the middle of my presentation, Pastor H.B. loudly asked, "Why has this not been covered before now?"

I was stunned. I answered, as politely as I could, "We received the study material last week."

"No good reason," he answered.

It took me and our teachers a few minutes to get back on track, but the effectiveness of the meeting had been killed. After six months, one of our neighboring pastors called. He asked me to meet him for breakfast. I had done a leadership training event in his church. I thought that was what he wanted to talk to me about.

When we had finished our meal, he began. "You know you have

serious problem," he said.

"Which one?" I laughed. He then informed me, "I have known H.B. for a long time. You need to look now for another church. He is not going to let you stay in Woodward."

"Why?" I asked. "We are growing. We are now the largest church in the county. We have even started a new work in the north part of town. The offerings are off, but the drought regularly causes that."

"It is simple. He cannot control you. You are too popular with the people in the church and community. I have a friend who is pastor of a growing church in Missouri. They are looking for someone like you to take over their church education program. I would like to send him your name."

"You think this is that serious?" I asked.

He laughed and told me that he liked me, but that he was not about to drive forty miles just to eat breakfast with me. I gave him permission to contact his friend in Missouri.

Several of the church members began to ask Flo and me how they might help us. Flo and I were last to see the seriousness of our problem. When the former pastor left, I had become their acting pastor by default for three months. I had counseled, visited the sick and reached out to people. Many still came to me for discussions that a pastor would normally handle. A church can have only one ministerial leader; no one, regardless of his title, could ever be the pastor while the role was filled by someone else. Our congregation as a whole had not released me from that ministerial role.

Six weeks later, I was asked to come to Springfield, Missouri, to meet with the pastor and church leaders. I had bought a new car, a Plymouth, from the wrong dealer.

My former friend, the sales manager for General Motors, was now chairman of the deacons. H.B. had gone to him to talk about my unwillingness to cooperate and the other problems I was causing. A meeting of the deacons was called, and, for the first time, I was purposely not invited. Flo and I talked. She was as much aware as I was, and maybe even more, of what was happening between H.B. and me.

"What are you going to do?" she asked.

"Three things," I said. "One, I am going to that meeting and handing the deacons my written resignation. It will be effective in four weeks. I will walk out with no questions and no discussion. Two, tomorrow I will drive to Fort Worth and enroll in two classes at the seminary to clear up my graduation requirements. I am two points below the grade average necessary for my master's degree. I can bring that average up with one short course, but I want to take another while I am there. Three, I want you and the boys to be ready to go to Springfield when I get back from Fort Worth."

"You have no way of knowing if the church in Missouri is going to ask you to come as part of their staff," she said.

"Well, if H.B. does not get to them, I have a good chance," I replied.

I did walk in and give the deacon my resignation with no hello, no goodbye and no discussion. The next day, we left for Kamay. Flo had decided to go to Kamay and spend time with her parents while I was in Fort Worth. I had filled our new Plymouth with gas the week before. I had driven to two farms, and the fuel gauge showed over half a tank of gas. We drove south through Elk City, and the gauge showed over a quarter of a tank of gas. There was an all-night station thirty miles south of Elk City that I had used before.

Ten miles south, we were climbing a hill, and the car began to shudder. Just as we reached the top where the ground leveled out, the car's motor quit. I turned off the ignition switch, waited a minute and turned it back on. The fuel gauge now showed empty. Flo, our three boys and I were stranded late at night and had no help. I had not been able to pull off the road. Flo and I, thankful that this car was lighter than our previous one, were able to turn the car around and head back toward Elk City.

Those of you who have lived on the plains will see no problem with this. The wind was blowing steadily at thirty miles an hour. We opened all four doors. Flo was driving. I got behind the car and began to push. With the wind blowing, I got the car rolling and had to run to get inside. On the downhill slope, we coasted ten miles to a service station. We filled the gas tank, picked up some food and went to Kamay. I spent the night there and left the next morning for Fort Worth, where I spent the night with my aunt and cousins who lived a mile from the seminary.

The next morning, I went to the seminary and visited the office of one of my favorite professors, Dr. T.B. Maston. I told him about being two points short of getting my master's degree.

"Is that dumb rule still on the books?" he asked.

I told him what information I had received. What I wanted now was to enroll in one of his ethics classes and in one other Bible course.

"We can work that out," he said as he picked up the phone. He called registration and made the arrangements for both classes for me.

I thanked Dr. Maston and was on my way to the office to finish my registration when I met Dr. Foy Bernard in the hall. She had been a timely and God-sent messenger for me when I left Grand Prairie. She stopped me in the hall and said that, if I had time, she would like to talk with me. I told her that all I had to do was sign a couple of papers and I would be free. I went to registration, finished enrolling in my two summer classes and then went to her office.

"I am so glad to see you. How are you doing?" she asked.

I briefly told her of my work at the Star Telegram and the present situation in Woodward.

"You have any prospects?" she wanted to know.

I told her about my invitation to come to Springfield to be interviewed.

"I told you it would work, didn't I?" she said.

We both laughed, remembering an earlier conversation when everything had gone wrong at Bowles Memorial Church and I had lost two jobs. I had come to drop out of the seminary. After I had then been turned down for the insurance adjuster job, I knew that I was in a hopeless situation.

I had lost all faith in myself and knew that, while God had not made a mistake, I had. I had not told Flo why I went to the seminary that day. I came to cut all ties with the seminary and then to find some secular work. I was convinced that I was not the type of person God could use in any kind of church-related work. Dr. Bernard had intercepted me that day and invited me to her office. She had asked me to pull up a chair across from her at her desk.

"You look down and defeated. Do you want to talk?" she had asked.

Poor woman, I had unloaded on her. All I could think of was my repeated failures and how they had continued to multiply and how I felt like I made a mess of nearly everything I touched. Of course, my grandfather's words had never been erased from my mind. In response, Dr. Bernard had said with a big smile, "So you think that you are a failure and have no future in God's work and you want to quit. Well, I have a guaranteed solution for you."

I looked at her like she was crazy, but she just sat and smiled and repeated, "I do, and I will give it to you if you will agree to take it."

"How can I agree when I don't know what it is?" I stammered.

"A little faith in me might help," she said, smiling again.

I was desperate; I did not want to quit, but I could not go on the way I was going. "Okay, I know you, I appreciate what you are, and I do trust you."

She had then put her hands on her desk, leaned forward and said, "If you are asked to do God's work, whatever it is, try. If you are as bad as you think you are and you fail, you will not be asked again. You will not have to make the decision to quit; it will be made for you. Now, look at me. Will you not give up trying?"

The memory of that conversation came back as Dr. Bernard and I stood together many months later. I was crying. We did not hug, but the feeling expressed was more than that of just a handshake.

I regained some composure and said, "Well, I am going to Missouri this weekend and will find what there is to learn."

We walked out together. At my car, Dr. Bernard put her hand on my arm, turned me to face her and said, "You have potential you have not yet discovered. Don't you quit on me or on God." With that, she smiled and left.

I left to get Flo and the boys in Kamay. On my way, what Dr. Maston, Dr. Barnard and Dr. House had done for me began to register. Those three people, who knew me well, had not given up on me even though I had given up on myself. While it was not public, I made the fourth and fifth commitments of my life.

Number four was that I would not let my three boys go through life feeling unloved or unworthy of what they felt God wanted them to do.

Number five was that, if those three recognized leaders in education and ministry thought I was worth salvaging, I was going to do whatever I felt God leading me to do and quit worrying about whether I was worthy or not.

I drove to Kamay and spent some time with Flo's family. We then loaded the car and headed back to Woodward. We took time to wash our clothes and reload our car and then continued on to Springfield, Missouri. We had rooms in a nice motel and went to Grant Avenue Baptist Church on Sunday morning. We met some members and attended a young adult Bible class. The boys went to their Sunday school rooms. Flo and I were introduced at the morning worship service. We were taken to lunch by Bob Burrows and his family. Bob was the Sunday school director, a deacon and the assistant manager of the J.C. Penney store downtown.

After lunch, we returned to the church. Mrs. Burrows took Flo and the boys to the nearby park while I met with the pastor, the deacons and church leaders. We talked, and I answered questions for two hours. At four o'clock, the interview was over, and my family and I left for home. We stopped in Tulsa for the night and drove to Woodard the next day. On Friday, the pastor, Glen Bryant and Bob Burrows called to tell me that the Springfield church had voted for me to come as Minister of Education in four weeks.

H.B. wanted me to leave immediately. The young adults and other members rebelled. They insisted I be paid for the month. They set the date for a church going-away party. All I remember was that the church grounds were full of people. There was more food than twice as many people could eat. They showered us with gifts and a money tree of three hundred dollars.

I had begun attending my classes in Fort Worth. Flo and the boys would go with me half the time and stay with Flo's parents in Kamay. On our way to Woodward one night, we came over a hill and found eight cows in the middle of the highway between Kamay and Electra. I hit my brakes and thought I was safely through the herd. One cow abruptly turned back and ran toward the headlights of our car. The right front fender of the car hit her head, which turned her rear end into the right side of our new Plymouth. You can imagine what that side of the car smelled and looked like.

Gratefully, no one was hurt. The right fender and headlight were heavily damaged. The door jamb between the two doors on the right side was bent inward about two inches. It was not raining, but it was cold. People in a car well behind us drove to Electra and came back with Texas Highway Patrol. After taking statements, the officers gave me a copy of the report: "Plymouth sedan collided with one Hereford cow. Cause of accident: cow had no lights."

We went back to Kamay and spent a restless night with Flo's parents. Wayne ran to their house shouting, "Grandma, we had a cow wreck!"

With no problem, we drove on home the next morning. For the rest of the week, our cow wreck was all Wayne could talk about. The insurance company took care of the repairs. I had a rental to use for going back and forth to Fort Worth for classes.

Our car was repaired in time for us to move to Springfield. One of the members of the church had a truck with a covered bed; he and two others moved us to Springfield for the cost of gas. We insisted that the least we could do was to take care of their meals. The house the church wanted for us was not ready, so we were placed in boarding house half a block from the church. I still had three weeks of classes at the seminary. I would catch the "Katy" passenger train at the station a mile from our house after services on Sunday evening. I would sleep on the train and arrive at Fort Worth at seven the next morning. I could catch a bus to the campus and eat breakfast in the cafeteria. There were no classes on Monday; I spent that day in the library.

My aunt and cousin still lived a half mile from the seminary. I spent my nights with them. I had classes early in the morning on

Tuesdays and Thursdays. Wednesday was another library day. On Thursday at two o'clock in the afternoon, I would catch the train back to Springfield.

Most of my three-week trips were routine; however, on one of my trips, the first passenger car going home was crowded. In the car behind, there were only a dozen people. I found a double seat with no one close. I took out my books and began to study. When the conductor came through to punch my ticket, he looked at me and seriously asked, "Fellow, you sure you want to ride in this car?"

I looked around the car. It was half-empty, and I asked him if there was a problem. He just shook his head, punched my ticket and, mumbling to himself, walked off. I did not realize until we stopped in Tulsa that the car I was riding in was segregated for blacks.

My last trip was for exams. I finished mine in time to go by and thank my two professors. I looked for Dr. Foy Bernard, but she was off-campus. I went to my aunt's home and packed my clothes. I took her and my cousin to a nice restaurant. We shared our week's events with each other. I took a bus to the train station and went home. Three weeks later, I was notified that I had received two A's and congratulated by my two professors. I was six points above the necessary grade for my master's degree. The next graduation was set for January, five months off.

Flo and the boys enjoy the Ozarks.

While I was yo-yoing to and from Fort Worth, Flo, with help from ladies of the church, was able to spend time with the kids at a large park three blocks away. She became acquainted with most members of the church. On Saturdays, when possible, we had family day. We explored the Ozarks and the river country west and south of the city.

The church furnished our housing and provided four hundred dollars a month salary. We still owed some on Steve and Wayne's hospital bills, and we had bought some furniture. The money tree funds had kept us current. In two weeks, we were moved into a house with a fenced-in backyard, four blocks away from the church. We had not unpacked everything while in the apartment. After we moved into our new home, I had stacked the packing boxes just outside the back door. I was going to break them down later for the dump. I came home one afternoon, and the boxes had been moved. I went outside and started to get after the boys for messing things up. Before I could say anything, all three began to laugh and holler, "You it! You it!"

They had made some kind of obstacle course out of the boxes. I had to crawl through the boxes while they chased me around the yard. I played until I was tired out. I sat down and looked.

The boys had toys, but they had pushed them aside. They made their own game by themselves. They were learning to do for themselves rather than have someone else do for them. I forgot about getting rid of the boxes until the rains came and destroyed them.

I was concerned about our reputation for honesty. I wrote my (banker) Uncle Eck who lived in Dalhart and asked if he could loan me five hundred dollars. I told him that I did not want to leave any unpaid bills in Woodward or Fort Worth. Two weeks later, I received a letter from him, telling me to go to a certain bank a mile from the church and to ask for a specific man. At the bank, I told the clerk who I was and who I needed to see. In a few minutes, the bank manager came and introduced himself. He took me into his office and handed me a bank book with an opening account of five hundred dollars. We talked and visited for a few minutes; he gave me four of his business cards and told me to take them to three different stores close by. The manager at each store would open an account for me with discounts of up to twenty percent for my purchases.

We paid our bills in Woodard and settled my school accounts. We repaid my uncle in six months. We had bought new clothes for all of us and began to fit into the community. (Two years later, my aunt refunded that five hundred dollars to us.)

I was asked to lead the churches in our association in a vacation Bible school clinic. It went well, I thought. I did my thing, not someone else's, but one lady did not like that. She called and complained to my pastor. I did not do a thing right. I was completely unprepared. I thought nothing about her or what she had said and prepared for our own VBS.

We had a large group. We took them to the park for recreation and picnics each day. The kids, the teachers, the workers and the parents were pleased and expressed appreciation for the school.

A week later, the pastor called me in and asked why I did not have more crafts. I thought I had enough. He disagreed, but I just put that off as us having two different opinions.

Our church was growing. We did not have space; something had to be done. One suggestion was to build a new nursery and children's facility, which we desperately needed. I asked about the space for the youth, because we were running over as it was.

The chairman of the deacons, Bob Borrows, asked if I'd had any church building experience. I told him of the courses in church planning and construction I had taken in seminary and how I had been involved in three church education building projects. The deacons wanted to know if I could I come up with a balanced plan for growth.

I agreed to try. My plan was to sit in on different classes, to talk to the teachers individually and to get their input on what was needed now and what would be needed in three to five years. Our Sunday school teachers helped me, and we began watching, questioning, and learning what we might need. In eight weeks, we reported what all of us working together had learned.

Every age group, from infants to seniors, had a regular attendance of between eighty and ninety percent of capacity. Eighty percent is usually the ceiling for any continued growth. I shared pictures to show the crowding problem in all age groups. I then suggested that a committee be elected by the church to develop and bring before the church some recommendations.

The new committee interviewed leaders in other churches and began a study on our necessity for enlargement. For any plan to work, it has to be balanced. If you provide for babies, you have to provide for parents; if there are brothers or sisters, they have to be considered.

In six weeks, I was given the task of sketching out an organization to show what we would need to do in each age group to take care of increased attendance. The committee also brought the results of their study to the church in six weeks. The first response to the chairman was that the committee's proposal was crazy and impossible and should be redone.

"People, we are not recommending anything. We are just reporting on what you asked us to do," the committee chairman (not me) reminded them. It was suggested that everyone get a printed copy of what was outlined and take it home, talk it over and come back with their suggestions in four weeks. In the meantime, the church continued to train leaders and teachers. We crowded people into a house across the street and into some living rooms close by.

I received a letter from the Baptist Sunday School Board in Nashville, Tennessee, asking me to be part of the teaching staff for a week at Ridgecrest Baptist Assembly, east of Asheville. North Carolina. I went to the pastor and asked about my going. He told me that I would have to take my vacation time if I went.

I could not believe that, but I did not respond. I talked to Flo about it. We had never had a real vacation and agreed we should go. I notified Bob Cook, who was in charge of the conference at Ridgecrest (he was also the son of the family that had given us the food in Grand Prairie), that we would come. I received my course plan, and we were ready to go in three weeks. The boys, even Bruce, would look at pictures in travel magazines and tell us which places they wanted to add as stops on our trip. Springfield was the furthest east we had ever been.

Our first stop was St. Louis. We spent a day at the zoo and walked along the Mississippi River. We then spent two days driving through and making occasional stops in Illinois, Indiana and the coalfields of the northern Appalachian Mountains. We spent one day at Gettysburg and the next day in Washington, D.C. We went to the Smithsonian, walked around the grounds of the White House and toured the Capital building. From D.C., we drove to the coast and followed it as closely as we could to Kitty Hawk, North Carolina.

We rented a cabin on the beach and spent two days resting and swimming. We went to the Wright Brothers Flight Center in Kitty Hawk and to the Lost Colony historic center as we made our way southwest to Ridgecrest, North Carolina.

We were amazed at the trees and foliage and miles and miles of mountains. We had a cabin in Black Mountain a short distance from Ridgecrest. I attended my first staff meeting, where I learned the rules and met the other faculty members. Flo enrolled the boys in their programs and chose a conference for herself. We ate our meals in the dining hall.

On our day off, we went to Chimney Rock National Park and visited the family of Ginny Mae, Uncle Prof's wife, in Easley, South Carolina. We spent the day with the Christophers. It was late when we arrived back at Black Mountain. We put the boys to bed, relaxed and shared our feelings about our trip. Flo and I both love history and geography and had become aware of our rich heritage in the South.

The last day at Ridgecrest, the families of the staff were invited to a special appreciation meal. Our hosts in Black Mountain were descendants of one of the early doctors who had moved there before the Civil War. We thanked our hosts for their hospitality and took three days to drive back to Springfield to work.

While we were gone, the committee had developed a basic concept of what they thought the church ought to and could do. I was amazed at their thinking and planning. We hired an architect, and plans were made to move ahead and build.

After our architect submitted his plans, the committee suggested that the church have an open meeting so the plans could be discussed. While most wanted to move ahead, a few of the older folks were cautious; however, after receiving assurance that the worship center would only have upgrades and the downstairs would only have some remodeling, they became part of the team.

The new education and recreation building would have a full-size gym with a commercial kitchen. The gym would serve as the youth center on Sundays, as a place for weekly church meetings and as the church fellowship hall. There would be a new modern nursery and children's facilities with child-size toilets. The youth and young married couples would have new larger rooms upstairs.

A church library, the church offices and classrooms for senior adults would be on the ground floor with easy access. We would not have to change our places of worship or study until the new building was finished. Bids were called for, and three were submitted. The committee looked at the price range, and we all knew that we could not afford a half million dollars. We had to look for where we could cut back and save.

I was in my office, mulling over possibilities, when my phone rang. A builder who was a member of another Baptist church called and asked if he could come by to talk. He came with a new approach for the church to consider. He would take the job and use any of our people who had expertise in various trades and give cost credits for their work on the church. He would do the same for any others who would volunteer their services. Together, we would keep a log of volunteer labor and credit their time back to the church. I had worked some with volunteers on smaller projects but never dreamed of an arrangement like this. The Bible Baptist National Headquarters and Training School were in the northeast part of Springfield. The builder had built most of their buildings and a few of their churches. The committee met and recommended that the church work with him. The church voted to do so.

We had some people with concrete experience and others with foundation background. One member owned a steel erection company and had construction equipment. After a week of checking references and volunteer availability, the projected cost was close to 200,000 dollars.

We had brochures printed and distributed to church members with enough copies to go to suppliers, neighbors and anyone else who might be interested in knowing what was going on. The local paper took pictures and gave us an excellent write-up. Some pastors of other churches began to criticize us for putting a gym and an eating place in a church building when "God has called us preach, not play."

Other digs followed, but the criticism created publicity that actually helped us instead of accomplishing the critics' intended purpose. Our committee worked with the contractor on prices of materials. The contractor submitted a list of the jobs on which he could use volunteers in the construction of our building.

We broke ground with a celebration on the building site. Charter members, committee chairmen, our pastor and city officials conducted the ceremony after Sunday worship. Early Monday morning, tractors, digging equipment, dump trucks and volunteers were there for the real ground-breaking.

While the building was being built, Bob Burrows and representatives from each age group met and planned for the furnishings that would be needed. Rooms were mapped, and chalk boards and electric outlets for visual presentations were placed. Cribs for infants were tested and priced, and the training of new workers to staff the new organization was increased.

While all this was going on, I received an invitation from the Missouri Baptist Convention education department to help with training conferences they conducted throughout the state. I kept the work at our church primary. There are always people who look for something wrong when everyone else is rejoicing over what God is doing; I have to admit, though, there were times I gave them reason to find fault.

According to a few, I was unfair to my wife and children. I was involved with the wrong people, especially college students, and spent too much time on sports (our young men's baseball team had placed second in the state playoffs). A major complaint was that I spent too much time with minorities. Our church was only six blocks from a black neighborhood, and I spent a fair amount of time with members of that church. This was happening the same year that, after much debate, the Southern Baptist Convention voted at the meeting in

St. Louis to back desegregation of public schools as ordered by the Supreme Court. I had been at that meeting, and my critics were sure they knew the way I had voted (they were right).

Since I was already not in my office as much as my critics thought I should be, I went way too far when I accepted a position as program director for a weeklong training event for teachers and leaders of the churches in the Green County Baptist Association. The fact that our church would be the major beneficiary was not important. I was not doing what some members expected or wanted.

The committee of Green County Baptist Association had asked me to lead training and help in enlisting qualified instructors from whatever source I could. We would invite leaders and teachers from all age groups, from infants to senior adults, to come and work with us for a week. We sent letters and made calls and enlisted capable, experienced leaders. We obtained permission from First Baptist Church in Springfield to use their facilities for the training.

The dates and hours were set, and our advertising went out. Not only did our Baptist churches and other churches respond, the Assembly of God Bible College president asked permission to bring faculty. We had a pre-enrollment of over eight hundred adult leaders. Our average attendance was just over 750.

On opening night, I was asked to bring the challenge. After the moderator introduced our staff and just before I was to preach, the youth choir of First Baptist Church sang. The song they chose was "It Took a Miracle." The solo part was sung by a young Jewish man, a college student who had become a Christian. He had been disowned by his family. His singing was so heartbreaking and yet victorious that I had trouble speaking. The mood of the congregation was the same.

After the week was over, we paid all our bills and gave the faculty their honorarium. The offerings the people gave paid over eighty percent of the cost. The associational budget paid the rest. We had a banquet for our faculty in a restaurant close by. The staff of the Assembly of God College had reserved the large room next to ours. The president of the college asked to speak to us for a few minutes. He came and expressed his gratitude for our willingness to let their faculty participate, and then he commented, "If you want to know why we wanted our people to be involved, I will tell you. No other Christian organization or conference can produce and train workers like the Southern Baptists, and I wanted the professors and teachers at my college to learn from the very best."

We shook hands, and he left. We all rejoiced and had a good dinner and a good time and went home.

I began to get more invitations than I could accept. While the church building was being finished, I made two big mistakes. To use a baseball analogy, I did not cover all my bases.

My first mistake related to a church training banquet. The church leaders planned the event; I had nothing to do with the planning, nor did I check with them. At the banquet, I sat at the head table and received recognition, along with three others, for attaining the most awards for leadership and teaching studies in the past year. Our pastor was there, but he was not recognized nor invited to speak or even pray.

My second mistake happened when the pastor had invited a professor from Midwestern Baptist Theological Seminary in Kansas City to a three-day church development workshop. The professor had asked our pastor to send him information on the strong and weak points of the church and to rate them as to their importance. The request included attendance, ministerial ministries, education programs, music ministry, community services and outreach, as well as a few other items about the church and our community.

The pastor asked me to compile the information requested. Instead of compiling and rating the list myself, I developed a questionnaire and went to each Sunday school class and department. I explained the survey to people sixteen and older and asked for their responses. I did that for two Sundays.

Two of our leaders and I eliminated the duplicates and wrote up the report. Bob Burrows, the Sunday school director and deacon chairman, and I went over the responses. Bob saw the red flag before I did. The education and music programs were overwhelmingly approved; the ministerial leadership was barely above acceptable.

We were moving into a new building that I had basically, with the architect, designed. I had been on radio and TV for two major city-wide Christian training events. Bob and I had to do some honest evaluation. We compiled what we thought was fair and sent our report to the professor, but I did not send a copy to the pastor.

When the professor came, he unknowingly lit a fuse. As the guest speaker, he thanked the pastor and told the congregation of their long and excellent relationship. Then he turned to me and said, "Mr. Brown, I want to say to you in front of this congregation that I have been doing this type of work for several years and have always asked for information about the church, its ministries and its health — but I have never received such an adequate and complete summary as you have provided."

I looked at Bob, and we both knew what was going to happen. It would only be a matter of time.

It was a bright sunny day when our new building was approved by the city and we moved in. Our church building was mostly finished. All positions in our teaching and administration staff, new or old, were filled with trained workers. We had a reserve of leaders and teachers trained to take over as needed.

Some older people and newer members began to ask if I was still needed. They reasoned that they could use the money from my salary to pay off the cost of the building. Others began to complain about being run over by new people with new ideas.

I was agitated and upset at what was going on in our church. I had to get away before I said or did something stupid. I could not get in touch with the pastor. I had vacation time, so I left a letter with the church secretary and asked her to get it to the pastor. I wrote him that I would be gone three days for a family emergency in Fort Worth. Flo and the boys were ready, and we drove to Fort Worth. I had forgotten about my graduation ceremony, but Dad had learned that the ceremony would be held while I was there to help him. He and Flo were in attendance as I was handed my master's degree diploma.

Dad then asked me to drive him to Deming, New Mexico. His car was with Mom and Janie. The only way for him to get his car and bring Mom and Janie to Fort Worth without jeopardizing his new job was for me to drive him to Deming.

I called Grant Avenue in Springfield three times and could not locate the pastor. I talked with the church secretary and asked her to please let the pastor know that I was taking a full week of vacation to care for my family. The secretary was one of the older group that was still unhappy and critical of me for messing up the church. I thought nothing about that at the time.

It took us two days to get to Deming. Flo and I helped Dad, Mom and Janie load their car to go to Fort Worth. The next day, we drove to Albuquerque, spent the day with my grandparents and then drove all night and the next day to Springfield. I went to the office the next morning.

The pastor wanted to see me. "Where have you been?" he asked.

I told him that I had left him a written letter in the church office about a family emergency and had called three times to get a message to him while I was in Fort Worth.

"In fact, I will probably have to go back to Fort Worth in two weeks and move my parents here to be with us until my dad can find regular work."

"You should have asked," he said.

"I know, and I tried," I replied. "I left you that information in the letter, and I called and left you a message before I left Fort Worth so you would know what was happening. Dad had no car with him, and this was the only way I could help him get my mom and my sister to Fort Worth."

"I never received any call or message," he said.

"I tried, and if I have to move my parents here, I will not leave until I am absolutely sure you get that information." I was then dismissed.

I went to work. The chairman of the association nominating committee called me. The committee wanted to recommend to the association that I be the Sunday school training director for another year.

Without thinking, I told him that they needed to look for someone else because it was possible I would not be there the following year. That information flew to all the Green County Baptist churches. Pastors and church leaders began to call me. They wanted to know why I might be moving. Our pastor was one who heard.

"What is going on?" he asked.

"I turned down the position of Sunday school director for next year because I may not be here. That was all I said," I told him.

"Well, it has caused a stir, and some are already blaming me," he responded, and he walked out.

The next week, the pastor was awarded his doctoral degree from Midwestern Baptist Seminary. Flo and I went to the ceremony, gave him a graduation card and congratulated him on his work.

Two weeks later, I had to go to Fort Worth and bring Dad, Mom and Janie to Springfield to live with us. Dad had a pickup; what we could not move, they put in storage. We were doing finish work on the church kitchen cabinets. I received permission from the committee and the pastor to hire Dad to complete the work. Dad stayed with us for six weeks; he then got a new job in an antique and used furniture store in Fort Worth. I helped him move Mom and Janie back.

An interesting event happened on the day I was to return to Springfield. I went to where Dad worked to say goodbye. The owner of the store was in his office with an antiques dealer. The door was open, and this is what I heard: "You want that antique desk in two weeks? I can do that, but you will not be happy. Now, if you want a good-quality authentic antique, that will take me five weeks to build."

Flo was four months pregnant and beginning to show. Her diet included some crazy foods. A church leader found a watermelon in November and brought it to her.

Relationships at church became worse. During a meeting with the deacons, the pastor said, "There is a rumor among the Baptist churches in our area that our deacons want to terminate Edd Brown's relationship with our church. I want it known that it is I, not the deacons, who wants his resignation within thirty days."

The chairman of the deacons suggested that I leave the room so they could discuss the pastor's request. I learned later that four of the nine deacons agreed with the pastor, three did not, and two were undecided. Their final decision was that I would have three months with pay to relocate. I would have no church responsibilities and did not have to attend services. I was free to find a place to move.

With no help from me, several pastors in the area were made aware of this decision. They began to offer me help and suggestions.

One told me he had a friend in California whom he was going to contact.

In two weeks, I received invitations from two churches in Missouri and visited both. One was in Moberly, in the northern part of the state. Flo and I visited the church. The leadership and pastor wanted us to come, but budget problems interfered. The second church was in Clayton (close to St. Louis). They asked me to come in two weeks and spend five days with them. I agreed to go.

That same day, I received a letter from Gene Harrell, pastor of the First Baptist Church in Norwalk, California. He requested a letter about my family, work history and references. I sent the information he requested. The next week, I received letters from St. Petersburg, Florida, and Los Alamos, New Mexico (home to the atom bomb facility). Within two weeks, I had four options.

Gene Harrell called me from California and asked me to come in three weeks to lead the music at their annual revival meeting. I now had two definite requests. I notified the churches in St. Petersburg and Los Alamos that I needed to determine if either of the two churches that I had already agreed to visit were where God might be leading. In my own mind, I had eliminated any church in California. I would go to Norwalk, lead the music for their revival and collect my honorarium, but I would not move there. I did not like California's fog, traffic or pace of life.

I went to Clayton and spent Sunday through Thursday with church members. I led the music in two services on Sunday and had lunch with church staff and leaders. I participated in a community survey and visitation program for non-churched people in the community. I also brought the message on Wednesday night. The search committee met with me for two hours on Friday morning and voted to recommend me to the church. I explained to them that I had already agreed to be in a revival meeting in California. If the California church asked me to come, I would try to give the church in Clayton my decision within two weeks.

I drove home, spent some time with the boys and went to bed. I was up at five on Friday morning. Flo drove me to the airport, and I flew to Fort Worth. Mom, Dad and Janie were there to meet me between flights. Charles, my younger brother, was out of the Navy and lived in Long Beach, California. He had asked our parents to move to Long Beach and live with his family. He was sure Dad could find work there. Mom and Dad had decided to go. They were leaving within three weeks.

I boarded TWA's new Stratocruiser. It flew at 12,000 feet elevation and cruised at 180 miles an hour. I had two free meals and soft drinks as often as I wanted. My seatmate was the head bishop of the United Methodist Church, USA. We had a great visit. He wished for me a new and challenging ministry. We prayed together when we deplaned at LAX.

I had been at LAX ten years earlier but had no memory of it being so large. I did remember the fog. I recovered my luggage. Gene Harrell had asked me to wait outside the baggage claim area. It was cold, and I had only a light jacket. I could not see more than a block ahead. I had no telephone number for the church. After waiting in the cold drizzle and fog for thirty minutes, uneasiness became a real problem. I made up my mind that, if I ever made it to this place called Norwalk, I would stay the week and never set foot in this part of the country again. Just when I had given up hope, a car stopped, and a guy came running.

"You Edd Brown?" he asked. I just nodded.

He grabbed my suitcase and headed for the car. He opened the back door and pitched in my bag, and I got in after. He jumped in the front passenger seat, and the driver took off.

The non-driver turned and said, "Sorry we are late, but the fog and traffic held us up. I am Gene Harrell, and this (pointing to the driver) is Rex Browning. We will have time for a more formal introduction later. We are already late for our dinner."

"If we are already late," I thought, "all this fog and traffic will not help." I had never seen anything like it. Cars were backed up for miles. All I could see were headlights of hundreds of cars creeping toward us and red taillights ahead of us. The fog became denser. We crept along for an hour.

"I will never put my family in a mess like this," I said to myself.

We pulled into a cul-de-sac in front of Browning's home and got out. The two men's wives were there. Helen and Ruth introduced themselves. We had a light meal and just talked. There were no serious questions; we just discussed family matters and other general topics that new people talk about. I had no pictures, so they were not bored with that.

Gene and I had been at Southwestern Seminary at the same time; we may have had classes together but were not sure. Our jobs and churches were miles apart. Helen, Gene's wife, and Rita, Flo's best friend from high school, were friends when Gene and Helen were in East Texas Baptist College in Marshall, Texas.

Rex and Ruth were from Missouri. Rex worked at a large aircraft factory in Long Beach. He was the interim church music director, and Ruth was the pianist and church secretary. We had a great meal and good fellowship. After the meal and conversation, we got down to business.

There were two worship services on Sunday mornings, and the choir sang at both. I would lead the congregational singing. Rex would lead the choir only this Sunday morning. All other services would be led by me. Ruth went to the piano, and we practiced together for fifteen minutes. Gene and Helen joined in, and we practiced all of Sunday's music. I agreed to sing with the choir that Sunday morning.

I was to stay with the Brownings that week. Their girls, Martha and Barbara, had moved into one bedroom, and I had the one they left. Surprisingly, I had no problem going to sleep. At seven on Sunday morning, we all got out of bed, dressed and had breakfast. I had not met the girls the night before. They were close in age to Steve and Wayne.

Rex and I went early. I could not believe what I saw. There was an old building on the corner that looked like an old school building; it would seat no more than two hundred people. There were two classrooms that would hold fifteen people each. There was a store-room and three small rooms used for offices. There was a greenish old house fifty feet away that was for toddlers and babies. Behind that house stood an unfinished two-story building that I assumed was to be used for Bible study and training. Along the edge of the church property were eight small shacks made with two-by-four studs and covered with tarpaper and sheet metal roofs.

I had been told in a letter and by other sources that the church had a regular attendance of close to three hundred people on Sundays. I could only see enough room for 150. At eight o'clock, cars overfilled the small parking lot on the church property and filled the parking lot of the bank across the street. I went into the auditorium and met many of the choir members. I took my seat, and the service began. After a couple verses of the opening hymn, I began to enjoy the way they sang with openness and joy.

I was formally introduced. The choir sang, and a visiting lay preacher from Oklahoma brought the message. After the early morning service, I walked the grounds and spent time observing.

The tarpaper shacks began to fill with children. Cars were pulled up onto the church property, and the doors were left open. Four to six older youth would crowd into the back and front seats of the car. The teacher would be in the front, and there they would have Bible study.

When Sunday school was over, other people began to arrive. A large number of them were young and middle-aged adults. Their Bible study classes met in living rooms of houses close by. Some met in restaurants that were closed on Sunday morning. Others met in a civic center and clubhouses as much as a mile away. Over three hundred people met and studied the Bible, but only half of them met on church property.

The early service had been great, but the later service was unbelievable. Without my realizing it, some of my resolution to never come back to California began to melt away. On Sunday evening, the house was packed. I led the music and marveled at their response.

On Monday, I received a telegram from the church in Clayton, Missouri. The church had unanimously voted to ask Flo and me to become part of their church staff. They offered an overwhelming salary, with up to six weeks a year for vacation and further study. They would send us to the Baptist World Congress meeting in London later that year with all expenses paid. They wanted to hear from me as soon as possible so they could find us a home in the exceptionally nice neighborhood where the church was located. I had to sit down. I had not believed anything like that could happen.

I sent a telegram to say, "Pastor, I am overwhelmed, but I must first talk to Flo and must be fair to the church here. You remember I told you that I could not make a decision before I fulfilled my promise to come here and see what God might want me to do. I will get back to you later this week."

In my mind, I was already moving to Clayton. I notified the

churches in St. Petersburg and Los Alamos that, while I appreciated their interest, I could not consider their invitations at this time.

The lay preacher for the revival did an excellent job; he was able to explain the Bible in a way that normal, everyday working men and women could understand and apply to their own lives. There were just under a hundred decisions for acceptance of Christ and for membership in the church that week. The small building was packed every night.

On Tuesday, Gene had asked me to make a hospital visit with him. We went to see a highway patrolman who had been injured in an accident. A car had made a sudden stop in front of him. Doug Wilson's motorcycle rammed the car, and Doug was catapulted over the car. He had a slight concussion and a broken leg. We visited for a few minutes. He inquired about why I was in California and shared how much he loved music. He played a harmonica. I told him how well the church members and choir sang and invited him to come and bring his wife to a service.

Pointing to his leg in the cast, he said, "No way could I come to church like this."

"You learned how to use crutches?" I asked.

"Of course," Doug said. "I could not be released from the hospital before I could use them."

"Okay. You come," I said, "and I will meet you at the front of the church building. I will reserve a parking place for you, escort you to your seat and have a chair set up for you to rest your leg on."

He asked if that was possible. I assured him that, with the pastor's help, it would be done. We three agreed on a night for him to come. He and Elda, his wife, came. After the service, they waited to thank me and exclaimed that they would be back.

On my last Sunday afternoon, the church planned a business

meeting. I was to publicly share about my personal life, including my salvation experience and my feelings of being called by God to full-time church ministry. I answered their questions. After an hour of honest two-way discussion, Bill Williams (one of the church leaders) spoke up: "Pastor, I have heard all I need to know — and if I am not out of order, I would like to make a motion that we call Edd Brown to join our church staff as soon as possible."

Ballots were distributed. Rex led some singing and a report was brought by the committee chairman. There were 158 votes cast: The results were 158 in favor and zero opposed.

"Lord, You had better let me know what to do, because I sure don't know," I prayed.

At the Brownings' house that afternoon, we had a light lunch. No one bugged me; they let me eat and think. I was grateful for their understanding. I had to talk to Flo. I had called twice, but the call would not go through. I called the local telephone office, and they told me that there had been a heavy ice and snow storm across northern New Mexico, Texas and most of Oklahoma. The lines were down, and they had no idea when service would be restored.

"Do you know anything about air travel?" I asked the operator.

"All we have heard is that flights are canceled in that area for the next two days," she answered.

I was on my own and did not like to make any decisions, much less this one, without talking to Flo. My brother Charles came from Long Beach to the evening service. The people had been generous in their praise and expected to soon see me again.

Charles, the pastor and his wife, and the chairman of deacons and his wife went to the Brownings' home for fellowship. We had finished our meal and were sitting around the table, talking. The doorbell rang, and the search committee chairman and his wife arrived. I knew what was coming. I knew I could not avoid the question that was on everyone's mind. We discussed the week — how I felt about the church, the people and the future of the church and how I would fit in. I do not remember who asked the question, but it was the one I did not want to answer.

"On what basis will your final decision be made?" I was asked.

I had been fighting with God for three days about that question, and I wanted to talk to Flo. I had to be honest with these people. No group had been more considerate and accepting of me. Other churches had been kind, but here I already seemed to be one more member of a living and loving family; however, I still did not want to come back to California with its traffic, smog and rushed style of living.

Everyone waited. I wanted to leave the room but knew I could not, so I waded in. "All week I have been seriously thinking and praying about what my decision would be if you asked me to come here. There is no way you could even come close to what the church in St. Louis is offering; however, that cannot enter into my decision. If I am to be honest with God and you, the basis of my decision has to be the needs of the church and the gifts that God has given me to help meet those needs."

Before anyone else could say anything, my brother, piped up and said, "I am going to call Babe" (his wife).

I looked at him, and he could see how I felt. Here, in one of the most serious moments of my life, he would say some dumb thing like that.

Charles looked back at me and said, "Don't look at me like that. You just told them you were coming. Babe and I will drive back with you and help you and Flo move."

Everyone but me burst out laughing. Rex Browning said, "Edd, there is not a church anywhere in this country that needs what you can do more than we do. Welcome aboard."

I was stunned and could not cover my feelings. Deep in my heart, I knew that this was where I should be. I looked up, looked at everyone in the room in turn and finally stopped at Charles, saying, "Okay, go call Babe."

The whole room erupted. I was sore for a week from the hugs and friendly punches on my shoulders. Charles left to get Mildred (Babe). I, with more help than was needed, packed and was ready to go. The deacon chairman gave me my honorarium check and laughingly said, "I plan to sign a few more for you down the road."

An hour later, Charles and Mildred returned in their station wagon. Rex helped me load my stuff. We three left Norwalk and started the fifteen-hundred-mile journey east at midnight on that Sunday.

We had checked the weather and decided to stay as far south as we could. The three of us took turns driving, changing drivers at every gas or rest stop. We rotated sleeping on the mattress in the back of the station wagon. We ate and drank what we had in an ice chest. As we went through Phoenix and Springville, Arizona, and then Albuquerque, New Mexico, we had only rain to contend with.

We began to see snow and some ice in Tucumcari, New Mexico. Fifty miles west of Amarillo, the ice and snow was one to three inches deep on the highway. We crept along behind trucks though the rest of Texas and most of Oklahoma. In Tulsa, the rain began to melt the ice, and we began to make better time. We arrived in Springfield early Wednesday morning. We stopped just inside of town, and I rented a trailer. We hooked it onto Charles' station wagon and drove to our house.

Flo and the boys, even in the cold sleet, came out to see what was happening. After everyone had hugged and kissed, Flo backed off, looked at me and said, "I know we are moving, but would you please tell me in which direction?"

I called the pastor in Clayton and expressed regret that I could not get to him earlier. I had to tell him what he already knew. I had to follow where God was leading. I would be leaving today for California.

How they knew, I don't know, but four of the men and two of the women from Grant Avenue Church came and helped us pack and load the trailer. We gave away a lot of stuff and loaded only the essentials. We were ready to leave for Norwalk by two o'clock that afternoon.

I went to the pastor's home and knocked on the door. His wife welcomed me. I went to his office. He looked up from behind his desk and said, "I was told you were back with a trailer. I have had calls from St. Louis trying to locate you."

"I know. All the telephone lines were down. I called and talked to the pastor this morning," I replied.

"I don't think it would accomplish anything for you to come to the services tonight," he said.

"I had not intended to attend. All I am here for is to give you my resignation," I stated.

"You have one ready?" he asked.

"No," I said. "You write it out however you want, and I will sign it and be on my way."

I sat down. He looked at me, grinned, picked up his pen and wrote something. He handed it to me. I did not bother to read it; I signed it and said, "I guess that takes care of everything." I stood and offered him my hand; we shook hands, and I left.

Charles and Mildred (Babe) had to leave early and left with the trailer hooked to their station wagon. Flo, the three boys and I left an hour later. Charles would leave the trailer in Albuquerque, New Mexico, with our Uncle Tom and drive on to California. We would be in Albuquerque two days later; there, we would hook up the trailer to our car and drive on to Norwalk.

I have to interject something here that is important to me. The men and women I met along my journey, although they seemed to oppose me and my service to God at times, were good people. It is so easy to judge and be critical of others when you do not know what they are going through in their personal or professional lives. I owe each of them a debt of gratitude. God put me with them for a purpose. They were His tools to shape (and pound some sense into) me so He could accomplish His will in my life. I learned more from those three than I ever did from many of my friends who overlooked my stupidity and stubbornness. Those three God-directed pastors (and others like them) helped me to stop making the same dumb mistakes over and over.

Flo had a nephew who was a woodcarver. One day, I was with him at his home when he brought in a hardwood limb that he had picked up in the desert of Baja, Mexico. He handed me the five-foot-long limb and asked me to look at it. All I saw was a brightly colored tree limb that had a large knot where a smaller limb had been.

Halfway exasperated, he asked me, "Don't you see that bear in there?"

I had to say something, so I replied, "I can see something (a knot to myself), but I cannot make out what it is." I handed the limb back to him.

A few weeks later, we were in his home in San Diego. He brought out an absolutely beautiful, highly polished five-foot walking stick and handed it to me.

"What do you think?" he asked.

I did not know what to say. How can I express my feelings for a walking stick? I turned it over, and a miniature bear looked as if it were ready to jump out at me.

I stammered and finally asked, "How did you do that?"

He shrugged and modestly said, "It's no problem. I just cut out the wood around the bear and there he is."

He had cut out, gouged out, sanded out and scrubbed off all the residue that covered up his bear. He then polished it until anyone could see the bear, which had been hidden from me.

I know the Bible message of the potter and his clay. Now that I am older and looking back, I see human tools, not enemies, that God used and is still using to make me into what He intended for me to become. There are yet other trials, cuttings and sanding ahead for me. He is still preparing me for His work in my days and years to come.

NINE

1955-1964

NORWALK, CALIFORNIA
MARCIA

Flo and I had two additional traveling problems. She was seven months pregnant with our daughter, and our three boys had the mumps. We explained this to service people every place we stopped to eat, go to the bathroom, get gas or spend the night. All were understanding and went out of their way to assist us.

Two weeks before I went to California to lead the music for the week in Norwalk, a deacon in the Baptist church in Lebanon, Missouri, east of Springfield, called and asked me to see him before I left for the church revival in California. I had led a leadership clinic at his church and spoken at their annual Valentine's Day banquet. He knew of my problems at Grant Avenue.

When I arrived, he told me he wanted me to have a new car to go wherever God led. With my frequent travel to Fort Worth and state leadership clinics, my Plymouth, which had 92,000 miles on it, was worn out. The deacon owned a Chrysler dealership and had earlier helped me in other ways. This time, he outdid himself. He took me into the showroom and showed me a new black four-door Plymouth.

"I want to move that car and put our new model on display. Here is what I want to do. I will give you the Blue Book price for your car and will sell you this car at my cost. Actually, since it has been on the showroom floor too long, I will give you ten percent off that price." I could not keep up.

"Come to my office, and we will get this on paper. Then you can see what I am talking about," he said. After we had gone over all he had said, I drove home with our brand-new car. My total cost was the price of our car and 680 dollars.

His last advice as he handed me the keys was, "Enjoy this car and use it for God's work, but do not pull a trailer or drive over fifty miles an hour until your car has five hundred miles on the odometer."

Flo and I were still in shock; we could not believe the timing of us getting a new car, just when we needed to move to California. We would hook up the trailer to our car at Uncle Tom's house in Albuquerque, New Mexico, after Charles had pulled it that far with his station wagon. I had a trailer hitch and lights installed on our new car; it would have been driven over six hundred miles when we arrived in Albuquerque.

At a restaurant in eastern New Mexico, the waitress seated us at a table in the rear of the dining room away from other customers. We had a relaxed meal; all three boys were getting over the mumps but had settled down. We were ahead of our schedule and relaxed for an hour. As we left, I went to pay our bill. Our waitress looked up, smiled and said, "Sir, your dinner has already been paid for."

"What?" I asked.

She pointed to a husband and wife outside in their car, driving away. "They told me to tell you that you have the best-behaved, nicest boys they have ever seen. They wanted to help you on your trip."

We told the boys what had happened, and they thought it was funny. For most of day, they kept asking why those people would do what they had done.

We made an overnight stop before we arrived at my uncle's house. Our plan was to take two weeks for our trip. The church leadership in Norwalk had insisted on paying all of our expenses. I had also been warned, in a friendly manner, that I was not to be back for two weeks. Our family was to enjoy and rest on our trip.

In Albuquerque, we stayed with my Uncle Tom, Aunt Ann and their three children. We also visited my other aunts, uncles and cousins.

We took a day to go to Los Lunas and visit with my grandparents. While we were there, my grandmother and I walked outside. My grandfather was playing with the boys. Flo, seven months pregnant, was resting.

Grandmother stopped, turned me around so she could look at me and said, "Edd Lamoin, I want to tell you something. When your granddad and I learned that your mother was pregnant with you, I began praying for you that night — and I have been praying for you every night for thirty years, that God would protect and use you. You and Florene and your three boys all being here with me today has let me know that I can thank God for answering my prayers. I am not going to quit praying for you; I just want you to know that you and your family have made my life worthwhile."

Uncle Carnice (Prof) now lived in Albuquerque. We spent the next day with him and his wife. Flo and I tried to verbally express to them our appreciation for all he and Ginny Mae had done for us at Hardin-Simmons. We had not only lived with them; they had opened doors for jobs and shared their lives with us. They listened as we tried to tell them how deeply we felt.

"Prof," I said, "we owe you so much, and there is no way on earth that we can ever repay you."

He smiled and said, "Oh, yes, there is a way. In your life and work, if you will look for others who are now where you were when you needed our help and will do for them what we have done for you, you will do more than pay us back."

Flo and I both sat there and cried. We made our commitment to Prof and to God that, to the best of our abilities, we would do our best to honor his request. More than fifty years later, we are still trying to keep that promise to him and to remember a grandmother who would never give up.

Early the next morning, we went to Uncle Tom's house. After a two-hour visit, we hooked the trailer onto our car and drove to the Grand Canyon. We spent part of two days marveling at its majesty and beauty.

At the campground, we unloaded our bed springs, mattress and bed linens. (They were the last items we had loaded into our trailer.) We placed them upwind from our small campfire. We five spent the night outdoors in the open on one big bed. We did not even try for sleep. For a few hours, we simply watched the moon and stars; we talked about the heavens, God and people as long as we could. We and the boys all enjoyed that time even more than seeing the canyon.

We drove south. The heat in Needles urged us to keep on traveling. We drove two hours more and spent the night in a motel in Barstow. Because of the heat there, we left early in the morning.

We drove a hundred miles and reached the five-point intersection of Norwalk. Ten minutes later, we pulled up in front of our house on Potter Street. Two cars were parked there. Ladies from the church were cleaning the house, and the men were working on the yard and had mowed the grass. They helped us unload our car and trailer and brought us dinner.

Our house had two bedrooms, one bath, a kitchen and a living/dining room combination. Later in the week, we went to a community show, and an entertainer asked, "How many of you have seen our latest subdivision, Orange Peel Acres? They are able to build two houses on one large orange peel!"

Our house may not have been that small, nor were the houses that close together, but the analogy fit anyway. I had never seen so many houses in such a small area. It was a long way from the two-hundred-acre ranch I had lived on years ago, with the closest neighbor two miles away. The house the church provided was adequate for our needs, well-kept and in a good neighborhood. With the help of the men and women, we were set up for living in five hours.

The next day, we five walked around outside and met our neighbors. By noon, all five of us were ready to collapse, so we went back to our house and to our beds. Late in the afternoon, the pastor and Helen, his wife, came and spent some time with us. They met Flo and, of course, were more impressed with her than they had been with me. Their and Flo's connection with Rita Storie, Flo's best friend from high school, helped build our relationship.

Gene told me that I need not worry about Sunday; it was all taken care of. The church members would help us get Bruce (age four), Wayne (age six) and Steve (age seven) into Sunday school classes. Flo and I, in our late twenties, would be escorted to the young married class and be introduced in the worship service. We had nothing to do our first Sunday but sit together, get acquainted with the congregation and relax.

The construction of an education building showed very little progress. It could be a long time before the church would be able to get rid of the tarpaper shacks and move the cars they were using for youth Bible classes. There were two dozen young couples our age, and they all had children. We fit in and were quickly accepted. At the close of the morning service, Flo and I joined the First Baptist Church in Norwalk, California.

Several things had to be taken care of — change of address, auto insurance, banking, shopping and locating the schools that Steve and

Wayne would attend. The most pressing issue for me was figuring out how to get around on such confusing and congested roads.

On Monday, I went to the bank across the street from the church, where we had permission to park on Sundays. I went to open an account and to move our banking to Norwalk.

The lady at the desk asked me more questions than I felt I needed to answer. When was I in the Navy? When and where was my first job? After a few minutes, I was getting tired of being asked about little things that had no relationship to my banking.

"Ma'am," I said, "I now work at that church across the street and have answered your questions at least three times. All I want to do is to open a checking account."

She looked up at me and said, "Mister, where you work is your problem, not mine" (Welcome to California).

I just stood and said nothing. One of the managers came over and asked if there was a problem. Before the lady could answer, I told him that, if this was the way the staff treated new customers, I could go to another bank a block away.

He looked at her written questions and shook his head. He motioned for me to follow him. He apologized, and in ten minutes, I had opened a bank account and made a new friend.

In 1955, almost all homes had trash-burning barrels or concrete trash burners in their backyards. The Los Angeles area is surrounded by mountains with only a few passes for the traffic and polluted air to escape. If the winds off the ocean were strong enough, the smoke was blown through the passes in the surrounding mountains. The smog was then forced to higher elevations and dissipated out over the desert. If the wind did not blow that briskly or that often, the fog would roll in. The fog would mix with vehicle exhaust and the smoke from backyard burners, and the smog would become thick enough to limit vision. Breathing became difficult for many people; for some, the smog could be life-threatening. The backyard burners were soon banned; however, the highways continued to become more crowded with cars, busses and trucks as more people moved to the enclosed basin of the Los Angeles area.

My first job at the church was to learn the names of the church leaders, their positions in the church and what they did for a living. If they were married, I also needed to learn the names of their spouses and children. Most importantly, I wanted to know what they saw in the future for our combined ministry.

In my second week, I was on my way to see a new family a mile northwest of our church building. The maps did not help. My year-old map might as well have been ten years old for its accuracy. I stopped at a service station and asked for directions. The clerk was very nice and helpful. As I walked out the door, she laughed and said, "You better hurry; those directions may be out of date tomorrow."

That was no joke for me. I walked out to my car and looked up. I now stood on the corner of Imperial Highway and Telegraph Road. Ten years earlier to the month, in that same location, the young salesman had picked me up for my ride to San Diego. He was the one who told me that I was building my life on a lot of coincidences and that there was no such thing as faith. He had said that, while he wished me luck, he also wished he could find me in ten years. He would then learn that I had given up on my concept of God and my belief that any God could be directing a person's life. How I wished that I could find him.

Our first full week had been overwhelming and constantly busy. We enrolled Steve and Wayne in a school three blocks away. Bruce was doing fine and had friends his age at church. Flo met with her new doctor, and the pregnancy was doing great. The church people and neighbors kept coming. They welcomed us and brought food and gifts to us.

Other than some breathing problems, I was doing okay. I worked with our people two days a week on the construction of the education building and urged others to follow suit.

A meeting of the deacons was called, and I was asked to attend. I was informed that no church meetings were closed to me. If I was needed at a meeting, I would be informed. The others were optional and open for me to attend. This meeting was mostly informational for my benefit.

In my second week, my office telephone rang. The person identified himself as a pastor and the Sunday school director for the Los Angeles Baptist Association and said he needed some help. A vacation Bible school (VBS) training program for the church leadership of our association was scheduled in three weeks. He asked me to take charge. If I agreed, he would work with me and help me all he could. I had not even completely unpacked, and I told him I would call him back.

I talked to Gene and told him what I had been asked to do.

"Can you do it?" he asked.

I told him I could if he and the other pastor would help me enlist the age group leaders. Gene immediately agreed to help, and I did not know how to react. Not only did I have the freedom to accept, but he would help me in any way he could. This was a new kind of working relationship, and I was not going to mess it up.

I called the neighboring pastor, told him that I would take on the responsibility with his help and asked when we could meet. We agreed on lunch the next day at a nearby restaurant and both arrived early. We visited and talked about our work and our backgrounds. At that time, I was still cautious about my future.

After lunch, he shared what he had done to get ready for the training program. He handed me a list of experienced people who could be division leaders and suggested I meet with them to become better acquainted before I asked them to help. With Gene's encouragement, we enlisted four women and four men from different churches to be our group trainers and set a meeting time to train the eight conference leaders.

We intended to keep our training conferences small to give as much personal help as possible. We planned for four hours of training on a Saturday morning three weeks away. I would lead the general officer and pastor training, but I had no idea how many of the churches would bring workers. I thought fifty people would be an exceptional response, but 123 laypeople and eighteen pastors came and participated. Their response was remarkable and a record attendance in VBS for the association of churches was set that year. My telephone began to ring constantly.

In four months, I was asked to be the director of Sunday school leadership and teacher training for the Los Angeles Baptist Association of sixty churches.

I was not going to make my same mistakes. I would make mistakes, but they would be new ones. I set up a meeting with Gene. I told him that we needed to make some things clear before possible trouble could begin. I told him about some of the misunderstandings (which I had probably caused) with former pastors. I wanted a clear idea of what I should do about requests for help from other churches. I went further and told him that I knew my primary responsibilities were to my family and First Norwalk; I would not violate either of those. I knew that my family would suffer if I took too much time away from them.

"Good," he said. "We are in agreement. My thought is this. If your outside invitations will help you grow in your ministry or benefit another person or church, don't just turn it down. What you learn by helping other churches will also help us. If you are asked to take a group of leaders to a church or to several churches, take as many of our people with you as you can. If you develop them as leaders, they will be better teachers and leaders for us.

"Here is my suggestion. You give your family one full day a week, away from church. You take a day for yourself. If you want, we can golf together; that is up to you. Give one day a week to kingdom ministries away from our church. The other days, do your job here. If I can help in any way, I will.

Even though the suggested days were not set in stone, I did have a pattern to follow. I was one of less than a dozen full-time music or education staff members in all the Baptist churches in Southern California. There were only thirty in the entire state. Our church developed a core group of leaders and helped build another group for the association churches.

In six months, I had my first experience as a conference leader for ethnic church leaders. I worked with two Chinese churches, three African-American churches, four Hispanic churches, and one Japanese congregation. Two Chinese pastors from Orange County association had also asked me for personal help.

As a result of my personal contact with those pastors, I agreed to help do an international cultural training event for our association. With the pastors' help, we enlisted leaders from five ethnic churches to teach, with interpreters if necessary, the different training classes. We enrolled forty-six people from ten ethnic churches and twenty-five from English-speaking churches. I would have my welcome message translated into five languages so everyone would understand me. On the day before our training conference, I received a call from our leader for the small children and infant workers division. She was sick, and the doctor had told her she should not lead her conference. I called everyone I knew, but no one was available. Flo was in no shape to help; our daughter was getting ready to meet the world.

We met for our workshop; I gave my introduction and challenge for our international training event and dismissed the people to their conferences. I was almost praying that no teachers of young children or infants would be there, but eight ladies of three different ethnicities were waiting. I, as the director, had promised training for everyone and had to step up. Fortunately, I only needed two translators for my group — one Chinese and one Spanish. There were two other ladies who were bilingual, and the others could understand some English. I am only sure of one thing: God took over. For two and a half hours, with two fifteen-minute breaks, I led the conference for those who work with small children and infants.

Requests began to come from other areas, such as San Diego, Orange County and even some distant ethnic churches. Most of these requests were for evening meetings. By rotating our trained leaders, we were able to help with most requests.

The progress on our church education building was incredibly slow. Volunteers would come and find no one there to give them instructions or to help them find materials. I was asked to attend the next meeting of the building committee. My first question of the meeting was, "Who is responsible for the actual construction of the building?"

From my experience in Springfield and Woodward, I knew that we needed to establish who was in charge. No one person had that responsibility. I did not make any suggestions. The discussion moved on, and a decision was made to hire a foreman who would oversee the completion of the building.

The church hired an experienced contractor who had worked with volunteers. The building was finished and occupied in three months. The cars went back to the parking lot, and the tarpaper shacks were eliminated. Our problem now was people. They continued to come, and the nursery population exploded. We had to do something. I was asked to spend time with parents, nursery workers and members of the building committee. A recommendation was made to the church to construct a building to care for eighty young children. Because half of the church members were parents and grandparents, there was no question it would pass.

Construction began, and in two months, the building was dedicated. We had seventy-eight children in the new building the Sunday it was opened. We were grateful but knew we were going to have to make other decisions soon. One of the workers asked, "What will we do?"

I remarked without thinking, "We will have to do one of two things or maybe both. We will have to make more room or slow down the production of babies."

Our weekly attendance was now at five hundred. The bean fields and dairy farms around us were disappearing, and more and more young couples were moving into our area. The pastor and I each made over fifty home visits a week, and we did not duplicate our efforts. It was not uncommon to have as many as twenty new families visiting our church each month.

At the peak of all this, Flo went into labor. I hurried the ten miles to Whittier Hospital (with not even a fender bender) to get Flo admitted. After fifteen minutes, the doctor came out of the examination room and told me to go eat breakfast, because it would be another hour before the baby came. I walked three blocks, ate breakfast and was back at the hospital in thirty minutes. I walked in, and the doctor was waiting for me.

"We tried to catch you, but we felt that the baby came first. You were just leaving the building, and she started coming out on her own. Your daughter and wife are doing fine. You will be able to see them both in thirty minutes," he said.

Marcia Ann Brown was here. I went in and visited with Flo and Marcia for a few minutes. The doctor came in and told us that both mother and child could go home in two or, at most, three days.

With three older brothers, Marcia was continually watched and entertained. She began to mimic her brothers early on. Before she was walking, she was talking, using words they had taught her.

I was asked by the Chinese Baptist Church in downtown Los Angeles to spent two hours an evening for a week with Tommie Lee, the pastor, and church leaders. I was to help their workers and teachers in Bible teaching and an outreach program to people in the Los Angeles area.

During the week that I was with the Chinese church, I received a call from Alvis Strickland, the Sunday school training director for our state convention. He asked me to partner with him and charter a bus to take fifty people from our churches to the Baptist national training center in Glorieta, New Mexico.

I talked to Gene, who said, "Do it, and take as many people from our church as possible."

We sent letters, and I made calls. Seven people from our church and

Edd and Flo's daughter, Marcia.

thirty-eight from other churches (including Tommy Lee and two others from First Chinese Baptist) joined us.

Glorieta Conference Center was located in the Glorieta Pass, east of Santa Fe, New Mexico. The Civil War battle site is close by. The center was under construction while we were there — and while our housing and meals were fine, we were crowded into limited space for our eight forty-five-minute meetings.

We led a four-hour teacher training event on the bus ride to and from Glorieta. At the conference, there were two meetings in the morning and two in the afternoon; there were also worship services in the evening, with great music and special interest programs. On two of the days, we had no afternoon meetings. On the free days, our chartered bus took us to Santa Fe. I had visited relatives in Santa Fe while in high school, and it was where I was inducted into the Navy.

Just as I had in my Navy days, I toured the old capitol grounds with the group, talking to American Indian women and men who sat on woven blankets under the porch of the old capitol building and displayed their handmade jewelry. The old capitol had been converted into a museum of the cultural history of Santa Fe.

On our way home at the end of the week, the conversations were about how much our people had learned about the history of New Mexico, how they would improve their teaching and what they planned to do in their local churches.

Our church kept growing; even with two services, we were out of room. If

Close friends Peggy and Jack DeShirley.

we were to do any more building, we would need more parking. The church bought a quarter-acre parcel behind the education building and put in a parking lot. We had grown to be one of the largest Southern Baptist churches in California, with a regular attendance of over seven hundred.

I received two letters: One was from the Kansas and Nebraska Baptist Convention, asking me to come on as their director of training; the other was from the Sunday School Board in Nashville, Tennessee. I was asked to become one of their staff to help build a new department focusing on the use of visual aids for training leaders and teachers.

I was flattered and honored; however, I had only been at Norwalk for nine months. I reasoned that, if Norwalk was where God wanted me, I should stay long enough to get the job done before I even considered going anywhere else.

I showed the letters to Gene and then responded to the Kansas and Nebraska Convention: "Thanks for the invitation, but no thanks."

"You better not go and leave me alone with this mess," Gene laughed as he walked out.

I was ready to refuse the offer from the Sunday School Board, but Dr. Bill House, my former seminary professor who was now head of the National Sunday School Department, asked me to wait and talk to him personally. He was coming to the Los Angeles area in a few weeks to lead the citywide training and outreach program. I was to be the local coordinator for this training event, working with the four missions directors and more than 120 churches of the greater Los Angeles area.

Before Dr. House arrived, I was contacted by one of the people I would be working with in the new department in Nashville. He was coming to Hollywood to meet with the managers of movie and television studios. He asked me to meet him in the restaurant of the Hollywood Roosevelt Hotel at six o'clock. I asked Ruth, our church secretary, how far it was; she told me that Hollywood was thirty miles away. In Springfield, thirty minutes would have been ample time. To be on the safe side, I set aside an hour. I left at five o'clock, and the traffic going into Los Angeles was not bad. When I entered the center of Los Angeles, I tried to follow the signs to Hollywood. I drove ten minutes and was back in the center of Los Angeles. I tried one more time, and the same thing happened.

I pulled up to the same traffic light for the third time and had no idea of what to do. A uniformed patrol officer walked over, and I rolled down my window. Very nicely, he asked, "Mister, where are you trying to go?"

I told him my problem, and he said, "I thought so when I saw your out-of-state license. Watch me; when I give you a signal, drive straight ahead for one full block, turn right, and you will be on the Hollywood Freeway" (the only one in California at that time).

I thanked him, and he went back to his post. He stopped all traffic and signaled me to drive through, motioning for me to hurry up. I floored my car and flew through the intersection; I drove the full block, turned right and was on the freeway (Bob Hope called it the only eighteen-mile-long parking lot in the U.S.).

I followed my map and arrived at the Hollywood Roosevelt thirty-five minutes late. My host was waiting for me. He introduced himself and took me to our table. While we were waiting for the waitress, several men and women came and talked to my host; I was introduced to heads of film companies, marketing people, salesmen and a production supervisor. Two people gave me their calling cards and told me to contact them. They would get me set passes to sets to see the filming of movies and TV shows. We ordered our meal, and when

I saw the prices, I was glad I was not buying.

He began, "Bill (Dr. House) has told me you probably will not accept our offer to come and work with us at this time; however, we wanted you to know and see what we are trying to do. Who knows? Things might change later."

We met a few more people who talked about their work and what the Southern Baptist churches were thinking of doing. An hour and half later, I drove home.

In a few days, I received a call from one of the executives who had given me her card. She invited me to meet her at one of the studios the following week. My calendar was clear, so I went. I was met at the gate and given a visitor's pass; I spent the day on the lots watching two movies being made. For lunch, I was taken to the cafeteria where the actors, actresses and production people mingled and ate.

My guide introduced me to many people, but I have no memory of who they were. I was assigned another guide, a female business agent, for the afternoon. She took me to a set and left me for an hour. I was standing a few feet off the set while a fake outdoor scene was being shot. About halfway through a fifteen-minute shoot, the sound man called for a new take. They redid the shot, but there was still an issue. One of the stagehands walked over to me and signaled for me to follow him.

"Do you have change or car keys in your pocket?" he asked.

Both hands had been in my pockets. Without my realizing it, the slight movement of my hand on my keys was being picked up by a mike ten feet above where I had been standing. The stagehand patted me on the back and walked away. The third shot was fine; the sound man had solved his problem.

At the end of the day, I thanked Georgia, my guide, for the experience and left early to keep ahead of the traffic.

That summer, when we had our VBS, I called Georgia and received permission to take sixteen of our youth to spend the day watching a movie being made. Later, we were invited to watch a few westerns and a drama being filmed; however, we did not see any actors or actresses that we could recognize.

The dates of the citywide leadership training and outreach program arrived. We had sixty-two churches participating. Each of the churches had four guest leaders to assist the church in its week of training.

Dr. House had sent word to me that the Sunday School Board in Nashville was sending me a young man from Grand Canyon College in Arizona to work as an intern and assist me in my responsibilities as the local program director.

The day after my time at the movie studio, I was an hour late getting to my office. When I walked into the building, Ruth stopped me in the hall. "Edd, there is a teenage young man in your office who says he is here to work with you this week," she said.

I had known someone was to come but had no other information. Ruth handed me a note with his name, and I walked in and introduced myself to Wendell Foss. Wendell, in spite of his youthful looks, was a senior at Grand Canyon College in Arizona. He was planning to enroll in Golden Gate Baptist Theological Seminary the next year after he and his future wife, Emily, were married. When Wendell asked me what he was to do, I had to tell him that I did not know. We talked and decided that we would make decisions and meet problems as they came. We ended up dealing with misunderstandings, presiding at group meetings and encouraging pastors and leaders when things broke down. Twenty years later, we both were on staff at the Baptist Convention offices in Fresno. Thirty years later, Wendell became my supervisor. After we both retired from the Convention, we worked together in the International Baptist Church in Munich, Germany. He and his wife became close friends with Flo and I, and we all traveled together in England and other European countries.

Dr. House and I (usually accompanied by Wendell) traveled around to interview conference leaders and as many of the people who were attending one of the conferences we could.

At lunch one day, Dr. House and I were alone, and he shared with me, "When I came here for this week, I was still hoping you would come to Nashville and work with us. After being here for this time, I can understand why you feel you cannot leave. To be truthful with you, you are where you belong — and if I were your age, this is where I would want to be."

That statement from one of my seminary professors, who was a recognized Christian education leader and one of the people I most admired, helped me to finish wiping out the years of doubt and uneasiness in my life. I was choked up. I thanked him and told him that I was pleased by his confidence in me and that his support, along with that of others, had kept me from giving up in the past. I had the privilege of working with Dr. House twice more in major city events before his retirement and early death.

Our church in Norwalk was now the largest and one of the most influential Southern Baptist churches in California. We were bursting at the seams. We led our state convention in baptisms, in gifts to the Cooperative Program and in special mission offerings. Gene and I both had to turn down invitations from all over the state. We built a new worship center, and our attendance increased to over nine hundred in Bible studies and well over a thousand in our worship services.

Gene had not been accepted into the Army during World War II because of a heart problem. His heart would slow down so much that he could pass out from getting too little blood to the brain. He was a great guy and, like me, one stubborn individual. When his blood pressure would drop too low, he would still force himself to keep going. He would refuse help. Oftentimes, his brain seemed to shut down, and he would respond to pressure without recognizing what he was doing or saying.

There were times when Flo and I would go to church and the pressures on him had been more than he could handle. He and I would have had some strong arguments. He would blow up and walk off. When these confrontations happened, Flo would know and ask, "Are we going to have to stand at the front of the congregation again?"

When Gene's blood pressure went back to normal, his way of apologizing was to have Flo and me stand at the front of the church while the people came by and let us know how much they appreciated us.

In March of 1959, we received a call from Flo's sister Jo in Wichita Falls, Texas. Their father had died. He had been having breathing problems for two weeks; because of his age the doctors could not do enough for him to recover. Jo wanted us to come. We made arrangements for the boys to stay with church members and took Marcia with us. We drove to Texas with Norma, Flo's sister in San Diego, and spent four days with family. We were there for their dad's memorial service. John, Flo's half-brother and a pastor, conducted the service. We helped Flo's mom as much as we could before driving back to California. Marcia, age three, was fascinated and asked a lot of questions about where Granddad had gone and if she would see him again.

Back home, Jack Combs, a state worker with Baptist foreign language churches, called and asked me to meet him in downtown Los Angeles. He wanted me to check out a building that had been the meeting place for a deaf ministry.

I met him, and we went through the building to evaluate its location and structure. With some upgrading and cleaning, it would be usable. It could possibly pass a city inspection with some minor improvements in the electrical and plumbing systems. With that and some scrubbing and paint, the building should be fine.

We had lunch, and he asked me to go with him to meet Don and Esther Kim. I knew both of them. We had been at Southwestern Seminary in Fort Worth at the same time. Don and Ester arrived, and we took them through the building and talked about using it to begin a new Korean church in downtown Los Angeles. Don, Ester and I had a great time together and renewed a relationship that would continue to grow over the years. Esther gave me an autographed copy of her book, "If I Perish, I Perish," which was about her time as a Japanese prisoner of war.

A few weeks later, the small congregation of the Korean Baptist Church moved into that building downtown. The church would later move twice and become Brenda Street Korean Baptist Church, which became one of the largest and most influential Korean Baptist churches in California. I was honored years later when I was asked to be the main speaker at a ceremony for Don and Ester's retirement and the appointment of the new pastor.

I cannot be positive, but I think it was either Dr. Staples or Dr. Maderas who phoned me. Both were former presidents of California Baptist College in Riverside. Whoever called asked me if I would be able to pick up a person at LAX and bring him to the college. J. L. Hardin was flying to LAX from West Texas. I was given Hardin's flight information. I had no conflict and agreed to meet him.

J.L. Hardin was coming to the California Baptist College as its new business manager. I met J.L. at the airport. We talked as I drove through Southern California traffic. J.L. knew my Uncle Prof and others I had known or worked with. We stopped at the church in Norwalk, and Gene joined us for lunch. During our conversation, Gene invited J.L. to come the following Sunday and preach for First Baptist Norwalk. Gene then volunteered me to be J.L.'s chauffeur for the day. J.L. agreed to return. I took him to his hotel in Riverside, and we agreed on a time for me to come and get him on Sunday morning.

Our church strongly supported California Baptist College (CBC), and we encouraged our young people to seriously think about enrolling there. On Sunday morning, J.L. did a great of job preaching on the importance of training pastors and church leaders; he focused on the need for educated Christian laymen and women to become involved as political and business leaders in our national and local communities. This, he emphasized, was something that CBC could help accomplish.

That summer when our youth were asked to choose their mission trip, they decided to go to CBC to meet with the students, professors and staff. In the next five years, nine of the high school graduates in our church went to CBC. Two of those were our sons Steve and Wayne.

Pat Patillo was the new director of the Sunday school department of our state convention. Alvis Strickland had retired and moved on. Fifteen years earlier, Pat had been studying for the ministry in a small college in central Texas. He was a close friend of Flo's and of my pastor in Kamay, Texas. Pat came to Kamay in the early 1940s and preached at a revival in our oilfield church when Flo and I were teenagers. He met with the young people after services during the week, and he and I became acquainted. He and I had renewed our friendship when Flo and I moved to Norwalk.

Pat called and wanted to set a time when he could come to Norwalk to talk to both of us. Pat came, and after we had caught up with each other, he asked Flo and me to become volunteer leadership trainers for our state convention. I would work with adults, pastors and church leaders. Flo would work with the teachers and leaders of young children in our churches. If we agreed, we would be sent to Salt Lake City for four days of special training and later to Glorieta with our expenses paid. He wanted us to work with him in four regional training events a year. To be safe, I talked to Gene.

"Do it. We will have two specialists in our church at no cost to us," he encouraged.

Another couple and a single lady from our area were asked to join the team as well. The other couple would take the single lady in their car, and Flo and I would ride with another man. We would drive to Las Vegas for the first night and then drive on to Salt Lake City the next day. We would be in Salt Lake City for five days and return home. With travel, lodging and a day off in Salt Lake, we would be gone eight days. Our driver had been a salesman in Nevada, and he had made our hotel and meal reservations. He drove most of the way. I drove some in the deserts to give him a break.

We left around noon and got to Las Vegas five hours later. Flo and I were wide-eyed; we had never seen anything like this place. Thousands of neon lights flashed day and night. Scantily clothed men and women walked the streets. There were hawkers for every show and gambling place. Some would even try to physically herd us into their establishments. After we walked through the crowds for an hour, our driver took us off the "Strip" to a nice restaurant he knew, and we had a great meal.

After we ate and checked into our hotel, we walked three blocks back to the Strip and went into one of the large casinos. It was bedlam; there was loud music and even louder voices. There were slot machines by the hundreds, and all of them were occupied. Dozens of other gambling devices that I did not recognize were being played by people who were in some kind of a trance.

One good thing stood out. The place, while crowded, was controlled by enough bouncers and security people to prevent any abusive activity. We watched a short magic show, listened to a band and then walked back through the crowds to our rooms.

As we drove to Salt Lake City the next day, our reactions to what we had seen and heard in Vegas kept everyone laughing, including Flo and me. We were more than surprised to learn of the number of churches in Vegas and their ministry to workers and patrons of the casinos.

In Salt Lake City, our driver pulled up in front of our hotel. I knew we must be lost; we were on the street that was part of Temple Square, directly across the street from the Mormon Temple. I asked our driver if we were where we should be. He was not sure either.

Pat Patillo and one of the conference leaders walked out of the front entrance of the hotel. They were going out for a walk. They saw us and helped us unload and directed our driver to where he could park his car. Flo and I had a room on the third floor that overlooked Temple Square.

The conference and training lasted five days, with workshops in the mornings and evenings. During the afternoons, we were free to explore the city. Our problem was that the temperature was below freezing. The streets and sidewalks were kept clean and sanded. We had to bundle up and could only walk a few blocks because of the intense cold.

Our local hosts had arranged for us to have a private tour of the Mormon Temple. We were welcomed by three young ladies and, for two hours, were told an excellent and thorough history of the Mormon trek across the country, the founding of Salt Lake City and the work of Joseph Smith, Brigham Young and John Taylor, the early President-Prophets of the church. There were huge dioramas that pictured the major steps of Mormon history. Throughout the tour, our temple guides subtly told us that, as Christians, we had been led astray by people who had misread and misinterpreted the Bible; however, nothing was overt or condescending.

The next day, we went to the "This Is the Place" monument that marks where Brigham Young pushed his walking staff into the ground to show that the long trek from Illinois had ended.

On Wednesday evening, Flo and I were guests in one of the local Baptist churches. The church was small, with just under a hundred members. Our purpose in going was not to tell them how to do their work. We went to learn and to share what we had learned over the years in situations like theirs.

While the Mormons did not openly object to the presence of Baptist churches, they did not entirely welcome the churches, either. The church Flo and I visited was in a developing neighborhood. The members were encouraged by their progress up to that point and anxious for any help we might be able to give. Flo met with the children's workers, and I spoke with the other teachers and church leaders. Their church was experiencing the same problem most churches have — an overwhelming need for trained and dedicated leadership.

I told them about one of my conversations with Gene Harrell just after we had moved to Norwalk. Gene told me how, on his way to church one Sunday, he watched the cars pulling into the parking lot with children and adults going to their Bible study classes. He said to himself, "God, if I am to help these people, You have to send me some leaders."

He went on to say that, though he was not actually praying, it was as if God spoke back to him and said, "You are looking at them right now. Get busy and train them." He continued, "I began to see not just people but potential leaders walking right in front of me. They were there, waiting for someone to lead them to become leaders. Preaching won't do it; they have to see and learn from our present leadership to understand."

He had then grinned and said to me, "That is our main job."

Our group of eight was now trained to be leaders for our churches in California, and we returned home. Over the next four years, Flo and I did our best to train leaders for new churches and older churches that were struggling in our area.

People kept coming to our church in Norwalk. There was no way we could build fast enough to provide for them. We began to enlist leaders who lived in new subdivisions to start churches in their own neighborhoods. We trained the people for leadership of small groups. We rented spaces in schools, warehouses and abandoned businesses and started new Bible study groups. As soon as it was possible, we would encourage the new group to call a pastor. We, the mother church, would help to provide the pastor's living salary for a year, to enable the new pastor to spend time with his people and family.

Three of our new church plants had difficulty finding a pastor. The result was that I would preach on Sunday mornings for one of the new congregations and work with them through the week until they were able to take on their own responsibilities. When a pastor was called, I would help with another church

Edd perched atop Norwalk's steeple.

plant. In the ten years that Flo and I were at First Norwalk, our church started eight new churches. Two did not make it, but six became strong congregations.

The community of Norwalk and our church were built up from new people coming to California; however, they soon could build no more. With no new houses, fewer new people were coming. New and larger homes in Orange and Riverside Counties became the destinations for most families.

Many members of our congregation were developing their work skills. Some now had much better paying jobs. They began to move into larger homes in less crowded areas. The community of Norwalk was changing, but our church, like too many churches, was reluctant to change. "Minorities" no longer existed. We were now the population center of multiple races. Our attendance was not increasing, and the younger people, the source of new leadership, began to move elsewhere.

At this same time, our family doctor called and asked me to come to see him. Mom and Janie were living with us, and Mom had been having medical problems for two months. The doctor had run tests and done x-rays. He reported, "Your mom has cancer of the uterus. She must have surgery and continued treatments."

Because of our personal finances and enlarged household, the thought of medical expenses was devastating. Mom and Janie had no health insurance. The doctor knew that and said, "I want you to call the City of Hope Hospital and see if we can get your mother in there."

He gave me their telephone number. "You tell them I have recommended that they should consider your request." The City of Hope is a national learning hospital. Doctors who are top in their fields are invited to practice and instruct other doctors in how to improve their skills. There is no cost to patients.

Three weeks before I received this news, I had been asked to speak on "Missions Are Our Mission" in five different churches at different times on Sunday mornings. Flo and I had applied to the Foreign Mission Board for overseas missions. Because of the age range of our children (five to sixteen years) and my lack of a continued preaching experience, it was their opinion that I should not be considered for overseas missions; however, my concern for missions and helping people in need was well-known.

I called the number our doctor had given me. The lady I was referred to asked my name and the reason for my call. I explained who I was and what my doctor had said.

"Would you give me your name again?" she asked, and I told her.

She asked, "Is that with two D's, and are you from First Baptist Church in Norwalk?"

"How do you know that?" I stammered.

"Just a guess. You preached in my church two weeks ago, and your voice sounded familiar. Now what can I do for you?" she asked.

I told her the details, and she put me on hold. I waited for what seemed ten minutes, although it was probably closer to three. She came back and asked, "Edd, you can bring your mom to see us Wednesday afternoon at two o'clock, and have her bring her doctor's reports." I could hardly speak but managed to say, "We will be there. Thank you."

Before I hung up, she said, "You think God might be involved in this?"

There was a reason that I, instead of my father, was taking care of Mom and Janie. When my dad moved Mom and Janie to California, he began to live a life of lies — lies to himself and to everyone else. His first open lie to me was that he had a job in a small town along the Colorado River. He said he would be gone for two weeks. Before he left, he moved Mom and Janie into the small two-bedroom house with me, Flo and our four kids. Mom and Janie had one room; Flo, Marcia and I had the other; and the three boys slept on pallets on the floor in the living room.

For ten days, we heard nothing from Dad. I called the police and entered a missing person report. After two weeks, they had found nothing. In my work at the Star Telegram in Fort Worth ten years earlier, I had developed skills in tracking down people who tried to skip out on some large advertising bills. I began to call law officers in areas where Dad could be living. I hit pay dirt in Fort Worth. Dad was now using the name "Jake," which had been his cowboy name on cattle drives as a young man. He had unpaid traffic tickets, and the police had located him in a small town in southeastern Oklahoma. They could do nothing as long as he did not return to Texas.

Janie, my ten-year-old sister, was in a hospital in Long Beach with some kind of infection. I told the officer that my call was a family emergency and convinced him that I was Dad's son. He gave me Dad's address and telephone number in southern Oklahoma. I called the number, and Dad answered.

"Dad ..." I said, but that was as far as I got.

"How the hell did you get this number?!" he yelled.

I heard a female voice in the background, "Who is it, Jake? Who is it?"

"I have ways," I told Dad, "but that is not important. Janie is in the hospital, and I thought you ought to know."

"She getting those damned shots?" he interrupted.

"I don't know, but Mom has no job. I have our four kids and I cannot pay Janie's medical bills."

"Well, that's your problem now. Don't call this number again." With that, he hung up.

His response to me, his oldest son, crushed me. Dad and I had been close throughout the years, and what I was hearing was devastating. I hoped I might have had the wrong number, but I knew better. I knew my dad was a proud man and had lost three jobs in the last two years, but for him to verbally disown me was almost more than I could handle. If God, my family and the people of our church had not stepped in, I do not think I could have held on.

Mom was accepted into City of Hope, and the surgery was successful — but soon after, we had another disastrous event to contend with.

Tom, Mom's youngest brother, had lost his only son, Tommy, in an accident a few months earlier. Around the time of Mom's surgery, Tom was flying in his private airplane with his wife, Ann, and their two youngest daughters over the hills of the Carolinas. They encountered bad weather along the border, ran out of fuel and crashed into the mountains. All four were killed. Sue, their older daughter, was the only one left.

I had to deliver the news to Mom two days before she was to be released from the hospital.

Our church rallied around us. They moved Mom, Janie and our family into a much larger three-bedroom home. Church members were there to help and brought food every day for a week.

In two months, Mom had recovered, and she took a job at the Baptist bookstore in Huntington Park. Janie, a year older than Steve, was doing well at school, and things looked much better. Three months later, a widow friend in the church asked Mom to consider moving in with her. She had vacant rooms, and they could share the utility expenses. Mom and Janie moved in with her.

In March of 1964, Flo received a call from Norma saying that their mom had been taken to the hospital and was in serious condition. Norma was going to fly back to Wichita Falls and stay with Jack and Jo, her sister and brother-in-law. She wanted to know if Flo could come.

I had vacation time. We made arrangements for church members to care for our four kids, and Flo and I drove to Texas. We stayed for a week. Flo's mom was in a coma and continued to get worse. The doctor told us that her strong heartbeat was all that was keeping her alive; otherwise, she would have died a week before. Flo did not want to stay any longer; she could do nothing to help, and she was worried about our kids. It took us three days to drive back to Norwalk. The day after we returned to Norwalk, Flo's sister called with the news that their mother had died and that the funeral would be in three days. Everyone would understand why Flo could not be there.

The church decided to give the pastor and us a housing allowance instead of providing homes for us. With the help of a realtor in our church, Flo and I bought our first California home close to a new high school and a nine-hole lighted golf course. We were on a cul-de-sac that the kids could use as a small playground. It was the nicest house we had ever had. We had great neighbors, including a Catholic priest whose church was only a block away. Our church members celebrated the move with us.

Our church was not growing in numbers. In one year, 112 new people joined our church, but 125 moved away. In spite of this, our youth ministry continued to grow. We took trips to Catalina Island, the mountains and, our favorite, San Clemente Beach. We would camp out and spend the day. I knew I was where I ought to be. Even with all our family problems, we were on our feet financially, in good health and in a loving and supportive church fellowship. That summer, we enrolled 560 children and youth in our summer Bible school.

Gene's heart problems began to get worse. He made bad decisions (and some good ones at the wrong times). He began to alienate people, especially the youth and their parents. I tried to help, but he resented it. I had to back off. I began to wonder if my years of ministry here were ending.

Around the same time, our family doctor called and asked me to come in to just talk. We had become good friends, so his request was not surprising; what he said, however, was: "Your youngest son, Bruce, has a major problem. He is allergic to plants and trees in this basin, and the smog is wrecking his immune system. I suggest you get him out of this area if you want him to live to be twenty."

He just looked at me and waited. I had been having viral pneumonia almost every fall for the last five years. Many of the people I knew had similar, if not more serious, problems. I did not want to move, but the church situation was not getting any better, and Bruce's health was the most important factor. I thanked the doctor and began to think seriously about the direction of my ministry.

During the past three years, I'd had as many engagements to preach as I had to train leaders. I still was not convinced that being a pastor was my calling. I was interviewed by two churches to come as music and education minister and had another invitation from the Baptist Sunday School Board to join their staff in Nashville. None of them seemed right.

Two churches asked me to come and preach, and both asked me to consider becoming their pastor. I considered and prayed about both, but neither could fit in with my responsibility to my family's needs.

My brother Charles, on his own and without any contact with me, bought Mom a house in Norwalk. He signed a long-term contract so Mom and Janie could have their own home. We cleaned and painted, and they moved in. He also bought Mom a car, which was fine with me; however, he did not continue to make the monthly payments on either. Mom had given him her payments, and Flo and I had written him personal checks for our share of the payments on Mom's car. The checks had been cashed, but no payments had been made to the bank on either the house or the car.

Mom had a new job in a women's store in Long Beach. This worked fine for about four months. One night, her car was repossessed. I had to take Mom to work and come up with three hundred dollars so we could retrieve her car. A few months later, I had to buy the house, refinance the mortgage and put the title in my name in order to keep Mom from losing her home.

When Flo's dad and mom had died, our travels to Texas and contributions to funeral expenses had caused us some financial problems. Flo, on a recommendation from a church member, found a job working for the new Oroweat Baking Company, not too far from Disneyland. She was the salesperson for their in-house sales. Marcia, our four-year-old, became my responsibility. Many church members stepped in and helped us, but most of the time she was with me. She had a place to play in my office. I would take her with me on many of my home visits. Because of her, I was able to talk to more people inside their homes instead of through screen doors. We would eat lunch together and sometime even cook dinner together before Flo came home.

One day, I was studying and working on a sermon when a telephone call interrupted me. A little annoyed, I picked up my phone. "This is Edd Brown. Can I help you?" I answered.

"Well, I hope so. My name is Ernest Smith, and I have been asked by our pastor search committee to contact you. We are a small church in Stockton. We have had a part-time pastor for two years. He is moving on, and we are now looking for our first full-time pastor. Your name was given to us, and we would like for you and your family to be our guests for a weekend. If you think you might consider talking to us, I will send you a letter with information about our church. We would then work out an acceptable date for you and your family to be our guests," he said.

I just wanted a break, but I agreed to look over their material. Their letter came, and I was not impressed. They had an average attendance of eighty people. Their congregation was made up of schoolteachers, law enforcement officers and business leaders. They had a small building that would not hold many more; however, the church was located in a growing area of the city. I talked to Flo and the kids, and we set a date to go.

Flo and I went with Bruce (age twelve) and Marcia (age eight), in Flo's car. Steve (age seventeen) and Wayne (age fifteen) were in the Volkswagen. We started out together, but Steve and Wayne passed us going over the Grapevine (a curvy mountain road) and were standing outside the restaurant in Bakersfield where we were to eat lunch. I had been president of the Western Religious Education Society that met in Berkeley and later in Mill Valley. Steve and Wayne had made several trips with me. They knew the road and our eating places. We had lunch and drove on to Stockton.

We checked into our motel in South Stockton, and I let Ernest know that we were there. He and his wife came and visited. Two hours later, we went to their home for dinner.

Ernest had been looking at Flo at the motel. As we entered his home, he stared at her for a couple of minutes, shaking his head, and then asked, "Would you by any chance be Florene Nelson from Kamay, Texas?"

Flo and I were both stunned. We looked at him and at one another. Before Flo or I could recover or answer, Ernest continued, "If you are, I have a picture of you and your sister Josephine sitting on a rock on your dad's farm. Our family lived in a rental house west of yours before we moved to California."

He went into another room and brought out the picture. Neither Flo nor I could remember the Smiths. That time was in the middle of World War II, when the moving of people was constant.

The next morning we were at the church early. Flo was dressed in her best. When she stepped out of the car, her foot landed in a four-inch mud hole that messed up her shoe and hose. My reaction was, "If I come to this church, the first thing we will do is to pave this parking lot."

We attended the adult Sunday school class that was taught by John Gorely, the church's volunteer music director. We were introduced and enjoyed the class and our reception. Steve and Wayne met with the youth and, without any effort, made a big hit with the girls. Bruce and Marcia had a good time with their age groups and liked their teachers.

The worship service was amazing. The small choir could have graced any church. John, the volunteer music leader, was as good as any paid music director in our state. I was again introduced before preaching my sermon.

After the service, the congregation and guests could not do enough for us. We had a big lunch with most of the church members and with several visitors who stayed to eat and fellowship.

An open meeting for all church members and other interested parties followed our lunch. Flo and I shared our personal history. The congregation was asked to raise any question they might have. One thing that puzzled most of the people was why would I consider leaving a two-thousand-member church and come to one of around a hundred members.

My basic and honest answer was, "It would not be my doing. God has to lead both you and me to respond. If and when God leads us to respond, you will have my answer."

Steve and Wayne drove back to Norwalk that afternoon. Flo, Bruce, Marcia and I spent the night in our motel. On Monday, we drove around Stockton and looked at schools and homes in the area. I met with four of the leaders of the church. We discussed our concepts of church business, music, services to the community, missions and church politics.

We were tired and left just in time to get home that evening. After school the next day, Steve and Wayne came home to talk about our day in Stockton.

Steve spoke up, "Dad, that church in Stockton is going to call you to be their pastor, and I think you ought to go."

While I was beginning to feel the same way, I wanted to know why he thought so. His answer was, "The building and grounds are a mess, and the entire place needs work. If they grow any at all, they will need a new building. You can lead them to do that."

I asked Wayne what he thought, and he said, "Steve may be right, but I don't want to leave my friends." He got up and walked away. Bruce and Marcia liked the kids but were happy whether we moved or stayed.

Flo, like Wayne, did not want to leave our friends; many were closer to us than family, but she knew and accepted the fact that, if I knew that God was leading, then we had better go.

The church unanimously voted for us to come. I could start in two weeks, and my family would move at the school midterm

The Brown family moves to Stockton, California.

break in eight weeks. I would be provided with meals and lodging until the family could move. I would be in Stockton Thursday through Sunday, although if there were a business meeting on a Wednesday evening, I might need to attend. We prayed and talked to Gene, the Norwalk church staff and the members.

We accepted the invitation to go to Stockton. We put our house on the market and made plans with Mom for Steve to stay with her until he could to finish his senior year of high school. Wayne was more than upset that we would not do the same for him. He had half his junior year and full senior year to finish, but there was no way we were going to have Mom take care of two high school boys for eighteen months.

The Norwalk church, at the pastor's leading, planned a huge going-away party. They loaded us down with gifts and money. A family in the church wanted our house, so one problem was solved. Val Prince, who had moved to Norwalk from Houston, Texas, was the educational director for the greater Los Angeles Association of Baptist Churches. He had a brother-in-law in Stockton who was a realtor and a prospective church member. We made contact with his brother-in-law. He located a house for us in a new subdivision and arranged for excellent financing. We paid the down payment and, with the help of people in Norwalk and Stockton, moved into our new home a week after Christmas. Our home was located along a river in the northwest section of Stockton. We were within walking distance to our church. Bruce and Marcia could walk to school, and Wayne's bus stop was only three blocks away.

On one of our Glorieta trips, we went to Kamay, Texas. The Baptist church where Flo and I grew up and were married had decided to ordain me to the gospel ministry. Flo's brother John, a pastor, was a member of the ordination committee.

TEN

1964-1967

STOCKTON, CALIFORNIA

HIGH SCHOOL, CALIFORNIA FISH AND GAME

Wayne continued to be very unhappy with our move. Two of the teachers at Stagg High School were members at Michigan Heights Baptist Church and had a son and two daughters close to Wayne's age. They went out of their way to get Wayne involved with the youth at church and at school.

When the rains had stopped, I shared with the deacons Flo's experience and hoped they could see what an incident like that could do for a possible new member. Since that had not happened to members of their families, they had not noticed the potholes. At the next church business meeting, the deacons asked the church to approve the finances to pave, curb and light the parking lot. A few of the ladies commented, "It's about time," and the church voted to began the project as soon as a contractor could be hired.

In four weeks, we had our new lighted parking lot, and the church's standing in the community went up a thousand percent. While Flo and our kids were still in Norwalk, I spent my time visiting church families and the neighbors around the church. Our church attendance began to increase.

Flo and I could not believe the way we were treated. When they were in season, boxes of fresh fruit or vegetables were left on our doorstep two to three times a month, along with cases of juice and canned fruit. Twice a month, Flo and I were taken by a church family to dinner, on a picnic, boating or camping. Most of the time, our whole family was included. This was in addition to the hunting and fishing that I did with our men.

One example of their treatment began early one morning. Our doorbell rang earlier than normal. I opened the door; two ladies from the church were there, and two others were in their car.

"We came to see Flo," they abruptly announced, and I welcomed them in.

Flo had only been up long enough to get breakfast for the kids and get them off to school. She was still in the bedroom and had not had time to dress. Flo came into the room wearing her robe. The ladies told her they were taking her shopping in ten minutes, so she had better go get some clothes on. Not knowing what was up, Flo hurried and dressed. I was told in no uncertain terms to stay home all day and make sure that the kids were cared for because Flo would not be back until late that afternoon.

When Marcia came home from school that afternoon, she wanted to talk to her mom. She was unhappy with me because Mom was not home. The boys couldn't have cared less, but they did question why the women would take Mom, half-dressed, somewhere all day.

Around four that afternoon, the women returned. I had to look twice before I knew it was Flo. They had taken her to a hairdresser and to an upscale women's dress shop. They had bought her new clothing, including undergarments, shoes and hose. Her old clothes were in a bag, which was handed to me. The ladies said, "Now, pastor, here is your wife. You had better treat her like the woman she is, or you are going to be in big trouble." They turned away laughing, got in their car and left.

Flo was almost crying. "How can we react to the love of these people? They won't let us just be human."

This was the beginning of three years of unprecedented ministry with a people who loved God and us and wanted to show it.

Six weeks after we arrived, the church budget for the current year had to be corrected to take care of a full-time pastor and his family. It was an opportunity to plan how to best use the increased offerings that were beginning to be given. The budget committee had purposely waited these six weeks to give themselves time to evaluate the necessary adjustments to the new expenses of a full-time pastor.

I was the moderator of our regular monthly business meeting. The budget committee chairman brought their recommendations. I was astonished. They increased most programs and missions a good amount. As a new pastor, I expected no salary increase, but the committee recommended an amount that shocked me. In discussing the proposed budget, the people only asked for clarification of a few items. No one even mentioned the recommended fifteen percent increase to my salary.

I felt I had to say something. I stepped aside as moderator. I reminded the people that I had only been their pastor three months. I could not think of any reason for them to give me any increase in salary; even five percent would have been too much, but fifteen percent was unreal.

The chairman of the committee, a professor of nuclear engineering at the University of the Pacific and the holder of two doctoral degrees, spoke up: "Pastor, while we appreciate your concern, look at the committee — a business leader, two public school administrators, three business owners and me. Do you think we are unaware of what we are doing?"

I was embarrassed and had to make sure that they knew that I had not meant any insult. I was just trying to share that I had a personal problem accepting that much of an increase so early.

"Okay, we understand. It may take us time to learn to trust one another," he answered.

This was a new world for me. I told them that I would stop questioning their decisions and that Flo would help us find the best way to use their generous salary increase.

Many families began to come and thank us for how much we cared for the community in which they lived. Our new curbs, parking and streetlights helped upgrade their neighborhood.

As we began to plan for VBS, our youth asked for the responsibility of advertising our Bible school. They created their own attractive flyers for the event. They planned to deliver the flyers a month before our Bible school to parents, children and young people in our area; they would also talk to the people about what was happening at their church. The parents planned a picnic afterwards for those who did the visiting and for any others in the community who wanted to come and get acquainted. Ten youth spent six hours over two afternoons talking to people in our community. We had thirty-eight people join our youth and parents at our picnic.

Ten days before VBS, there was a two-day mission conference at Golden Gate Baptist Seminary in Mill Valley. Six of the young people wanted to go. I drove my car. We checked into our guest rooms at the seminary and drove to Sausalito.

Sausalito, California, is the small town where the hippy/flower child movement began. It was later fleshed out in Haight-Ashbury and on the USC Berkeley campus. The business owners in Sausalito, a small village just north of the Golden Gate Bridge, had been seeing a major drop in tourism for the past two years. Some smart business people put together a scheme that they hoped would bring more business to Sausalito. They went to USC-Berkeley and two other nearby college campuses and hired students at a fair wage to come and help them drum up business in and for their town. There were very few limits to what the students were allowed to do. Girls wore short skirts; boys wore tie-dyed shirts and tight, worn-out jeans; and they played loud, off-key music. Open displays of affection were encouraged, and the idea caught on. The news spread rapidly on TV and in newspapers that were looking to increase subscriptions. The movement escalated. College kids in other parts of California and, later, all over the nation began to mimic what had begun as a local business advertising strategy.

The first day after our conferences and lunch in Sausalito, we went to Haight-Ashbury and walked the streets. After two hours, all of us were embarrassed enough by what we saw that we were ready to leave. While there was no open promiscuity, the innuendos and attire left no room for misunderstanding. We went back to the seminary and attended the general meeting and breakout conferences that evening.

At breakfast together the next morning, we shared our thoughts. The last message of the meeting was titled "Change Can Only Come From Personal Involvement." On our drive home, the difference between what we had seen in our visits to Sausalito and Haight-Ashbury and what we had seen and spoke about at the seminary were their major topics.

The week before our VBS began. Four of the six youth that had gone to the mission conference came to my office and wanted to talk. They were still disturbed at what they had and seen in the Bay area and wanted to do something.

"Okay," I said, "give me a reason why, and tell me what you want to do."

Their response was, "What we saw on our trips to town were young people who only wanted a life for themselves. They just don't care for anyone else. We are not like that."

"Have you looked at the outside of our church building?" one young lady asked. I had, but I wanted their answer. I waited.

"It has three colors of faded paint, and some of the plaster has fallen or been knocked off. With our new parking lot and curbed streets, the church now looks like a dump, and no church or home should ever look like that. We want the job of repairing and painting the outside of our church building to be our vacation Bible school project for the next two weeks. We want to help the teachers with the younger kids in the mornings, to have a quick lunch at church and to work for four hours each afternoon. We also want you come to one of our homes in the evening so we can have a light meal together and an hour of Bible study."

I could hardly keep up, much less believe what I was hearing. All I had done was to ask some questions. They had completely covered a need that I was hoping to present to the church at a later time. Now the question was, could we together get the church to turn eight to ten young people loose on that big of a project? It would take planning, supervision and money for materials.

We had only a week to find a way to let these young people tackle a job bigger than they were. I agreed to help them, but they had to help me convince the church that they could and would finish the job. Our building was an eyesore in a community of nice, modestly sized homes. The youth left our meeting pleased and began to work on their parents and the building and grounds committee. The project became so popular with our young people that parents and church members knew we would have an open rebellion if we did not go along and help them do the project themselves.

Men, women volunteered to supervise. We parents and other adults committed to provide meals and refreshments. The church agreed to buy the materials as needed.

On the first day of Bible school, after three hours of helping teachers and leaders with younger children, all eight teenagers changed into work clothes and had lunch.

I, along with two other men from the church, supervised and helped where needed and encouraged our young people as they began to scrape and clean a ten-foot-high, 120-foot-long exterior wall on the street side of our church building. With minimal instruction and demonstration, they began to make progress.

Teenagers in the community came by and watched. The second day, a fifteen-year-old girl came in work clothes and asked me if she could help. I put her with one of our girls who had gone to the mission conference. The next day, she came back and brought a friend. At the end of the two weeks, a professional re-facing job had been done on our church building by not eight but thirteen youth from our church and community. Five new youth began to attend our church regularly.

Three weeks later, the three older girls came to see me again. I had no idea what they wanted this time. The older one, who was the leader of the church painting project, spoke up.

"Edd, we have been talking about the mission conference and what we did for our church, and we are grateful for your support. Now we want to do something for others, not ourselves. Could you help us find something older teenagers can do?"

"Sure, I will work with you, but you have to be part of the decision," I responded.

They asked about the older lady who lived in a house nearby. The house had bad steps and a horrible paint job. Two rest homes, where elderly had no family and no visitors, were also close by. Additionally, the girls knew of migrant work camps where children had no supervision while their parents worked in the field.

"Now," I said, "you three talk it over with others who are interested.

Choose one project to begin. Make your plans simple. Let me know what you decide, and I will see what we can do."

Six days later, the three girls, accompanied by two boys, came back with a proposal. "We want to replace the steps and rebuild the entrance to the house on the corner where the older lady lives. After that, we want you to help us find us a small work camp close to town and get permission for us to visit. We will then see if we can do something to help those people."

With help from Les Range, a highway patrolman and chairman of our building committee, six young people and I did an excellent repair and upgrade of the porch and entrance to the house. The gratitude shown us by the lady more than paid for the work that was done.

With minimal help from me, the young people located a migrant camp three miles east of town on a river bank. The workers were there to prune fruit trees and grapevines for local farmers. Five couples with nine small children were in the camp. A twelve-year-old girl was left to watch the other eight children. Three of our girls and two boys took vacation Bible school materials and cared for the children for two hours every morning for a week. The children were ecstatic, and the parents could not find words to express their thankfulness. The young people continued to go two or three mornings a week until the workers moved on and our young people went back to school.

At a meeting with our young people a week later, we reviewed our summer. I had asked them to come with answers about what the summer had done for them and how they felt about it.

One of the younger girls was first to speak: "I watch the news and see hundreds of kids our age destroying themselves and others, and I get sick. Then I think of what we have done and are doing, and I feel good. You know, if we could get enough young people like us involved, we could change the world." Our group named itself "World

Changers."

In the present day, under the leadership of our denomination's Home Mission Board, over twenty thousand youth and adults are involved in short-term mission projects around the world every year. Neither a pastor, nor a denominational worker nor a group of adults began that ministry. The concept began with three teenage girls who wanted to make a difference and who unknowingly began a program that has made a worldwide difference. World Changers was picked up by the California Southern Baptist Convention and by other associations. A few years later, the Brotherhood of Baptist Men, which is now part of the North American Mission Board, bought the concept and program from California Baptist Men's Ministries for a thousand dollars. Teenagers might just surprise us if we listen.

A new house was built next door to our home. A captain for California Fish and Game and his family moved in. We had become good friends, and his family, on occasion, attended our church. One evening, he came to our house to talk to me. He asked if I would consider becoming a deputy game warden for California Fish and Game. It would be a volunteer position, with mileage and expenses paid. I would have to go through the regular California Fish and Game officer training and certification. I would ride with one of the regular wardens no more than one or two days a week.

I went to the deacons and told them of the request. I had ridden with the three highway patrol officers in our church

Deputy game warden Edd.

in Norwalk. Our church in Stockton had a highway patrolman, a federal officer and the county undersheriff as members. I was encouraged by the deacons to accept the invitation. Our church saw this as an outreach ministry opportunity. I attended the field officer training program and bought my uniform and gun. I passed the written test and the pistol range shooting test and was sworn in.

Most of my territory was Delta Valley County (where I lived), but it also included Amador, Calaveras and Tuolumne Counties in the foothills of the Sierra Mountains. Those counties were where much of the gold was discovered in the early Gold Rush. The historic Highway 49 runs through the counties where I worked. Waterfowl, dove, quail and pheasants were the main bird families to be protected; trout, bass, salmon, stripers and catfish were the main fish. We also saw to deer, bear, and the occasional cougar or mountain lion. As wardens, we checked for licenses, permits, alcohol and bag limits; we also monitored gun, campfires and boat safety. Most of the time, warnings were all that were issued. Only twice in four years did either my partner or I have to write a ticket or threaten to confiscate firearms.

I rode boats in the delta, inland lakes and waterways. The high point of my four years as a deputy was when I was asked to ride horseback into the game reserve west of Lake Tahoe for ten days, a week before the opening of deer season. I had not been on a horse in years. I wanted to go, and the church said to do it.

Jess Smith, a deacon, owned a service station. He asked if I needed to start riding a few weeks before I rode a horse over mountain trails for ten days. Did I ever! His teenage daughter had a horse and rode along the dikes close to where he worked. Jess was working more hours and offered me a horse with saddle and gear if I would take a couple afternoons a week and ride with his daughter. She was not allowed to ride in that area by herself. We worked out the times, and she and I went riding for two hours twice a week. Even though I had not spent time around horses for seventeen years, I thought I would only need a short time to recover those old habits. Was I ever wrong!

The first two times we went, I had to have help from a teenage girl with the bridle and saddle. I nearly fell twice getting on the horse. I had to relearn how to make him go where I wanted and at what speed. After six two-hour outings, it all began to come back, and I enjoyed a great, relaxing time. My relearning time gave me a dozen good illustrations for sermons on the importance of consistent Christian living. The soreness on my rear end, inside my thighs and in my shoulders began to disappear after riding for four days.

The day for me to go to the reserve came. The captain and a warden helped me load my camping gear, and we headed to Truckee and then south to Squaw Valley, where our horses were. I had told no one about my growing up on a ranch and learning to ride my own horse the summer of my fourth birthday. There were seven other riders, and everyone watched me like a hawk. They knew a preacher would need help and would have to be carefully watched to keep him from getting hurt around unfamiliar animals.

I did have some difficulty getting into the saddle. When I finally got on the horse, the wrangler re-cinched my saddle and handed me the reins. The horse did not know me, and I was not sure about him. I strapped my pack on the back of the saddle. I looked around, and only two others were on their horses and ready to go. Guess who they were watching. We were to take turns leading the pack mule with our gear. I would be the last one to lead the mule. Mules are usually more stubborn than some people.

We started up the mountain, going west into Desolation Valley on the border of the state game reserve. We were halfway over the pass when one of the horses bumped into a large rock on a curve and began to act up. I stopped my horse, but the rider behind me did not. We were overlooking a hundred-foot-deep ravine. We all began to work on settling down our horses. I was the first to get off my horse; I walked in front of him and stroked his forehead between his ears, and he began to settle down. I did not see what the others did, but in ten minutes, everything seemed calm. The captain then wisely suggested that we walk and lead the horses until we came to wider sections on the trail. We walked uphill for a half-mile, and the trail began to level. We got back in our saddles and rode five miles to camp without any more problems.

We unloaded our pack mule and unsaddled the horses and led them into a roped-off corral. We made sure there was food and water for the animals, and then we went inside our cabin.

The cabin was built for law enforcement people. It was set up for twelve. We eight had plenty of room and surprisingly good bunks. A dry well and a privy were out back. On the opposite side of the cabin, a stream bed had been cut out to bring fresh snowmelt water. The water would flow by our cabin once a metal pipe was connected to a small reservoir half a mile up a slope from our cabin.

We unpacked our gear and went to the reservoir to connect the pipe. The connector had been knocked off or thrown off a large flat rock into the eight-foot-deep settling pool. Several attempts were made to get a rope around the connector, and everyone was getting frustrated.

Without thinking, I took off my clothes, grabbed one end of the rope and jumped into the ice-cold water. The shock stunned me, but I was determined to get the water flowing and get back to the cabin. The water was clear; I tied the rope to the connector and headed for the surface. I jumped out to grab my clothes. Before I could dry off to put them on, the others put their coats around me and sat me down on a coat-covered flat rock. Not a word had been spoken. The connector was put in place, and water started flowing. I wore two of their coats, and they carried my wet clothes to the cabin. A fire had been built. Inside, I toweled off and put on dry clothes with heavy socks and a sweater. There was hot coffee, and I began to warm up.

Two of our guys had stayed behind and were cooking dinner. The others started clearing the water ditch. I made up my bunk and placed my clothes with other items in my locker at the head of my bed. The two cooks let us know that our meal was ready. After we sat at the table, the captain asked one of the men to lead a prayer of thanks before we ate.

The prayer was short, and we began to eat. A building contractor sitting across from me put his fork down and said, loud enough for everyone to hear, "I have to say something. When I found out some preacher was coming on this trip, I almost backed out. I knew we would have to look out after him. He would not know how to ride a western saddle even if he could find the front end of a horse. He might fall off and spook our horses on the trail, and that would be dangerous for all of us. It turned out that the trip up the mountain was no big deal to him. This preacher is better with horses than I am!

"I also thought he would not do any good camping out up here night after night. Things might become strained, and he could be a nuisance. But when he jumped into that freezing water and tied that rope as fast as he did, I changed my mind. I want you to know, Preacher, that not only do I owe you an apology, but you can ride with me any time."

Everyone but me clapped, and then it got quiet. Embarrassed but grateful, I had to say, "Guys, I am just another man like you. I may be a preacher now, but I was fortunate to learn many things as I was growing up on ranches, working in oil fields and serving in the Navy.

I want to do my part on this trip, but right now I am hungry, so let's eat."

We became a team. Even though I refused to drink anything stronger than coffee and did not use their choice of words, I was now a welcome member of the group. After the meal, whoever had kitchen duty cleaned up, and the rest of us made sure the horses were okay. We played dominoes, and I was questioned more about my background and the typical problems of religions, but there was no criticism of me or my profession.

All of us were tired and went to bed. I slept well and woke up smelling bacon cooking. I dressed, went to the privy and washed up with soap and ice-cold water. I was wide awake when I went inside for a country breakfast of bacon, eggs, potatoes, gravy, biscuits, butter, jam and boiled camp coffee.

We were there two days before deer season opened. As many people do when dealing with rules, some hunters think regulations and laws are for other people, not themselves. We made the rounds to check on camp locations, fire safety, hunting licenses, deer tags, alcoholic drinks and firearms.

The first day, we found three camps on the wrong side of the reservation border. They had to be moved. Two of us rode together on a seven-mile circuit and were back to camp for lunch. All teams were made up of two men. We took an hour-long break and rode out again. This would be our pattern for six more days.

State and federal park rangers came by and visited. We had a relaxing good time. We rode our horses eight to ten hours a day, rain or shine. I thoroughly enjoyed myself. We made no arrests and had no problems. Every day, we visited every camp. We found no violations. We varied our times of arrival to keep everyone lawful and safe.

A week after we returned home, I began to receive calls from the guys who were with me on the trip. One asked me to come to his house. I went to his home, met his wife and waited for him to speak.

He stammered and began, "We are having some problems that are my fault, and I need some help." He told me that, while he did not drink much nor often, he lost control when he did drink. He did and said things that sometimes took weeks or months to correct.

I asked his wife what she thought. "He is the best man a woman could have for a husband, but when he gets down on himself and drinks, he becomes the worst anyone could be stuck with," she said between sobs.

He had tried to quit on his own, over and over again, but he would never admit he was a weekend alcoholic. I knew some people in Alcoholics Anonymous (AA) and suggested that the man and his wife go and visit them — not yet to join, but just to visit. They agreed to go if I would make the appointment for them. The appointment was made, and they went. They then decided that both needed to change more than just his drinking problem. They called me and wanted to know if they should start going to a small church close by. They asked me to contact the pastor and to have him come and visit them. In a month, both were both attending AA and the local church on a regular basis.

Another fellow from the mountain trip called and came to my office. He came to convince himself, not me, that he did not need the church or God in his life. We had several meetings, and he did eventually begin to realize that his problems were with himself, not God.

Things were going great for our family. Several church members were teachers at the schools our three kids attended. Steve's high school football team won the district championship for Southern California. He was the starting tight end and first string defensive linebacker. We went to his regional championship game in Camarillo.

Their team lost by a few points. Steve graduated from John Glenn High School and came home for the summer.

Our director of missions for the Delta Valley Association moved to Nashville, Tennessee, to work at the Sunday School Board. I was elected moderator of the association. It was a non-paying job that took up a lot of time since we had no director of missions for our twenty-four churches.

The treasurer of the association was a pastor of a small church in Stockton. There had been some questions about some of the financial reports. As moderator, I asked someone from another church, a friend of mine who was an accountant at the local military supply base, to look over the books. Laurence Estes, an associational board member, agreed to help. The ledger showed a positive balance, but there was no money in the bank. A complete audit was ordered, and Estes was asked to handle it. Over five thousand dollars was missing. An official complaint was filed, and a court hearing was set. The pastor was found guilty and ordered to repay all funds and pay a substantial fine or else go to jail. He was put on probation for two years and was barred from handling any money that was not his own.

Laurence was later elected the treasurer of the association, and we developed a great working relationship. In our work together, Laurence and I became good friends. He asked about my family and learned that Steve was coming home from California Baptist College for the summer. Laurence had a daughter, Peggy, who was also at CBU. She was a year ahead of Steve. He asked if Steve had a job for the summer. I told him I doubted that he did. He told me to have Steve come and see him when he got home.

When Steve came home, he went to see Mr. Estes and was hired for a night maintenance position. Steve and Peggy had not been involved together in any school activities at California Baptist, but through mutual acquaintances in Stockton, they became friends.

I began to get more outside invitations, and our church continued to grow. At the urging of church members, I began to teach as a substitute at high schools one day a week. After a year, I was receiving more requests from the school district than I could accept. I had to resign.

I was contacted by the president of the ministers conference of Stockton, who asked me to be part of a pastor's committee to create a citywide emergency counseling program. We would have printed signs in the bus stations, telephone booths and other strategic places in the city. He wanted us to enlist and train fifty people to answer telephones for one week twice a year. If these trained people could not help the person calling, then one of twenty pastors would be on call no more than two weeks per year.

He promoted the idea at the first pastor fellowship that I was asked to attend. The pastors decided they wanted to study the concept and talk to their congregations about what was being considered. There was enough positive reaction that a three-person team of volunteers began developing the program.

The first thing the team did was to schedule a meeting three weeks off, in which the head of the California Mental Health Department would come and speak to us about the importance of such a program. Information was mailed to all the pastors. We were encouraged to come to the meeting and bring at least one layperson with us.

Sixty pastors and church leaders met in a large church near the campus of Pacific University. In his message, our speaker complimented the group on its plans and relayed the results of two studies his department had conducted.

He began, "I have two doctor's degrees: I am a medical doctor and have a doctorate in psychology. I was the medical director for two large health services for twenty years. When I was asked to take the leadership of the state mental health program, I wanted to know the best approach that we, as doctors and specialists, should take to help people in need.

"My staff and I wanted to find out who had done the best job of helping people with emotional and temporary mental problems and how they had done it. For six months, we did an in-depth study of people and groups involved with persons in need, and our results were clear.

"First, we reviewed the work of our trained specialists. We had a fifty percent success rate with our patients. One half made significant progress, and the other half showed little or no improvement.

"Second, we reviewed the work of pastors trained in counseling, school counselors and medical doctors. We were shocked to find that they had the same success rate as we specialists had.

"Third, we interviewed people who were connected with churches — pastors, lay leaders, Bible teachers and those who regularly attended church gatherings. We found that if a troubled person had a close Christian friend, someone trustworthy who would listen and offer encouragement, the result was the same as if the one needing help had talked to a specialist. One half of those with mental or emotional issues improved, and half did not.

As one person in our study group said, 'We shot ourselves out of our saddle with our own gun.'"

He continued, "Pastors and church leaders, if you have not trained your people in how to listen and show acceptance and love, you are going to have to explain yourselves to God. We found that Bible believers had already within them a special 'something' that enabled them to sense needs. All the believers needed was training in how to use that 'something' to help people."

For another hour, we dialogued with our speaker. When he left, most of us could see the training as a necessary facet of our ministries.

After the citywide program began, I was contacted by two individuals who had been referred to me by our trained first responders. The first was a distraught mother. Her son had become a real problem, and she wanted help. I agreed on a time for her to come to our church building. She came in and sat in the chair across the table from me. My personal office was in my home, but I used a small classroom at the church for counseling. The lady, in her forties, began to tell me about all the problems she was having with her son. The more she talked, the more confused I became.

When I could get a question in, I asked her, "Ma'am, how old is your son?"

Her answer was, "He has no reason to want to leave me and my husband. He is only twenty-six, and we never did anything to harm him. We have always given him everything he wanted, and now he is unhappy that we want him to stay and live with us."

After ten minutes of letting her vent, I tried to suggest that she look at what she and her husband had done by not letting their son have a life of his own. She refused to even discuss that. We both gave up, and she stormed out of the room.

My second referral was also a very distraught woman. Her husband was an alcoholic who stayed drunk half of the time. According to her, he was the sorriest man in the county. She went on about how he had never really loved her, was abusive to her children, had refused to take a promotion at his job and did not like her cooking. She said that the neighborhood they lived in was not good enough for her; then she commented that she had expected a counselor to have an office instead of an old table in a small room.

I had an unholy thought: "If I had to live with this woman, I would have to stay drunk all the time, too."

I gave her my card; why she kept it, I never knew. A week later, I had a call from one of the local hospitals, asking me to rush to the emergency room. The woman had shot herself but had not damaged any vital organs. Neither the doctors nor I could get through to her. She and her husband moved away as soon as she was released. I doubt that we helped her at all.

Seven weeks after I had resigned as a substitute teacher, the school district superintendent called me. He asked if I could help him with a short-term problem. The teacher of continuation high school was pregnant and needed to take a year off to care for the new baby. The continuation high school met four hours a day, five days a week. They wanted me to fill in for her. I again went to the deacons and church staff, and they said to do it if I could handle the pressure. I cut back my game warden time to two days a month and agreed to try.

On my first day of class, my twelve students had to see what I was made of and how I could be manipulated. After the first two hours, most of the students settled down; however, there is always one. This young man was there on probation from the California Youth Authority. He kept verbally pushing me. When he figured out that I would not let him take over, he came out of his seat and stood right in front of me. I was standing in front of my desk. While still mouthing off, he put his hand on my shoulder and gave me a light push to emphasize his contempt for adults who tried to push him around. The other students were horrified. An uneasy silence penetrated the room.

I did not back off. I got right in his face and said, loud enough for everyone to hear, "Young man, you either take your hand off me and return to your seat, or I will break that arm; and before you hit the floor, I will kick you so that you won't be able to walk for a week. If you think I care about getting fired, you had better think again. I have a full-time job and will resign from this one long before you can walk anywhere to file a complaint. You have five seconds." I began to count. By the time I reached three, I was still staring directly into his eyes. He dropped his arm and went to his chair.

I turned to the class and said, "In case you are wondering if I would have done what I threatened, the answer is — you don't need to find out."

We continued our work for the day. For the rest of the semester, I had no discipline problems. Two days after the confrontation, during our class break, the young man who had mouthed off came outside to where I was sitting and sat down across the table from me. I looked up, he asked if we could talk, and I agreed.

"Why do you like me?" he asked.

I had him repeat himself and then asked him, "What makes you think I like you?"

His reply was one I would have never dreamed of hearing. "I am seventeen years old. You are the first person in my life who cared enough about me to make me do what is right. No one else, not even my parents, has cared enough about me to make me behave and grow up."

I sat, wondered and prayed. What could I do? What could I say? After three long minutes, I said, "You know, maybe I do like you, but I sure do not like the way you act. If one of my sons ever pulled what you tried to pull on me, I would hope, because I love him, that whomever he tried to bully would put him down hard and make him think."

I put out my hand, and he looked up at me and smiled. We shook hands and held them longer than necessary.

Two days later, he came to me again. "I feel I owe you something, and I want to help. If either of those other two punks give you trouble, let me know; I will take care of them for you," he said.

While I appreciated his concern, I had to control myself to keep from laughing. I said, "You can take care of those two punks? If I remember correctly, I took care of you. You think I cannot handle them?"

He looked at me and then at the other guys standing nearby who were not convinced I was for real; then he said, "I guess you could."

We walked together into the classroom. The rest of the semester went great. All of my students passed their year's work and either returned to regular high school or graduated.

Even with all of my so-called "non-church" work (as some good members called it), Michigan Heights continued to grow, and we were soon out of space. We designed a multipurpose worship center and fellowship hall. It could seat two hundred people for worship with choir space for thirty. We had an upstairs room for Bible classes that could later be converted into a balcony for another fifty people when needed.

Flo had a job at the local military supply base and had received a promotion. Our kids were doing well in school. Friends, including church members, invited us to something every week. I went duck and deer hunting with our deacons. Our young people were pursuing more mission projects, and other young people from our community were joining them.

Our family was soon leaving for Glorieta, New Mexico. I was to be a conference leader. I was working my rear end and everything else off and loving

Edd checks fund-raising totals for Michigan Heights.

every minute of all that I was doing. We had two weeks of vacation that we could use in conjunction with the week of leadership training at Glorieta. We planned to rest, relax and enjoy the break.

When we returned home after a relaxing time of visiting family and seeing new country, the plans for our new worship center had been approved. We began to build. What was happening in our family and in our church was more than either Flo or I had ever dreamed God would provide. We were content to stay there and love those people until I died or retired.

Flo and I had made friends with Jim and Dot Warren (Rick Warren's parents) when we first moved to California. They had come to Golden Gate Baptist Seminary. Dot was the seminary bookstore manager, and Jim had two jobs. He was the pastor of a small Baptist church in Sausalito and the supervisor and maintenance director for the seminary grounds.

One day, I was on campus and walked into the bookstore. Dot walked over to me and said, "I guess you and Flo are doing a lot of praying right now." I looked up, confused, and she noticed my reaction.

Embarrassed, Dot said, "Oh, I guess I spoke too soon — but since I have started, I might as well finish. Four days ago, at the executive board meeting of Redwood Empire and North Bay Associations, we voted to ask you to become our director of missions for the two associations."

"Dot, are you sure?" I asked her. I was stunned and did not want to

Rick Warren's mother, Dot.

believe what had happened.

"Oh, yes, I am sure. I was one of those who voted for us to contact you," she answered.

Michigan Heights Baptist Church was my home, my life. It was all I could ever dream of for my ministry. Wayne had graduated from Stagg High School, and he and Steve were both doing exceptionally well at California Baptist College. Marcia and Bruce were close friends with international students and had excellent teachers. The community we lived in had many varied recreation opportunities. Flo had an excellent job, and life had never been better. I did not tell Flo what Dot Warren had told me, because we were not moving. No position anywhere could ever come close to what we already had.

To our young people, who had been great in their ministry and support of the church, Flo and I were not just leaders — we were their close friends. They came and asked to go somewhere and just have a good time. I called Jenness Park.

Jenness Park was a mountain camp that was given to three Baptist church associations in the north central valley of California. The camp had two days open. I reserved those days for our church youth. Eighteen youth and six adults signed up to go. I had been camp director for the greater Los Angeles youth camps for three years while I was at Norwalk. Most of the time, we had over four hundred campers. Taking eighteen youth with six adults would be a retreat for me. We gathered at the church, loaded two cars and two pickups, and headed for the mountains sixty miles east.

The adults and youth played tag football with a volleyball on the wet softball field in the meadow. We hiked the trails and were ready to eat at any time. In the evening, we had an open sharing time; any subject and any question or comment was permitted as long as it was not vulgar or judgmental. We closed with a prayer. Everyone was ready to call it a day.

The next morning, we had light rain and some snow on the mountain peaks. After breakfast, the rain stopped. Everyone finished their chores and cleaned their cabins. We took a four-mile round-trip hike up the mountain to the snow. Of course, a snowball fight started, and we adults were tackled and rolled in the white stuff. We came down the mountain singing and laughing. After lunch, we had a much-needed rest and personal meditation period.

At three o'clock, the rain began again. There is no way to keep eighteen young people cooped up unless it floods or gets bitterly cold. The youth, both boys and girls, decided that they wanted to play touch football on the already soaked meadow. Adult leaders could only watch, but I had to referee.

I came prepared; I knew what was going to happen.

After the game, two boys tried to move behind me. I waited until they reached out to grab me, then I ducked and rushed them. I grabbed one of the girls and pushed her into the boys. I then turned and bumped the other girl, and we five plunged into the four-foot-deep river. We surfaced dripping wet and laughing. Before we could recover, the others jumped into the freezing water. Dinner was supposed to have been in thirty minutes. Very few made it on time. Mud and water were everywhere. The furnaces were not built for drying clothes. Our kitchen crew for the day had been watching our fun time. The meal would be ready when it was ready. The rest of the day was spent inside, and we broke up in small discussion groups. After our evening devotionals and prayer, we were all ready for bed.

A few minutes after midnight, there was a loud knock on my door by Sam, the camp manager.

"Edd," Sam said, "We have a problem. The water is rising, and we have half an hour or less to get the people on the other side of the river over here."

There were no bridges across the river. Shallow crossings with gravel beds were the only ways to get our people across. We had only two four-wheel-drive pickups available. I grabbed my rain jacket, pulled on my shoes and rushed across the knee-deep water. I banged on every door and shouted, "Grab your clothes, bedroll, and all personal items! Do not take time to pack. Just get your stuff together. A pickup will be here in five minutes to move you and your gear to the dining hall. If you are not ready, you may be stranded here for a week."

Two other adults used flashlights to guide the drivers of the pickups across the river. Forty-five minutes later, in the pouring rain, everyone had been safely moved to the dining room. A fire had been started. Most of the girls had to put on wet clothes to stay modest. Soaking wet clothes, shoes and coats were laid out to dry on every table, chair and cabinet in the room.

One of the guys said, "I won't have to make up stories about this campout. No one will believe the facts."

We slept some and drank barrels of coffee and hot chocolate. The rain moved on, and the sun broke through in the morning. We washed clothes and dried everything we could get into the three dryers. After lunch, we went home half-wet and half-clean. Years later, when we had opportunities to get together with those who had gone on the trip, reliving it was the highlight of our conversations.

A few days after we returned, my telephone rang. I reluctantly answered, knowing who it was. I did not want to hear from him.

"Hi, Edd. This is Ralph." Ralph Longshore was the director of the missions division of the California Southern Baptist Convention. He said, "I will be coming through Stockton on Friday, and I want to take you to lunch."

Ralph was not aware of what Dot Warren had told me. I really wanted to tell him that I would be unable to meet with him, but I did not want to embarrass Dot. I agreed to the meeting.

After our lunch, Ralph told me that I was being vetted by the Home Mission Board in Atlanta and the state missions office for the position of missions director for two associations in the North Bay Area. He went on to explain that neither the Home Mission Board nor the state convention would have any authority over my work in the two associations. Vetting was for financial support (as if money were not a concern). My salary would come from the two associations. The other agencies would assist the associations to supplement my insurance, retirement, office and travel expenses. I had been the moderator of one association. This was not new to me, but formalities had to be covered.

My response was, "Ralph, I am familiar with all that, and I know you have to go over it with me, but I am not interested in leaving Michigan Heights Baptist Church."

As he prepared to leave, he said, "Edd, it is because of what you did in Norwalk and what you are now doing here in Stockton that we need you in the Bay Area. All I am here to do is to make sure you know what is going on and ask you not to cast our request aside when it comes. Take time to think and pray about what you ought to do. That's all we want."

He left, and I went home and told Flo what was happening. She responded, "I don't want to move, and you know why. I have a good job, and we have the best home we have ever had. We have never had people treat us like the ones do here. Besides, the new building is not completed. There is no way you could leave."

For two months, there was no news. Just when I was sure it was all over, that sometime devil's tool rang again. I heard, "Mr. Brown, I am Tom Crooks. I am chairman of the nominating committee for the two associations of churches north of San Francisco Bay. We have thirty-eight churches in Marin, Solana, Sonoma, Lake and Napa Counties. We are looking for a new director of missions, and we would like to talk to you. We have a joint meeting of our committee scheduled for this Saturday morning in Fairfield. We would appreciate you meeting with us for breakfast."

I had no conflict and wanted them to know my feelings upfront. I agreed to go. Our church construction was progressing well, and our attendance was close to two hundred in a building that legally could seat no more than one hundred. We could be in big trouble if the fire marshal came.

Flo was not happy with my going to the meeting, but I felt a face-to-face meeting was the right thing to do. There were twelve people there — six from each of the two associations. I knew some that were present from my work in the state. After the meal and formalities were over, the chairman, Tom Crooks, began the meeting by looking directly at me and saying, "We understand that you are very hesitant to consider our request to become our director of missions. Would you tell us why?"

I was caught off-guard. I stood, looked around the table and said, "Yes, that it is true. I do not feel I should leave Michigan Heights. You and God will have to convince me (and especially Flo) that we are to leave. We are not even close to that at this time. I am in the middle of a major building project. I cannot leave until that is finished. Flo has a good job and a recent promotion. Our two kids have excellent teachers and are making good grades. No one in this state has a more loving and committed congregation than I have the privilege of pastoring. I work one day a week for the California Fish and Game Department as a volunteer game warden. I am not sure that would work in the North Bay Area."

One of the pastors asked about our World Changers program for youth. He wanted to know if that could be expanded into a multi-church event. I had not thought of that but could see no reason why not.

When the meeting was over, I headed for home. Both the fog in my head and the fog outside became worse. I crept along at ten miles an hour and met very few cars and no trucks. I was exhausted mentally and physically. There was just no clear outcome.

On the following Sunday, highway patrolman Les Range came in and informed me, "When I found out where you were yesterday morning, I was worried! There was a head-on collision about the time you were coming across the delta. It took us two hours to find the wreck because the fog was so thick."

Our church building was enclosed, and the inside finish work had begun. One problem was keeping kids, including ours, outside to keep them and others from getting seriously hurt.

My meeting with the search committee was no longer bothering me. For two weeks, there had been no pressure — just an open and honest exchange of information.

I called a meeting of our deacons and church leaders and told them, "I did not want the information I am going to share with you to come to you secondhand. I want you to know what may or may not happen." I then related to them the discussions I'd had with the director of missions search committee. I closed by telling them not to listen to any rumors. "At this time, I have no intention of leaving Michigan Heights; however, I cannot at this time give you a permanent answer one way or another. I do need your prayers and understanding that I will make the right decision if it becomes necessary."

Two weeks later, I was asked to meet with the camp committee of Cazadero Baptist Camp, which is west of Santa Rosa in the redwoods on Austin Creek, ten miles inland from the Pacific Ocean. Flo and I had not been to that part of California. We decided to go for the day. We stopped in Napa, Sonoma and Santa Rosa. We drove miles through vineyards and fruit orchards. Because of our ignorance of the country, we ended up driving on an old logging trail that had been crudely made into a local road. We arrived an hour late but in time for an outdoor barbecue lunch.

The location of the campgrounds is unreal. It was bordered on the west by Austin Creek, which ran year-round. A small mountain covered by giant redwoods, cedars, firs and other types of trees and shrubs was on the eastern border of the property that ran a quarter of a mile downstream.

The campground had been given to four associations by a retired seminary professor. It was a beautiful place but in very poor condition. Every building except the dining hall and chapel was temporary. The sewer system had been "red–tagged" by the county. Use of the camp was prohibited at the time of our visit, but youth and children camps were to open in five months. My building and camp leadership experience came back to haunt me. "We need you to help us get this place ready for camps this summer," the committee told me.

On the way home (on a more direct route), Flo and I talked. Eventually, she asked the inevitable question: "What are you going to do?"

"I wish I knew," I replied. "Everywhere I go in this area, everyone keeps saying the same thing. We need you for what you know and because we believe you can lead us."

"I know," she said, "I don't want to move, and you know all the reasons. But if you become convinced that this is what God wants you to do, I will support you in doing it."

I kept the leaders of Michigan Heights up to date, and they

continued to pray with and for us. We finished and moved in to our new worship center and celebrated.

A week later, the director of missions committee chairman called. "We decided to recommend that you become our director of missions, and we want our pastors on board. We will have a vote from the pastors in each association. Four different groups will vote. We want you to come and meet with each of the four groups for an open sharing time. After each meeting, a ballot will be passed out."

The dates were set. I knew I was off the hook. The old adage — "Get two Baptists together, and you will have five opinions" — would give me my out. I told Flo we would not be moving. There was no way there would be a unanimous vote in all four groups. One negative vote was all I needed. I went to the first round and met with the pastors. When the votes were tallied, the result from thirty-two pastors from thirty-eight churches was thirty-two in favor and zero opposed. The next week, I met with twenty-five to thirty people from each association with the same result at each meeting.

I called the church leaders of Michigan Heights together and told them what had happened. I explained that I still believed God to be in control and needed to be willing to respond to what he was leading me to do.

"When would you be moving?" I was asked.

"My family will not leave until after school closes this spring and we sell our house. I will leave in four weeks and live in a small camping trailer parked at a church in Napa. I will be under an overhang at the back of the building. I will have use of restrooms, a small kitchen and an office with a phone until we get moved," I explained.

Our new church building was already contributing to an increase of new members, and the church elected a pastor search committee. The committee asked me to meet with them.

"Will you be preaching every Sunday in your new job?" I was asked.

"I doubt it," I replied. "This soon, they really don't know me that well."

"Could you serve as our interim until you move or until we call a pastor?" the chairman asked.

"I don't know, but I can ask," I answered.

The association's missions committees, to whom I would be reporting, agreed to the church's request. This gave me the opportunity to be home with Flo and our kids at least three days a week.

Eleven

1967-1976

NORTH BAY AND REDWOOD EMPIRE BAPTIST ASSOCIATIONS

I continued to preach at Michigan Heights on Sunday mornings and a few Sunday evenings. In my new job, I began visiting each of the twenty-eight churches I was responsible to. I went on Sunday and Wednesday evenings to get to know the pastors and lay church leaders.

For six weeks, I looked at homes in my four areas and found four possibilities. The fourth one was in Kenwood (in the Valley of the Moon, as the early American Indian tribes called it). Flo and family approved, and we bought a very nice new house halfway between Sonoma and Santa Rosa. It was on a half-acre lot in a developing area, as close to the center of the four counties as we could reasonably find.

We sold our house in Stockton and completed arrangements to move into our new home. The church building in Stockton was completely finished, and the first wedding in the new building was that of Steve Brown and Peggy Estes. I performed the wedding. After their honeymoon at the Glorieta Conference Center in New Mexico, they helped us move into our new home in Kenwood.

Our leaving Michigan Heights could have been like a funeral or a family breakup. We were that close to our people. They wanted us to stay but accepted our call from God to go where He wanted us to minister. We had a banquet, and they loved and encouraged us to do the best we could in our new field of service. They asked us to come back as often as we could. They had a fun time honoring Flo and our kids and lampooning me. Then they gave us gifts and money, which was hard for us to accept. Flo, the kids and I tried to not overreact, but we could not hold back our tears. A few weeks later, the new church worship center was dedicated, and I was asked to be the main speaker. Our family was honored again.

Cazadero Baptist Camp was the main item that I had to attack. I met with the county health department people and convinced them to list what they had determined we had to do to make the camp acceptable. With their report, we drew up plans and went to work. We hired a sanitation company to transfer the refuge of old cesspools to a special dump. We then filled each hole with packed clean sand and small rocks. We replaced the old system with a completely new septic system. We had to sign an agreement to replace the cabins and upgrade the kitchen in a year. Volunteers from fifty churches in our four associations came to clean the camp for the summer. The housing was still in tents on rotting wood floors, but they would be safe for a year. Our camps were well-attended, but I and others knew

Oldest son, Steve, and wife, Peggy.

we could not expect kids or adults to keep coming unless new cabins were built and the kitchen enlarged and modernized.

In my first year as director of missions, Jim Warren was called to be the director of missions of the association just north of mine. He and his family moved to the small town of Redwood Valley, northeast of Ukiah. He had twelve churches scattered across an area almost as large as the two associations that I was responsible for. He and I shared the leadership for the development and improvement of Cazadero.

Dot Warren was the high school librarian in Redwood Valley. Some of the students she helped were from families who lived in the Jim Jones settlement. This was the settlement that would later move to the Bay Area and then on to South America where the mass suicides took place.

Jim Warren and the pastor of the Baptist church in Ukiah arranged for a loan of forty thousand dollars from the local bank. We used the money to upgrade the housing and kitchen at Cazadero. We replaced the tents with cabins. We added a conference center and enlarged the dining area. With the help of a Christian contractor in Sacramento and a large number of volunteers from our churches, the camp was approved by the county for the following year.

Steve and Peggy Brown and Rick and Chaundel Warren worked with us and enlisted others to help. Wayne, our second son, had graduated from California Baptist. After fifteen months in Vietnam, he was honorably discharged from the Army with the rank of sergeant. The summer after his return home, he worked part-time for sixty dollars a week as the supervisor of volunteers at Camp Cazadero.

A problem for me was my limited formal education. I had a four-year bachelor's degree and a two-year master's degree in education. I'd had good and bad experiences in my four previous churches and had gained a lot of practical knowledge; however, I had been the pastor of a church for only three years and was nowhere near the academic level of the pastors in the churches I was now working with. Half of the pastors in my two associations were enrolled in graduate work at Golden Gate Seminary, an hour away from home. Two professors encouraged me to enroll in a course on contemporary theology and an updated course in church history. Both professors were members of churches in our association. While they were considerate of the difference between my age and that of other students, they made no change in the requirements that all students were expected to follow.

For eight weeks, in addition to learning my new job, I began making unannounced visits to churches I was responsible to on Sunday mornings and evenings. I did this for two reasons. I wanted to hear the pastor and to get a feel for the congregation and their reaction to a new unknown person.

Other than the pastors and a few members of the church staff, very few people in the churches knew who I was or what I did. In order to accomplish my purpose, I waited until after the music was finished and offerings were taken and entered the church building as the preacher was moving to the pulpit to bring his message. That way, I could not be introduced without a serious interruption of the service. I would sit close to the back of the worship center (which, in some churches was almost impossible to find). At the close of the service, I would stand at the end of an aisle near the exit that most people used as they left the building.

The few who knew me were courteous, and others nodded. Some made a quick introduction and moved on. Unfortunately, most people either ignored me or, without intending to, gently pushed me out of the way so they could get to where they could talk to someone they already knew. I tried to dress the way the people of that particular membership dressed. I made extensive notes for future reference. After three months, I began to accept invitations to preach in those churches.

Because of the different services times, I could visit or preach in three or four churches on one Sunday. Of our thirty-eight churches, three were African-American congregations, one was Philippine, one was Indonesian, one was Japanese, two were Chinese, and three were Hispanic. Very few of the other churches were comprised of one ethnic group; instead, they represented the mixture of the people in their community.

When I was asked to return to a church I had visited earlier, I would as kindly as I could relate to them how I, as a visiting stranger, was treated. I did not do that to be mean or judgmental, but to help them see how their actions could easily and unintentionally cause a new person to feel that he or she was not welcome.

Another thing I discovered was that each of our pastors and their wives were so involved in school, ministry, family and other jobs that there was very little time for the pastors and wives to get know one another. The pastors might occasionally be together for some association meetings, or the wives might see one another at an associational Christmas party. I began to search for a way to catch their attention and encourage them to become better acquainted. Hopefully this would provide support for the couples in their ministries and help them to develop personal relationships with others who were on the same journey in life.

After several dead ends, I was ready to give up — but then I remembered Bill Williams. Bill was the member of First Baptist in Norwalk who had called for the vote on my coming to that church and our moving to California. He had later become manager of the Hawaii Baptist Convention Camp on the coast of Oahu. I called Bill to get a price for us to use Camp Puukahaa on Oahu for a week. We would take care of our own meals.

Bill called later and gave me a price. I contacted a charter airline and explained what I was trying to do. They gave me a price. I checked with a food supplier and received an estimate of the food costs for ninety people for six days. I compiled all this information and added money for van rentals and fifteen percent to be safe. I came up with a figure of 150 dollars for each person for a round-trip ticket and a week in Hawaii.

I went to both executive boards and asked them to help with the cost of the trip so that we could keep the price as close to a hundred dollars per person as possible. They approved half that much and voted to ask each church to care for the additional cost to help its pastor and wife go. In the fall of 1967, twenty-eight ministerial couples and ten other couples who were part of church leadership agreed to go.

We had room for nine singles; my mother was one who decided to go. Our committee of five had organized the people into three groups. Each group would do kitchen and clean-up chores twice during our stay. They would be free the rest of the trip. We planned to have breakfast and a supper together. For lunch, everyone would be on their own. There were several small eating places and a 7-Eleven store close by. Our camp was across the coastal highway from a military recreation area on a huge sandy beach. There were bathhouses and dressing rooms. The area was guarded day and night but would be made available for our use at any time except between midnight and an hour before daybreak.

We rented two vans for the groups to use. We encouraged smaller groups to use the bus. It was not expensive, and they would avoid traffic and parking problems. The bus circled the entire island of Oahu, and anyone could ride all day for one dollar.

Every night after dinner, we would share about our day and exchange information about sights to see and places to shop. We would have a brief worship service led by various groups or individuals that the committee had enlisted. The only other joint meeting planned was a short Bible study that I would lead each morning.

When the groups and individuals were off-duty, they were on their own. Even those who had kitchen or clean-up duty would be free after a few hours. They would have access to the military beach area or could walk the trails around the camp or along the coast. These plans were only ideas; we would modify them if needed or requested during our stay.

Everyone was at the airport on time and ready for a relaxing, enjoyable trip. An hour before we landed, the pilot came on the P.A. system. He thanked us for traveling with them and wanted us to have gifts from the charter company. My name was called. Flo and I were each presented a gorgeous lei and a large box. Everyone else was given leis and smaller boxes. We entered the holding pattern for landing. We concentrated on the windows and saw Diamond Head, Waikiki and the beaches. We crossed over Pearl Harbor and the Arizona Battleship Memorial. We landed and all wore our leis as we left the plane. We were given other leis when we entered the airport.

Three of us men went to the rental agency, and I signed and paid for our rental vans. The others went though baggage claim and, with help from some friendly officers, were able to park and load our luggage into the vans. We drove to Puukaha and were met by Bill and the camp staff. Edmond Walker, the executive director of the Hawaii Baptist Convention, was also there to welcome us.

We went to our assigned cabins and unpacked. We took showers and put on cooler clothes. We were ready for an introductory meeting with the camp staff and convention officers.

Flo and I opened our box. Inside were a smaller box of macadamia nuts and a large bottle of champagne. I opened the cabinet door in our small room to put away our things. On the inside of the door was a large sign with bold letters: "ANYONE ON THIS CAMPUS CAUGHT WITH ALCOHOLIC BEVERAGES OF ANY KIND WILL BE ASKED TO LEAVE. NO EXCUSES ACCEPTED!"

I have no idea how much our champagne cost, but it was lost as we emptied the bottle down the drain. I hid the bottle in the bottom of the trash container outside our door. When we went to our meeting, others wanted to know what was in our gift box. We answered, "Just some small stuff that we really had no need for." We appreciated the gesture and did get a large box of chocolates. Our answer ensured that we not have to explain what had really happened.

The others were in cabins that were close to eighty years old. I had suggested that, in addition to bringing their own bedding, they might want to bring blankets to hang up in their cabins for privacy. The camp was built on property that had belonged to one of the early island princesses when Hawaii was an independent nation. The princess' mansion was now the conference center. The upstairs had a large screened balcony that had been converted into bedrooms, and the downstairs held the kitchen and dining room. Some small houses on the grounds had been converted into cabins that each had two baths and two bedrooms.

While the camp could take care of 150 people, couples' quarters were limited. I had sent Bill the names of married couples and single people. He and the camp staff had done a good job of rearranging beds to accommodate our group. Other than roof leaks in the cabin for single women, the arrangements were fine. Flo and I and another couple were housed in a duplex built with unfinished block walls, but each couple had its own bathroom.

The beautiful foliage and sea breezes, coupled with the relaxed atmosphere, opened new doors of communication that lasted for years. Eight people decided to take an airplane to one of the other islands. A van took them to the airport and picked them up later that evening. Everyone went to the Arizona Memorial, to Waikiki Beach and to the Polynesian Cultural Center, sponsored by the Mormon Church. The water was warm, and the beach at the military retreat area was usually private.

Flo and I had two exceptional experiences with Mom. Gene Harrell, who had been our pastor in Norwalk, was the interim pastor of Downtown Baptist Church in Honolulu. Flo, Mom and I went the first Sunday to be with Gene and Helen and stayed for lunch. We also spent a day with the family of one of the children Mom had looked after in her in-home daycare in Norwalk, the daughter of a young Hawaiian couple who were then schoolteachers in Norwalk. The couple had returned to Hawaii, and both were teaching school there. We had a great time with their family.

For our last evening in the islands, we wanted to do something special. We had saved enough money to invite the pastors and wives and the staff of the Baptist Convention of Hawaii to our final evening dinner.

Two days before, two of our deacons had gone for a walk along the shore and met the leader of a group that was celebrating the finish of a political campaign circuit they had been on for four weeks. When the leader heard about Flo and me, he was interested in meeting us. He learned we were leaving in two days and were preparing for a special night with guests. He talked with his traveling companions, and he and two leaders returned to camp with our deacons. They wanted to help us with our special meal and do a Hawaiian luau program for us on our last evening in the islands.

The three co-leaders and I met with them and worked out what seemed like an impossible deal. Their group would take over the cooking for our special dinner; we would pay for the food, but they would prepare the meal and do the cleanup and let us enjoy the night. They would also provide the music and entertainment. After agreeing on the food and a program, we asked them to come.

The last day, we set up tables and chairs for 150 people in the garden area; we would use a covered porch as our stage. We decorated the tables and the porch area before the entertainment group arrived. When we had finished decorating, Flo and I started to leave to dress for the evening. One of our co-leaders stood up on the stage and asked everyone in our fellowship to stay for a short meeting. I knew nothing about this and wondered what was going on. Everyone stayed, and Flo and I were asked to come to the stage. Everybody was laughing, and a joyous (and somewhat ridiculous) mood took over.

The leader calmed everyone down. Four ladies dressed in muumuus came forward and presented Flo and me with a thank-you card signed by the group, as well as three boxes. There was a large box for Flo, a smaller one for me and a smaller box to both of us. We were told to open the two larger boxes first. The group had bought Flo a brightly flowered muumuu. (The natives describe a muumuu as a long dress that covers everything but touches nothing.) They gave me a matching shirt and gave both of us a huge box of Hawaiian chocolate-covered macadamia nuts. We were instructed to wear our new clothing with the leis they had made for us to the program that night.

Our guests for the evening were Edmund Walker (the executive director of Hawaii Baptist), his wife, four convention staff members, eight pastors and their wives, and the camp staff. The entertainers did a fabulous job. For the meal, we had our choice of chicken, pork or beef, all which had been barbecued over open fires. Pineapple, mango, papaya and various nut dishes made

Flo and Edd in Hawaii.

a superb dessert. The ukulele and guitar music, led by a Mexican man and his Hawaiian wife, could not have been better. Of course, the hula dancing was the highlight of the entertainment; everyone enjoyed watching me try to follow a young lady as she showed me how to do it. No one left hungry, and our local guests enjoyed the evening as much as the people in our group did.

Flo and I had never had so much happen in one week in our life. Flo, on one of our private trips to town, shared her mysterious feelings about our work and marveled at how God seemed to be in complete control of our lives.

We returned to California loaded down with fruits and nuts. One of the church members in Hawaii was manager of a wholesale export company. He loaded us down with merchandise and took care of the customs for us. The joke among our group was that we would be the first group to fly to California with a U-Haul trailer attached to the rear of the plane.

That week of fellowship and relaxing together opened doors for relationships with pastors, their wives and church leaders that continued through years of ministry and into retirement. I began to get more requests from churches and pastors to preach and lead conferences for them. Requests for help in planning for construction and remodeling of church buildings doubled; however, financing church buildings was off the list for many banks and building loan agencies. The common argument was, "What could we do with a repossessed church building?"

While we were in Stockton, I had made friends with one of the vice presidents of Bank of America. He helped us to finance the building at Michigan Heights. He was later promoted and moved to Fresno. Milton Woodall, pastor of one of our churches in Vallejo, asked me to work with the church in a weeklong revival. The church was out of room, and the building they were in was not suitable for remodeling. During the week, in addition to preaching and visiting, I worked with the building committee on building plans. The church accepted the plans. Permits for the building were approved by the county. When the plans were ready, we went to the local Bank of America to talk to the manager; however, the manager was not interested in talking to us. His bank was not offering loans for church buildings.

The next morning, I called my friend in Fresno. I told him about our reception at the local bank and asked if this was a new policy. He asked me some questions and said he would call me back. That afternoon, he called and asked what my schedule was for the following day. I told him I was free.

"Okay, you go back to the bank in Vallejo and be there at eleven o'clock," he directed.

I went by the church, picked up Milton and took him with me to the bank. As we walked up the bank steps, the manager opened the door and invited us in. The church was able to negotiate a loan, and the new building was built. During the next eight years, I was able to help over a dozen churches in our associations with the planning, financing and construction of worship and education facilities.

I was visiting some of our pastors at Golden Gate Seminary, and Dr. Atkins came and asked me to visit him in his office. Dr. Atkins was a professor of languages and Old Testament history. He had been a pediatrician before becoming a professor. He still worked part-time at the Oakland Children's Hospital.

After our greetings, he said, "I hope you don't mind my meddling in your life, but I have been going over your academic records and want you to think about something. If you would take one course in Hebrew, one in Greek and one other of your choice, you would be eligible for a master's degree in theology. This would put you on the same academic level with most of the pastors you are working with. I know you have a master's in religious education, but this would help to update you in theology."

I knew he was right and wondered how much study time it would take. He explained that my visits to the seminary for meetings with pastors would only add four hours a week to the time I was already on campus.

I talked to Flo and to the missions committees; with their approval, I enrolled in Hebrew and in a course on ethics. My grades were not the highest, but they were not bad. I moved onto campus I enrolled in a two-week Greek immersion course that met for four hours a day. I was grateful that the only grade was pass or fail. I accused my friend and professor, Dr. Harrop, of passing me simply to get me out of his class because I was an embarrassment to others. He never denied that.

Dr. Richard Cunningham and I were friends; his wife taught in our VBS training program, and he supported pastors in our association. His course in contemporary theology would fit into my schedule, so I enrolled. The course was an eye-opener; I learned many details about theologians I had never even heard of before.

As a World War II veteran, I was fascinated by Bonhoeffer and his "Letters From Prison." I knew several people who had been prisoners of war. I had tried to help two people in their readjustment to life and family. Bonhoeffer's approach to unjust suffering and his down-to-earth way of writing about his firm faith in spite of horrible circumstances began to wake me up. My so-called bad experiences with pastors, church leaders and family members were already known by God. I could let those traumatic experiences make me bitter and resentful, or I could learn how to live the better life that God had for me. I graduated that semester, alongside nine pastors of the churches that I was privileged to work with, with my second master's degree.

Our summer camps at Cazadero grew larger every year. We had no more space to enlarge and had to increase the number of camps we held. Our new churches were asking for help with vacation Bible school and youth outreaches. There was also a need for more summer workers in our newer and smaller churches.

I had wrestled with the idea of expanding World Changers, begun by the young people in Stockton, into a multi-church program, but it had not been a priority. I approached the missions committee, and we worked out a possible plan. We normally had eight college students from across the U.S. come and work with churches in our associations for ten weeks each summer. With teams of two, this gave me only four teams to share among our thirty-two churches.

My idea was to develop a training camp one week before Bible schools and camps usually began. We would have specialized training for our guests and summer workers. We decided to encourage the senior high school students in our churches to volunteer for the summer. Two of our students would work with one of our summer college guests. That way, we would have enough workers to serve sixteen of our churches for two weeks each. We would pay our students the same thirty dollars a week that the college volunteers were paid.

The students were excited about the idea, and a plan was hurriedly adopted. I was given the responsibility of enlisting leaders to come the first week and train our youth with the summer college students. I called the national Baptist agencies,

College students serve as summer missionaries.

local college and seminary professors, and church and denomina-tional leaders in neighboring states for help in enlisting eight leaders for our teams.

Our first year, twenty-two high school students applied. Sixteen were accepted to be in the first associational World Changers program. Trainers came from the home missions board in Atlanta, from the Brotherhood Commission in Memphis and from our state office in Fresno. Two professors from the seminary and a teacher from California Baptist College came to help. For six days, the eight teams were taught as teams and practiced as teams. We focused on relationships, teamwork, music leadership, camping, counseling and leader responsibilities. Flo and I would host the entire group in our backyard in Kenwood before they went to their first assignments.

The program was continued for eight years, and lifetime rela-tionships were formed; I conducted four marriages and attended two others. Many of our young people also became missionaries, pastors, professors, business executives and community leaders, all called by God to continue what He wanted for their lives.

Rick and Chaundel Warren and Tom Holliday (now at Saddleback Church in Orange County) were among those who worked with and were changed by the program. Our children Marcia, Bruce, Wayne and Steve, along with Steve's wife, Peggy, made crucial life decisions that were influenced by knowing those young people.

Most of the time, requests to lead training events were for me. Sometimes the invitations included a request for Flo to come and train leaders of young children. This time when I answered the phone, it was different. Pat Patillo greeted me and then asked to talk to Flo. He asked her to be part of a special teaching and training group. The group would be gone two weeks to Alaska and Hawaii. This was the first direct invitation of many that she would receive.

I encouraged her to go. She was the associational office secretary, but we could make adjustments in our schedules. Steve and Peggy were at Petaluma, and Wayne was at California Baptist. Bruce had graduated from high school and was at Baylor. Marcia was in high school, and she and I would be all right.

Our twenty-fifth wedding anniversary would occur at the end of her trip, and I made arrangements Flo was not aware of. After she and the group had left San Francisco for Anchorage, I would fly to Hawaii on the last day of their teaching tour. She and I would stay four days to celebrate our wedding anniversary. A family in Santa Rosa wanted Marcia to stay with them.

I flew to Kona on the big island of Hawaii. I rented a small RV and went to the hotel where the team was supposed to be, but a heavy windstorm on Maui where the team had been teaching had interrupted their flight. They were delayed until the next day. I went to the Baptist church where I was to meet Flo and met with James Sambi. James was one of the young men who had worked with me as a church custodian in Abilene, Texas, when a university building burned at Hardin Simmons. He and his wife had been classmates with me. We had a great visit, and he was busy getting things ready for the team to come the next day.

I had nothing to do, so I drove the RV to Hawaii Volcanoes National Park and did a three-hour private walking tour. When I came back to the parking lot, there was not one other vehicle in sight. I drove out of the park over huge electric cables that had been laid across the roads. I was surprised. I could not imagine why I was the only one in the park or why those cables had been placed on the road. I drove to Black Beach on the ocean side of the park and spent the night. The next morning, I drove to town for breakfast at a restaurant close to the church where Flo and the rest of the team would be teaching. I picked up the local paper and read the details about the volcanic eruption at the park the previous night.

I hoped my showing up at the church where Flo was teaching would not cause any difficulties. Walt Crabtree had no one in his conference, so he and I toured the area and climbed to the top of a valley where one of the major waterfalls of the island was located. We relaxed and had a great time. He shared about the Alaska tour and the team's physical reactions to the temperature changes they had endured the past week — freezing for five days and sweltering for four. They were headed back to California after another day in the islands.

We went back to the church. I had lunch with the team and agreed to take them to the airport in my RV. At the end of the conferences, we loaded their luggage into the RV and drove to the airport. Their flight was delayed for three hours. They did not want to spend those hours in the airport. They received permission to check their bags, and I took them to Hawaii Volcanoes National Park. When we arrived, half of the park was off-limits because of the eruptions.

There were a few places that were safe enough for us to walk. We could see the lava exploding up to a hundred feet into the air. We drove to a place suggested by one of the officers and parked in the same lot that I had parked in the day before. The first thing I saw was a tree at the far end of the parking lot, less than a hundred feet away. It was the tree that I had parked under the day before. It was now burning from the lava flowing around its roots.

While we were watching the lava flow across the ground seventy feet away, a crack opened, and we could feel and see the lava flowing under us. Red-hot melted rock and earth were flowing like syrup under eight feet of hardened lava from previous eruptions. The ranger watched with us for a few minutes and then advised us and others to move back with him a hundred feet to where it was safer. We spent an hour walking in safe areas of the park before I returned the team to the airport.

The rest of the team flew home. Flo and I toured the rest of the island and spent the night under coconut trees at Black Beach. Early the next morning, we heard a sizzling sound. It sounded as if someone were frying meat — but that was not possible, because we were the only ones in the campground. We dressed and walked outside. Steam was everywhere, like a thick fog.

We walked along the beach and found the answer a hundred feet away. We watched a river of lava, ten feet wide and one foot thick, flow into the ocean. The lava did not cool until it was thirty or forty feet deep in the ocean. The colors and shapes of the cooling lava were beyond any description. The only thing I can compare it to was what I saw on our ship the day we celebrated Japan's surrender. In all the lifeboats and rafts on our ship were emergency signal guns with shells of phosphorus that burst into brilliant lights when they exploded in the air. They were like giant, slow-burning firecrackers. We had an overabundant supply, so we fired them off in celebration. Most were fired into the air, but one shell fell into the water. As it sank, the phosphorus made the sea around it glow red, yellow, blue and green until the phosphorus burned out. The colors we saw when the lava entered the water was like that of the signal guns but magnified.

Flo and I watched for an hour and decided we needed to leave. Lava flowing from the park above us could close the road before we drove out. At two places on our half-mile drive to the highway, we saw lava flowing in the bar ditches.

We spent the rest of the day at the City of Refuge and the coffee plantation. The next morning, we flew to Maui. When I went to pick up the small motor home we had reserved, the middle-aged Hawaiian clerk asked me where we had flown from.

When I told him, he looked at me and said, "This is probably your first trip to the islands, and you saw the show the volcano put on. I have lived here all my life and have never been able to see a single one." He shook his head, handed me the keys and wished me luck.

We spent two days on Maui. We camped on the beach and at the top of a mountain. There was far more to see and enjoy than time permitted. We began to make plans to come back for a week.

Our last day, we flew to Honolulu and spent most of our time on the far side of the island at the Polynesian Cultural Center. Flo was tired, and we were ready to go home. We returned our rental van and went back to the motel. The next morning, we caught our plane and returned home.

Edmund Walker, the executive director of the Hawaii Baptist Convention, called a week after we returned home. He asked me if I could bring a work team to Hawaii and help them rebuild the cabins and remodel the main building at the camp. Flo sent letters concerning our invitation to churches and individuals on our mailing list. We had over a hundred replies. We mailed out information on housing and the types of work to be done. We had forty-five requests for further information. We enlisted a team of thirty-eight adults and seven young people and used the same rotation of jobs and days off that we had on our previous Hawaii trip.

We demolished the decaying houses we had used on our retreat. For ten days, we removed termite-destroyed beams and changed out damaged wall supports and paneling. We rebuilt over half of the buildings. This was my first out-of-state building program. I never dreamed that this was another phase of education for future plans that God had for me. To me, it was just another opportunity to guide our people in using their God-given physical abilities to serve Him by helping others. We had good team leaders, and Flo and I decided to take two days off.

We flew on an inter-island plane to Molokai and rented a car. We found a nice room at a motel on a large beach, and she and I were the only ones there. We did our swimming in the early morning and late evening to stay out of the hottest sun. We visited small villages and spent two hours at the deserted former leper colony.

In the early days of the settling of Hawaii, people with leprosy were put on a boat and taken to a bay on Molokai and forced over-board with whatever possessions they could carry. After several years, the settlement was abandoned, as was the secluded beach. Flo and I walked the beach and visited with some of the descendants of the original settlers.

The next morning, Flo and I flew to Lanai, home to the Dole pine-apple plantation. We visited our friends, the pastor and pastor's wife of a small Baptist church on the island. The church building is set in a dream location. The sun, the palm trees and the variety of flowers make it an unmatched place for wedding ceremonies and pictures. The pastor spent as much time doing weddings as he did preaching.

It was late in the evening when we flew back to Honolulu. We were the only passengers on the small plane. Flo's dislike for small planes changed on this flight. The moon was as bright as the sun. The reflection off the ocean and mountains blended with the lights of boats and ships on the water and homes on the mountainside. All this was highlighted by the ripple of waves along the shore. It was so captivating that we both almost forgot about being on the plane until we landed.

When we returned, we found that the team had continued their good work. They were glad that we had taken time off. We finished our work at the camp that day and all flew home the next morning.

Our churches were doing well. I had cut back on my outside ministries and (as far as I knew) had finally finished my formal education. I had taken two extra classes at Golden Gate and at a neighboring school to keep current and to try to understand the radical cultural change of our youth, with their anti-everything mindset. I had a bachelor's and two master's degrees, and that was enough. I was fifty-one years old and had enough formal schooling.

I received a conference call from three of my professors and close friends — Dr. Fisher, Dr. Dubois and Dr. Elkins. They asked me to come to the seminary for a personal conference. Dr. Fisher had been my Bible professor at Hardin Simmons University in Abilene, Texas, in the late 1940s. He was a member of the one of the churches in our association. Dr. Dubois and I had worked together in San Francisco on inner-city mission problems and projects. Dr. Elkins had been my Hebrew professor. I had even taken a second Hebrew class with him. I met with them as a friend, with no idea what the meeting was about.

Dr. Dubois began, "We have been authorized by the National Accreditation Committee of Graduate Universities to offer doctoral degrees as part of our educational program. We want to start with fourteen people in our state and region, and we want you to be one of those fourteen."

I was so shocked, I could not speak. He continued as if I had no choice.

"Your coursework will be supervised both in the field and in classes. You will recommend your field supervisor to us, and we will judge his or her qualifications; if satisfactory, we will approve them. You will present a prospectus of your proposed work, and it will be cleared or sent back for revision. There will be four three-week seminars and two months of supervised work on special projects each year. You will be required to submit a journal and evaluation of all programs."

When he had finished, all three laughed.

"This is nothing more than you are already doing, so it should not be that difficult," one of them said. While they were joking, they were not too far off concerning what took place over the next three years.

Dr. Akins walked out with me and said, "Edd, we hope you will take this offer seriously."

These three professors had been my coworkers in churches and associational groups. If they thought that much of me, maybe I had better do some serious praying before I turned it down. The three-year program would not start for four months, but some preliminary work needed to be done. I called the two association missions committees together and asked for their input. Their consensus was that they had no problem with my being part of the new program because it would be an asset to my work.

Our college summer missionaries had gone home. We evaluated our first year of using our high school young people as World Changers. We found some areas that needed to be improved, but the associations wanted to continue. We made plans to expand our training and to get out our invitations earlier.

On April 4, 1968, I was in Fresno for a workshop for missions directors. Jack O'Neal, the director of African-American churches for our convention, came into our room. He signaled that he needed to talk to Bob Hughes, our state executive director. Coming from Jack, Bob knew it must be important. He left the room. In ten minutes, they both returned. Bob asked Jack to share with us what he had learned.

Jack, whom I had known since college and seminary days, had made exceptional progress in helping churches of different races work together to reach people and improve relationships among their members.

Jack, worried and restless, said, "I just received the news that Dr. Martin Luther King Jr. has been shot and killed on the porch of a motel in Tennessee. While we may not agree with all Dr. King has done and said, to black people and black churches in our country, their 'Moses' has been killed."

He continued, "You know of the racial problems we have had in our state and in our country. Frankly, I do not know how this will affect our work and relationships with the blacks in California. I need your prayers and help to make sure that we do all we can to help our people through this critical time. If there is any way I can help you, let me know."

During the rest of our meeting, we focused on our responsibilities where we lived and ministered. The afternoon meeting was cancelled, and we went home.

The first black Baptist church in the United States to become part of the Southern Baptist Convention was Community Baptist Church in Santa Rosa, California. Reverend James Coffee was its pastor at the time, and his church was in my association.

I arrived home late that night, and Flo and I talked about what we should and could do. James and his family lived in Oakland, but the church had a home in Santa Rosa for their long weekends. I called James the next morning and told him of my concern and asked when we could meet.

We set a time, and I drove to Santa Rosa. We talked and prayed. James then said, "The city mayor called me. He wants us to host a special day of remembrance here next week. He and I and others from the community will speak, but I want you to close the meeting if you would agree."

"James, you don't know me that well. Are you sure you want me to do that? What will others think?" I asked.

"I know you well enough. This is my church; as pastor, I approve of who uses my pulpit. Will you speak?" he asked.

I am not sure if my emotions showed or not, but I have never felt more humbled and unqualified. I answered, "My brother, if that is what you want, I will do it."

We stood and hugged for a long time, and I went home. My mind was reeling. What could I say? What could I do?

Three days later, Community Baptist Church was so overcrowded that the windows were opened so people could hear outside. The mayor, a developer, and two other community leaders spoke. After the choir sang, James walked to the pulpit and thanked the choir and the other speakers. He then said, "I have asked one of my closest friends and fellow workers to come and speak to us. When he is through, we will gather out front and plant a tree that has been donated. It will be our local freedom tree in honor of Dr. Martin Luther King. Reverend Brown, would you come and speak to us?"

I walked to the pulpit and discarded my prepared message. I began, "We have been in this meeting for two hours, and it is enough." I then thanked the mayor and others who spoke and thanked Community Baptist Church for their work and their presence in our community.

I turned back to the congregation and said, "Yes, it has been a long day. We have heard several speak, and now we are going to plant a tree. I am grateful for the service today and for those who have donated and will stay to plant that tree; however, if that is all we are going to do, then Martin Luther King's dream dies in us when we go home. It is easy to plant a tree, water and tend it — but to change our lives and our attitudes will be long and difficult. If we just plant a tree and do nothing else, we have wasted our time here today and dishonored a great man. God help us if that is the only way we leave here today." I prayed, the choir sang, and we planted the tree.

The response from the people, especially the other ministers, was overwhelming. I went home relieved and conscious that I had simply spoken from my heart. I was now responsible to our people and myself to do my best to live by my own words.

The Sunday edition of the Santa Rosa paper covered the event and had a picture of the tree planting with a quote from me: "It is easy to plant a tree, but it takes a lifetime and commitment to change relationships." They were not exactly my words, but they were close enough.

I began to get more invitations for speaking and training events from minority groups. We started a new African-American church, a second Japanese Bible study, an Indonesian church and a new mission program for farm workers from the Philippines.

Ray Ozasa, the pastor of the Japanese Baptist church in Tiburon, made contact with the Baptist church leaders in Japan. He and Dr. Ashby, the pastor of Tiburon Baptist Church, wanted to know if our pastors and church leaders could be of help to the Baptist churches in Japan.

The result was a letter of invitation from the Baptist leaders in Japan. Their request was for pastors and workers from our churches to come for three weeks and help them in outreach and training of church leaders.

The two associations voted to send Flo and me. One smart pastor laughingly asked if the plane fare could be round-trip for Flo and one-way for me. Our family was cared for, and Flo and I agreed to go on our first out-of-country mission trip. On May 17, 1972, we and fourteen other ministerial couples and church leaders would fly to Japan. We committed ourselves to do whatever we were asked to do to help our Japanese brothers and sisters.

Twelve

1974

My Return to Japan

Flo and I began to get letters and pictures from Japan with information about the churches that had sent requests for help in children's work, general outreach, and the enlistment and training of Bible teachers. We took care of passports and travel arrangements and were anxious to go.

With an interpreter, I had been teaching a weekly Japanese Bible class in Vallejo for three months, but I had no idea what to expect in Japan itself. All I could remember was the devastation I had seen twenty-five years earlier.

Most members of our team had been involved with me or Flo when we were helping churches in four different states and ten associations in California. This was the first time we would work with internationals in their own country and culture.

Our team met and boarded a plane in San Francisco. Our plane made one stop to refuel in Anchorage. Flo took me to the observation tower and pointed out the places she had worked during her earlier trip to Anchorage with the California leadership team.

Our plane flew along the Aleutian Islands. They looked much different than I remembered from my time on the Escambia, when we were fueling warships there for the possible invasion of Japan. We arrived at the Tokyo airport with no problems and were met by twelve Japanese pastors and church leaders. They literally grabbed our bags from us and carried them to our train. Fifteen minutes later, the train stopped, and we were taken to a restaurant.

We were seated across the table from our hosts. We all ordered lunch. If any cultural problems existed before, they were immediately erased. All the members of the Japanese team had ordered potatoes with their meals. All the members of our team had ordered rice. We laughed as we recognized our mutual concern for our different cultures and eating habits. This consideration remained constant throughout our four-week stay. After lunch, we were escorted to the Prince Hotel on a main rail line and were given the rest of that day and the next to adjust to the time change and to become familiar with our surroundings.

Our team wanted to get oriented, so some took a walk of the area. Flo and I and three others took a taxi to the Ginza, the main commercial section of the city. We walked the busy streets in markets and rode escalators in shopping malls. We bought very little and only stayed two hours. We took the local train back to our hotel. Flo and I were standing just a short way from our group, waiting for our train, when a young lady who was maybe fourteen years old stopped in front of us.

"Could I help you find your way to where you are going?" she asked, in excellent English.

I assured her that we would be able to take the right train back to our hotel.

"I could help you and even go with you to make sure you get off at the right stop. It is so easy to get lost in this big city," she said.

I agreed with her but assured her we would be fine.

"I am glad you are here in my country, and I wish for you a happy and safe time," she said, smiling. She bowed to both of us and went on her way. We caught our train and were back to our hotel in plenty of time to eat dinner with most of our team and to get a good night's rest.

We spent the next day exploring the area where we were staying. We were to be the guests of Tokyo Baptist Church that evening. At four that afternoon, two deacons from the church came to our hotel. Flo and I and eight of our pastors had received personal invitations to make this trip. We met with them for an hour; we discussed our trip and what they hoped would happen as a result of our being with them.

At five o'clock, our group boarded the train. We were to be at the church, which was on the other side of the city, at half past six. Halfway to our destination, our train stopped; the electricity was out on a train ahead of us.

We sat for twenty minutes, and the train slowly moved to an exit. We left the train with our two guides, boarded a bus and rode six blocks. We boarded another train and were an hour late for dinner. The church leaders knew about the problem and apologized. We told them that we were not upset and that this happened in our cities, too. They served us an excellent Japanese dinner, although it was Americanized in some ways: There was less seaweed, no raw fish and knives and forks for those who needed them.

After dinner we all shared our hopes for our trip and had an extended prayer meeting. Our guides escorted us back to our hotel. The train problem was fixed, and we were in our rooms by eleven o'clock.

The next morning, we were escorted to the center of the city and to the top of the Tokyo Tower. At first, we had trouble getting to see any of the city. A class of fourteen-year-old girls from one of the local schools was there. All wanted to talk to us.

"Speak English, please — we want to learn to talk English. Where are you from? How long will you be here? Have you been to our country before? What do you want to learn here?"

The questions went on and on. We talked to them for thirty minutes before their teachers were able to herd them to the elevator, then we were able to enjoy the panoramic view of the massive city.

I saw the Emperor's Palace, which was now a museum. There was also a huge new market center and new fish markets on the wharfs along the bay. I was amazed; nothing I could see indicated the total destruction of that section of the city that I had seen the week after the close of World War II. We spent two more days in Tokyo; we ate in special restaurants, were honored at a tea ceremony, visited museums and toured the Emperor's palace and gardens.

The next morning, our teams were sent to their first church assignments. Flo and I were sent by plane to Kyushu in the southern part of the main island. We met our host pastor and his wife and boarded a sixty-year-old train to Moji-Kitakyushu. We were then escorted to a *ryokan* (a Japanese inn) that was owned by graduates of the Baptist girls' school in Japan. We were given our speaking and teaching assignments for the week and were introduced to our first interpreter. Our interpreter had graduated with a degree in business from the University of Texas in Austin.

His story of becoming a Christian was unreal. While he was attending the University of Texas, he was hired as a driver for a wealthy family, and they became close friends. They arranged his work around his class schedule. When he had left Japan for Texas, he was warned by his friends and family to stay away from Christians and especially Baptists. He was told that these people would be nice but would try to lead him away from his religion and culture — and if he strayed, he would no longer be Japanese. While in Austin, he did attend church, but only to better understand American religion and culture. He had dismissed all religions as just different ways of life.

After four years in Texas, he graduated and returned home. He tried three businesses, and all failed. As a true Japanese, because he had failed three times and was an embarrassment to his family, he decided to commit suicide.

He tried first with poison, but it was too old to work and just made him sick. He then bought a gun, but it misfired. He could not swim and, in desperation, went to the end of a dock late one night when no one would see him and jumped into the water — or so he thought. The tide was out, and he landed in deep mud. He crawled out, muddy and hardly wet, a complete failure to his family and country. He found a hydrant and washed off the mud as best as he could. Not knowing what to do next, he wandered aimlessly around.

In his words, "I passed an old building and heard some music that I had heard in Texas. I stopped and listened. It was a hymn, 'What a Friend We Have in Jesus,' in my language. I was tired and dirty and had nowhere to go. I went inside and sat on the back row. I listened to the gospel of Jesus in Japanese and began to seriously think about Christianity for the first time. When the service was over, the people paid no attention to my wet and muddy clothes. They just welcomed me and encouraged me to come back. I went back because I needed friends. I began to attend regularly. Six weeks later, God became real to me, and I became a Christian. I went home to my parents. They knew of my suicide attempts, so they accepted me back home. I was surprised when they began to listen to my story and were open to hearing about Christ."

He opened a small jewelry shop, and it grew. A year later, he added another store. His business kept growing, and he now owned several wholesale jewelry stores. When he started his business, he provided an hour with pay for all his employees who wanted to attend a daily Bible class. Those who chose not to attend had that hour free, also with pay.

The interpreter traveled with us for four days. Two of those days, I led the Bible study for his employees. I had asked him to help Flo and me learn some basic Japanese customs so we would not embarrass our hosts. One day, we returned from a teaching assignment at a nurses' school and found a small mat that we had not seen before on the floor of our room.

We would soon have our noon meal brought to us. Our host and interpreter looked at me and asked, "Do you really want me to correct you when you do something wrong?"

"Of course," I replied. "That is what I asked you to do."

"Okay. Would you mind stepping off our dining table?" he said, grinning and pointing to the mat that I was standing on.

After I moved, he explained. Our dinner would be served on the special mat, and we would sit on the floor around the mat to eat. Our feet and legs would hang over into a recessed area.

After that, our host was not hesitant to advise us of possible cultural problems.

Our food was traditional Japanese fare — excellent fish, foul, some beef and local produce, with rice at every meal. Desserts were fruits and pastries, of which we could have all we wanted. It was almost too good to be true.

Our evening meals would begin with a notification from our hostess that our bath was ready. In the traditional Japanese hotels, bathing is open to both sexes at the same time. Since we were not Japanese, Flo and I would bathe before the bathing room was open to others. We undressed in our room and were escorted, in only our robes, to a large room with a twelve -by-ten-by-four-foot hot tub in the center of the floor.

There were small stools for sitting and small pans for dipping water from the hot tub. There were separate drains for washing. We dipped water from the hot tub and poured it over our bodies. We then washed our bodies with brushes and soap. After we rinsed off all the soapy water with fresh water from the hot tub and were squeaky clean, we soaked in the hot tub for fifteen to twenty minutes. Fresh, warm towels and large terrycloth robes were waiting for us. We returned to our room, and our evening meal was set out for us on a low table on the special cloth on the floor. Our hostess, a young lady, sat across from us on the floor and served us from dishes of food we indicated we wanted. It was relaxing and unhurried, with excellent food and casual conversation. Our hostess spoke enough English that we had good communication.

Regardless of when Flo and I returned from a teaching or preaching assignment, there would be hot tea and cookies waiting for us in our room. Flo wanted some coffee. We decided to go to a market a mile away and stunned our hosts by insisting on walking. We finally prevailed and went to the market and bought a few things. On our way back, a half-mile from our *ryokan*, we stopped at a coffee and tea shop. Flo bought some ground coffee beans. When we returned, we were greeted by our hostess. We went to our room, changed into lounging robes and went to get our tea and cookies. There was hot water and cookies but no tea.

I remarked, "Well, they are human. We have been here three days, and they finally made a mistake; we have a pitcher of hot water but no tea."

We went to our assigned church that evening. It was a branch of our host church that met in a ladies beauty shop. Over thirty people, mostly middle-aged adults, came and sat on the floor with cushions. Flo and the pastor's wife sat with them. The pastor and I sat on a low bench with cushions in front of the group. We sang hymns in English and Japanese. I brought a simple message on love and personal responsibility. We had an informal thirty-minute question-and-answer period and closed our time with tea and cakes.

The next morning, when we were leaving to teach at a medical school, our hostess stopped us. "Brown-san (Mrs. Brown), we must apologize to you for the coffee merchant where you bought coffee yesterday. He charged you too much. Here is your change."

We had walked two miles, and they knew where we were all the time. They knew we had bought coffee, so they had brought only hot water and cookies to our room.

When we completed our work in that area, I had preached eight times in four locations in three days. Flo had led four children's leadership conferences.

We met with our team for a two-day break and then went to Nara and toured the Golden Pavilion and the Kasuga Shrine. We walked through miles of *torii* gates, which marked the place as sacred. We attended a traditional tea ceremony and learned how to hold the cup and to slowly drink and taste the tea.

We spent the next night in an Americanized hotel in the neighboring city of Kobe. We walked the streets, window-shopped, ate lunch and toured a doll manufacturing plant. I was guest speaker at the local church.

Our last morning in Nara, Flo and I were on our way to lunch when it began to rain. We were on the sidewalk, waiting for the traffic light to change. When the light changed, a nicely dressed Japanese man took Flo's arm and, holding his umbrella over the two of us, escorted us across the street to an awning. He said, "Glad you are here; enjoy your stay in our country." He smiled and, with water dripping off his clothes, walked away. Everywhere we went, that was the way we were treated.

Eating in restaurants in Japan became no problem. Most menus were in Japanese, but there were pictures at the entrance of the restaurant of each dish that could be served. With a little practice, we could point and get what we wanted.

We returned to Mojiko that evening. The next day, our pastor host and wife came and ate an early lunch with us. When we finished, he asked how we were feeling, if we were tired and if we were having any health problems. We both assured him that we were fine.

He continued, "The reason I ask is this: We have been asked to include another meeting for the two of you. The Japanese Navy Midshipman's Academy has asked for you to come and speak to the cadets."

"When?" I asked.

"Tomorrow morning if you feel you could go. You have two meetings this afternoon and one tonight, but we should be finished early. Your new interpreter will be here tomorrow afternoon. I would be the interpreter for you in the morning at the Academy."

Flo and I looked at one another and agreed to go. That afternoon, we went to the Baptist girls school, and Flo and I both spoke. They made Flo an honorary graduate of the girls' school. We went to another nurses' school for dinner, which Flo and I shared with the young men and women. That night I preached at the main church body that was the sponsor of all of those ministries.

The next morning after breakfast, we were driven to the Academy. We met with the deacon of our host church. He was a professor at the Academy and a Gideon. Two weeks earlier, a Buddhist monk had spoken and given out copies of the Buddhist holy book. The deacon had heard Flo and me speak and wanted us to address the cadets. He also had enough Gideon Bibles to give to all the students and professors.

The superintendent who had asked for us to come welcomed us

to Japan and to the Academy. We shared our background. He had been on the staff of the Navy command in World War II; I told him I had been in the U.S. Navy and was in Japan at the close of the war. He was especially glad that Flo was there. She would be the first female to formally speak to the cadets, and we were the first non-Japanese couple to address the student body.

We were ushered into an empty auditorium and given seats on the front row. Our pastor and his wife were with us. The superintendent took his place and gave a nod. We stood as the doors opened and four hundred young cadets marched in as one and stood at attention in front of their seats in less than five minutes. They stayed at attention until they were commanded to sit.

Flo and I were introduced. Our pastor, his wife and the deacon who had requested our coming were presented to the young men. The pastor's wife went to the piano and began to play. The pastor had given out song sheets and asked everyone to join him. He and his wife sang a hymn. The pastor then announced in Japanese and English that Flo and I would sing for them his favorite hymn, "What a Friend We Have in Jesus."

I looked at Flo and asked, "What did he say?"

"He said we were going to sing 'What a Friend We Have in Jesus,'" she answered.

"What are we going to do?" I asked (I am not a soloist).

"I guess we will sing," she replied. We went to the podium and sang our first and last duet.

Our pastor asked Flo to stay at the podium and address the student body. She thanked the officers and professors for letting us come. She then shared her personal story and told of the gifts that others had given us so we could come to Japan. She shared about the gift of life that she had in Jesus and what His gift could mean to them if they were willing to accept God's invitation.

It was my turn, but she had already stolen the service. I simply related to them my personal history with Japan: "My intent during World War II was to destroy as many of your soldiers as I could. I did that to keep them from destroying me, my family and my country. This time, I did not come to fight or hate but to learn and accept. All I want to do today is to share the love that God has for me and for you. I am here on this trip with forgiveness and love. I now pray that our two countries and we as individuals will learn to love and trust one another. Only then can we work together for a better world and for the kind of life that God has promised to all of us. We can have that kind relationship through the gift of Jesus Christ, God's son, if, with God's help, we will turn our lives over to Him."

When I finished, I had Flo come and stand by me. We bowed to the young men. Before we could move, the entire student body stood and applauded. We stood transfixed. The superintendent came and stood beside us until the applause stopped. We bowed again, and they applauded again.

The superintendent thanked us and told the young men that he had been reading the Bible that was given to him. He then suggested that they do the same. The students were dismissed and moved out in formation. The superintendent turned to us and asked us, along with our escorts, to come to his office.

We entered his office. Tea and cookies were served. He looked at me and asked, "What makes you so different?"

I had to ask him to explain. He said, "I have been here for over ten years, and we have had statesmen, government leaders and some well-known authors speak. None have ever gotten an applause. Today they not only applauded but stood to honor you. Why?"

I had to struggle for an answer. "I do not want to be glib about this, but the reaction from the young men was not my doing. In some way, God used our words, and they struck the hearts of your young men. Why us? I really do not know."

He looked at me for a few minutes, nodded his head, reached across his desk and shook my hand. We visited for awhile longer. He gave us gifts and asked if there were any way we could come back before we left for the U.S. We were to be in Sasebo the next day, so we had to thank him and move on.

Our interpreter for the latter half of our trip spoke five languages — Japanese, two Chinese dialects, English and Russian. His mother was a Japanese princess, and his father was a Chinese merchant ship owner and commander. While our interpreter was living in China, the communists took over and he was assigned to a work camp. He was later brought before the Russian authorities for questioning. He had been listening to the noise going on outside; he heard gunshots when a Chinese was sent out the right door but no shots when a Japanese went out the left one. His turn came, and after a few minutes of questioning, he was asked about his nationality. In Russian, he replied that he was Japanese and was released. He became involved in the Communist Youth Movement. Because of his language abilities, he was moved into leadership and sent to Taiwan to infiltrate their National Youth Movement. He was later recognized by local police, arrested and sent to prison for life.

His told me, "A Baptist Navy chaplain began visiting me in prison. I called that Bible thumper everything I could think of, but it did not bother him at all. He kept coming back and brought me books and nonpolitical material to read. One day, he left a Bible. I was not going to even touch that book.

"Later on, I was bored and even thinking of suicide. I picked up the Bible and thumbed through it. A few days later, I began to read and make notes. The chaplain continued to come and help me with the answers to my questions. In six months, I became a Christian and began to tell others about the change in my life. The guards and prison officials really began to watch me. Other inmates would foul my food and push me out of line. I did not fight back, and they eventually gave up. I read the Bible more. The chaplain got permission for me to attend his regular Bible study group, and I was soon assisting him.

"A year after I first met the chaplain, he returned to the United States. Before he left, he asked me to take over the Bible class. The prison officers were skeptical but agreed to give me a three-month trial. At the end of three months, I became the teacher, and some of the officers began to attend our study. In two years, my sentence was reduced from life to ten years. I was later given leave from the prison, but I could not leave the island.

"A group of Japanese pastors came to Taiwan last year and held evangelistic meetings, and I was asked to be one of their interpreters. Three months ago, I was called into the island warden's office and asked what I knew about Edd Brown. I told the warden I had never heard of Edd Brown and wondered why he would ask. The warden held up a sheet of paper and told me that he had a letter from Baptist churches in Japan; they were requesting that I come to Japan and be with Edd Brown for two weeks as his interpreter.

"I again told the warden that I knew nothing about that letter and had no idea who Edd Brown was. The officer reminded me that the condition of my release from prison was that I could never leave the island of Taiwan. I told him that I was well aware of that restriction and asked to see the letter. He handed me the letter. It was in English. It had been sent to one of the Taiwan government officials, who had sent it on to the chief of police for the island.

"The letter was from one of the pastors in Japan who had come to

Taiwan the previous year and hosted the evangelistic meetings where I had been an interpreter. This pastor had asked one of our government leaders if there was any way possible for me to come and be Mr. Edd Brown's interpreter for two weeks. After I explained to the chief what had happened, he became interested. He contacted the government officials and, to everyone's amazement, I was given two weeks to go to Japan to be an interpreter for Mr. Brown and another two weeks to visit my brother whom I had not seen in twenty years."

I have preached and taught in over thirty countries and have been interpreted in as many as twenty different languages, but I have never had another interpreter like him. Flo and I were amazed and fascinated by this young man's ability not only to translate my words but to match my emotions and movements as I spoke. At times, I would be so interested in watching him speak that I would momentarily lose my concentration on my message. Once, to everyone's enjoyment, I became so engrossed in watching him that I completely lost my train of thought.

On that occasion, he had waited a minute and then turned to me; in both Japanese and English, he said, "Preacher, it is your turn now." I waved at him. Everyone laughed, and I resumed my message.

With our interpreter, Flo and I visited an island just off the coast, where a Catholic priest was the leader of the oldest Christian church in Japan. The priest and his wife (they were a long way from the Vatican) were very friendly, and I was asked to come and preach for him the following Sunday. I would have loved to do that, but our time for leaving was coming soon.

The next day, we had a break. Our interpreter came in a car and picked us up. He drove along the coast and bought us lunch and took us to his mother's grave. He walked around and looked at the monument. In an whisper, I heard him say, "Mom, how I wish you could have heard what I have learned about God."

He and I worked together for eight days in churches, schools, businesses and community meetings. His personal testimony opened doors to talk with skeptics and people who had no idea what a Christian was.

A young executive for the Japanese rail line had read the advertisements in the local papers that Flo and I were coming to her area. She came to hear English so she could become more fluent in her dealings with American tourists. She later laughed that my English had a Texas accent with California overtones, but she continued to come to every service.

She took vacation time to take Flo and me to different restaurants, local events and tourist sites. In the middle of the week, she came and told us we would be gone for several hours. She took us in her car across a new bridge to the south island. We had our picture taken by a local tourist agency as we toured the island. We were very close to where the Escambia, my ship, had anchored two days after the Japanese had surrendered to end World War II.

We went to an older restaurant for lunch. All the waitresses were in kimonos, and we sat on the floor. We three had our own waitress to prepare and serve our food: some things Flo and I chose, and others our hostess ordered for us. We had several meats and pan-braised vegetables, followed by pudding with fruit and nuts. Some things we did not recognize, but all were excellent. Our guide had two more things she wanted us to do.

She drove to a secluded valley and through an open gate to a giant brass Buddha in the center of a fenced-in five-acre lot. We got out of her car and walked to a small, open, decorated shed at the foot of a smaller Buddha. She pulled out some coins and handed them to us. She clapped her hands three times "to wake up the gods." We were then told to pitch the coins into the large brass bowl at the feet of the sitting Buda. We three did that. She then bowed and turned away. I thought we were returning to her car. Instead, she walked past the car to a large barn-like building. There was no one around that I could see. She walked up to two large doors, opened one, stepped inside and indicated that Flo and I were to follow.

We entered a long, large hall. Across the front was a platform one foot high, twelve feet deep and forty feet long. To one side was a replica of the Buddha outside. There were non-perishable foods, flowers, fruits and beverages in colored papers and wrappings that covered the stage. There were no seats or tables in the room. The room was beautifully decorated with multicolored ornaments, pictures and statues. I knew instantly that we were where we did not belong and was ready to leave. Our hostess began to explain to us the meanings of the multiple drawings on the walls and the ceremonial rugs we were standing on. The food was for the resident monks and the needy.

She was interrupted by a loud voice in perfect English, "Who are you and what do you want?"

I thought, "I am already in trouble, so I might as well get put out for a good reason." I replied, "I am Edd Brown from California, and this is Flo, my wife. Our hostess brought us in to see the Peace Pagoda. We are here working with Baptist churches in Japan on leadership training. I also preach Jesus to people who come to the churches and schools to hear me."

The speaker put out his hand and welcomed us. He turned to our hostess and said, "I am so glad you brought this couple to our place. Would you three please come into my office? I would like to talk to you."

We went into a sparsely furnished room. He found three chairs for us and asked about our weeks in Japan — what kind of responses we had received and how we had been treated. We were now his honored guests. We answered his questions as best we could, and I asked him who he was, where he had learned English and why the giant golden Buddha was outside.

He smiled and answered, "The Buddha was a peace offering from Burma to Japan after World War II. I was sent here by the Burmese government to be its caretaker." Japan had sent a similar Buddha to Burma.

He had no family, and this was his life assignment. He had been raised in a Methodist school at home. He now wanted to talk with us so he could practice his English. We shared about our lives for an hour. He gave us gifts and a small gold-covered pagoda to thank us for coming.

"We both have people waiting on us," he said, and with a short Christian prayer and a firm handshake, he sent us on our way.

The second thing our hostess wanted us to do would be after the evening church services. She wanted us to come to her home for a meal and fellowship. In her earlier life, our hostess was a geisha. Geishas are not prostitutes; they are professionally trained musicians and entertainers. Some turn to prostitution, but that is not the purpose of their career. Our friend still had her special kimonos and musical instruments, and she wanted to dress Flo in her favorite kimono after the service that evening.

Several people at church that night inquired if Flo and I could come to their home for tea. This was our last night with them. I had to tell them we could not come because we already had another commitment. In the service, before I brought my message, I shared with the congregation our appreciation of their love and acceptance of us and then explained why we could not come to their homes. I meant to say, in my practiced Japanese, that we had been invited earlier to tea and that our hostess, a former geisha, had a special kimono that she wanted Flo to put on and have her picture taken.

I had used all the right words, but the inflection of my voice did not communicate what I had intended. I had told the congregation, "Flo and I have some problems, and I am going to put her in a cage with a tiger."

The horror of the idea was received with gasps and worried looks. My interpreter stepped forward. He was laughing so hard, he could hardly speak. He interpreted what I was trying to say, and the result was hilarious. The service that followed was a joyous one. Our lasting friendships with the pastors and laypeople of Japan taught us a great deal and would change the direction of our lives in a way we could never imagine.

We went to the home of our hostess. She laughed so hard that she had trouble getting Flo into her kimono. She insisted that I take pictures and that we both stay for tea. The kimono fit Flo perfectly. Our hostess did not powder Flo's face but did change her hair. Flo looked amazing.

The next morning, we were loaded down with gifts and escorted to the train by over a dozen people. On the small regional train, we made our way to Kobe. There, we boarded the bullet train for Tokyo. Traveling at over a hundred miles an hour on the ground through tunnels and over bridges convinced me that flying was a much safer way to travel. Seeing the coastline with Mount Fuji's snow-capped peak rising high above it made for another joyous and unforgettable experience. All but one team arrived on time. The last team would be joining us early the next morning.

Between sharing stories, visiting and packing, we did not get much sleep that night. The next morning, men and women broke tradition: They hugged us and cried as we left.

If mission trips are to be judged by immediate growth in the churches, our trip to Japan was a failure; however, the Japanese pastors and leaders were not of that opinion. One Japanese pastor had explained to us when we arrived, "Our people do not move to new or different ideas quickly. They will come and watch us and see if our lives are real or any different. They will want to know how we act towards one another and towards others who are not like us."

At our farewell dinner, the lead Japanese pastor and mission leader left us with this message: "You have planted more seeds here in three weeks than we have done in five years. We have to water and care for those seeds, but in time, we will harvest."

Thirteen

1974-1975

Berkeley, San Francisco
Napa State Hospital, Doctoral Program

Once home, I had to make a decision about the doctoral program at Golden Gate Baptist Seminary. I was fifty-two years old and had three degrees. Flo and I talked, and she left the decision to me and God. The seminary hired a new professor to begin the doctoral program. After three meetings, we decided that I would do a study on the need and resources for continued education for pastors and church leaders.

After consulting with the pastors and church leaders in my associations, my prospectus was accepted, and I entered the program. Four candidates dropped out. The other ten of us had classes on methodology, personal record keeping, relationships with our field supervisors and our concepts of ministry. Our four eight-week seminars were helpful and interesting, but my fieldwork was especially intriguing. I interviewed pastors and church leaders. I did surveys of church members and pastors about needs and the content of continuing education programs. The response was not what I expected. Congregations were overwhelmingly in favor of continued education for their pastors and church leaders. They were especially concerned about their leaders' ability to relate and about the way church leaders and members were sometimes treated.

The most common comment from church members was, "Most know how to preach, but many forget we need to learn how to live with jobs and contrary bosses, how to make a marriage, how to protect our children from the garbage they hear, and how to relate to other Christians and people not like us."

One chairman of deacons stated, "I will never vote for another pastor who has been to the Holy Land or knows Greek. We don't get sermons, just language lessons and excursion reports. I need help living with my family and putting up with my job and other issues of daily life."

Another wrote, "We are not chess pieces; we are people. We have a right to be consulted before we are asked to move to new programs or change our buildings."

The responses from most pastors were almost the opposite. I heard responses such as, "I have enough formal training; I already know more than I use," and "More education would be a waste of time, because most of my people know so little about church and the Bible that I can do fine with what education I have."

I interviewed state and national leaders and applied to attend a meeting of a national association for continuing education for ministers. Twenty-four of us met at a university in Tennessee. I was the only Southern Baptist, although two other Baptist leaders were there. After the first two days, we began to better relate and enter into open discussions.

The major result of the week for me was that I learned that what I had uncovered in my study with our churches and leaders in California was a common problem across nearly all religions and Christian groups. Jews, Catholics and Evangelicals were struggling with the same situation. In most churches, there was a vast gap between the expectations of pastors and expectations of their lay leaders and congregations. This was the topic we wrestled with.

Another event marked the beginning of a three-year relationship with the staff and patients at Napa State Mental Hospital. Napa was in my area. I spent extra time there and became friends with the doctors, specialists and patients. After our required three months, I remained a welcome observer, participant and learner. I maintained contact with the hospital and visited and helped when requested.

I began receiving invitations from pastors and directors of missions in the inner cities of San Francisco, Oakland and Berkeley. I learned firsthand the difficulties of street people and the reasons that many live a nomadic life in an industrial, crowded city environment. I was accepted and spent time at the University of California at Berkeley. I visited the downtown churches and helped in ministry centers throughout the Bay Area. I became more proficient in relating to pastors and their families and more conscious of my responsibility to my own church and family. I visited prisons and helped set up three ministries.

The more I learned, the more I was reminded of how a seminary professor in Fort Worth had opened on our first day of class with him: "Young men and young women, I am not sure what you expect to get out of this class, so let me set you straight. I do not and, I repeat, do not intend to teach you anything new (My thought was, "Then why am I here?"). I will guarantee you this — you will be more ignorant about more things than you ever knew possible when you leave this class. In our process, maybe I can point you to places and people that can help you find some answers."

After I finished the prescribed classes and was approved for my fieldwork, the hard part for me began. I had to write a thesis and submit it for approval to get my doctor's degree. While my doctoral work had fit in perfectly with most of my work with pastors and church leaders, some major events happened as a direct result of my involvement in the program.

One morning, I was called by one of the doctors at Napa State Hospital; he asked me to come by when I could. When we met, he explained, "We have a problem with a patient here and have run out of options; hopefully you can help. We have a young lady who is in a 'bad fairy' state of mind. She sees bad fairies in everything. Some, she says, even have the faces of gods. We have tried medications, counseling and therapy, but we cannot get through to her. Could you find time to come and talk to her for us? Maybe that would help."

Since the staff and doctors had been good enough to let me attend a few staff meetings and some evaluation sessions and treatment procedures of patients, I agreed to try with this young lady, although I knew that failure was staring me in the face.

Two days later, I dressed in causal outdoor clothes and went to meet the unknown. The patient was a nice-looking young lady in her early twenties. She was in a neutral state, with no outward indication of emotion. She was not sad, not happy, not angry, not anything. She was clean and modestly dressed. I was impressed by her physical appearance and instantly became concerned about her. Her lack of any feelings bothered me just as it had the doctors. I was just one more object in the room.

I started by telling her my name and asking what I should call her.

She looked at me and then at the window in the door. The window was made of one-way glass. An orderly outside could see in and give help if needed. At my insistence, all my conversations were to be private. They could watch, listen and respond if there was any problem or danger, but nothing the girl or I said would be recorded.

She told me, with no smile, that she was Sue (which was not her real name).

I replied, "That is a nice name. Sue, I was born in Texas. Where were you born?"

She answered, "California."

I continued with simple questions, and she began to expand her answers. We talked for twenty minutes about her sister and where she had lived. I asked if she would like me to come back to see her in a week so we could talk more.

"Maybe," she said.

I took out my pocket calendar; it was blank. I studied it for a few seconds and told her that I could come back next Tuesday at the same time if that was all right with her. She looked up, turned away, looked back, shrugged and nodded.

I thanked her for her time and signaled to the person outside that I was through. An orderly came and took her to her quarters. As she passed by me, she gave me just the small beginning of a smile.

A week later, I went back. Nothing much had changed; however, she seemed happy that I came. On my third trip, I went expecting rejection from the doctors or from Sue. I was probably wasting everyone's time. I was met with good news, though: Sue had begun to talk some and had only mentioned bad fairies and their punishing her a few times. She had not changed in any other way, but the doctor's opinion was that, with my just being there for her, she had begun to make some progress.

I went to the conference room and was surprised by what I saw. Sue's hair was done up, and she had just enough makeup on for me to know she had used it. She smiled and asked the first question, "What do you do?"

Thinking she was asking about my occupation, I kept it simple: "I am a Baptist minister."

She looked at me curiously, waited and then asked, "Do you believe in the devil?"

"I sure do, but I believe in God and Jesus a lot more," I answered.

"The devil ever bother you?" she wanted to know.

I replied, "All the time. He tries to foul me up, but my God is a lot stronger than the devil. I just turn the devil over to God and move on with my life."

"Your God can take care of the devil?" she stammered.

"All the time, if I let Him do it. If I try to whip the devil by myself, I lose," I said.

"The devil ever throw you up against a wall and beat on you?" she asked.

"No. Some people who did not like me tried — but it was people who did that, not the devil," I answered.

"The devil uses people to be mean?" she asked.

"He has to use people, just like God has to use people. We have to chose who we want to use us."

While I answered, her face became pale and worried, then she broke down. I slowly moved to her side of the table and sat beside her. Hoping that someone was watching through the window, I placed my arm around her shoulder; she leaned into me, and the tears flowed. For five minutes, she shook and wept. There were Kleenex boxes on the table, and I handed her some tissues and said nothing.

After another five minutes, she blubbered, "I ought to be ashamed for behaving like this. I was told that I was too big to cry and was always slapped for doing it."

"Well, I am sure not going to slap you — and you know what? When I cry, I do not want anyone to slap me. If I hurt for someone like you, I cry because I hurt for them."

She turned and saw real tears on my face. She was the age of my daughter. Her story and her pain had torn me up. In few minutes, we both stood and walked around the room, trying to get a hold of our emotions. After a little while of silence, I was ready to leave. She walked up to me, looked me in my face and asked, "Can I hug you?"

We hugged. I left with a promise to come back in two weeks with a dry shirt.

I met with the staff and told them what had happened. They were encouraged. It was three weeks before I could get back, and I could not find Sue. The staff was no help at all. They kept telling me to go to the dining area and relax for a few minutes, to get a cup of coffee or something and let them do their work. I was stunned at their reception and thought about leaving, but I knew I could not abandon Sue, regardless of their actions. I went to the small eating area where patients could buy coffee and snacks and socialize with one another. I was looking at something in one of their brochures when I heard a clear, almost sing-song voice say, "Oh, Mr. Brown, I am so glad you came today!"

I looked up and saw Sue. She was not just working in the small dining area; she was its manager. While I stood there speechless, the staff walked in. Sue came around the counter and joined us. We all laughed and hugged. Anyone not knowing what had happened and why we acted the way we did would have thought that the patients had taken over the hospital.

I went back three more times and continued to work with Sue and the staff. In three months, Sue was released and moved to Southern California. I never heard from Sue, but the staff kept me up-to-date for a few months on her progress. As far as they could tell, she was fully recovered. We were not allowed to give out any personal information about Sue, and she was under some of the same restrictions.

A week later, an invitation came from an American Indian Baptist Church in South San Francisco. They wanted someone who had experience with the culture (and maybe even some American Indian heritage) to come and spend a week with them in a special revival and outreach to other native peoples in the community.

The members and friends were descendants from several different tribes, some from tribes who in past years were blood enemies. My wife's mother was part American Indian, as was my grandmother. I had been privileged to have close ties with tribes in New Mexico and north Texas. I agreed to go.

I lived that week with an American Indian family from southern Arizona. The pastor and wife were from Oklahoma, and the music director from the Carolinas. The members had occupations of all types in the South Bay Area. Most families spent their vacations and off-time back home on reservations or at the "old home places" where their families had lived.

I visited in homes and met people at their jobs. I met their children and became a part of the church family. We had a great time of church fellowship and blessings, with four new additions to the church and three others waiting for baptism. They had a powwow and barbecue with venison and flat bread for me at the end of the week.

I had been on the USC-Berkeley campus while racial unrest was making national headlines and had met with some leaders of churches in the area, but one telephone call really shook me.

"Mr. Brown, I cannot give you my name, but I represent a group of African-Americans in Berkeley and Oakland. You are aware of the problems we are having in our area. I have been asked to contact you and ask you to come to a closed meeting with some of our leaders. If you would consider coming, we will guarantee your safety and find an agreeable date."

Ever since my time with Dr. Foy Bernard, I had followed her advice and had always gone where I was asked, but I had never been in a heated situation like this. I hesitated and replied, "Sir, since I do not know you and have no idea why you called me, I will have to give some serious thought and prayer to your invitation. Give me a tele-phone number, and I will call you back in four days."

He replied, "I understand your reluctance and will look forward to hearing from you. Let me emphasize again, you will be well-protected and cared for if you will come. I will call you in four days. We just want to talk to you; that is all." With that, he hung up.

I told Flo about my call, and she was understandably concerned. I had two other people whom I trusted and knew would keep a confidence. I talked twice with my trusted friends.

The call from Oakland came, and I talked again to the person who had called before. For some reason, I began to feel that maybe God was in some way behind this. I had no idea how they got my name, but the more important question for me was, what good could I do? After days of much prayer and thought, I agreed to go.

He called me back with instructions, and we agreed on a date a week off. I would be contacted the morning of that day and given the time and place where I was to meet my escorts.

I was more than just concerned; to be honest, I was scared. Oakland and Berkeley were hotbeds of protest with some serious riots. Flo was still uneasy but supportive. I waited for an hour that morning and no call came. I began to relax and hoped the meeting had been called off.

Fifteen minutes before noon, the phone rang; a different voice said, "Mr. Brown, I have been instructed to call you with these specific instructions. Do you have a pencil ready?"

He told me in detail what freeway to take, what turn-off to use, what street to take and what garage to park in; he even specified which level and space I was to park in. He gave me the time I was to arrive, with only a five-minute window. He gave me the names of two men who would meet me. I was not to open my car door until those two men arrived and identified themselves. I gave him a description of my car and my license number, and he hung up. I left in plenty of time and arrived fifteen minutes early. I circled the block and, at the agreed time, drove to the third floor of the parking garage and parked in the assigned spot. I sat for ten minutes and was ready to leave.

A big black man appeared at my window and held up his name card. I lowered the window. He said, "Reverend Brown, will you come with us? We will escort you to our meeting."

With one man in front and one in back, I went out the back entrance of the garage. We three walked down an alley for two blocks, up two flights of stairs and into a dimly lit room. There were four or five others there. They all stood up and shook my hand, but they did not introduce themselves. They welcomed me and served me coffee and some excellent pastry.

The leader began, "While no names will be used, we want you to know that you are welcome and that we appreciate your coming. It may be late when we are through, but you will be escorted back to your car with four of our men. Once you are in your car, two of the men will get in another car and will lead you out onto the freeway. Another car will follow you until we are sure you are safe. Now, we just want to talk."

He paused, and I said, "Before we start, let me ask one simple question. Why me?"

The leader answered, "We asked around about a white Christian leader who would be open and honest with us, and your name was given to us. Our policy here is that your name will never be mentioned outside this room and that our names will never be used today or later." I nodded my head and sat back.

We discussed some politics but mostly focused on relationships between blacks and whites. I refused to get into police relations and stayed away from personal feelings. They had some serious and justified problems. I had some difficulties with the way they were trying to use those problems for the justification of their riots. As one said, "We would not get anyone's attention otherwise."

After almost two hours of discussion, it was over — but before I was ready to leave, I wanted to ask a personal question: "How do you get so many people to show up for your protests?"

The leader answered, "Brown, you ought to know the answer to that. It is what your whole movement of Christianity is built on. Jesus called twelve men to him and got them totally committed to his cause. Each one of them recruited a dozen others and so on down the line, and His movement grew. You give me a week to ten days ahead, and I will have a dozen men hit the streets. Each of them will have a dozen others, and in a week, I can put thousands anywhere we need them."

I had to smile. We stood and shook hands all around. With my four guards and two car escorts, I headed back home from my meeting with the Black Panthers of Oakland, California. To this day, I have no way of knowing for certain how or why they contacted me.

The next week, I had a meeting at Golden Gate with one of the professors, who was a member of one of our churches; we needed to talk about a problem concerning one of our young pastors and his relationship to his church.

We talked a few minutes, and he agreed to speak to the young man and get back to me. Maybe the two of us working together could help him. I left and was going down the steps. At the landing halfway down, I heard a voice just below me say, "It can't be you! It can't be!"

I looked down, and a beautiful young woman ran up and grabbed me; she began to cry, laugh and kiss me on both cheeks. She suddenly stopped as quickly as she had begun. She backed off, embarrassed; I, however, was enjoying myself.

"You don't have any idea who I am, do you?" she stammered.

"I don't, but I am not unhappy that you remember me and choose to express it this way," I answered.

"I have to talk to you. I want to tell you a story that I think you want to hear. Do you some have time?" she anxiously asked.

There was no way I was going to turn this down. We went to the cafeteria and took a table away from the others (many were there studying).

She began, "Do you remember, at the youth camp in the mountains east of Los Angeles, when you had to take the dagger away from that teenage boy who threatened you?" she asked.

When she mentioned it, the experience came back to mind; I had never dreamed that the hand-to-hand combat training I had learned in the military would ever be needed in a Christian camp. But what had that to do with this young woman?

She then asked me if I remembered three girls who had been "hell-raisers" (her term).

"Oh, the ones from Bellflower, the ones the camp director was going to send home. You were one of those three?" I asked.

"I was not just one of them; I was the leader. That is why I may have made such a fool of myself on the stairs. You have no idea how much I have wanted to find and talk to you."

She began, "That night at camp when the entire staff was ready to call our parents and send us home, I was as scared as I have ever been. You see, the church had paid my way, and my dad was mad at me and the church. When I left that morning, he said, 'Well, Miss Troublemaker, go ahead, but you won't last a week with people like that.'

"I knew that, if I was sent home, I would be grounded for the summer, and my hopes for school and college would vanish. I would be constantly reminded that I could not even stay with those 'self-righteous bigots' for a week. Dad would not even tolerate my wanting to go back to church."

"We three had been a problem, and we knew it — but we were not like the young man who challenged you. We were fighting with ourselves, and we made everyone around us miserable. Even so, I could not blame Miss Waters for coming to you with the demand that you send us home.

"However scared I was, I was going to stand up to you and make you the goat for us being sent home. You came to our room and had us all sit around you so we could talk. For what seemed like an hour to us (it was probably five or ten minutes), you just looked at us and waited.

"One of us (I don't remember who) finally spoke and asked you what you were going to do. You just continued to look around for a few more minutes and told us you did not know. Then you asked us what we thought you ought to do.

"It seemed funny to me. You wanted us to determine our punishment, and that threw me. I wondered, 'What would I do if someone treated me the way I had treated our leaders and other campers?' I had never thought of my effect on others; I just wanted my way. We did not have an answer, and you gave us none. You leaned back and told us that we needed to think and talk or we would be there for a long time. While we all waited, you just sat and said nothing.

"I, for the first time I could remember, began to dislike myself. I was ashamed but did not want to admit it. Since none of the other girls had responded, I spoke up and said, 'I don't want to go home and embarrass my parents or my church. Is there any way we could stay?'

" 'I don't know. What do you think you would need to do to be able to stay?' you asked.

"One after another, my tears came — not for being expelled, but for my attitude and behavior. We began to talk among ourselves, and you pretended not to hear or care. Later, I looked up and asked if you would help us. You asked how, and I answered, 'Ask the camp leaders to let us apologize to them, and we will promise to become a part of the camp like we should have been all week.'

"You said, 'I will do it on one condition. All four of us will make a covenant — not just a promise, but a covenant — here, together, tonight. It must be a lasting agreement that this will be the beginning of a new way of life for you. I am not interested in a short-time promise that you will forget before you get home; I do not want to see you repeat your sorry life the way it has been this week.'

"We all looked at you like you were crazy, but you said that was your position. We could take it if we wanted; if not, we would go home that night. You then held out your hand and said, 'Here is my hand. If you mean business, take my hand; if not, there are no hard feelings, but I have to have a commitment from you before we go talk to the staff.'"

The young lady who was telling the story had been the first one to reach out and grab my hand, nearly crushing it. The others had followed. We all held hands and each prayed for forgiveness. The girls made a promise to God and to each other that, whatever else happened, a change in their lives and actions was going to be made.

The next morning, the staff heard their request to stay, and I encouraged the staff to accept their apology and not talk about it among the campers. The girls, like the young man I had taken the dagger from, began to fit in with the other young people; we had no more problems with those four or any others during the last two days of the camp.

The events that followed had partially blocked that camp from my memory. It all happened around the time that I left the church in Norwalk and moved to Stockton.

After the young woman had explained why she was so overwhelmed to see me, I had to know why she was on campus. She answered, "To the annoyance of my father, I went back to church the next Sunday and asked for help to become a Christian and a member of our church. I graduated from high school that year and enrolled in California Baptist College. Even though my father could have helped, he refused to pay any of my expenses. I graduated this year and came here today to enroll in the seminary. I now hope to become a missionary."

She again burst into tears and said, "I had to find you and thank you for saving my life!"

As I drove home, a feeling came over me that I still cannot describe; all I know is that the world looked a lot brighter than it had in days. There were stories of other young people and adults that had not turned out this way, but this one would keep me going for a long time.

That summer, Dr. Staples, president of California Baptist College, was our preacher at Cazadero Baptist Camp. I had hired a long-haired kid with holes in his jeans to help in the kitchen and lead music at our evening watch around the campfire. The hippies camping in the redwoods began to come to our evening campfire services. The next year, I was asked to marry one of the couples who came and was a guest at two other weddings.

Two other major events happened at camp that week. At dinner one evening, Dr. Staples and I sat together. He asked me, since I traveled a lot and made many contacts, if I knew where he might find a graduate student completing a master's degree in economics who would consider coming to California Baptist for two years. The current head of the economics department at CBC was taking leave for two years to finish his doctor's degree. The interim director of the department would be one of the current professors. What Staples wanted was someone to teach basic economics for two years and maybe even longer.

I laughed and replied, "I just happen to know one who finished his bachelor's and is now is teaching first-year economics as part of a grant to finish his master's degree. He should be done this year."

"Who is he, and where is he now?" Staples asked.

"He is my son Bruce, and he is at Baylor University in Waco," I replied.

He looked at me, and I nodded. He laughed and asked for Bruce's phone number. I reached in my pocket, pulled out my address book, wrote down Bruce's information and gave it to Staples. Staples looked at the information and asked, "This for real?"

"So far as I know, that is his status," I answered.

That summer, Flo and I helped Bruce move to California Baptist. The now Dr. Bruce Brown taught at California Baptist for three years. He then went to Gardner Webb College in North Carolina for two years and completed his doctor's degree at the University of South Carolina. He has been a professor of economics at Furman University in Greenville, South Carolina, for over twenty-five years.

The long-haired kid I hired decided that his life was to be dedicated to God in ministry. Rick Warren had been

Harry Williams, Rick Warren and Edd.

approved for an internship in Washington, D.C. At a late date, it had been cancelled. The job I offered him was his last chance for a summer job. That summer, he worked in the camp kitchen and led music at night by the campfire. Hippies continued to come to our camp in the evenings. Rick was used by God to help some turn their lives around. Rick left for California Baptist that year. He became youth director at First Baptist in Norwalk. After he graduated from college, he moved to Southwestern Baptist Seminary in Fort Worth. He graduated from the seminary and moved with his wife, Kay (whom Flo and I had known since she was born), to Southern California. They, with twelve local people, began Saddleback Community Church. Its worldwide ministry now involves thousands each week. Rick and Kay and Tom and Chaundel (Rick's sister and brother-in–law) are as close as family to Flo and me. They and our four children were together in college, and we have worked with them and members of Saddleback Church for years.

Our greatest blessing that year was that our son Wayne, who had graduated from California Baptist and become an Army sergeant, came home from Vietnam. He worked in the Riverside area as a house parent in a boy's home while studying for his master's degree at a nearby college. He later became a family counselor for military complexes in the deserts northeast of Riverside, California. Later, he became a family advocate for the Riverside County Courts Juvenile Division.

Of course, other things happen.

Son Wayne returns from Vietnam.

Flo developed problems and had to have a hysterectomy. Flo did not want anyone to know about her being in the hospital. Our doctor, a close friend, told me to relax while Flo was prepared for surgery. He said the surgery would last less than an hour. An hour passed, and I was worried. After two hours, the doctor came into the waiting room.

Before I could ask, he said, "Edd, Flo is all right now. You don't have to worry."

"What do you mean, now?" I asked.

He replied, "I would have been here sooner, but her heart stopped, and we had to get it restarted and make sure it continued to function. She will be all right, but she will be sore for several weeks. I may have used too much force to restart her heart, but I did not want to waste any time. We watched her on the monitor for an hour, and everything is working the way it should. We will continue to watch her for two more days before she can go home." He gave me hug and said, "She is going to be fine."

I had to wait for half an hour before I could see her. In two days, she came home and did recover.

Fourteen

1974

The Streets of San Francisco: Another Move?

We had a nice home in Kenwood in the middle of the Valley of the Moon. Marcia, our youngest, was at California Baptist College. Bruce had graduated from Baylor University and was teaching at CBC. Wayne was home from Vietnam and was on staff at California Baptist. Steve and Peggy were in Napa, and we had our first grandson, Matt, close by. North Bay and Redwood Empire Associations had begun eight new ministries. Eleven churches had made new or major improvements to their facilities. We were on good terms with our pastor and our church. We were loved where we were and loved where we lived.

Again, that phone rang. "Edd, this is Bob Hughes (the executive director for the California Southern Baptist Convention). Richard Kay (the associate director) and I would like for you to come to Fresno for two days. You bring Flo. We have hotel arrangements for you."

We went, thinking our visit was for another short-term project. Bob and I had been friends and coworkers for twenty years. Once, he had asked me to be co-pastor in the church where he was the pastor.

Flo and I took our time in getting to Fresno and checked into our hotel. Flo went shopping at the mall across the street, and I went to the Baptist building to meet with Bob and Richard.

After greetings, Bob began. "We have asked you here because we want to enlarge our program of outreach to men. The music and brotherhood departments are both being handled by one person, and he cannot do either department justice. We want you to think and pray about joining our state staff. We will not push you, but we want to begin the new program in January of 1975. We need your answer by the time of the convention's annual meeting in October, which is six months away; we do not want a yes or no from you at this time. You will get our letter next week, but we wanted to let you know personally that we pray that you will seriously consider our invitation. We feel you can do what needs to be done to improve the involvement of men in our church ministries and missions."

Flo and I spent the night and drove home the next morning. We did not talk much. The idea of moving back into the valley and leaving our new home, in one of the choicest places in the world, was not one we wanted to consider.

Their letter came, and I wrote back a nice reply. I told them that, at this time, I did not see how I could move. I was in the process of completing my doctoral work at Golden Gate Seminary, and I was closely involved in the founding of two new mission churches. Flo, who worked as my secretary, sent the letter, and we were satisfied that it would take care of their invitation.

The next week, I received a call from one of my fellow doctoral candidates. He had been a real pest when we first began our training at

Edd, Marcia and Flo.

Napa State Hospital. I was ten years older than him, and he had constantly followed me for two weeks before I could guide him away to work with the people there on his own. He had since begun a new work in North San Francisco, reaching out to homosexuals and street prostitutes. He asked me if he could meet and talk with me at the seminary. I had a meeting with my supervisor and agreed to meet him.

After we had greeted each other, he began. "I want to talk to you about two things: One concerns you, and the other is my work.

"It is the knowledge of four of us in the doctoral program that you are being set up to fail your doctoral work. Please don't ask me how we know; we just know. Your thesis will not even be read. It will be turned down by the director, and the graduate committee will never see it."

He had my attention. I already knew from my meetings with the director that something was wrong, but surely he could not bypass the committee. I thanked the man for telling me, and he moved on to the next item.

"My wife and I live on the second floor of a huge house in North San Francisco, which the mission board is supporting. We have six young ladies on the top floor and seven men in partitioned-off rooms on the ground floor. We would like for you to come and live with us for ten days and talk with our people. We have eight other people who come regularly to our Sunday worship and a few others who come to our evening Bible study. Would you come and work us, if we worked out the dates?"

I asked him to send me a letter with details and told him I would think and pray about his request. I went home. Before I could talk to her, Flo handed me a letter from Bob Hughes.

He said in his letter that he understood my reluctance but asked me to reconsider. In his opinion, the change to a full-time ministry for men would be approved by the convention only if I was to be the director of the new department. Reluctantly, I agreed to rethink my answer.

I agreed to go to San Francisco and help my pastor friend and his wife in their ministry. I met with the pastors in my association to make sure that potential reports of me being seen on the streets of San Francisco with homosexuals and prostitutes would not become a problem in their churches. A few pastors asked why I would even consider wasting my time with a bunch of losers; however, once word of my trip to "Baghdad by the Bay" was known, the overwhelming response from pastors and church members was support for my going. They encouraged me to do the best I could and said they would be praying for me.

I went to San Francisco two weeks later. After lunch with my friend and his wife, I met with four of their houseguests. We had our first meeting with ten people that night. I had asked that our first meeting be informal. There were no songs, no prayers and no Bible study. It was just a time to get acquainted. I had asked the pastor to have name tags for the people so I could learn who they were. I started the meeting and told them a little about my life, including the impact of my grandfather's statement that I would never be worth a damn. We talked. I answered their questions, some of which were personal. Then, one by one, I asked them to share with me their full names and where they were from and anything they wanted to tell about their early lives. We all then told some crazy or fun thing that we remembered about growing up. We laughed and had refreshments, and they went to their beds or homes.

The next night, I gave out sheets of writing paper and asked them to list for me, anonymously, what they wanted to discuss and what specific questions they might have that would be best handled in private. The group increased to fourteen the next night; by the end of the ten days, we had twenty people.

During the day, I would go to the beach or Golden Gate Park or downtown with a few people from our group. We just talked. After four days, they became very open and honest. We dealt with family backgrounds, ministerial perceptions and rejections. I tried to show them love, strength, forgiveness and acceptance. I did not leave any of my foundational Biblical beliefs, but neither did I lay blame or condemn.

At our nightly meetings, one young lady would wait until everyone was in our conference room; she would then come in and take a back seat. She would pull up a chair in front of her and prop up her feet on the chair. If I had been totally ignorant of the female body before, I would have had a complete education those first three nights. She was always dropping something on the floor and stooping suggestively to pick it up. I did my best to ignore her actions, but I did not ignore her. When she came on the fifth night, she had cleaned herself up so much that I did not recognize her. I walked up to her and introduced myself. She was embarrassed to tell me her name.

I backed off, looked at her and said, "My, my, young lady, you are one good-looking gal. I am sorry I did not recognize you."

"Not your fault," she laughed and sat on the second row.

My partitioned room was on the ground floor, and I was the most protected person in the city. When I was with individuals or small groups — whether at the zoo, the beaches or the Japanese gardens — I never had one indecent approach or word to me. I had a great time while I was there.

Out of the sixteen men I tried to minister to, four were what I would deem truly homosexual. Three were not happy about their situation and were thinking of a change. Three had accepted their condition but were not practicing sex. The others were either experimenters or just antisocial. They were using the "homosexual" tag as a way to protest against an unfair (in their minds) society.

Eight of the women were between sixteen and twenty years old; the other six were older. Out of the fourteen, four were prostitutes and said they enjoyed sex. Two of those later told me that they were worried about their future, when they would no longer be marketable. The others were there because of family problems or because there were no jobs they could compete for.

Two things I learned in San Francisco have stuck with me. One was that difficult circumstances often lead to bad decisions. Too many of the women (and a few of the younger men) were on the streets as a direct result of abuse from family members, church leaders or other so-called respectable men and women who took advantage of their trust. Many of the men and women had been rejected by their families and pushed onto the streets. Their experiences with overly religious zealots had become the last straw. They decided they might as well become what they were accused of being. They received no counseling and no help from family or others.

Half of my ministry in the Redwood Empire and North Bay associations had become counseling parents, siblings, extended families, pastors and church leaders. Far too many leaders and parents would rather give up on their family members than admit they might have contributed to the cause of the problem.

The other thing I learned was to never give up on people. One evening, the young lady who had made such a transformation came and asked me if I would come to her apartment. I was stunned, and it showed!

She turned red in the face and quickly said, "Not for that reason. I have someone I want you to meet. You can bring the pastor with you so there will be no questions."

I agreed to go. The pastor drove us to the boarding house where she lived. I knocked on the door. A beautiful young girl, about seven years old, opened the door and then backed up and looked up at me.

"Are you that nice man that Mom has been telling me about?" she smiled and asked.

I stammered, "I don't know."

She asked us to come in and said, "You must be. Some men who come here are not very nice."

We walked in, and the girl began to ask more questions. I got down on my knees in front of her, and we talked about everything. After ten minutes, her mother came to my rescue, and I went to my chair. When I sat down, my new little friend came over and wanted to sit in my lap. I looked to her mother, and she said it was okay. The little girl crawled up into my lap and, in ten minutes, was fast asleep.

The pastor and I stayed and talked for over an hour. The young lady had put her daughter to bed. She thanked the pastor for coming and for inviting me to be with their group. She then told me that the week had helped her far more than she ever imagined. With the pastor's help, she wanted to get back into society and hopefully back with her family.

At the end of my time with the group, they decided on their own to prepare a special dinner. They also wanted to meet Flo and get to know her. I called Flo, and she agreed to come. I drove to Kenwood that night, and Flo and I returned to the big house the next afternoon.

When we arrived, I could not believe it was the same place. It had been scrubbed, cleaned and decorated. The houseguests had their special meal laid out on long tables across the front of the room. I was asked to introduce Flo, and she was welcomed. After thirty minutes of talking with her, they asked Flo and me to be first in the serving line. One of the people was a chef, so we had a great meal.

After two hours of fellowship, Flo and I were asked to stand at the front of the room. Several stood and spoke about being glad I had come and how I had understood and accepted them. Then, in no hurry, everyone stood and lined up to come by and thank Flo and me. They took their time to share some personal thoughts. They thanked Flo for letting me be with them, and they were especially grateful for her willingness to come and be there with them that night.

The young lady who had changed so much waited until all the others were through the line and then came. She gave Flo a big hug, looked at her and said, "Mrs. Brown, I want to thank you for coming — and I don't want you to misunderstand what I am going to do, but I have to do it."

She turned, hugged me, kissed me on both cheeks and then backed off. With tears streaming down her cheeks, she stutteringly said, "Thank you for treating me like a human being!" She held my hands for a few more seconds and then turned, still sobbing, and walked away.

Flo and I were so moved by those people, who just needed someone to accept them, that we hardly talked on our way home. Yes, they were broken, battered and rejected — but they were still some of God's people and needed help. Flo's and my thoughts were the same: without God, our parents and family, we could be in the same situation.

Another letter from Bob Hughes was waiting when I returned; he asked me to contact him if I was still having problems with joining the staff in Fresno. I called and asked some questions; he explained that, if and when I came to join the staff, I would be working with Pat Patillo three months as an associate in the Sunday school department and would be the part-time director of the current brotherhood department. At the beginning of the new year, I would be the director of the men's department.

I had never allowed salary or benefits to influence any of my decisions. Wherever I went, I went because I was personally convinced that it was where I ought to be and that God would take care of me and my family. This time, I tried to use finances as the reason to keep from moving. I felt God needed a little help in decision-making.

Our daughter would lose her scholarship at California Baptist. Our health insurance with the convention would not begin until the first of the year. We would be three months without medical insurance, and Flo's heart was still a concern after it had stopped beating for two minutes during surgery four months earlier. The travel allowance I would be allotted was no more for all of California and northern Nevada than it currently was for the four counties north of San Francisco. The salary would be very little more than I was already getting. With my current job, I could be home at night and most weekends. I put in writing my uneasiness about taking on a large project that I was not yet completely sold on.

Flo said, as she typed the letter, "You really don't want to move, do you?"

"Not unless God really makes it abundantly clear to me that this is what I have to do," I replied. "I am having enough problems with the supervisor of my doctoral program and with three new pastors in our associations. Besides, I do not feel I am ready or able to head up their new program."

We mailed the letter, and I hoped I had not alienated some good friends. A week later, Bob sent me another letter. He asked, "If you were the new leader, what would you do? I need some suggestions."

Dumb me. I did not realize the trap he had set. In two weeks, I mailed him two pages of what I thought the leader ought to do in beginning the new program. I left for a leadership workshop I was doing in a church in Richmond, California. Pat Patillo was doing the same in a neighboring church. Pat called and asked me to meet him later that week for lunch.

As I have mentioned, Pat was one of Flo's and my closest and oldest friends in California. We met, and Pat asked if I had replied to Bob's letter. I replied that he must have left before Bob received the letter that I had sent three days ago. Pat had been on the road and had not seen the contents of my letter.

"What did you put in your letter?" he asked.

I told Pat that I had thanked Bob again for his confidence in me and had listed, at his request, five things I thought needed to be done with the men's department, by whomever they enlisted to be the director. My suggestions broke with most of the present concepts and purposes of the current program. Pat wanted to know what my suggestions were. I told him in order the five suggestions I had made. Pat had his fork halfway to his mouth but stopped and dropped the fork on his plate.

"You put that in writing?" he asked.

Wondering at the shock, he had expressed, I told him that was what I had done.

"Edd, we have known each other for over thirty years. Have I ever lied to you?" he asked.

What a question. He never had, but what did that have to do with our conversation now?

"Of course not," I replied.

"Okay, I want you to listen carefully to what I am going to tell you. Two days before I left Fresno, Bob and I sat down and came up with five reasons that we wanted you to be part of our state staff and to lead the men's work. We not only listed the same five items you say you wrote to Bob, but we also listed them in the same order. My friend, you have dug yourself a hole that you cannot get out of."

Before I could respond, he asked, "You going to Glorieta?" I told him I was going.

He continued, "Bob will be there. Why don't you let him know that you just want to talk to him and nothing more?" I agreed and began a troubled two-hour drive home.

I had finished my draft copy of my doctoral ministry project and made the mistake of having my supervisor (at his request) look it over for content, not form. He had briefly glanced through it and then pitched it back to me. "Just what I expected. This will not do. Redo the entire paper," he demanded.

Two hundred pages, which represented hours of hard work and fact-gathering, were gone. I had been warned he would do this. In fifteen minutes, he had evaluated my work and rejected it outright.

When I told Flo, who had also worked hours on the projects and reports, she was as disheartened as I was. I had done what he had asked: "Do a preliminary draft for me before you start the final one."

Almost in tears, Flo said, "Why don't you just quit? It is not worth what he is doing to you, and it is becoming just another burden instead of a learning experience."

I replied, "I know that, and I was told by four of my good friends that he was going to do everything he could to block me; however, I am not going to let him determine what I can or cannot do. If I can do nothing else, I will outlast him."

I am not sure my motive was right, but after overcoming the effects of my grandfather's harsh words, I became determined that no other person had the right to make that assessment of me. I hired a professional writer, and she did an excellent job of reworking my paper. I had several of my friends and coworkers review the revised work, and they were impressed

Flo and I went to Glorieta. On our way, we stopped at a rest stop in Arizona. A close friend and fellow director of missions was there with his wife. Joe Bradley decided to ride with me, while Flo would ride with Anna. A convention board member was a member of a church in Joe's association. Joe knew about me being asked to join the state staff and wanted to know if I had made a decision about the men's department.

I told him the number of times I had said no and that Bob and Richard kept coming back. After a few minutes, Joe said, "You are afraid you can't do what you said needed to be done, aren't you?"

I had to agree. I knew the present men's leadership would be up in arms and that many would want to do away with any kind of layman's program they could not control. I would have not dozens but hundreds of people after me from both sides.

"Have you ever backed down from doing what you knew had to be done?" he asked.

"Joe, you know the answer to that better than I do," I replied.

"Then why are you thinking about backing off now? You can do what they want because you know it needs to be done, and we will get you a lot of help," he said, smiling. I stayed quiet.

I knew then that our being at the same rest stop on the same day was not just a coincidence. I met with Bob, and in September of 1975, I was elected to be director of the new Men's Ministry department of the California Southern Baptist Convention. The name change was my first move.

Before I took the office on January 1, 1976, and even before the convention I was elected at was over, the rumors began. People thought that I was out to destroy the brotherhood or to make it into something equivalent to a women's mission study group or a self-help program.

That was just one of my problems. My supervisor for my doctoral program would not accept or even read my revised dissertation.

Without even opening the report, he rejected it outright in September. He maintained that what I had submitted to him could not be accepted and that any project report had to be based on my new position. I was not to begin for three months. I was more than upset; I was mad, and I had to leave to keep from telling the professor what I thought of him and that I did not appreciate his lying to me for the past year. I walked out of his office, feeling defeated and not very Christlike.

I went to Fresno and talked to Bob about what happened. He suggested that I not contest the rejection of my work, which I could do. We both knew that the graduate committee would overrule my supervisor. He suggested I use the development of the new men's ministry department and its mission and purpose as my new project. Since what I was beginning was a new concept for California Baptist men, I had to keep records and make reports. I also had to enlist and train leaders. I could do two things at once. Bob agreed to become my field supervisor if the graduate committee would approve the change along with my new project. I contacted the chairman of the graduate committee, not my supervisor. The committee looked at my new proposal and approved the change with only one negative vote.

The Old Testament story of Joseph's reunion with his brothers after they had sold him into slavery came to mind. Years later, when the brothers met, Joseph told them, "What you intended for me was bad, but God intended what you did for good."

Our friends, Ted and Sue Lindwall, called. They were missionaries to Guatemala. He was a guest professor at Golden Gate Seminary. They were taking a week off and wanted Flo and me to go with them to Victoria and Vancouver Canada. Flo and I both had to have a break, so we went. We toured the country and small towns and stopped for movies. The women shopped, and we ate and slept whenever we wanted. We took the ferry to Victoria Island and had a ball. Ted and I went to the harbor and looked at boats while the ladies had tea at the Queen's Hotel. We drove to the north end of the island and looked at cabins that the early settlers had built and lived in. While we were tourists, we forgot about study, work and problems. We returned home and were ready to do whatever needed to be done in our ministry.

Fifteen

1975-1977

Men's Ministries

I resigned my two positions as director of missions. The pastors and churches of both associations had special farewell dinners and programs for my family and me. We moved to Clovis, a nice community east of the Baptist building in Fresno. Our finances, scholarships, insurance, buying and selling of houses, and moving all fell into place with very little effort from us. We celebrated Christmas with family in our new home. Flo and I, as a team, were asked to be part-time ministers of education at Temple Baptist Church in Fresno.

Bob Hughes had made arrangements for me to be in meetings with staff members two months before we moved. He had sent me to the national Brotherhood meetings in Memphis, Tennessee. I met other state directors and had a mixed reception. Most were open and encouraged me to join with them.

One ministry caught my attention — Texas Baptist Men's Disaster Relief program. When I returned to Fresno, a staff member told me about a similar group in San Francisco called NOVAD (National Volunteers Active in Disaster). I attended a meeting and was intrigued by how they helped people in earthquakes, floods and other disasters. They held quarterly meetings. They knew that Southern Baptists were a church group but little else — and as little as they knew about us, I knew less about them. I invited them to hold their next meeting in Fresno, and they accepted.

I shared with Bob what I had done. He was encouraged but told me that I needed to check the calendar before scheduling meetings at our building. That was lesson one learned, and there would be others.

My job description was broad and open. I was free to do what I needed to develop the new program. I was to stay within my budget, be in-house for a monthly staff week and make written monthly reports. I was to let Helen Martin, my new secretary, know where I was at all times so she could locate me when needed. At that time, cell phones were just dreams, and computers were unthinkable.

I wanted to find out what the laymen of our state thought we needed to do. We sent letters to all the Baptist pastors in California and the northern half of Nevada. The letter asked for the names and addresses of two men from each church who may be interested in developing and participating in an expanded program of ministry.

I was surprised by the number of pastors who responded. After receiving their responses, we mailed letters to over six hundred men whose names had been given to us. Our follow-up letter asked the men if they would be willing to attend an all-day meeting to help us develop a program for men in California and Nevada. Over four hundred men responded and attended eight regional meetings to begin the development of an acceptable program for men in our convention's churches.

Twenty-four men who had been selected by the regional meetings met in Fresno and went over in detail all the suggestions submitted by the larger group. That information became the basis for the men's ministry department of the California Southern Baptist Convention. A summary of the Fresno meeting was mailed to over seven hundred participants and others for review. They were asked for a detailed response to express support of or opposition to the proposed agreement. The response to the idea of a men's program was overwhelmingly positive.

After six months and thousands of miles of driving, the format of men's ministries began to take shape; it was refined as we went along. The basic concept was twofold. First, since we heard preaching twice on Sunday and once during the week, we would not need another meeting once a month just to eat and hear another sermon. We wanted pastors and church leaders to help us find ways to be involved in ministry and put in practice what we had been taught. Second, we wanted to do something that would be worth our time and energy and helpful to others. We needed hands-on challenges for personal development and outreach opportunities.

It was now our job to "sell" the new program to the pastors and members of churches in California and northern Nevada. Many pastors were unaware of what was happening, and others did not care. I used my connections with directors of missions to get invitations for me and/or layman to speak at their church meetings. That way, the pastors could hear firsthand about what we were doing and why we were trying to get the men of our churches involved.

Because this new program was the basis of my second doctoral thesis, Helen and I kept meticulous records.

Ted and Sue Lindwall called again. They were going back to Guatemala in five months. They were taking a ten-day vacation to Mexico in two weeks and asked if we would go. I had vacation time. I cleared the time with my supervisors, and Flo and I went with our friends to Mexico.

The plan was that Ted, Sue and Flo would drive to Tucson, Arizona. I had two training meetings in Southern California. I would take care of the meetings and fly to meet them in Tucson in four days. Ted had some stops he needed to make, so the timing would work well.

I finished my meetings and met them in Tucson. We spent ten

days vacationing in Mexico. Ted and Sue both spoke fluent Spanish. We stopped at the coastal resorts of Los Mochis and Mazatlan. We moved on to Guadalajara for three days. There, we ate twice at "No Name Restaurant" on "No Name Street," but it had excellent food. We shopped in markets and filled our trunk with merchandise. We spent two days in Guanajuato, one of the most beautiful small cities that we have been privileged to visit. Our hotel had the charm of old Mexico, and the inside was modern and comfortable. At one stop, Flo bought eight hand-hammered copper plates to use as hot pads for platters of the special enchiladas she makes for family occasions.

We spent two days north of Mexico City. We climbed pyramids and walked through museums and the surrounding countryside. We toured San Miguel and visited with the local historian. We spent our last night in Zacatecas and returned to the U.S. through one of the largest Mormon settlements outside of our country. In the desert they had created a deep-well agricultural compound. They produced an abundance of fruits and vegetables, most of which were shipped to the southern states of our country.

We stopped at a converted railway station for dinner. The place had been renovated and was beautifully decorated with old Mexican and Indian artifacts. There was an eating place in the center of the former station. We were led to our table and given menus. There were over thirty items to choose from.

We gave the waiter our orders, but he came back in a few minutes to apologize and tell us they were out of that food. We ordered again, and he was gone a few minutes longer. He returned with our bottled drinks and informed us that our second order was not available either. In my broken Spanish, I (thankfully helped by Ted) asked, "Out of the more than twenty items on your menu, what is available?"

He smiled and gave us the two choices we could have. We held in our laughter until we had eaten and were outside. We spent our first night back in the U.S. in Tombstone, Arizona. We did the town, including the sites of real and imagined western stories. We visited the huge open pit copper mine just out of town and the agriculture fields in Southern California and Arizona on our way home.

When we arrived back home, we found that a weird arrangement had been made. Ted's field supervisor for his doctor's degree had moved. Since both of my doctoral programs directly related to Ted's doctoral work, Ted had (without my knowledge) asked the committee to assign me as his field supervisor until he returned to Guatemala. The graduate committee recognized my completion of the required work on my first project as sufficient experience for me to be Ted's supervisor, and they approved the change. Five months later, as Ted finished his doctoral work, he and Sue moved back to their mission field. They insisted that Flo and I begin planning to visit them in Guatemala City.

Our new men's ministry program was taking shape. A large number of pastors saw the value of having strong, mission-minded men's ministry groups in their churches. I began receiving requests to come to churches and present the program. My only requirement was that each pastor let other pastors and churches in his area know about our meeting and invite them to be a part of the conference. I was driving over a thousand miles a week to make those meetings. All this was happening at the same time that President Jimmy Carter, in an address at the Southern Baptist Convention, challenged churches to put volunteers into communities where hunger and bad housing were an embarrassment to our nation and to our Bible message. I was able to ride that wave of commitment in our churches in California and northern Nevada.

I went to my office and went through my mail. There was a letter from the executive board of the Southern Baptist Convention. I had been elected to the national board of directors for the radio and television commission and invited to their annual meeting at their headquarters in Fort Worth, Texas.

I have written about the difficulties I had and was continuing to have with my father. Those problems had become worse. He was then living somewhere in northeast Texas. I had held onto my negative feelings about him and had waited ten years for him to make some movement toward reconciliation. Mom, Janie, Flo and I were still living with the results of his abandoning Janie and Mom.

I had been telling the men in all my conferences for a year that if we were going to make any difference in our neighborhoods or our world, we needed to quit talking, get off our rear ends and make the first move to find needs and meet them. A ready-mix concrete company in Fresno had as its slogan, "Have a Need That Needs Filling? Call Us!" While I had adopted that concept for our program and had begun to promote it to the men, it dawned on me that maybe I needed to practice what I preached. I asked Helen to schedule me four extra days in Fort Worth. I wanted two extra days before and after my meeting. She arranged for my lodging and a car.

When I arrived in Fort Worth, my first visit was to the local police department. Sure enough, Dad had two traffic tickets there (with one more, he could have his driver's license revoked). I got his Fort Worth address and located the house, then I went to the radio and television office, reported in and received program guides. I left the office, drove to Dad's house and parked across the street from it.

Fifteen minutes later, Dad drove in. I waited and prayed for another ten minutes, and then I walked across the street. I had no idea what kind of reception I would get. I knocked on the door. He came, disgruntled because he knew it was salesperson. When he opened the door and looked through the screen, he knew that it was not a salesman.

At first he could not figure out who it could be. He cautiously opened the screen and then, with open fright, asked, "How did you find me, and what do you want?"

Before I could answer, Pauline, his new wife, called out, "Who is it, Jake?"

"It is Edd Lamoin," he answered.

"Well, don't stand there like some stupid dummy. Ask him in," she hollered.

Still cautious and unsure, he pushed the door open. He stepped back and nodded his head, and I went in. Dad was speechless and worried. He had no idea of what to do or say.

I had never met Pauline. She came over and introduced herself and asked why I was in Fort Worth.

"Three reasons," I answered. "I have never met you. I have not seen Dad in over ten years, and I have a meeting here." I told her the address. It was two miles from them.

"You mean that television building there?" she asked.

I told her, "Yes, that is where I will be meeting."

That broke the ice. I had to explain that I was one of a committee that oversaw the operations and that I was not involved in any production or acting.

Dad then asked if those were the only reasons I was there. I told him I was also going to Wichita Falls to see Flo's parents and sister and wanted to visit his sister and her daughter who had helped me when I was studying at the seminary here in Fort Worth. With that settled, we visited for awhile, and Pauline insisted that I stay for dinner.

Eventually, the conversation included Mom and Janie. I assured him that they were all right and that we all were doing fine. Janie was married and had a new baby. Our boys and Marcia were either in college or had good jobs. As we ate dinner, Dad's defenses began to drop and my anger lessened — but I still had a long way to go.

He asked me how I was getting around. I told him I had a rented a car.

"That will cost you too much money. I will take you to the rental place. You can turn the car in and use my pickup while you are here. I have another way to get to work and back," he said.

I did not want to do that and started to turn him down, but then it hit me — I had made the first move toward reconciliation in coming here and had no right to turn down his first move. After dinner, he and I went and exchanged cars, and I went to my hotel. I did not sleep well that night.

The next morning, I drove a hundred miles north and spent the day with Flo's family. On the drive back, thoughts flooded my mind. If Dad had had a broken leg or arm, I would have been there regardless of how much time or money it cost me; however, I had overlooked a broken spirit (and maybe even broken morals) because I could not or did not want to see. Dad did not know of my anger or my unforgiving spirit; they were not hurting or bothering him at all. Those and other feelings were eating at me alone. If I kept feeding those feelings, I would soon destroy myself as a person and as a minister. I had to pull off the road at a rest stop until my sobbing stopped.

I continued to use Dad's pickup. I visited Dad's sister and her family. I went to a bookstore and bought two thank-you cards, one for Pauline and one for Dad. I enclosed them in a box with a New Testament for Pauline. I thanked her for accepting me and wrote that I was glad that she and my dad seemed happy. I also was glad to now know her.

I left a similar note for Dad with a special invitation for both of them to visit us in California. Dad took me to the airport. I encouraged him to come to visit us. I was fortunate that, on my long flight home, I had two seats to myself. A feeling of relief that I did not yet understand began coming over me. Flo met me at the airport and wanted to know about Dad and me. I shared how Dad had opened up and talked. After three years of hard work on my part, my relationship with Dad had been restored.

Sixteen

1976

Guatemala

On February 4, 1976, a massive earthquake struck Guatemala. The ground not only shook, it heaved and dropped — and, in some places, split open. Although it lasted less than two minutes, hundreds of people died, and a third of the population was forced out of their homes.

On the fifth of February, my phone rang. It was Ted Lindwall, who said, "Edd, we need help. The mission boards in Richmond and Atlanta are going to do all they can, and Texas is mobilizing to come. Could you bring a team and work with us? We would house you at our seminary, which was not badly damaged, and move you to and from your worksites. Do not bring women on this trip. There will be other trips later, when we can house them. If you think you can come, I will send you more information."

"How soon do you need us?" I asked.

"Yesterday, of course — but if you could be here in three weeks, it would be a great help," he said.

I asked Helen how soon we could get out a notice to the people on our mailing list. She answered, "Give me what you want, and it will be in the mail by tomorrow at noon."

With that taken care of, I called four people. First was Jim Warren, the Mendo Lake Association director of missions; I told him what I needed and then called the music director of the First Baptist Church in Vacaville, who had been an Air Force doctor. Next, I called a furniture salesman in Fairfield who was bilingual. Lastly, I called Werb Stamfli in Napa, who was a fire captain and a rescue specialist.

To all I said, "I need two things. One, if at all possible, I need you to go with me to Guatemala. Two, I need you to help me enlist at least five people to be on our team." I then gave them the dates.

Helen sent out our letter, and I made an appeal to my church in Fresno. I went to a travel agency and got prices. We would pay our own expenses and would take enough money to care for our meals in Guatemala. In ten days, we had a team of nineteen with passports who would go in two weeks. I collected their money (which most of their churches had donated) and bought our tickets. I then notified Ted when we would arrive in Guatemala City.

We left Los Angeles on time; ten hours later, we were in Guatemala City. We were met at the airport by Ted and two others with two vans and a truck to take us the ten miles to the seminary.

We had been told to bring our own sleeping gear and to expect to spend time in tents away from the city. I was not just scared — I was petrified. The streets and highways were packed with people living in cardboard and paper shacks, cooking on fires in the center dividers. The traffic was horrendous. What few traffic lights there were that worked were ignored. Crying babies and small children were everywhere; adults were half-dressed and had no food. Dozens of people stood in line at scattered fire hydrants for just a bucket of water. There were portable toilets, but the stench made them almost impossible to use. Horses, donkeys and milk cows were crowded in with the lost and weary humanity. The smell of smoke and refuse was almost overpowering; the devastation was worse than anything I could remember, even worse than the aftermath of the bombings in Japan.

It took us an hour to go ten miles. We arrived at the seminary and were given the rooms of students who had gone to their villages to help their people. We unloaded our gear, went to our rooms and cleaned up as much as we could to be ready for a briefing for the three weeks we were to be in Guatemala.

We walked outside to settle down and walk off the stiffness from our ten-hour flight. We had light refreshments and drinks in the kitchen and were informed of when supper would be ready. Ted informed me that Sue was sick, but she had insisted that I come by for a few minutes. I went and spent ten minutes with Sue. She wanted to make sure we were there and that I was all right. She asked about Flo and then told me to go on back to the men. She felt better knowing that the men from California and I were there to help their people.

After supper, we met with our local leaders and learned what we would be doing for our three weeks. The plan was for us to work in four villages. We would take a trip tomorrow to see the people and to determine what equipment and materials would be needed to help them. We would only take what we needed to each job. Materials and tools not needed at a particular job would be locked up at the seminary.

After our orientation and meal, our team gathered upstairs in a large classroom. Nothing about it was formal; it was just a chance to talk about what we had seen and what we thought we were going to experience during the next three weeks. After twenty minutes, I asked for their attention. There had been no time for formal introductions at the airports or in the brief time before our evening meal.

I asked each person to share five things: who he was, what he did for a living, something about his family, something about his church and why he came on the trip.

Their responses were open and, I felt, honest. They said things like, "I felt I was needed," "I have never been out of the U.S.," "I like to travel to new places," "I love building," and "I felt this is what

God wanted me to do." The result was that a feeling of a teamwork began to form. We had three medical people, including a doctor. We had construction workers and a mason. We had one other minister besides me. We also had a truck driver, a salesman and a male nurse who spoke Spanish.

To most on the team, I was an unknown. They had only received letters or telephone calls from me or Helen. They had no idea of who I really was or how to relate to me. I shared with them the same information I had asked of them and then added, "Guys, I want you to know upfront that I have never done ministry on this scale. I have not had training in disaster response. I do not know what to do. I pray that you will help me learn."

They sat silent for a few minutes, and then one spoke up: "Edd, thanks for sharing that with us. I thought I was the only ignorant one here."

Others laughed and began to share their fears and worries about being able to help in such a mess. After twenty minutes, we decided that, instead of just talking amongst ourselves, we should spend some time in soul-searching prayer. For a half hour, with no guidance, we prayed; then all were silent. Everyone was deep in thought. I closed with a short prayer for God's presence and our patience. As we closed, one team member spoke up. "I always wondered about what might have gone on in the upper room when Jesus and the disciples met. I may never know for sure, but I know this: after tonight, I will never be the same."

The men stood and began to hug one another. On their way out, everyone came and told me not to worry. With God's help, they would take care of me, and we would get done what He had for us to do. For three weeks, in horrendous situations, there was not one single instance of bickering or refusing to take a job or help someone.

My personal conviction is that people with needs should be involved in the solution to those needs; no outsider can know their feelings and struggles or what they see as their primary need. We toured each village where we were to work and talked to the locals. The people in each first wanted assurance that we would help and stay until the promised work was done. They wanted their families safe. They wanted to be with others who had suffered; they needed a place for community support. They wanted their dead to be recovered and buried according to their religious and family traditions. They wanted medical, spiritual and community assistance.

This was my first experience in a disaster situation, and I began to appreciate how large of an impact the actions of voluntary organizations had in those situations. Medical supplies were supplied by Wycliffe. Seventh-Day Adventists took over the clothing distribution. Methodist and Catholic services helped with field kitchens. The Mennonites took care of delivery and cleanup. The Salvation Army had placed mobile kitchens in the city where the Guatemalan refugees had fled. We all worked together to meet needs and forgot our differences.

We divided our group into three teams — medical, recovery and building. We set up tents for our doctor, who had an ex-Army medic as an interpreter. We sent local runners into the communities to let them know we had medical care for them.

Our second crew helped with body recovery and cleanup

Jim Warren, crew leader in Guatemala.

of the homes. Most homes were old adobe clay with very little straw for strength. Most roofs were sheet metal, held down by rocks, old tires or heavy tree limbs. The high death toll was mainly caused by roofs collapsing onto sleeping families and killing them.

Our third group became somewhat controversial. As I have mentioned, the people wanted spiritual and community support for themselves and others. They wanted us to help rebuild their temples (church buildings). We helped to rebuild three church buildings and built two new ones.

Some other agencies saw church or community buildings as a waste of time and money; to the local people, however, the church buildings were visible signs of strength and recovery.

I was given an older station wagon, and an unhappy fourteen-year-old boy was assigned to be my guide and helper. He spoke as much English as I spoke Spanish — but with hand signals, we could understand each other fairly well. He and I picked up and delivered building materials, medical supplies, drinking water, food, coffee and tea. We also moved people to where they were needed.

The roads before the earthquake were not the best, but now they were the worst. One major problem we had was trucks; unfortunately, most of the trucks were not necessary. Many people with good intentions had sent clothing, shoes, underwear, old cans of paint, canned food (but no can openers) and other stuff that the Guatemalans did not recognize or could not use. The result was that the volunteers spent hours sorting stuff and sending too much to already overfilled dumps. The unnecessary supplies were shipped in trucks that blocked many of the roads. The food, blankets and building supplies that we needed were tied up in that mass of traffic. Good intentions and a desire to help should not be overridden by ignorance.

My young guide had ridden horses through the country, herding family cows. He knew the back trails. We took the trails; while they were rough and dangerous, they were much better and faster than crowded highways.

We worked for five days in the first village, took a one-day break and then moved to a village in the upper foothills. My young guide was with us. His family's house had escaped major damage; however, their yard backed up to a twelve-foot-high concrete block wall, and a building on the other side of that wall had been destroyed by the earthquake. We stayed in tents adjacent to the concrete wall and ate outside. The food was prepared by the family in the house.

Because of the traffic and distance, we moved into tents provided by the seminary. We lived in five waterproof canvas tents; four of us were in each tent. We now knew why we were told to bring air mattresses. Most members of our group were campers or ex-military, so it was no great problem.

The water mains were broken. We and forty village families shared two bathhouses and two restrooms. The bathhouses and rest rooms had been set aside for us for an hour in the morning and an hour after work. The rest of the time, they were shared by us and the families.

We had a light breakfast in a small house close by. Our noon and evening meals were at the house where my guide's family lived. Our food was basic — tortillas, black beans, rice and either lamb, beef or chicken; the meat was cooked over an open fire on small wooden skewers. Coffee and tea were made with boiled water.

I tried to put men in jobs that I knew they could do. One of our men was a medical salesman to doctors and clinics; however, when I asked him what he did, his response was simply, "I am a middleman."

"Okay," I said, "I will assign you a middleman job if that is all right." He agreed.

We had a professional block layer, and he was fast. He used up mortar and blocks as fast as we could get him the material. He was working on a scaffold five feet off the ground. The young fellow on the mixer used a shovel to place mortar on the scaffold floor. We needed someone on the scaffold in the middle to shovel the mortar up another five feet to the mason's mortar board. The salesman laughed, saying that surely was a middleman job, then he crawled up on the scaffold and went to work.

The next day, my young guide and I had to go after more cement blocks. When we came back that evening, our middleman was sitting in a chair. He had his swollen feet in a small tub of warm saltwater. I asked why he had not told me that he was not used to heavy physical work.

"You would have pulled me off and given that job to someone else. I made up my mind when I came on this trip that I was going to do whatever I was asked and get it done even if it killed me," he said. Then he looked up, laughed and said, "And it nearly did!"

We moved to our last assignment higher in the mountains. Our sleeping quarters and the doctor's "office" were in tents. Our team had been divided in two. Half of our group was helping to build new homes in a village twenty miles away. We now had three tents, with three to a tent. We had plenty of water to wash with, and the restrooms were clean and not crowded. This arrangement was fine, but it increased my driving time threefold.

The mayor of the new town where we were to work did not

U.S. Army doctor at the medical clinic.

send out runners; he had a man and a big drum. The drummer and mayor would walk around the city and countryside; at major intersections, the drummer would pound on his drum. The people would come out of their homes or businesses and listen to the news as it was read out loud. The people carried that news back to where they lived. This was how they learned of the doctor and of our rebuilding homes and temples. The people came in droves. We had over three hundred come to see the doctor each of the five days.

We had help from people in the town to mix concrete, lay blocks and pour a concrete floor for a new temple. Our men, along with local men and women, built walls and put a roof on the temple. We would have a dedication service the day we left.

The information of our progress got back to the federal district office. The district police chief came to see what was going on. He inspected everything. He said nothing until he went to our medical clinic and watched a few minutes. He called me and the mayor over and asked me for our permits. We had been in Guatemala two weeks, and this was a first. We had only their request to come and help; we had no permits.

The chief decided to shut us down, and a heated argument began. It almost came to blows. The village people began to gather and were on the verge of rioting. People were picking up stones and sticks. The two officers unbuttoned their holsters. Everyone got eerily quiet, including the chief and mayor.

Working together to install a new roof.

They then continued to quietly talk for a few minutes. The chief nodded, and the mayor came to me and asked how many more days we would be in their community. I told him three. He grinned and walked back to talk to the chief, and the chief and his two officers left. The mayor came back smiling. The police chief had agreed that he had to have papers from Guatemala City to prove that he could stop what our medics were doing. He would be back in four days. We laughed, and I told the mayor that, if he would send the chief to California, I would accept his order.

We finished our jobs and returned to the seminary; there, we washed ourselves and our clothes. We went to the city and did some shopping. We walked clean streets and marveled at the determination of the people.

I was asked to a wedding and another reception, where I met several local pastors and their wives. They could not say enough good things about our team and expressed their thanks for what we had done. I spoke at four churches and helped in the dedication of two new temples. On Sunday, we divided into small groups and went to six different churches; all received the same gratitude that I had received.

On our last workday, our team went to dinner at *El Pico Loco*. We had fried chicken, iced tea and ice cream; we then returned to the seminary to pack. We were never sure whether it was the food, a virus or just a nervous reaction, but half of the team became sick afterwards.

I got what medicine I could at a *farmácia*. If you could tell them what you wanted, they would sell it to you. Our doctor and I began to make rounds. By morning, with help from pastors, we were all able to board the plane. Halfway home, the medicine and exhaustion began to kick in, and everyone began to feel better. I had an empty seat by me and slept for awhile. Later, for a period of two hours, people from our group came to thank me for letting them come and to share with me what the trip had done for them.

Jim Warren, Rick's father, came and sat with me, and we shared our feelings for half an hour. As we began to approach Los Angeles, he turned and said, "Good job, old man. You may not know it, but you have started a long overdue revolution, and I want to be a part of it."

We landed and went to our homes. We had become completely different people than we were when we left. In fifteen working days, our team had helped to recover five bodies and had cleaned out and rebuilt twenty-four homes and three temples. We ministered to over nine hundred people with our medical clinic and participated in the dedications of three new places of worship and community service. The missionaries and local people were open and helpful in all that was done. We were asked to come back in six months if possible. It would take years for Guatemala to get back on its feet, but we could help. Our prayer was that this experience would be the beginning of a long-term ministry program that men could do and be justly proud of doing. We all were exhausted, but even the ones who had been sick asked me to let them know as soon as possible about our return to Guatemala in the fall.

On my second day back in my office, Bob Hughes asked me to share with our convention staff and office personnel a report on the attitude change of our team on their return home.

Elmer Gray, my longtime friend and former seminary professor, was editor of the state Baptist publication. He did an excellent job of reporting the reactions of the team members, along with a description of the work they did in Guatemala. I was then asked to make a one-hour visual presentation with time for questions and answers to three hundred pastors at our annual pastor retreat. Requests from pastors for me or other team members to come to their churches and share our experiences filled our calendars.

My immediate problem was twofold: I needed time to personally accept requests, and our program needed trained workers. I asked Helen to contact the Red Cross and NOVAD and find out what information she could about training disaster workers. The result was that I was asked to meet with the leaders of four other groups; together, we would determine what training was needed.

Most of the Baptists in California had never been directly involved in disaster response, and we were dependent on those who had experience to do our training. The Mennonites, Salvation Army, Catholic World Services and Red Cross all had manuals and their own materials. We studied them and then developed a basic program for our on-the-job training of workers. My Depression experience of doing what you could with what you had and creating solutions for problems with no outside help became the basis of my approach. With four of our area directors, I developed a three-page basic training guide. Our concepts, listed below, eventually became the foundation for all of our ministries.

1. We do not do for others what they can do for themselves. We only help; the needs are theirs, not ours. Our work is determined by their needs, not by what we want or like to do.

2. Physical needs are primary, but emotional and mental needs must be considered. Most anyone can do some physical work. Our objective is personal support of the total person. A cup of coffee or water and a few minutes of listening may be more important than finishing a roof.

3. Christian witnessing must come from a deep concern for the total person and at a proper time.

4. Never attempt anything on the job beyond your expertise. If you do not have training in first aid, get someone who does. If something

has to be done and you are not sure what to do, get help. Local people may know how to make your task easier and maybe even better.

5. While we may want to verbally share our faith, we must be guided by the old saying: "Preach always, but only use words when necessary." People's physical and emotional needs are primary and must be met first.

There has never been a time when we took a job or were involved in disaster response that we were not asked, "Why are you here helping us?" That is the time for an honest answer.

Our approach to training was too basic and in a constant state of flux. The equipment we needed for our ministry was just as limited. We knew we had to start somewhere. In most instances, we trained our workers and found materials and tools while on the job.

We did return to Guatemala in November. Our crew of twenty-three people included seven new men, eight women and eight men who had been on our first trip. Flo insisted that we take food for a Thanksgiving dinner for our team and the missionaries, staff and teachers at the seminary. She bought a huge frozen turkey, canned pumpkin for pies, canned cranberries and packages of dressing mix. We packed two sea bags full with food and requested materials. We took a generator for electrical work in mountain areas.

On our plane to Guatemala, one of my seatmates was a Guatemalan man returning to his former home. He was going to help rebuild his parents' house. He asked me why I was going to Guatemala and who all the people who had been coming to ask me questions for the past hour were. I explained to him who we were and why we were going to his country.

"You have relatives there?" he asked.

"No," I replied and told him again why we were going.

"You will do that for my country and our people? Why?" he asked.

I spent the next twenty minutes sharing the reason with him.

He shook his head and said, "Your God and your beliefs are different from what I have been taught. Maybe I need to start reading the Bible for myself. I want to personally thank you and your people for coming. Our world needs more like them."

We landed in Guatemala City. This time, Sue Lindwall came to the airport to welcome Flo and the other ladies. We went to recover our baggage, and one of our sea bags was missing. I had warned Flo that this might happen and that the frozen turkey would never make it to Guatemala. We had housing for our team in the dorm rooms. The students had gone home for the holidays. Flo and I were to stay with Ted and Sue. We unpacked and found that we still had the sea bag with Flo's turkey. The other sea bag held some equipment and school supplies we had been asked to bring.

The next day, I drove to the airport. After twenty minutes of my refusing to pay the clerk a bribe, he grabbed my passport, stamped that I could not return to Guatemala for six weeks and tried to throw the bag at me.

This trip, we were to build twenty-eight homes in a small mountain village. The homes were designed by the government and would have two or three rooms. The materials were delivered to our jobs. The homes had concrete foundations and floors. The reinforced concrete block walls were five feet high. On top of the concrete blocks were vertical two-by-four studs covered with large three-quarter-inch-thick tongue-and-groove plywood sheets. Window openings were cut in two sides, and shutters were made to fit the openings. A community bathhouse, a laundry facility (a large circular reservoir fifty feet in circumference and three feet deep) and drying rings to hang clothes on were built in the center of the village.

When one of the families moved into their new home, the young mother began to cry. We all worried about what we had done, but she said, "I knew you were going to build me a new home, but not a palace." Her "palace" had three rooms and a concrete floor instead of pounded dirt or clay. It had windows that shut and opened. All one had to do to understand was see what she had been living in before.

Some personnel from the International Mission Board came to see what was happening. In a private conversation with the leader of the group, I was asked what I saw as the greatest need.

"You will not like what I will tell you, but I am going to tell you anyway," I said. "You either must stop sending volunteers to Guatemala for three to four months or prepare to replace half or more of your missionaries. They are compassion-drained. Their physical and mental condition is almost at the breaking point. You have good people here, and you do not want to lose them."

He looked at me, shook his head and said, "I was afraid of that. We will have to do something."

Flo and I did not wait for the mission board to respond. We insisted that Ted and Sue take us to Atitlan in the mountains for a day. Ted balked at first, but we did not let up. This would be his first day away from people and destruction in over four months, and he was dragging. We drove to the small town in the high country. We stopped twice and had tourist breaks; we shopped and ate a leisurely meal.

We arrived at Atitlan on market day. We slowly walked through the crowds and visited with the people. In our moving around, I became separated from Ted, Sue and Flo. I saw them a half block away and began waving to get their attention. They saw me and signaled where they were going. An elderly man who was watching me grinned and said in a heavy accent, "Americana, buy some my peanuts; mine much better than President Carter's." We both laughed, and I bought a bag of his peanuts.

We spent an hour or more just looking around and sampling some of the local foods. We sat under a large tree and reviewed the past week. We drove to the Atlantic Coast and stopped for a leisurely evening meal at a spot overlooking the ocean. After dark, we drove back to the city and went to bed, rested and with a renewed focus for the days ahead.

The next morning, Ted and Sue both thanked us for getting them away. Our crew was finishing the homes we had come there to build. Flo, Sue and one of the other missionary wives began preparing our Thanksgiving dinner. While they were doing their thing, I cleaned the backyard and set up tables for the more than forty people we were expecting. I reached for a board to level a table, and a scorpion decided to jump onto my left arm. I quickly knocked it off and stepped on it. I was not aware at the time that I had been stung. I finished setting up tables and chairs and began to get dizzy.

It was hot. I sat down, and one of the ladies brought me some iced tea. In ten minutes, I began to sweat, and my arm felt numb. I attempted to get up, but my arm would not function. I was only able to get up using my other arm. I went inside and asked Sue for some aspirin. I took two and lay down on our bed. Ted came in to see how I was doing; I was not well. He wanted to call their doctor.

I asked if they had any Benadryl. They had a new bottle. I asked that they let me try that for half an hour; if that did not work, I would go and see the doctor. I took a safe dose and went to sleep. Flo came in and woke me up an hour later. I sat up, still dizzy, but my eyes could focus and my arm had stopped throbbing. I felt that I could tough it out. I drank some iced tea and put on clean clothes.

The swelling in my arm was less noticeable, and I could move my fingers without any pain. I tried to help finish the preparations for dinner, but my feet would not go where they should. I walked around close to the wall to keep my balance.

One group was late for our Thanksgiving dinner. We visited and mingled and waited. After a half hour, I suggested the rest of us go ahead and start. We had prayer, and I helped the ladies bring out the food. We had two huge turkeys, three pans of dressing, four serving bowls of gravy, and plates of cranberries and sweet potatoes. We had freshly washed (and safe) salads and finished with pumpkin pie, ice cream and tea or coffee, which we could have either hot or cold. The dinner was excellent, and Flo was told over and over again how much everyone appreciated what she and the others had done to make this a great day.

The late team that had stayed to finish their house arrived and helped to make the day a complete success. I had almost forgotten about my arm until I bumped it against a door. I had to take two more pain relievers and let the others finish my job. It was three days before the swelling was completely gone.

Our teams, with local help, had built thirty-eight homes and a school building with two classrooms. Only one person had been sick. I was one of two who had been injured in some way. The eight women on the work crews were admired and openly praised by the local men and women.

On our way home, the women who had come on the trip expressed to me that they thought I could get more women involved if we had our mission activities under a generic name instead of "men's ministries." Churches all over California and northern Nevada began to write and ask for couples to come and share.

Helen had received a letter from the seminary, asking me why I was dropping out of the doctoral program. I called the chairman of the graduate committee and told him I had asked for an extension, not a cancellation. I needed extra time since my original project report had been turned down.

He was surprised. The letter he had showed a termination request. I assured him that was not what I had sent. Helen had copies of all my letters. He asked for the copies. I had Helen pull out all the records of my correspondence with my faculty supervisor, and we sent copies to the chairman. A week later, I was asked to come to the seminary. The committee (which did not include my supervisor) wanted to talk to me.

The meeting was cordial, and an apology was offered to me by the committee. They were not aware of the problems I had been having with my supervisor. They asked me to complete my degree work and to take all the time I needed. I was to send my thesis to the graduate committee chairman with a copy of any mail I might receive from my supervisor. I would continue to send reports to my supervisor; however, I was to ignore my supervisor's replies and to do only what the director of the graduate committee thought was needed. With another apology, the entire committee offered me their help.

Flo, Helen and Bob Hughes were the only other ones who knew what had happened. I went back to work to finish an unnecessary doctoral program.

SEVENTEEN

1976

TETON DAM, HAWAII, MISSISSIPPI, ALASKA

On June 6, 1976, a call came from a member of a Baptist church in Stone Mountain, Georgia. He was an inspector of dams for the federal government. He told me he had been given my name and needed some assistance in response to a major disaster.

He continued, "The Teton Dam in Idaho has collapsed. I am flying there tomorrow to see what needs to be done. I will work with local, state and federal offices. I would like for you to come with me and see what the churches of California could do for the people who have lost homes, farmland and livestock. Winter comes early there, and they will need more than food and clothing."

I told him I would do what I could. I enlisted Larry Hoskins, a retired police captain, and Bill Johnson, a local pastor and builder, to go with me. We left in my motor home and drove to Rexburg, Idaho, only stopping for food and fuel. We located the disaster center and received maps and directions.

The dam, built for hydroelectric power and irrigation of farmlands, had a troubled history. In 1964, basic construction began. The seventeen-mile river and lake became a popular recreation center. In 1971, against the advice of environmentalists and city leaders, a second phase of dam construction was begun. On June 5, 1974, large cracks in the dam face appeared. Warnings of a potential dam break were sent to people and towns downriver while repairs were being made.

Around noon on June 5, 1976, breaks in the dam began to appear; thirty minutes later, it collapsed. A wall of water three hundred feet high moved at thirty miles an hour into the towns of Wellford, Sugar City and Rexburg. It lessened in intensity but continued through Idaho Falls, Shelly and Blackfoot. Cars, trucks, tractors, buildings, trees, fences, crops and animals were swept away. Eleven people were killed, and hundreds of cows, horses and other living things disappeared — some were found later in basements of flooded homes and businesses. One local newspaper called the dam break "the single worst disaster in the history of Idaho."

We three, along with federal and local officials, were given a safe hurried tour. We studied the situation so we could make a decision as to what California Baptist volunteers could best do. The area is largely Mormon, and the LDS churches were on the jobs of nourishment and rescue. We decided we could do our best ministry in recovery and rebuilding. I called Helen and asked her to get a letter out to our churches and volunteers to let them know what was needed.

We three were asked to go to a farm close by and help a family. Their house and barn were not overly damaged; the potato shed was damaged and the inside was covered with sand and mud. Their fences were down, and most fields and irrigation ditches were under two to three feet of sand, rock and silt. No machinery was available. For five days, we rebuilt fences and cleaned barns and then returned to Fresno.

On our return, we mailed out pictures of the destruction. The three of us split up to go to pastor's meetings and churches to share the needs of people in Idaho. Over a period of nine weeks, eighty-seven people from our churches responded to the need and went to help. I could not be in Idaho all the time but went for three days every two weeks to help and encourage our workers.

On my last trip, I was asked by the feature editor of the local newspaper to take him to where our people were working at that time. I agreed on one condition. My people knew who I was, so no introduction would be necessary. I would carry my camera and be a photographer. When he interviewed the people that our teams had helped, I wanted an honest response; if they knew I had enlisted the workers, I may not be given an honest report. He agreed, and we went to six different places. Two places really stood out because of the people's response to the editor's questions.

The first was from a person the editor knew. He asked, "How did these folks who helped you rebuild do?"

The older man, seated on his new front porch, responded, "I have never met people like them. They worked hard, did not bicker and stayed until the job was completed to my satisfaction. They were more than a team; they were almost family. I thanked them, and then they thanked me for letting them work. We had a short prayer, and they left. I would still be living with my son miles away if it were not for those people."

The last of four places we went had been an almost hopeless job. It was a two-story house that I had seen on one of my past trips. The lower story of the house was a split-level basement apartment. The house was built on a slope, and the lower half of the basement was below ground level. The single lady had to move out of her basement apartment to live with family several miles away.

The apartment had been filled with dead animals, tree stumps and rusted machinery and had been red-tagged by the health department. It was unsafe and unlivable. Five of our people were finishing their work the day the editor and I arrived. Two of our couples, in their late seventies and early eighties, were there working. I did the introductions. Two of our ladies were not present. I asked where they were and was informed that the two would be back in a few minutes.

"They can't be completing the work on the ceiling," I thought. That was all that was left to do. The editor and I left the others and walked into the basement apartment. Two ladies, ages seventy-six and eighty, with help from the others only when needed, had stripped the ceiling and installed new insulation and sheetrock. They then taped and textured the ceiling and were now finishing the painting. The editor shook his head. They cleaned up, and the four of us went to where the others were sitting around a table.

The editor looked at the two ladies and asked, "Whose house is this? Does it belong to a relative of yours?"

They laughed and assured him that they were not related and had not even met the lady who owned the house.

"Who cleaned up this place so you could work here?" he wanted to know. They told him they were the first and only ones to work on this house. He had seen the impossible situation before and was stunned.

"You came from California at your own expense to work in an impossible situation like this, and you do not even know who the lady is? I don't get that," he said.

I am not sure, but I think it was Mrs. Pounds who looked at him and said, "What difference does it make who she is? She needed help, didn't she?"

A stunned editor (who was also a Mormon elder) and I left. We drove back to town but did not talk. When I started to get out of his car, he reached over and held my arm. "Brown, I am having some problems. I don't care what the people in Salt Lake City have told me. You have some of God's greatest people I have ever met working with you. I am going to have to rethink my relationship with God."

I was sent a copy of his feature story in the next week's paper. The headline read, "It Makes No Difference Who She Is. She Needed Help, Didn't She?"

Six years later, Flo and I were on our way to one of my Navy reunions in Chicago. We went through Rexburg and visited the Teton Dam Museum. While the report of the needs and recovery was detailed and accurate, very little was said about the response of any group other than the Mormon Church. However, it really makes no difference that our people were ignored; they went to work and help, and that was enough.

Later, at a national meeting for state directors of Baptist men's programs, the director for Alaska and I were getting acquainted. He wanted to know about my background and what we had done in California with the new men's ministries that had been initiated. I told him what Jim Warren had asked me: "Why do we have to wait until someone is hurting to try to help? Why can't we do some good work in addition to disaster response?"

Jim and I had discussed the request from women who wanted to be involved. Out of that discussion, "California Baptist Volunteers," a separate cooperation was born. While the cooperation was under the umbrella of men's ministries, it had its own board of directors. One of those directors was to be the executive director of the convention. This corporation was to support disaster response, World Changers, Campers on Missions and volunteer mission projects. Each group had a volunteer leader who worked with Helen and me to provide education and opportunities for people to be involved in direct mission activities. California Baptist Volunteers was open to anyone who wanted to be involved — men, women and even non-Baptists.

Edmund Walker called and asked for another team to come to Hawaii. I had already agreed to do a mission involvement workshop in Portland, Oregon. After much discussion, Helen went as the team leader of eight couples and four single women to work at the Pu'u Kahea Baptist campground. Other than falling out of a bunk bed, she did a great job. Helen did have one major problem: The temporary camp director from South Texas had refused to let a woman be in charge of a work party at "his camp."

The camp director refused to feed our group even though he knew about the arrangement. Since a man was not there to run the job, he knew that something must be wrong. He locked the food pantry and refused to give Helen or any of our crew the key. Helen had spent all her money, but others had helped. For three days, they had no food and nothing to do. They became tourists and bought their own meals.

When I returned to Fresno and learned what was happening, I was able to get a flight to Hawaii the next day. I called Edmond Walker, the executive director of Hawaii Baptist. I told him what was happening, and we met at the camp. Edmond almost fired the guy right then. Edmond made arrangements to refund the group's money. He gave the pantry key to Helen and told the camp manager to stay away from the kitchen and let Helen do the job she was there to do. I flew back to Fresno. Helen and the crew completed their work without any more interference.

Later, at a training conference in Atlanta, the Alaska director shared with me the need for some people to come to Kotzebue, Alaska. The local church building needed a new roof. Another team was needed to assemble a pre-framed building for a church 125 miles northeast in Amber, just inside the Arctic Circle. Women were welcome to come and work on the building, conduct a vacation Bible school for children or help with the meals.

Our volunteer group leaders thought it was a great idea, and we agreed to go. Figuring out the logistics was going to be a headache. The food and supplies for our team had to be bought in Anchorage, shipped to Kotzebue and ferried by small plane to Amber. Opportunities for buying food in remote Alaska were extremely limited, and the cost was prohibitive. I would have to order enough food for twelve people for fifteen days. It had to be in Kotzebue the day after our arrival there. The locals in Kotzebue would take care of the food for their team. Eighteen men and four women from California and Nevada signed up to go.

I had agreed to go to Mississippi for a two-week mission education event. I would be speaking in fourteen different churches and attending several meetings with association and church leaders. I knew that Paul Harrell, the men's leader for Mississippi Baptist, had been in Alaska after the Anchorage earthquake and could offer some good advice.

I flew to Jackson, Mississippi. When I arrived, the bag with my glasses, notes and toiletries was missing. I was given a fifty-dollar check and went on my way. Two days later, the bag was brought to me but without my glasses. I was to preach at First Baptist Church in Macomb the next morning. I can read without glasses, but it strains my eyes and takes several hours for them to recover. I made it through the service, and two important things happened afterwards that made my day.

One was that an optometrist was sitting close to the front of the auditorium. After the service, he asked me to come to his office the next morning; he would take care of my need for new glasses.

The second thing was that one of the ushers came and asked me to meet with two young ladies who had heard my message on their car radio. The two graduate students had stopped and waited to talk to me. They heard me emphasize the need for churches and missions in California. They pointed out that California was a world leader in culture, economics, entertainment and fashion. If we could use those avenues to spread the Christian message in California, it could open the door for Christian influence around the world.

The result of our discussion was that the two ladies helped me see more clearly the need for a strong Christian presence in California. According to their research, much of what was good or bad in our world either originated in or was made popular by the social and business structure of California. Our opinion was that the bad far surpassed the good.

I had come to Mississippi with twelve requests from churches and associations for help in leadership training, community outreach and church remodeling and construction. I preached messages and led open discussions, and the response from pastors and church leaders during those two weeks was overwhelming.

By Thursday of my second week, I was exhausted and ready to go home. I had one more church to be in on Friday evening, and I was to preach at a church on Sunday morning and fly home early Monday. I had planned to have a free day to rest on Saturday.

I arrived at my church assignment on Friday evening and was walking around outside to relax. I had a breakfast meeting with a group of men, a lunch with pastors and a conference that afternoon, all after having driven over two hundred miles. I was beat.

The pastor's wife came and asked me to come inside. She had received a telephone call from the First Baptist Church in Picayune. They wanted me to call back. I did not want to call back. I knew a meeting would be requested. The pastor's wife gave me some refreshments and volunteered to call the church and get the person who had called for me. In a few minutes, she gave me the phone.

The person on the other end said, "Mr. Brown, I am the chairmen of our church mission committee. We are not on your list of churches to visit, but would it be possible for you to meet with our missions committee at five tomorrow evening?"

I wanted to say no but knew I could not, so I agreed to be there. I had a good meal at the church where I was, and the people had a lot of interest in doing something in the future; California would be their priority for the next year.

I had not made room reservations for that night. I had planned on driving halfway to my next appointment and having Saturday to relax before being in church Sunday morning. Instead, I was now driving in the opposite direction through a hundred miles of swampland in southern Mississippi. I stopped at a small town and stayed in a nice, clean "Mom and Pop" motel. I woke up around ten the next morning and looked over my files after breakfast. Of the twelve requests for help, eleven were already taken care of. No church had been interested in Jenness Park, a camp owned by our state Baptist convention.

I read through my sermon notes for Sunday and then left. I drove for an hour and ate a light lunch. I spent two hours walking through a park and visiting a Civil War museum. I arrived at the church in Picayune early and spent some time admiring their church building. At fifteen minutes before five, two couples arrived, introduced themselves and asked me to come inside with them. In a few minutes, the rest of the committee arrived; after more introductions were made, we had our meal.

After the dishes were removed, the chairman began by asking me, "Would you tell us something about the request for Jenness Park?" I nearly fell out of my seat.

I shared with them, "It is on the eastern side of the central valley of California, five thousand feet in elevation. It is surrounded by 6,000-foot mountains. The camp is open all year, as long as the camp roads are passable."

I had brochures and passed them around. A member asked if any group or church had asked for that project. I shaded the truth just a little and replied, "Not yet."

After a few more minutes of questions, the chairman said, "The reason we did not initially ask to be on your list for visits was that we could not really get interested in any other project. This past Wednesday, we decided to do something. That is why we called last night and asked you to come today."

The First Baptist Church of Picayune, Mississippi, accepted the Jenness Park project (and I had almost refused to come and meet with them!). They came that year and the next; after their third year, I met with them and told them the real story of how Jenness Park was the only project that not been taken. For twenty years, a team from Picayune has come to Jenness. They have helped with upkeep, repaired snow damage and built new facilities for campers and conferences. This helps to keep the cost down so more of our youth can be a part of a Christian camping experience.

After our meeting, I drove halfway to my Sunday morning church assignment. I spent the night in a motel and had a good night's sleep. On Sunday, I ate breakfast and drove to the church, which was almost in the middle of nowhere. At that time, it was the largest rural church in Mississippi.

The three hundred people were gracious and attentive. I enjoyed the fellowship, their acceptance of me and their attention and response to my message. After a big lunch, I thanked them and went to get in my car. I had opened the door to get in when a middle-aged, nicely dressed lady stepped up and asked me to wait because she wanted to talk to me.

"Your message this morning made me mad, and I have been waiting to talk to you," she said.

I prepared to take whatever was coming. She broke into a smile, and then tears began to form in her eyes.

"While I was waiting here for you, God got a hold of me," she said, and she turned and pointed to a small village across a small river.

"You see those run down houses over there? That is where the poor people live. For years, I have resented them being so close to our church. You spoke of God's love and said that, if we had any love at all, we had to show it and share it where it was needed. That area there, that I wanted to get rid of, struck me. I immediately thought that you had no right to come as a guest and make me feel guilty, and I have been waiting to let you know how I felt."

Her tears really began to flow. "Just now, I realized that I should be mad, but not at you; I should be mad at myself. I want to thank you for letting God use you to show me how selfish and bigoted I have become. I want to tell you that, this week, I am going to get some people to go with me and see what we can do for those people. If no one else is willing, I will go by myself."

I just stood there, not knowing what to do. She wiped her tears away, looked up at me and said, "I have one more question. Would you let me hug you?"

Before I could respond, she grabbed me and held me, sobbing; then she stood back and said, "Thank you." She turned, her head high, and walked back to her car.

As Elvis would say, I was "all shook up." I got back in my car, now not nearly as tired, and drove to Jackson. I went to my room at the hotel. Paul Harrell came by, and I brought him up to date, still marveling at what God had done.

The next morning I flew back to California and home. I had three weeks to get ready for Alaska. I checked on our team and our travel arrangements, ordered our food and supplies, and tried to catch up with family and office work.

Flo and Steve drove me to SFO, where I met our California team. The others from Nevada (Northern Nevada was part of the California Southern Baptist Convention) would join us at SeaTac in Seattle.

We flew to Anchorage and were met by the Baptist state leaders and taken to lunch. After hearing introductions and valuable suggestions for our trip, we flew to Kotzebue and met Harley Shield and the local church pastor. Harley worked with all Baptist churches north of the Arctic Circle as advisor, coordinator, counselor and supply pastor.

Our crew enjoyed an evening meal together and was assigned to homes for that night. The next morning, after meeting local leaders and receiving instructions, we gathered materials for the roof and a new closed entryway for the local church building. We loaded and delivered the materials and part of our crew to Amber in Harley's Cessna 210.

I flew with him and four others on the first trip. After an hour of flying over tundra, we circled the small town and landed a mile uphill from Amber. The Eskimos heard the plane (their signal to come to the airstrip) and brought two pickups to help us move our cargo to the National Guard barracks. The barracks would be the home for the Amber team.

Gerry King and Mrs. Wilson sorted out the materials for Bible school and food for meals. They checked the cooking utensils and planned to begin a Bible school the next day.

Harold King, Ed Bailey and I checked the plans and location site for the new church building with the mayor of the village. This was the first volunteer mission project for the three of us. Harold was a builder from central California and Ed was an electrician and builder from Orange County. I was learning non-disaster assistance.

Much of the food that I ordered would be brought on the next flight. Some was perishable and had to be frozen; there was no refrigeration. We found a level place out of traffic and dug a hole two feet round and four foot deep through the permafrost (frozen ground twelve to eighteen inches thick). We stored the frozen food on the bottom, the food to be kept cool was halfway down, and the rest was stored at the top. We covered our refrigerator-freezer with a tarp and weighted it down with a sheet of plywood and sand.

Harley and I flew back to Kotzebue, and I went to his house for the day. It was a warm day with no wind, and I took a picture of the thermometer in July: It read 79 degrees. I had a problem going to sleep. It did not start to get dark until around eleven at night, and the sun came up again at one o'clock in the morning. The kids in the community stayed up almost all night and played right outside my window. On the longest day of the year, the sun never goes down in that part of Alaska. That day, the people of the community had a ball game with no man-made lighting; the first pitch was thrown at midnight.

The next day, I helped to load the food and some additional supplies on the plane, and we took three more workers to Amber. The rest of the day, I worked with the Kotzebue team, laying out the foundation for the new entrance to the church building. (I had, at that time, some real problems with us building a new entrance.) We then removed half of the old roofing, re-nailed the sheeting onto the rafters and covered the new entrance with plywood decking.

The third day, Harley and I flew back to Amber with the rest of the food and more materials. The team in Amber had laid out the area and dug holes for the footings. In the Arctic, footings and foundations have to be protected from heat radiating from the building above, which can melt the permafrost. If the permafrost becomes mushy, the building will begin to settle in that area. The entire building could eventually become unusable. Insulation, much thicker than what is used in the ceilings of homes in the lower states, is used in the floors of buildings in the Arctic.

The building we were there to erect had been pre-assembled in sections and shipped by sea to Kotzebue. It was ferried by boat, dog sled or plane (depending on the weather) to Amber. The building was originally to be a radio and telephone relay station that would double as housing for the operators; however, satellites and new technology had now made the building unnecessary.

Rather than spending money to ship the building back, the radio company sold it to the church at a bargain price of five hundred dollars. Many of the panels and sections had been left in the open; they had been covered by sand in the summer and left under ice and snow in the winter. Arctic weather is like that of the desert — snow-melt is almost all the moisture the area gets.

The ladies began a Bible school with twelve children and had a ball. Most of the men and women of the village were away at fish camp and would be gone for a week. Summers are so short that all daylight must be used to raise vegetables, catch and cure fish, and hunt caribou for winter food.

Harley asked me to fly the plane back to Kotzebue. I had been flying for thirty minutes when, with an explosive noise, the plane's engine began to miss. Harley grabbed the mike and called the airport to declare an emergency. His son was on duty as the tower operator, and he cleared the airfield area.

Harley took the controls and eased the plane in for a good landing. We tied the plane down and removed the cowling. A three-inch oblong hole was in the left manifold. It was beyond repair. Harley reported the problem to the local authorities and called his mechanic in Anchorage. The mechanic had a manifold and would get a pilot of the Alaska airline to bring it to us the next day.

While much of the food was there in Amber, the meat and other items that needed to be cooked longer — roasts, hams, pies, bread and cakes for ten people — were cooked in Kotzebue. Either Harley or I would fly the cooked items to Amber on our daily flight, along with materials and mail. The team in Amber was notified by a local pilot that we could not bring any part of their meals until the plane was repaired.

Three days later, Harley and I replaced the manifold and flew to Amber. We knew we were going to catch it for abandoning our team without enough to eat. We were picked up at the landing site by the mayor in an open-bed pickup. The guys and gals of our team were working hard and thoroughly enjoying themselves. The floor joists were down, and they were installing insulation. Not one word was said about the food.

We learned that, for the first time in years, the village people had returned home from fish camp three days early and had fed the team all they could eat of freshly caught salmon and caribou steaks. They had flat bread and kale, along with wild berry pie. We were not even missed.

I walked out on the floor joists to see how they were joined. My foot slipped, and I fell and straddled one of the floor joists. Everyone stopped their work. I had to sit and wait while all got their cameras and took pictures. Afterwards, every time I showed up at a job, the workers would holler, "Get out of the way and watch for broken lumber! Here comes our clumsy boss."

After dinner the second day, we had a sharing time. I spent my time between the two teams. At both places, we talked and prayed. I asked each man and woman, "Why are you here, and what do you want to learn? What made you think that coming here at your own expense was worth it?"

Most of their answers were about liking to travel and wanting to see Alaska. Most also added that they wanted to do something that would benefit others, that they felt was worth their time.

One expressed it this way: "I have never worked so hard and so long, but you know what? I have enjoyed every bit of it. I thank God for this privilege."

On Saturday morning, Harley asked if I would go with him to Selawik, a seaside village sixty miles southeast of Kotzebue. We prepared the 210 for flight, and I took off. Thirty minutes later, Harley landed the plane on the very small landing strip on a small island nearby. We tied the plane down and stepped into a twelve-foot metal boat. After priming the engine and pulling the starter cord three times, we got the engine started. We rounded the small island and pulled up to a dock in front of a small, well-maintained church building. Harley unlocked the door, and we went into a worship center that would hold forty people. We gathered some dry wood out of a closet and built a fire outside. He walked into a small room behind the pulpit area and pulled down a ladder to a room in the attic.

I still wondered why he wanted me on this trip. We climbed the ladder to the attic. In the middle was a large wooden casket. It was made like the ones in western movies — wide at the top and narrow at the bottom.

We wrestled it down the folding stairs and into the worship center. I assumed it was for a funeral and that Harley was preparing for the service, but we had left the cover upstairs. He placed two folding sawhorses in front of the pulpit; he then went to the back room and brought out two five-gallon buckets. He handed me a bucket, and we went to a small creek. We filled the buckets with water and placed them on the fire. We went back inside, and I helped him set the casket on the sawhorses. We then put some heavy plastic sheeting inside the casket and moved a small set of steps to back of the casket.

I had to ask, "What are we preparing for?"

His answer caught me completely off-guard: "We are having a baptism tomorrow, and I have to make sure that everything is ready."

We filled the casket with boiling hot water that would cool down to comfortably warm by morning. We covered the casket with more plastic and heavy blankets. We locked the door and took the boat back around the inland lake. I flew us back to Kotzebue. The symbolism of being buried with Christ and risen to a new life took on a new meaning for me, and I pondered it all the way back.

Two days later, we flew to Amber. We had finished the construction of the building there and put on the new roof in Kotzebue. We flew the next day on Alaska Air to Anchorage. We checked into our hotel, had hot showers and changed into clean clothes. We then went to a local church, where I had made arrangements with the members to provide the team and local guests with a full dinner of fresh fish, caribou steaks, fresh vegetables, ice cream and pie. We all had hot coffee and tea. Everyone shared about their humorous experiences, and many laughs were had at my expense. Afterwards, there was serious talk about what this trip had done for us.

The next morning, a tired and happy bunch flew to San Francisco. We were glad to get home. Ed Bailey had come without Alma. She wanted him to find out if this type of program would be worth their time. Ed and Alma became regular volunteer leaders for our mission trips. Harold King and Gerry wanted to be involved in this ministry as often as possible. For the next twelve years, those two couples recruited and participated in ministries in California, other states and over twenty foreign countries.

Eighteen

1977-1978

Cessna 182
Samoa, Fiji

I arrived in Fresno and gave Helen a full report of the trip. She handed me a stack of mail and a list of telephone calls I needed to return. One of the calls was from a young man who owned a heating and air conditioning business in town. He had planned to go on our last mission trip but had to cancel because his wife was pregnant. I called him, and we had lunch together.

"You have to travel a lot to get to churches in California and Nevada," he began. I waited, interested to see where this conversation was going.

"I have not been able to go on any mission trips, but I want to help. I and two others own a six-year-old Cessna 182. It has been completely rebuilt and certified for fifteen hundred hours. One of our owners is leaving, and my partner and I want you in."

I sat there, stunned. There was no way I could be a partner in a Cessna 182, a four-person plane with a power plant that I could safely use on mountain runways; however, I listened, and the more he explained the details, the more it became a possibility.

While I was in Norwalk, I had bought a third interest in a rebuilt Porterfield for three hundred dollars, and I later became the owner. I flew it once to San Jose and back, but the rest of the time I flew it along the coast or out over the desert as a hobby and way to relax. I sold that plane when we moved to Stockton.

One of our volunteers on a mission trip to Hawaii was a flight instructor at the Vallejo-Napa airport. I had flown with him a few times and rented a plane there to keep my required flight time current.

This new offer intrigued me. I told my friend I would look into the possibility of buying in. I knew I would have to convince our executive director and Dennis, our business manager, of how it would help in my ministry. At that time, I was driving close to a thousand miles a week for meetings that, in some instances, were attended by fewer than five people. One time, I had driven three hundred miles to Northern Nevada for an area meeting, which only three people attended.

Bob was the easy one. If it would help the growth of men's ministries, he would go along with it. Dennis, the business manager, was against the idea. Three years earlier, a young man who worked for the convention and was not instrument-certified had taken off in heavy fog, crashed and killed himself.

I had to have insurance that would not hold the convention responsible for any accident that involved my flying. It would have to include a million-dollar rider in case something was challenged. The men who owned the 182 already had such a policy.

I bought into the plane and hired a certified flight instructor to conduct me through a complete training program. I passed my physical and made my first solo flight to Tehachapi. Kern County Baptist Association was looking at a site in the

Edd and the Cessna 182.

mountains for a possible associational camp. They wanted me to come, look over the site and give them my opinion.

I met with the committee in Tehachapi for an hour and flew back to Fresno. I secured the plane and drove home for lunch. Flo was surprised to see me.

"I thought you were going to Tehachapi," she said.

"I did, and I am back," I replied.

Instead of spending ten hours driving, I was finished in four. I made a deal with Bob; I could use half of the time I saved in travel for my family, and the other half would be for work.

Six months later, another partner dropped out, and the last partner left a year later. I now owned the plane. I cut my travel time by fifteen hours a week and was able to increase my personal contact with pastors and lay leaders at the same time. For me, this was a great situation.

My flight instructor had pounded into me, "You will be a safe pilot because you are still afraid of flying. If you ever get over knowing that you have no right to be up in the air, it will be time for you to quit."

The Brotherhood Commission called and wanted me to attend an orientation in Memphis. The meeting was for updates on world mission conferences. I had done two such conferences in my associations and one in another church. I had enlisted missionaries and developed my own program. This meeting would not only help me in planning; it would also give me direct contacts for enlisting overseas and home missionaries. I went and came home loaded with materials and new ideas. On my return, Helen and I prepared packets for each association in California and began promoting these conferences in our churches. We were able to help associations and churches host weeklong mission education programs. These programs were open to the entire church; they were not just for the mission organizations.

Within a few months, we had world mission conferences and On Mission Celebrations scheduled for the next three years. We had to set up a yearly rotation system so every association that requested a mission conference could have one.

I used my time flying on commercial planes and in hotel rooms to finish a new proposal for my doctoral work at Golden Gate. To my surprise, both the committee and Bob Hughes accepted my first draft. With Helen and Flo's help, I began to gather and sort materials and information.

At one of our early meetings in Bakersfield, a young man named Norm Tooman attended and was interested in what we were doing. He was a petroleum engineer and was building a large yacht to be used for taking Bibles and materials to small islands in the South Pacific. He suggested that we look into the possibility of going to the island of Samoa and helping them build a school and worship center.

Four men were selected to work with me to gather details for the possible project. Eight weeks later, we had a planned a trip to Samoa and contacted Ray Villiamu, the island pastor.

While information and plans for our trip to Samoa were being put together, I attended the Baptist World Congress meeting in Los Angeles. One morning, I was visiting with a friend who worked at one of our national offices when a young South Pacific man stepped up.

"Excuse me, sir, but would you be Edd Brown?"

Curious, I assured him I was. He said, "I don't want to interrupt, but when you have time, could I talk to you?"

I explained that the other man and I were just two old friends and that I could step away. The islander and I moved to a quiet place and sat together.

He introduced himself: "I am Enoke Kubulabola from Fiji. Ray

Villiamu in Samoa and I are close friends. I understand from him that you may be coming to Samoa sometime in the next few months. I would like you and your team to take three or four days and come to Fiji as my guest. If you think you could possibly come, I will mail you an official invitation from our churches and from our government. All on your team are to be our guests."

We talked more about the kinds of work my team did and how the team only did what people needed, not what they could do by themselves. We shared some personal history and parted company.

When I arrived back at my office, I asked Helen to let our Samoan Mission team members know that we had the possibility of a four-day trip to Fiji. Three team members could not stay the extra time, and four others were going on to other mission areas. The other twelve were anxious for the opportunity to visit Fiji. Four weeks before we were to leave, I received a call from a member of one of our churches in Hawaii.

"Mr. Brown," he asked, "when are you going to Samoa?"

I gave him the dates the team would be going. He asked again, "But when are *you* going?"

"I usually go with the team," I answered.

He continued, "If I may, I strongly suggest that you go at least ten days earlier."

He would not tell me why, but he was very insistent. He had just returned from Samoa and had been to our future worksite, but he gave me no other information.

"If he is this concerned," I thought, "maybe I should take him seriously." I made contact with a builder, his wife and a nurse and asked if they could go with me ten days early to get ready for the team. They agreed.

When we arrived in Samoa, I was very grateful for that phone call. The Samoans were supposed to have cleared the land where we would build the school and worship center. They had cut all the trees and banana plants to the ground, but the roots and some small growth were still left. Most of the potholes in which we were to pour concrete were small, but some were large enough that they needed to be filled and packed. We had to have metal stakes to hold forms; wooden stakes could not be hand-driven into lava. We two men, along with several Samoans, worked twelve hours a day for six days to get the forms ready for concrete.

Two interesting things happened that became sources of both concern and much merriment. I had to hire a bulldozer to move big lava rocks and to pack filler into cracks and holes to prepare for the foundation and floor. We had to level yards of clean sand (crushed lava) to form the base for the concrete footings for the 125-foot-long, thirty-foot-wide, six-inch-thick concrete slab.

The bulldozer owner and driver said he would be ready by nine. At nine, there was no bulldozer; at half-past, there was still nothing. At ten, we heard a rumbling sound; we grabbed our rakes, shovels and tampers to level and prepare the surface for the slab floor. The noise stopped, and I became worried. I got in my rental car and drove a mile down the road. I found the driver of the bulldozer talking to a man beside a new driveway to the man's house. I walked over to the driver and asked when he would be at our job.

"I am on my way and will the there in thirty minutes," he said and fired up the dozer.

I went back to the jobsite and waited along with our two men and the Samoans who had come to help. We had concrete coming (maybe) by one o'clock. I knew we would never finish this project on time. The three Samoans were not concerned. Finally, the dozer arrived, and we worked like mad to get the sand leveled and the forms in place. The driver was great and helpful. I found out later that he had left his shop at nine. Some of his friends on the way needed a little help, so he stopped and helped them. It was not a big deal; after all, he had left on time.

The other thing that happened was related to the propane stove we would use to cook on when the full team arrived. The gas bottles were empty. I took the bottles to the propane supplier. I explained that I needed propane as soon as possible.

"You will be the first one to get gas," he promised.

The four of us who were there had no problems with meals. The Samoan families fed us, and we ate in restaurants. Two days later, before the team arrived, I was in town and went to the propane place to pick up the gas. I asked if my tanks had been filled; the owner looked up and replied, "Sorry, not yet."

"You have any idea when they will be ready?" I asked.

"Not really," he answered.

I was stunned but held my temper. "Why not?" I asked.

"Don't know when the ship that is bringing the gas from New Zealand will be here, but when it gets here, you will be the first one to get gas."

I tried to smile and thank him honestly. I then told myself that I had better learn that I was on an island in the South Pacific and not in the U.S.

I had been told (or warned) by Ray Villiamu that the electricity for the island was erratic. To make sure we would not be stopped while cutting lumber, I had shipped two ten-inch gas-powered chain-saws that could be used when needed.

With the help of four additional Samoan men, we used wheel-barrows and screed boards to level each section. We had many local helpers to pour the footings and slab. Three Samoan women and four older girls helped us with the finish work. By midnight, the floors had been poured and smoothed with trowels.

Other Samoan women had continued to bring us snacks, water and drinks all afternoon and had prepared a late meal with plenty of fresh fruit for us. We decided we would not remove the form boards for three days.

Heat and humidity were dangerous for us. The Samoans had no problem working in the heat, but we Americans could very easily suffer heat stroke or heat exhaustion, which I did not want to happen. We took regular breaks. That night, we all slept well; we had a large late breakfast prepared for us by the Samoan women in the morning. There was no way that the footings and floor would have been finished if our friend in Hawaii had not called.

Our team arrived. Our housing arrangements were very interesting. There was a large meeting hall with two double baths and a large kitchen. Everyone had been instructed to bring sleeping gear and an air mattress. Lightweight shirts with long sleeves and full-length pants were necessary because of the sun. The team was to bring housecoats for coverings in case they were needed and two pairs of shoes that could be worn in wet weather.

It became my responsibility to assign sleeping arrangements. The four single women were assigned the eastern end of room. The five single men were in the western end. Five married couples were given the center space along the wall away from the kitchen. During the day, the large room would be used for meals and meetings if we could not meet outside. All bedding and clothes had to be moved to the walls and the center of the room kept clear during the day.

The contractor and his wife and I had been living in two rooms with one bath at a small Methodist Church a half-mile from the worksite. The church asked us to stay there while we were working.

Flo joined me when the team arrived. The four of us had some guilt for the disparity in sleeping arrangements, but not enough to move in with the others. We became the source of some good-natured jokes. The joke about the weather in Samoa was twofold: "Today we will have rain. Tomorrow we will have more rain — maybe heavier, maybe not."

Before we left California, I had asked for the building plans to be sent to me so that I would know what we would need to bring and what was not available on the island. Harold King and I had blueprints made. We took them to a truss company, which engineered the plans for us. The Samoans built most of the small buildings the same way they built their houses. They were on posts in the ground with enough uprights to hold the roof. Mats woven by the women formed most exterior and interior walls. They could be lowered for privacy or to keep out the rain or wind. There were wall sections inside the house that could be mounted or moved. Traditionally, floors were often made of packed mud or sand; wooden floors would be elevated a foot off the ground.

More modern homes were being built to current safety requirements. I took our plans to the building department to get a building permit.

"Are you the contractor?" I was asked.

"No, I have two with me," I replied.

"Who is really running the job?" he wanted to know.

"I am the team leader and will work with the two men's help," I replied.

"Okay, you sign here. We will give you the permit, and you will be responsible. If you come again, bring your own license. We will come and inspect your work every day."

I signed the permit and went back to the worksite. Ed Bailey,

Harold King and I decided that one of us had to be on the job every day our team worked. The inspectors would expect to talk to one (or maybe all three) of us when they came. We had poured the floor and footings according to the plans. The inspectors approved the work we had done.

We had to have concrete blocks for the two end walls of the building. I went with Ray to the block plant. We ordered the blocks and hoped they would be made and cured by the time we needed them. The lumber was ordered and delivered the next day. I thought my so-called kiln for drying lumber at home was bad, but the lumber in Samoa almost wept with sap. Regular saw blades gummed up. The four extra blades for our two small chainsaws were the only things we could safely use.

Harold laid out the pattern for our trusses on the concrete floor. Four men and two of the ladies began to cut and stack in place the pieces of lumber for the trusses. Ed Bailey, along with a Samoan and a member of our team, made plans for the electric service with a list of materials needed. Three women kept the worksite clean, and the Samoan ladies brought water, drinks and salty snacks.

The rains came, and our breaks were built around the weather instead of the clock. The first two days, I had to continually warn the workers not to do too much too soon. Everyone but me was doing fine. I kept seeing more problems than I could see solutions. I was over-tired and could not sleep. I began to take all the problems personally.

The van we would use for traveling to town for supplies and for time away from work was brought from Western Samoa, but it would not run. We had to physically roll the van onto the barge in Western Samoa and push it off when we brought it to our island. Norm Tooman and I brought the van the four miles to the worksite from the dock; I was pushing the van with my pickup, and Norm Toman was driving the van.

The third day, the weather was clear with a cool breeze. We had our first time for formal orientation. I went over the days' schedules and lined out our proposed progress for the week. I explained that Ed Bailey, Harold King or I had to be on the job each day. The result of that requirement was that we had to form three work teams and rotate our days off.

One of the single young men loudly interrupted and said, "I did not come here to work all the time. When am I getting my time off to see this island?"

Instantly, the devil got his licks in. I lost control and spoke when I should have shut up. I told him and any others that if they came to play and felt the same way he did, I would take them to the airport that day so they could go home. When I realized what I had done, I quietly apologized and walked off. I was totally ashamed and wished I could hide.

Either Ed Bailey or Harold King took over. I worked by myself the rest of the day. That evening, we got the van running, and a few of us (I was surprised they even let me be with them) went to Pago Pago for dinner. Our son Steve's father-in-law and mother-in-law were with me and Flo.

No one said anything about what I had done until after we ate and were on our way back to camp. Then Laurence, Peggy's dad, spoke up: "Edd, you got a little out of line this morning, didn't you?"

"Laurence," I said, "I got way out of line. Come morning, I will apologize and hopefully make it right."

"Good," he said. "Just admit you were wrong and shut up."

Everyone laughed, including Flo, who had not said a word about how big of a fool I had been.

At breakfast the next morning, everyone acted no different toward me, which cause me to feel even guiltier. Before we broke up for our morning prayer and sharing time, I told the group that I was ashamed and sorry for what I had said and the way I had acted the day before. I had been out of line. I wanted their prayers and forgiveness. I broke down and tried to hide my crying.

One of the men said, "Edd, when you walked away, we all stayed and prayed for you and for us. You don't have to ask for our forgiveness; we have already given it. Now, you tell us what needs to be done, and we are going to do it."

I just stood there and cried like a baby as they began to come and hug me.

Before we left home, we had requested that a mechanic come with us to rebuild the transmission on a school and church bus. Two churches in California had raised money to buy and ship the necessary parts. Charlie Apple from Orange County, a service manager for an auto dealership, and Norm Tooman from Bakersfield were both excellent mechanics.

It began to rain as usual when the mechanics went to work. They were on their backs under the bus and had lowered the transmission. They were able to remove and replace the broken pieces while still under the bus. They were lying in over an inch of flowing water but had to keep the transmission housing and internal gears dry. When they were replacing the pan over the transmission, the rain began to come down not in buckets but in barrels. It was almost impossible to see ten feet ahead, it was so heavy. The rain water ran off of the parking lot and through the low-lying area they were using as their workspace. The runoff was five inches deep. The water not only soaked them; it covered them everywhere except their heads. They had made wooden "pillows" to serve as rain barriers and to hold their heads up.

Charlie and Norm continued to work, raising the transmission pan into place and securing the bolts and nuts; then they, in their words, "swam out from under the bus." They took off as many clothes as they morally could. They got in the bus, drove it to their lodging and took a cold shower. (The only hot water we had for showers or washing was from hundred-foot sun-heated metal pipes that brought water to the house.) They put on dry clothes and then talked about repairing a transmission in a swimming pool.

After the transmission was repaired, two Samoans came and repaired the point springs on the brushes in the alternator and starter on the small van. The metal springs that keep the brushes in contact with the armature had rusted out. The Samoans removed the brushes, made sure the armature was not too worn and replaced the springs for the brushes with flexible bamboo strips that had been cut to fit. "Bamboo does not rust," they reminded us.

We now had the use of the school bus, since school was out. With the van and my rental, we were able to get supplies and materials we needed. We also had transportation for our crews on their days off. Our building inspectors came three days in a row and stayed for an hour each day. When they were satisfied that we knew what we were doing, they only returned for the final inspection.

Harold and I went to the concrete block plant. They were beginning to make our blocks. We had most of the trusses built and needed to start setting them, but we had to build the end walls first. We had set wall posts and installed the beams to which the trusses were to be secured.

Our concrete blocks had just come out of the molds and had not cured. It would be three days or more before they were safe to use. We decided to take the day off so everyone could go to a secluded cove on the island for a picnic and swimming in the lagoon. The Samoans were ready for a day off and went with us. Our team and twelve Samoans went on the bus and van to the northwest end of the island. We parked our vehicles and walked a quarter of a mile through banyan, banana, mango and bread fruit trees to a small beach that few tourists knew about. No one else was there. The multicolored birds and the splash of small waves hitting the beach was all the noise we heard. Even our chatter was muted.

The Samoans gathered tree limbs and built a small fire to heat water for coffee. Others spread cloths on the ground and laid out a feast for us. We had cold drinks and water to drink — and the chicken, beef patties, mangos, papayas, pineapples, coconuts and three kinds of bread were more than we could eat. Some went out into the warm water to swim, some waded, and some stayed back on the beach under the shade of banyan trees and rested on blankets. We all forgot our work. We walked the beach and watched Samoans casting their nets into the water. Two men came over to teach some of us how to cast the nets and pull in the fish. After untangling ourselves a few times, we actually caught a few fish six to eight inches long.

After four hours, we walked back to the bus and drove to Pago Pago. We walked though the outdoor markets. Most of the Samoans knew who we were and what we were doing and were openly friendly. Some were not that happy; they thought that, if we did not come to spend money and buy from them, we should have stayed home.

The day was therapeutic. A relaxed feeling of unity began to come over us. Our work did not slow down or speed up, but the way it was done was different. We were not individuals working; we were a team, sent here by God to help people.

The next day, the ladies needed to go to market and replenish some of our food. The Samoans fed us in the evenings, but we took care of our own breakfasts and lunches. Even so, several of the Samoans came to help our cooks. I took four of our ladies to the market. I made sure they had what money they needed, and we went to the village farmers' market, not too far from where we were working. I let them out on the south end of the village, went to Pago Pago for some more supplies and returned.

The women were to buy what they needed in the market and meet me at the opposite end of the village. Three of the women met me at the agreed time. They all had large sacks of foods. Helen Stampfli was not with them. I asked where she was, and they told me she was trying to buy some bananas and had to wait for someone to help her. It was hot and humid, and the ladies were sweating. I had parked under a tree and suggested they get in and drink some water while I went to find Helen.

I walked down a dusty street and was covered with sweat in ten minutes. I went another hundred feet and saw Helen. She was red in the face, her hair was matted against her head, and sweat was running off her face and hands. She was lugging a huge stalk of small bananas, the best kind for eating. I went to her and took the stalk of bananas. It weighed at least forty pounds. She stopped, took two or three good breaths, took my arm and signaled for me to not ask questions until we got to the van.

With the stalk of bananas on one side and her hanging onto my other arm, we just made it to the van. We got her to slowly drink water and waited until she could relax.

She said, "Everyone in our group likes these good-tasting small bananas. I could have bought twenty-five for a dollar; for two dollars, I bought the stalk, which has more than sixty. It was a good bargain, but I did not think about the weight or the heat. I am still glad I bought them."

Everyone was pleased, and we returned twice more to replenish our bananas. After that day, a man would always carry them to the van.

I was called by the owner of the gas station. Our ship had come in. I picked up the full tanks of propane; everyone, especially our cooks, was happy.

Our concrete blocks were ready, but their delivery truck would not run. It would be three days before they could deliver the blocks. I called Ray Villiamu and asked him to find six or eight young Samoans who would help me load and move the blocks. I was going to use the bus to move them to the building site. Four guys and three girls came. Harold and I and the seven young people went to the block factory. We needed seven hundred six-by-twelve-by-six-inch blocks and forty half blocks.

We made four trips, which was easier than removing the seats from the bus so we could make it in two. We formed relay lines, and the girls insisted on being a part of the loading. We loaded from both the front door and the rear emergency door. I had brought leather gloves for everyone, and the gloves were completely worn out by the time we moved all the blocks.

In addition to my working on the jobsite with Norm, Charlie, Harold and Ed (who were doing a first-rate job), I had been asked to teach a ten-day course for thirteen young men and women after dinner in the evenings for an hour and a half. While this was not a physical job, it did add more stress to my already taxed system. The materials I had ordered for the class had not arrived. I thought about canceling, but most of these young people had worked as hard on the buildings as our team had.

Four were from then Western Samoa ("western" has since been removed from the name). Samoans as a people were converted to Christianity by Methodists over 150 years ago and to Mormonism a hundred years later. Most are very religious in a cultural way. There was not much understanding about having a personal relationship with God through Christ. I was not dealing with just a spiritual quest but a cultural dogma.

I based my approach on understanding the Bible and the differences between it and other religious books. Christians should base their lives on Biblical knowledge and use it to interpret Christian ethics in family and personal relationships. We, as individual, have spiritual, moral and ethical responsibilities.

My method for the course was to take ten or fifteen minutes to lay out my concepts and related issues. I would then open up the evening for discussion. At first, I was put on the defensive; I was not sensitive enough to their ways and their understanding of life. They believed that, with no firm traditional religious laws, there would chaos. I did not challenge them, nor did I take a superior attitude. Instead, I asked them to help me understand their beliefs. Most did not know why they believed what they did, except that it was what they had been taught. We explored some of our concepts and laughed at ourselves.

After two of our meetings, serious questions began to surface: "Why am I here?" "What is my purpose for living?" "How do I know what I should do with my life?" "What about bullies, abusive parents and teachers?" "Why should I care?"

These were just a few of the questions they wanted to deal with. On a chart, I listed the ten most important topics for us to discuss.

I had from ten until twelve at night to prepare. We only dealt with two of their questions or concerns per night. For three nights, Flo came and sat through the sessions, just to observe. After the third night, Flo asked me, "Where are you getting your material and answers? You have no notes or teaching guides other than what you develop with your studying each night."

Please do not misunderstand, but something eerie happened

those eight nights. Answers that I needed from what I had learned in classes or in my experience with God would flash into my mind at just the right instant. Sometimes I could see in my mind the page of the book I had studied on the subject we were discussing. It scared me a little. I was thankful that, with everything else that was going on, I had the opportunity to grow to love and appreciate the Samoans and their culture. Flo and I still believe that God simply took over, and that I was just an instrument used by Him.

The first week was finished; to my overwhelming relief and to the others' satisfaction, we were a day ahead of our planned schedule. We cleaned up, put our tools away and rested for the day. In the morning, Ray Villiamu drove us in the bus to the airport. We boarded a South Pacific Airlines plane and flew to Fiji.

We were met at the airport in Suva by Enoke and two others — the airport baggage supervisor and her husband, who was a harbor pilot for the government. We had no problems getting through customs. Our luggage was waiting for us to claim and was loaded on the bus that had been chartered for us. On the bus, I introduced Enoke Kubulabola and shared what little he and I had discussed about our trip. I then turned everything over to him, sat back and relaxed.

Enoke welcomed us and gave us a running commentary about the island as we drove thirty-five miles to Lautoka, the capital city, where we would be staying for four days.

To me and most of our crew, Fiji was what we thought a South Pacific island nation should be. Fiji was discovered by Captain Cook on his first sailing trip around the world. It declared its independence from Europe earlier than most island nations. The Methodist Church sent some of its first missionaries to Fiji. The two main cities, Suva and Lautoka, are very modern but maintain their island culture. The nation is heavily populated by Indian refugees. Most of the economy is controlled by the Indians, but the land is owned by Fijians. There have been several bloodless uprisings from both groups over the years but very little fighting. While the elections are open to all citizens, the president has to be a Fijian Ratu (chief tribe); he has more control than most democratic leaders. He is also the supreme commander of the military.

Enoke was a friend of the president and was the director of the South Pacific Bible Society, with headquarters in New Zealand. He was also the leading layman in the Baptist churches in the islands. We circled the south side of the island and saw resorts along the coast that were comparable to anything in the U.S. The sea breeze was cool, and the humidity was much less than Samoa. We arrived in Lautoka and ate lunch at a restaurant beside the blue-green Pacific.

After lunch, we were driven inland through coconut plantations and pineapple fields to a modestly sized Lutheran church that had a school for young ministers. The ministers had gone home on vacation. We gathered our luggage and headed for the dormitory.

Enoke took Flo's and my luggage from us and started away from the group. I was about to say something when Enoke explained that Flo and I were to stay with him and his wife, Jue.

We were stunned, and I guess it showed. Enoke assured us that we would be with the crew for lunch and dinner each day. Our team would have a good breakfast where they were, and we would be together at ten each morning.

Flo and I were taken to a small village uphill from Lautoka and ushered into a nice, modest home. We were introduced to Jue. She had prepared a tea and several kinds of pastries and cookies for us.

We visited with each other and discovered a real difference between our cultures. While both were Fijians and Christians, Enoke was a Ratu, a descendant of the early ruling class of the islands, and

Jue was a commoner. In everything they were equal, except at mealtimes. Unless there were non-family guests present, they did not eat at the same time or at the same table.

The Ratus were always served first and away from women. If a woman was with her husband in a public place, she could sit with him and their guests; however, if she were alone, she sat at a place reserved for women and non-Ratus. The custom is off-limits for jokes or discussion by outsiders, but Enoke and Jue were very open about that part of their culture.

Flo and I had a room to ourselves with a big double bed and a huge net to protect us from mosquitoes. The net was suspended from the ceiling and lowered over us at night.

Flo and I were guests at several meals and discussions with government officials. Our team had its own guides and cooks. I met with students at the new school for Baptist leaders and was a guest lecturer for three days. Our team members visited with students and teachers as guests at outdoor barbecues. One of the older students asked me to go for a walk with him. We shared about our family backgrounds, and he asked how long I would be in Fiji. I told him we would be there four days but would spend two of those days in Suva.

"I wish you could go with me to meet my grandfather. It is a day's walk over trails in the mountains to his village. He would love to meet you and will be disappointed that you could not come. He is the village chief and a Christian. He is now the only former cannibal alive."

The nation of Fiji is made up of dozens of small islands. The island we were on is the business and political center. We were guests for their national day of independence. Their internationally acclaimed marching band marched through town. We enjoyed watching the fireworks and celebrated with the Fijians at an outdoor picnic. We went to see fire walkers and an island history show with simulated battles. We participated in the guava drink ceremonies and shopped in their open markets.

Our oldest volunteer, age eighty-two, would bargain and haggle with merchants until she got her price. One morning, I met the local Baptist leaders at a restaurant in the open-air market. When I arrived, the merchants wanted to know when the older woman would be coming to shop. They did not care if she bought anything or not; they just enjoyed having her around. I told them I would bring her the next day.

In unison, they said, "Not tomorrow; it will be a bad day."

I asked, "Why not tomorrow?"

They replied, "A cruise ship will be in, and prices on everything will be twenty percent higher. She must come the day after the cruise ship leaves."

The next morning, we packed and loaded our things on the bus. We had hoped for another scenic drive along the coast, but all we saw was heavy rain and small creeks flowing over their banks. The drive was slow, tedious, humid and hot. We had rented a small hostel from Youth With a Mission for one night and two days while we were in Suva. We had to wade through water three inches deep to get into our quarters.

The hostel had two floors, with baths on both. We let the ladies and older couples have the first floor and put the younger singles and couples on the second floor. We had air mattresses and our own bedding.

A small kitchen was sufficient for meal preparation. We had eaten at a nice restaurant on the way back to Suva, so no food or drinks had been bought. We would buy what we needed the next morning. Around midnight, someone got up to go to the bathroom and discovered that four to six inches of water was all over the first floor. We carried bedding and clothing upstairs, crowded in, and lay down to get some sleep. One of the men then asked if we had everyone upstairs. He turned on his flashlight (the power was off) and took a head count. Our older lady was missing.

Harold King and Ed Bailey went downstairs to check on her. The water was then over six inches deep, and our missing lady was sound asleep, floating around the room on her air mattress. They enlisted two other guys, and the four of them carried her up the stairs and placed her in a space on the floor. She did not wake up until the next morning. She said she was sorry that she did not get a chance to enjoy being carried upstairs by four good-looking men.

Harold and Ed waded outside in foot-deep water and found a bread store that had four large loaves of bread left. They bought the bread, a pound of ground coffee and a jar of jam and brought it all back to the hostel. That was our breakfast.

By noon, some of the heavy rain had moved on. We were able to get outside, but there was still three inches of water covering the ground. I was able to get a ride in a pickup to the center of town. I walked to the airport. All planes had been delayed by eight hours or more. No one knew if anyone would be able to leave, even if a plane did arrive.

I ate a light lunch at the airport and wondered what to do. I was surprised when an attendant came to me and told me that our people needed to be at the airport in forty-five minutes. With the help of our friend in the baggage room, I was able to round up enough taxis and small trucks to get us to the airport. I rushed back to the hostel, and we packed our stuff (including wet clothes) and rode the two miles back to the airport. The waiting room was jammed with people; however, we were asked to check our bags.

The floor was the only place to sit. A few men gave our older women their seats. I gathered all the tickets and passports and went to the counter. The agent had to check with her supervisor, and her supervisor had to confer with his boss. After fifteen minutes, they took our tickets and passports and disappeared into a back room. I waited and waited, and dozens more people filed into the overcrowded waiting area. Twenty minutes later, the agent came back, returned our passports and gave me fourteen boarding passes. He told me our plane was thirty minutes out. We had to be ready to board when our flight was announced.

I went back and gave each person his or her boarding pass and passport and told them all to be ready to move when the flight to Samoa was announced.

Harold and a few others (including me) wondered what would happen when the announcer called for our party to go to the gate and board a plane to Samoa. There were over a hundred people who had been waiting hours longer than us. My worry was how foolish we would look if there was a mistake and we had to make our way back through the crowds that we had walked over to get to a nonexistent plane.

The announcement came; we sheepishly picked up our sodden bags and went to our gate. The boarding person looked at me and called his supervisor. I was asked a dozen questions that seemed unimportant to me, but my answers satisfied him. We filled every seat on the small commercial plane. I later learned that one of the people I had met in Fiji was an executive with South Pacific Airlines, and he had made arrangements to get us to Samoa.

We worked long hours during our last week in Samoa and finished the building that would serve as both church and school. The building inspectors signed off on our work. We held the first service and had a huge party with music and dancing to celebrate and dedicate the new building. Our team was given gifts of wood carvings, dress and shirt material, and dozens of cases of canned white tuna that is kept in Samoa and not marketed anywhere else. We were one tired and blessed bunch, and we had no problems getting back to California.

Nineteen

1978-1979

Hayfork, California
Building Contractor's License

Two days later, I checked in at the office and brought Helen up to date. She handed me a stack of mail six inches thick. One letter was from our church in Hayfork. Their building plans were complete and at the county office for review. Another letter was from a church in the desert east of San Diego. They wanted me to come and meet with them about a new church building. We had two statewide boys' retreats, one in San Diego and one in the Sacramento area, planned around the same time. There was also a request from some adults and young people to incorporate World Changers into a statewide program.

I saw immediately that I had to make some changes. I contacted Jim Warren and Hugh Jameson and enlisted them to be my co-directors for Northern California. I enlisted Harold King and Norm Tooman to help with Central California, and Ed Bailey and Doug Crowder would focus on Southern California. I would follow up on matters at the men's request, but they would take care of the preliminary work. Helen and I would help only as needed.

Jim Warren called me a few days later and asked if Harold King and I could meet him in San Jose. A Chinese congregation was planning a new building and wanted help. I flew my plane to Madera, picked up Harold and then flew to San Jose. Jim met us at the airport. We had lunch with the pastor and building committee at the church building site. We looked over the property, explained our policies for helping churches and answered questions. They were satisfied with our arrangements and agreed to send us copies of the building plans.

Jim took Harold and I back to the airport. I did the preflight check, received permission to taxi to the runway and was cleared for takeoff. Once we reached the necessary altitude and leveled off, I cut back the engine to cruising speed. The noise of the engine and propeller was subdued enough that we could talk.

Out of the blue, Harold King asked, "Do you know how much you are blessed?"

I knew things were now going great for us. Flo and I were in good health, our kids were doing fine in school, and we had two great grandkids. We did not have any unpaid bills and had more than we really needed — but before I could say any of that, Harold spoke again.

"You really don't know what I mean, do you? You are a minister, but you do not have to beg or push people to work or teach. You are the only minister I have ever known whose main job was finding jobs for people who wanted to work. What a blessed job you have."

He was right. I had been focused on the immensity of my job and did not see that I was now able to provide a place for people who wanted to help others; I was enabling them to do what they believed God wanted them to do.

In a few minutes, Harold was asleep. Alone, I thought and thanked God for letting me be part of His work. There was no traffic going into the airport. Harold woke up as I banked for our landing. As he left, I thanked him for going with me. I also thanked him for giving me new insight into how God was directing my life.

Paul Harrell called from Mississippi and asked if I could come for two weeks and be part of a world mission conference. If I could, he wanted to ask the Brotherhood Commission to approve me as one of the home missionaries he was allotted. I had Helen and Flo check our calendars and agreed to come six months later.

We had received the plans from Hayfork and were preparing to build; it would be the first Baptist church in California built by California Baptist volunteers. Information was sent out to the people on our growing mailing list. Three weeks later, twenty-three different people, both men and women, came and joined us. In two weeks, we completed our first Baptist church building in Hayfork, California.

Requests came from ethnic churches all over the state. In the first three years, California Baptist volunteers had helped to save churches over two million dollars in church construction costs. In the second five years, we helped to build church buildings for four black congregations, three Korean congregations, four Chinese congregations, five Hispanic congregations and one for people from the Philippines. This was in addition to twelve white or mixed congregations.

While I was at the county office with a Southern California pastor, getting building permits for his church, I received a call from a man in Georgia. He was the leader of a group of men and women who were helping to build church buildings in newer work states, and they wanted to come to California. Borrego Springs Baptist Church had its permits and was preparing its building site. I called the leader of the Georgia group and told him we had church that would be ready as soon as they could come. I was informed that they had a cancellation on a planned trip and could be at the church site in Borrego Springs in six days. If the foundation was poured and the floors cured and ready to build on, they could have the church closed in and ready for worship in two weeks. It would not be finished, but it would be usable. The local people could finish the inside of the building.

I relayed this information to the pastor. He told me to call them back and tell them to come on. The church site would be ready, and the church members would provide housing and meals for the team.

Two days later, in Fresno, the phone rang; Helen came into my office and said, "Edd, you'd better get ready for this. It is the pastor at Borrego Springs."

I picked up the phone and could not believe what I heard. A shortage of crushed rock had put a strain on concrete plants. The result was that the cement company could not deliver the promised concrete mix to the church. The plant manager had no idea when they would be able to get the cement to fill the church's order. I tried to contact the team leader from Georgia, but the group was already on the road. No one knew how to get in touch with them or where they were.

The pastor had no idea what to do. I suggested that they finish the preparations for a monolithic pour and make sure all the stakes were firm and the footings were clean. I told them to call for an inspection and get permission to pour when they could get concrete. I added that they might want to call for special prayer meeting if they had not already done so.

While I was concerned, I had other pressing things I needed to do. Some counties were putting pressure on us to have a California-licensed contractor overseeing the work of volunteers. Two volunteers had licenses, but they had to work for a living and could not always be available. I asked Bob for a conference. I explained what this potential problem might mean. He asked me what I would need to do to be licensed. I had no idea, and he suggested I find out.

I had to have five years of building experience and three licensed contractors who could vouch for my skills; I had ten years and six contractors. I would have to take two written tests, one on construction and one on legal requirements. I shared this with Bob. He said, "Let's it get done. The state convention will cover all your costs."

I wrote letters to the building contractors I had worked with in the past five years. All five sent back recommendations. I presented the letters to the local office, and in a week, I was asked to go to Pasadena for the exams. I had two weeks to get ready. I borrowed books and studied like crazy before I was to be in Pasadena. I took the tests and was comfortable with the building test, but the legal one was a bear.

I went to Norwalk, spent the night with Mom and drove home the next day. In ten days, I received my grades. I could not believe what I had done. I had scored an eighty-five on the legal and a seventy-eight on the building tests. Eighty was passing. A notice was enclosed; I was asked to return in two weeks and take the building test again. I now knew how the questions were phrased and studied better. The second time, I scored a ninety-two. In three weeks, I was asked to present my proof of insurance so that I could be issued my California builders license. The convention would pay for my insurance.

I was home finishing the paperwork to get my license when Helen called and told me to call the pastor at Borrego Springs. She laughed and hung up. I called the pastor and made immediate arrangements to go Borrego Springs. I had to see what was happening to believe it. The church was in a near panic when I had left them. There was no concrete available; the team from Georgia was expected in two days, and there had been no way to make contact with them.

The pastor told me, "Yesterday, my office phone rang four times before someone in the hall answered it, just before whoever was calling hung up. The caller asked to talk to me. I was called in, and I took the phone. The man calling was the manager of the concrete plant. He asked me how much concrete we would need to pour the full slab floor, and I told him it was something like seventy yards.

The manager then asked how soon they could deliver seventy-five yards of concrete. An order had been cancelled because of form failure at another job. They had to find somewhere to use that mix before it began to set up, and the plant was forty miles away. The manager told me he could have the first load on the way in an hour. Church members called other church members, friends, neighbors and anyone else who might help. The original plan had been to make the pour a third at a time; now the entire floor and footings had to be a monolithic pour and finished as one. While this was happening, the first of the three teams from Georgia arrived. In twelve hours of difficult work, seventy-four yards of concrete was delivered, poured and finished. Everyone in town knew what had happened, and thirty or more non-church people from the community gave their time and helped."

I arrived the day after the floor and footings had been poured. The concrete had not set up enough to be worked on without scarring the surface. Men and women had formed teams. Church members and neighbors were busy cutting and laying out lumber so they could begin erecting the building in two days. The church building was finished and occupied within two weeks, just as the volunteers from Georgia had promised.

TWENTY

1978-1980

ALASKA, WEST COAST FLOODS

Monterey and Salinas counties have had problems with flooding, high winds and rain as long as they have existed. They are located between San Francisco and Santa Barbara on the coastal inland mountains. In February of 1978, a larger-than-normal storm moved in and left damage for a hundred miles along the coastline. I was called by the state Red Cross director and asked to meet her in Boulder Creek the next day. When I walked into the disaster assistance center, I heard someone who was there for the meeting say, "We can relax; the Southern Baptists are here."

I have no idea who made the remark, but I was pleased by the recognition our volunteers had earned. We got to work, giving assignments to different organizations. Our volunteers were coming the next day. I was asked to begin a damage survey of the area.

My first thought was that the main damage would be in the valleys below the mountains. With my map, I drove a mile and was stopped because a bridge was washed out. I put on my raingear and walked the stream bed. I was shocked at the amount of debris that had been washed downstream. Parts of houses, furniture, dead animals, clothes, pieces of machinery and a torn-up bridge filled the small river. I went back to my four-wheel-drive vehicle, drove uphill for a mile, parked and walked into what had been a small neighborhood of maybe twenty homes in a cove in the mountain. Half of the houses were washed off their foundations. Water had been funneled into the area from three streams that came together at that point. The flash flood had lasted less than ten minutes, but the damage was unreal. In two hours, I discovered two more areas with similar or worse damage.

I went back to the disaster assistance center and gave my report. They had a topographical map of the mountain area. Where I had been was a low point for the water from three creeks, which had merged into a rolling flood. I was studying the map when the director told me I had a telephone call. I answered, and it was Helen.

"Edd, I had call from Mennonite Family Services in Modesto. They want to join our team and asked where you would want them," she said. I asked Helen to call them back and tell them I would get that information to them within two hours.

The other survey workers returned, and we compiled a list of needs and locations. We then determined which group would be responsible for work in each area. The Salvation Army would have four feeding units placed at strategic locations for families and workers. The Seventh Day Adventists would take care of clothing sorting and distribution. The Red Cross would handle medical care. Southern Baptists and Mennonites would focus on recovery. I called the director of the Mennonites, and they agreed to come the next day.

I drove home to get clothes and personal equipment and returned early the next morning. There were two teams of Baptists and two teams of Mennonites. We studied the map and made assignments. As supervisor, I would check with each of the four teams once every two hours to make sure that what we were doing was okay. I also carried food and water and prayed that there were no injuries.

I asked two of the older Mennonite men to handle the telephone. There was no other way I could stay in contact and know of additional needs. I could not send people to help without that information. When I returned to the disaster center late one day, the phone was ringing, and no one was in the office. I rushed in and picked up the phone, and a man said, "I have been calling for thirty minutes, and no one has answered."

"I am sorry," I replied, "but we have been very busy. What can we do for you?"

The caller had no water and no electricity, and he could not get out of his driveway because of a downed tree. I was taking down the information when the two men who were supposed to take care of the calls walked in. In our talks that followed, they apologized. They explained that they thought they had come to help people. They did not see that answering a telephone was helpful. I did not argue with them but gave them a different job. I asked them to get two others from their group and to help the man who had called. I then called the local pastor and asked him to find me someone as soon as possible to come and man the phone.

We worked there for a week and learned a valuable lesson. In cleanup and damage repair, you only do what is necessary for the safety of the people. You only help with their permission. The repairs you make must only be in response to immediate needs. Insurance companies may balk at honoring claims if something else is damaged or destroyed. They may determine that the work was unnecessary and not for safety reasons. In two weeks, our people had done all they could, and the residents of the area were grateful for our team's efforts.

Three weeks later, I attended the national training for state disaster leaders in Atlanta, and my friend from Alaska was there. He asked me to come back to Alaska with another team in three months if I could. I agreed, even though I knew I would have to rearrange some meetings.

Our workers were to go to Cross Roads Baptist Church, eighteen miles east of North Pole, Alaska. The town of North Pole is not named for its location; the town is forty miles south of Fairbanks. The church was meeting in a residence but had permits to put up its own building. They needed help to get it built. I would see what our people in California wanted to do.

Twenty-six men and women agreed to go. We had no coordinated travel arrangements. Groups and individuals were to make travel plans on their own and to let me know when they would arrive in Fairbanks to join our team. Our main group of ten drove in two cars and a van to Seattle and took the Alaska Marine Highway Ferry from Seattle to Hanes, Alaska. We then drove to North Pole and Crossroads. The others either drove all the way or came by air. No one came by dog sled.

Flo and I rode in a van with two other couples and one single man from Easton. We were part of the group that rode the ferry from Seattle. The ferry made several stops to unload passengers, cargo, trucks and other vehicles. While they were loading and unloading, we had time to walk the streets, eat in restaurants and shop.

Our ferry went by Vancouver Island and continued up the coast of Canada and the U.S. We stopped at Ketchikan, Petersburg, Sitka and Juneau. Later, we would follow the ALCAN Highway, which runs through Canada and joins Alaska to the rest of the U.S. At each of our stops, a park ranger would come on board and ride with us to the next city. He or she would give lectures and answer questions about the mountains, the sea, the birds and the wild animals we would see. We toured old Gold Rush towns, Russian settlements and the homes of different Eskimo tribes. Many families had lived in the same place for hundreds of years. We saw bears, elks, wolves, caribou and bald eagles by the dozens. The water was clear and, most of the time, exceptionally calm. We entered into channel for Haines, escorted for about an hour by a mother whale and her calf.

The director of missions for Alaska had arranged for us to be guests of churches on our drive from Haines. Our first day on land, we drove to Delta Junction. The church there provided us with dinner and beds. Their pastor was sick, and Jim Warren volunteered me to preach that Sunday morning. It was Flo's and my thirtieth wedding anniversary. A family in the church told us of a nice restaurant an hour north where we could enjoy a good meal. We thanked the people and left. When we arrived at the recommended restaurant, it was closed.

North Pole was the only other town between us and Cross Roads. We bought gas and ate lunch at the only place that was open. It was a soup and sandwich shop. The group got off easy, since they had decided to buy Flo and me a nice lunch for our anniversary.

We drove sixteen miles east to Cross Roads and arrived in time for the evening service. We met the pastor and were introduced to the people with whom we would be living for the next three weeks. Someone had made them aware it was Flo's and my anniversary. They had a cake and hot drinks for everyone to celebrate with us. We met our host families, went to their homes, unpacked and tried to get a good night's sleep. It never did get completely dark, and the sun was all the way up when we ate breakfast.

We went to the jobsite and I was overwhelmed. The concrete slab for the two-story building had been poured and was covered with a quarter of an inch of ice (in August). We could clean that off, but what really disturbed me was that there were no roof trusses. I had sent the plans six weeks early and asked for delivery two weeks before we arrived to make sure we had them on time. We had to build framing to get the building closed in, which was our job. We had to start setting trusses and roofing the building as we finished securing each section of the wall frame.

The lower part of the outside wall was eight feet high; it was made of poured concrete and had to be waterproofed. The ladies took that job. The ten-foot wood frame that formed the upper part of the wall had to be built and secured on top of the concrete for the outside walls to be finished. Studs had to be cut to length. Sections of the wall frame had to be assembled on the floor and then secured in place. Everyone had plenty to do.

The pastor and I went to the truss factory and asked for the manager. He came out from his office. I introduced myself and asked what had happened to our truss order.

"Our frame cutting saw and one of our nail guns broke down, and we had to order parts from the lower states. The parts are not yet here," he explained.

I thought that he could have let me know sooner, but that was now beside the point. "We have twelve work days before the team leaves. I have to have trusses in two days, or we cannot get the building closed in. Can you make plywood gussets and cut the length lumber for the trusses and get that to us in two days?"

He called in his foreman, they talked, and he came back and said, "We can bring you enough material for two days tomorrow and keep ahead of you on a daily delivery, if you can handle it. I will even send one or two of our people to help for two days."

We agreed and went back to work. The floor was two feet above ground level, with the building foundation built through the permafrost. Piers had been driven ten feet into the ground and were joined to the foundation with mesh and half-inch rebar at the junctions of the reinforced floor and the wall.

A well had to be hand-drilled twenty feet deep though two feet of permafrost. The well and pump would be closed in under the steps at the entry to keep the pipes on top of the well from freezing. The heat of the earth (fifteen feet down) would keep the lower pipes from freezing. Three of the ladies who were going to help assemble trusses asked for the job of drilling the well. Using a hand auger, they began to dig through the gravel and clay. I do not know how they did it, but they were through the two feet of permafrost and four feet into the ground in three hours.

The next morning, materials for a dozen trusses were delivered; however, the gussets were not. The driver knew nothing about them. I called the mill owner and told him that the gussets and nails were not in the delivery. He explained there had been a mix-up and that a truck with the materials would be there in an hour. An hour and a half later, the truck came with the gussets, nails and ten more pieces for trusses. They also sent two more men to work with us for the rest of the day.

The women and I sorted the truss lumber by length and stacked it where it could be reached as needed. I had laid out a pattern for each frame, and they stacked the pieces accordingly. The trusses had to cover a forty-foot span, with a three-foot overhang on each side of the building. We needed two fifty-foot clear spaces on the level floor to assemble and stack fifty-two trusses. The top and bottom rails were two-by-sixes. We were building for heavy snow loads. The support timbers that completed the trusses were two-by-fours. The center post of each truss was two by six by eight feet. The roof would be made of smooth-cut plywood and covered with metal sheeting. Because of complications caused by long-term freezing, there was no tarpaper or other covering between the plywood and sheeting. The trusses were spaced every two feet. Volunteers, supervised by me and two other builders, had to build, set and secure these monsters on twenty-foot-high walls.

I assigned two people to each place where a gusset had to be nailed; three others were to place the board or gusset cut for that particular joint. One of the two would hold the joints in place while the other nailed. These jobs were rotated to give workers variety in their positions.

There were seven joints to each truss. We would put together one side, take a break, and then turn the trusses over and nail the gussets to the other side. Everyone would then help to move the completed trusses to the finished stack, lay out the cut lumber and nail another truss. After five trusses were done, we would rest and then do five more; we continued this way until all fifty-two were assembled and nailed. Jim Warren, Harold King or I would double check every joint on each truss to make sure all were safe and done right. We only had to set aside three trusses to be redone.

Another team of California volunteers was working south of Anchorage at the same time. I needed to go and meet with them and check on their progress. Flo went with me. We rode the scenic Alaska Railroad from Flagstaff to Anchorage. It had begun to rain, but it was not snowing. The train runs through part of the valley around Mount McKinley and through the edge of the national park. We had lunch on the train and enjoyed the scenery of timber, small streams and the running river. There were a few bears and elk and a lot of eagles. We relaxed for the first time in a week. The crew at Cross Roads was to finish all the outside walls and brace them so the trusses could be set and the roof could be started on Monday. That would give us one week to close in the building and have it ready for the next crew that was coming to finish the interior work in two weeks.

Flo and I spent one night in Anchorage. We met with our crew and Baptist convention leaders. I got good reports from both groups. They had no problems and were ahead of their time estimate. We had a relaxing breakfast and enjoyed visiting.

We headed back Saturday afternoon. The ride to Fairbanks is normally around three hours. I had planned on us being back around five that evening. The train had cleared the city and was headed north when the rain began to get heavy. Because of poor visibility, the engineer slowed down. Soon, we were almost at a crawl. I was seated at a window where I could see the river and the railroad tracks. The train tracks were laid out six feet up from the river on top of the banks. I watched water being sprayed from under the cross ties as the wheels rolled over the rails above them. The train slowed and came to a stop. We were on a curve, and I could see the locomotive ahead. The engineer and conductor were out on the tracks, walking ahead and talking. After a few minutes, the engineer returned and climbed back into the engine cab. The conductor walked slowly ahead, looking at the tracks and the track bed for a hundred yards. He then signaled the engineer to move the train forward. This went on for a mile, then the conductor climbed back into the cabin. From there on to Fairbanks, the train moved at twenty to thirty miles an hour.

At one point, I saw a large rubber boat come down the river, circle a dark shape and turn upstream into the current. As I watched, the dark shape was grabbed by two men and pulled aboard. When they separated, I saw that the thing was another person who was being helped out of his clothes and covered with blankets and raingear. We went around another bend, and I lost sight of the boat. The rains never let up, and we arrived in Fairbanks seven hours after we had left Anchorage.

We were met at the station by the pastor, the chairman of the church building committee and a member of our crew. They took us to dinner in a warm, dry place; we all shared about our experiences of the day. I picked up on some concern from the group but thought nothing about it. The next day was Sunday; for a pastor or deacon to be concerned the night before services is not that uncommon. We had been on the road twenty minutes when one of them told me that there was a problem. They and our crew needed me to make a decision. My ears perked up. I wondered what had happened. I decided to jump in and ask, "Okay, what has happened?"

The pastor answered, "All trusses are made and are on the ground. The only day we can get a crane and an operator to set them on the top of the building is tomorrow, Sunday. What do you want to do? We, our members and your crew decided that we would do whatever you think best."

"Why me?" I thought. This was a hopeless situation.

I waited for maybe five minutes and then replied, "I may be stretching the truth a little, but I have a great deal of trouble seeing much difference between an ox in a ditch and a truss on the ground. Let's get those trusses up where they belong."

I thought the driver was going off the road as he pounded on the steering wheel and the deacon pounded him on his back. They looked at Flo and then at me, and one said, "We were sure that you would decide that way. The crane and driver will be there at one o'clock tomorrow afternoon unless we call him by ten tonight and cancel."

The team and a dozen church members were waiting when we got to the pastor's home. They were excited when I told them my decision. We had a prayer time and went to bed. The rain continued. The next morning, we had breakfast and dressed for church. The rain had not stopped nor lessened. We had a Bible study and then a worship service, and it continued to rain. Our team and church members had lunch, changed into work clothes, put on raingear and went to the worksite. There were sixty people standing around in the rain. All looked at the trusses, at the building, at one another and then at me.

I turned to Dot Warren, Rick Warren's mother, and asked her to lead us in prayer. Dot kept it short and to the point. I motioned for the crane operator to get the machine going. As he crawled into the cab, the clouds and rain moved on, and the sun came out. The first crew to work on the top setting the trusses rode up on the crane ball. We hooked up the first truss, and the crane operator lifted it to the top of the twenty-four-foot wall. Our crew on top set it in place and braced it; three trusses followed and were secured. With the rain stopped and the ground crew working well, I rode the cable ball up and helped to align and secure the trusses as they were lifted to us. In an hour, both end trusses had been secured. In another three hours, the other trusses were lined up, leveled and secured.

In another thirty minutes, we built four level platforms for the packs of plywood sheeting. The packs were lifted to the roof and secured on the platforms. Workers were lowered to the ground by the crane operator. He backed the crane away from the building, secured the ball and cables, shut down the engine and climbed out of the cab. As he shut and locked the cab door, the rain began again.

That night, we had a celebration dinner and a special prayer meeting. We thanked God, the crane operator, the church members, and our team for being there and doing what had to be done. During the next two days, in some light rain, the roof was sheeted and nailed. We finished our part of the job a day ahead of schedule. The local roofers were ready to do their work.

The next morning, we spent hours washing and drying clothes and visiting with friends. Those who were flying left for the airport in Fairbanks. The rest of us who were driving loaded our van and cars. The local people began to come and bring us food, water and gifts. We had so much food given to us that we had to turn part of it down. Gifts and thanks were more than we needed or expected.

We drove south on the ALCAN Highway and stopped below Sheep Mountain to spend the night. Flo and I slept outside in our sleeping bags on air mattresses inside a small tent. We stopped at the mileage marker and found the name of a couple from Pioneer. We added our names to the sign.

The next day, we stopped at the one-mile marker. It marked the place where the Seabees and Army engineers and over a thousand servicemen had completed the construction of Highway One to ship war supplies to Russia for their battle against Germany and Japan in World War II.

The Alaska Highway is still rough in places but is one of the most scenic drives in the world. We saw snow-capped mountains, rushing rivers with salmon jumping upstream and black bears waiting to catch a fish for lunch. We stopped in several small villages, where we were always welcomed.

Three of us rotated driving, so we moved along at a fairly rapid rate. We stopped for gas but ate most of our donated meals on the road or at outside picnic areas. One couple who was with us on the trip up had flown back home. With just five of us in a van, we were not crowded. We could sleep if we wanted to, but most of us did not want to. Fall was coming, and we did not want to miss the colors of the leaves or the animals that were roaming and searching for food.

We took the longer route and went through Vancouver. We spent several hours having lunch in the old town and enjoying the rose gardens that were being developed on the slopes of an old stone quarry. Two days later, we arrived home, exhausted and still marveling at what only God could do. We received many calls from churches and individuals about our work in Alaska, Samoa and the South Pacific.

The response from these trips and the reports from Guatemala and Teton Dam gave me a good problem. In the months and years ahead, I would have more volunteers who wanted to be involved than there was room for. I had to begin limiting the number of people who could travel with a team to where our help was needed.

At a Royal Ambassadors camp for boys ages twelve to sixteen,

I met a young man named Charles Reynolds. Charlie was a friend of our son Steve. They were both students at Golden Gate Seminary, where I was (hopefully) finishing my work for my doctoral degree. Charlie was beginning a new church in Cameron Park, forty miles east of Sacramento on Interstate 80. He had some knowledge of World Changers and wanted to know more about the program. Charlie was a graduate of Richmond University in Virginia. He had been active in camp work, and his dad was Baptist pastor.

Around the time I met Charlie, I also met a young lady named Dona in the church where Flo and I were members. Dona was the youth director and had also become interested in World Changers.

I had begun what was known as Christian High Adventure, a mountain hiking program for older youth and young adults. The program placed people in strenuous but safe environments to teach them resourcefulness and openness to one another's needs.

All of this began to come together at the same time young people were asking for something they could do that was important and worth their time. I set up a meeting with Charlie, Dona, two other interested adults and three young people. At the meeting, we decided to have a weeklong camp for youth and youth leaders to explore ways for them to be involved in meeting people's needs.

Our state WMU (Woman's Missionary Union) director, Dixie Hunky, also wanted to be involved. You would have thought we were going to explode an atom bomb. Edd Brown had not only nearly destroyed the Brotherhood Commission, but he had corrupted Dixie Hunky into joining him. "They want a state camp for teenage boys and girls — together! Can you imagine the discipline problems they will have with teenage boys and girls in a camp in the mountains for a week? And they'll have them going on so-called 'work projects' instead of studying the Bible and doing mission work."

Again, the publicity from our horrified opponents helped us reach out to our youth. More parents began to support our first California World Changers Camp, which was held at Jenness Park. Youth leaders from churches in our associations came with their youth, and many parents offered to help. We brought in youth leaders from across the nation and had our own youth band. Rick Muchow, who would later be the worship leader at Saddleback Community Church with Rick Warren, was our music and worship leader. Around 240 youth came to study, share and plan specific ministries in their communities. They were to lead others at home to help with their projects. One interesting project that they decided to do was to go to a large recreational lake, fifteen miles up the mountain, and talk to people who were there on vacation or out for the day.

Several national leaders became interested in our program and were involved with us from the beginning. For two years, we camped and encouraged our youth to get involved in finding solutions instead of complaining about parents and other things that they could not control.

More youth became involved, and we adopted communities where elderly people needed help and served migrant workers in their camps. Churches began to join together so the youth could do ministry in more neighborhoods where people needed help. Local adult mission programs began to focus on action as well as study.

Our daughter, Marcia, was working in Southern California at a home for abused children. Part of her job was taking a mandatory break; all the workers were required to "get back to reality" periodically. The pressure of the job and the horror of what parents and adults do to children were both extremely difficult to deal with. Marcia came to our home in Fresno, stayed three days and went on to Sacramento to be with Steve and Peggy and the two boys. Steve and Peggy had planned a dinner for Marcia and invited Charlie Reynolds to be their guest.

Charlie and Marcia both felt like they were being set up and were not overly pleased. In the years to come, that casual meeting gave impetus to World Changers, changed the lives of Charlie and Marcia, and caused some major changes in Flo's and my ministry.

Other events followed. Charlie was searching for a project for his doctorate in ministry. In conference with his faculty advisors at the seminary, they questioned him about World Changers. This interest came from the positive reports the professors were getting from some of their students. Charlie approached me and asked permission to use our development of the concept of World Changers for his doctoral work.

I had no problem with that and encouraged him to develop something definitive out of our basic concepts. We had no guidelines and no planned programs as such. We were flying by the seat of our pants, hoping we were going in the right direction. Not only was the program heartily approved by the graduate committee, but some of the professors wanted to be personally involved.

Later, I was contacted by one of the directors of youth ministries from the former Brotherhood Commission. The Home Mission Board wanted to buy our concept and copyright World Changers as a national program; they would purchase our program for a thousand dollars.

I knew I had gone as I far as I could with the program. With the permission of our state executive director, we sold the program to them. No one would have thought or even dreamed that three teenage girls could come up with an idea that would eventually involve over twenty thousand youth in mission projects every year for thirty years and counting. We sent the money from the mission board to Charlie, to help him in his research and development of a comprehensive format for the program.

We planned a Royal Ambassador retreat for school-age boys at California Baptist. Some of the boys slept in dormitories, and a few slept in tents on the grass area next to the dorms. In addition to their other activities, the boys met professors and teachers. Dr. Staples came to a few meetings and met our counselors and staff. He asked me for a brief meeting and took me to an abandoned room above what was then the school cafeteria.

It was a mess. Some rooms were used for storage and as extra classrooms if absolutely necessary. He explained the need for an office and lab area and wanted to know if I could get some volunteers to come and help. Dave Swift, one of the older students, was a builder and would work with me if I thought this was a possibility.

I told Dr. Staples I would try. Helen and I sent out letters, but only a few people even responded. I received a call from Mr. Weidner, a retired teacher who had moved to California from Arizona. He, his wife and his daughter said they would like to come and help. Another man also responded favorably. Ed Bailey agreed to come and help with the electrical work. Two students had time and wanted to be involved. We eight tore out walls and ceilings and cut out openings for new doors. The walls were covered with roughly finished stucco. We removed floor coverings and put in electrical outlets, windows and doors where needed. In ten days, we were done: The rooms were painted and new flooring was being installed.

We all went to dinner together. Mr. Weidner asked if I knew anyplace that needed two teachers for a year, and I asked if they had any preference. They did not and were even open to going overseas. When I left Samoa eight months earlier, Ray Villiamu asked me to help him find one or two teachers. He and his wife, Lena, were working in a new church in Fagali'i and a Korean church in Pago Pago in addition to ministering at Happy Valley and teaching in the school.

"We need any help you can find," Ray had said.

I gave this information to the Weidner family, and the family was in Samoa six weeks later. They stayed the year and then two more before retiring to northern Arizona.

I had finished my doctoral thesis and, with Helen's much-needed help, had submitted copies to Bob Hughes and the graduate committee at Golden Gate Seminary. I waited for three weeks and heard nothing. Graduation was just six weeks away, and I still had to do my oral exam before I could receive my degree. Three weeks before graduation, I was asked to come to the seminary and meet with my professors and the graduate committee. How they managed to schedule my oral exam while the supervisor who had given me a difficult time was in Southern California, I never knew nor asked.

Included in my report was a section on the relationship between pastors and laymen. I had quoted a church leader who had told me honestly how he sometimes felt about his pastor. He had said, "If there is a small insignificant need, like a mouse in the kitchen, I would probably be called; however, if the need were major, like a tiger, my pastor would say, 'Fellows, just stand back. I can handle this by myself.' Damn it, I am not a child. I don't care for recognition, but I am capable of doing more than chasing his mice."

The professor's comment was, "This is the first time I have accepted a doctoral thesis with 'damn' in it."

I laughed and told them, "That was one of the man's nicer statements."

I went home; in three days I was invited to the seminary for graduation. Helen, Flo and I had completed our work, I had finished my oral exams, and we could prepare for the reception of my doctoral degree. Flo insisted that I have a new suit. I arranged for Helen to have two days off. Helen, Flo and my mother went with me to Mill Valley. Steve and Peggy met us there.

At my graduation, I was the only one of the three to get a diploma. I made sure that those two and others got more than just a thank-you.

An interesting event happened after the ceremony. The faculty supervisor who had done everything he could to block me met me on a path outside. I put out my hand to shake with him, but he ignored it. Instead, he looked at me and said, "I see you are wearing one of those new lawyer-type business suits." With that, he walked away. I never saw him again and was disturbed when I later learned that he had taken his own life.

We went to a nice restaurant in San Rafael. My family and Helen had an excellent meal, and all were grateful that the ordeal was over. We were ready to focus on other matters.

I received all kinds of gifts and made sure that Helen and Flo were recognized for the work they had done. I remember later, when someone asked me how I felt about all the awards and degrees I was getting, my answer was and still is, "It does not seem fair or right to me that I get recognition and awards for what other people have done. They do the work and pay their own way. I get paid and then am honored for the work that they do."

A week after graduation, I sat down long enough to think through the past eighteen months. In that time, I had acquired a pilot's

"Dr. Edd" and his mom at graduation.

license and a California builders license; I had finished two graduate programs and received my doctoral degree. All of my children had graduated from college, and I had two grandchildren with another one on the way. I thought about how God had kept His promises and wondered if anything He would do could go beyond what He had already done for Flo and me. We had been blessed far beyond any of our dreams. I remarked to Flo that I could not see how our life could have been any better than it had been in the past ten years. I knew we had reached our limit. We would have other ministry opportunities, but nothing could be more rewarding than what we had experienced. Besides, in five more years, I would be ready to retire.

Was I ever wrong! In the next twenty years, our ministry would take us to thirty-two countries in every section of the world. Our awards, licenses and degrees opened doors for ministry that no one could have ever imagined. We began to realize that the previous years of struggles and confusion, as well as those of good times and blessings, were preparing us for the next step of our lives and ministries.

So that you may understand what I am trying to say, I have included on the next page an outline of my follow-up book, which will cover most of the times when we were called by God to go "To the Ends of the Earth."

If you have questions or comments, email me at elb64ffb@gmail. com, or send a letter to the following address:

Dr. Edd L. Brown
4 Mizzenmast Court
Greenville, S.C. 29617

To the Ends of the Earth

I want to thank the staff of Courier Publishing for moving this book from manuscript to finished form. They are top-notch people as well as great Christians.

CPSIA information can be obtained at www.ICGtesting.com
Printed in the USA
LVOW04s0301280515

440204LV00003B/6/P